IMPERFECT U

IMPERFECT UNIONS

*Security Institutions over
Time and Space*

Edited by

HELGA HAFTENDORN

ROBERT O. KEOHANE

and

CELESTE A. WALLANDER

OXFORD
UNIVERSITY PRESS

*This book has been printed digitally and produced in a standard specification
in order to ensure its continuing availability*

OXFORD
UNIVERSITY PRESS

Great Clarendon Street, Oxford OX2 6DP

Oxford University Press is a department of the University of Oxford.
It furthers the University's objective of excellence in research, scholarship,
and education by publishing world-wide in

Oxford New York

Auckland Bangkok Buenos Aires Cape Town Chennai
Dar es Salaam Delhi Hong Kong Istanbul Karachi Kolkata
Kuala Lumpur Madrid Melbourne Mexico City Mumbai Nairobi
São Paulo Shanghai Taipei Tokyo Toronto

Oxford is a registered trade mark of Oxford University Press
in the UK and in certain other countries

Published in the United States
by Oxford University Press Inc., New York

ISBN 978-0-19-820796-2

PREFACE

This book is a truly international collaborative endeavour by American and German academics. It owes much to the commitment and support of a number of institutions and persons on both sides of the Atlantic. First of all, it would not have been possible without the generous support of the Alexander von Humboldt Foundation and the Max Planck Society which awarded Helga Haftendorn the 1995 Max Planck Prize (Forschungspreis für Internationale Kooperation) and of the Weatherhead Center for International Affairs at Harvard University which, over a number of years, supported both the project and the study group on alliances that preceded it. Helga Haftendorn enjoyed the Weatherhead Center's hospitality as a Visiting Fellow during the spring semester of 1998 with the generous support of the Fritz Thyssen Foundation, and Robert Keohane and Celeste Wallander were guests at the Center on Foreign and Security Policy Research of the Free University of Berlin in November 1995 and May 1997 respectively.

Since 1995, editors and participants in this joint project on security institutions have met a number of times. At three conferences, in May 1996 in Berlin, and in March and September 1997 in Cambridge, the outline of the book and the individual chapters were thoroughly discussed. In this process, a number of Americans and Germans participated who could not contribute chapters, but who gave very valuable inputs into the discussions: Robert Art, Peter Barschdorff, Marc Busch, Nikolas Busse, Colin Elman, Page Fortna, Susanne Feske, Gunther Hellman, Otto Keck, Vera Klauer, Michael Kreft, Jeff Legro, Lisa Martin, Andy Moravcsik, Dan Reiter, Tim Snyder, Olaf Theiler, and Reinhard Wolf. Of special assistance were Genevieve Libonati, Michael Hoch, Lois Kaznicki, George Scialabba, and Heidi Strecker who checked the manuscript for style, transcribed corrections, or organized meetings.

It has been a demanding project for all who participated. It was also great fun; it increased our mutual understanding for the different academic cultures on both sides of the Atlantic, and it will, as the editors hope, further our thinking about international institutions, how they change, and the impact they have on states.

H.H., R.O.K., and C.A.W.

Berlin, Durham, and Cambridge

CONTENTS

I. FUNCTION AND FORM
OF SECURITY INSTITUTIONS

II. EFFECTS OF SECURITY INSTITUTIONS

CONTRIBUTORS

CHRISTOPHER DAASE is Assistant Professor at the Department of Political Science and a Faculty Associate at the Center on Transatlantic Foreign and Security Policy Research at the Free University of Berlin. He specializes in international relations theory and security studies. He has published widely on regionalism and the theory of war. His most recent publication is *Kleine Kriege: Wie Guerillakriegführung die internationale Politik verändert* (Small Wars: Explaining Unconventional Warfare and its Impact on International Relations) (Baden-Baden: Nomos 1999), for which he received the Free University's Ernst Reuter Prize for best dissertation. Currently, he is working on a project on time and space formations in international relations.

CHRISTOPHER GELPI is Assistant Professor of Political Science at Duke University. His research and teaching interests centre on international conflict and conflict resolution. He recently published work on the role of norms in international crisis bargaining and is engaged in revising a book manuscript on this topic. In addition, he has recently published research on the influence of democracy on the international use of force and is engaged in several article-length research projects on this topic. His previous publications concern diversionary wars, deterrence theory, and the influence of the international system on the outbreak of military conflict. His works have appeared in the *American Political Science Review*, *Journal of Conflict Resolution*, and *Political Science Quarterly*.

HELGA HAFTENDORN is University Professor of Political Science and International Relations, Free University of Berlin; and Director, Center for Transatlantic Foreign and Security Policy Studies. Her research interests are German and American foreign policy, security and arms control, NATO, European-American relations, contemporary German history, international relations theory. She is the author and editor of numerous articles and books, most recently *Kooperation jenseits von Hegemonie und Bedrohung* (Baden-Baden: Nomos 1997, with Otto Keck), and *NATO and the Nuclear Revolution: A Crisis of Credibility* (Oxford: OUP, 1996).

ALASTAIR IAIN JOHNSTON is John L. Leob Associate Professor of the Social Sciences in the Government Department at Harvard University, where he teaches courses on international relations theory, East Asia, and Chinese foreign policy. He is the author of _Cultural Realism: Strategic Culture and Grand Strategy in Chinese History_ (Princeton: Princeton University Press, 1995). He is current working on a book on socialization in international arms control institutions.

ROBERT O. KEOHANE is James B. Duke Professor of Political Science, Duke University. He is author of _After Hegemony: Cooperation and Discord in the World Political Economy_ (Princeton: Princeton University Press, 1984) and _International Institutions and State Power_ (Boulder, Colo.: Westview 1989), and co-author of _Power and Interdependence: World Politics in Transition_ (Boston: Little Brown, 1977) and _Designing Social Inquiry: Scientific Inference in Qualitative Research_ (Princeton: Princeton University Press, 1994).

INGO PETERS is Associate Professor at the Department of Political Science and Executive Director of the Center on Transatlantic Foreign and Security Policy Research at the Free University of Berlin. He has published widely on German foreign and security policy and European security, including his recent edited volume _New Security Challenges: The Adaptation of International Institutions. Reforming the UN, NATO, EU and CSCE since 1989_ (Münster: Lit Verlag/New York: St Martin's Press, 1996).

LOUISE RICHARDSON is Associate Professor of Government and Faculty Associate at the Center for European Studies at Harvard University. She is author of _When Allies Differ: Anglo-American Relations During the Suez and Falklands Crises_ (New York: St. Martin's Press 1996) as well as a number of articles on foreign and security policy and international terrorism.

HENNING RIECKE is a Ph.D. candidate at the Department of Political Science and Research Fellow at the Center for Transatlantic Foreign and Security Policy Studies at the Free University of Berlin. In 1995, he was a Visiting Fellow at the Center for Science and International Affairs, Kennedy School of Government, Harvard University. He has published various articles on nuclear non-proliferation and international security affairs. His dissertation deals with international institutions and US non-proliferation policy.

CARSTEN TAMS is a Ph.D. candidate in the Department of Political Science and was a Research Assistant at the Center for Transatlantic Foreign and Security Policy Studies at the Free University Berlin. His research focuses on the theoretical problems of European integration, alliance transformation, and transatlantic relations. He is currently a German McCloy Scholar at the Kennedy School of Government at Harvard University, where he is a student of the Two-Year Master in Public Administration Programme.

CHRISTIAN TUSCHHOFF is a Visiting DAAD Associate Professor at the Political Science Department of Emory University. His research interests are alliances, European integration, and foreign policy. His publications in clude *Einstellung und Entscheidung* [Attitude and Decision] (Baden-Baden: Nomos 1990); *Machtgewinn auf leisen Sohlen. Deutschland, NATO und die Kernwaffen 1949–1967* [Tiptoeing Up the Power Path: Germany, NATO, and Nuclear Weapons] (Baden-Baden: Nomos, 1998).

CELESTE A. WALLANDER is Associate Professor of Government at Harvard University and Director of the Program on New Approaches to Russian Security at the Davis Center for Russian Studies. Her research and teaching interests include international relations theory, national and international security, and Russian security. She has published articles on Soviet use of military force, Germany's trade policy toward Russia, and the role of international institutions in Russian military operations. She is the author of *Mortal Friends, Best Enemies: German-Russian Cooperation after the Cold War* (Ithaca, NY: Cornell, 1999), and editor of *The Sources of Russian Foreign Policy after the Cold War* (Boulder, Colo.: Westview, 1996).

ABBREVIATIONS

AMTC	Allied Maritime Transport Council
ARF	ASEAN Regional Forum
ASEAN	Association of South East Asian Nations
BDIHR	Bureau for Democratic Institutions and Human Rights
CCG	Contingency Coordinating Group
CEEC	Central and East European Countries
CFSP	Common Foreign and Security Policy
CIS	Commonwealth of Independent States
C/OSCE	Conference on Security and Cooperation in Europe
COW	Correlates of War
CPC	Conflict Prevention Center
CSCA	Conference on Security Cooperation in Asia
CSCAP	Council of Security Cooperation in the Asia-Pacific
CSO	Committee of Senior Officials
DCP	Defense Counterproliferation Initiative
DPRK	Democratic Peoples Republic of North Korea
EDC	European Defence Community
EPC	European Political Cooperation
ESDI	European Security and Defence Identity
FAZ	*Frankfurter Allgemeine Zeitung*
FCO	Foreign and Commonwealth Office
FRG	Federal Republic of Germany
FRUS	Foreign Relations of the United States
GDR	German Democratic Republic
GOC	Committee of Good Offices
HCNM	High Commissioner for National Minorities
HEU	highly enriched uranium
IAEA	International Atomic Energy Agency
ICB	International Crisis Behavior
IFOR	Implementation Force
IMF	International Monetary Fund
ISG	intersessional support groups
ISM	intersessional meetings
KEDO	Korean Peninsula Energy Development Organization
LWR	light water reactor

MFA	Ministry of Foreign Affairs
MFO	Multination Force and Observers
MF	Multilateral force
NACC	North Atlantic Cooperation Council
NATO	North Atlantic Treaty Organization
NNWS	non-nuclear weapons states
NPT	Non-Proliferation Treaty
NWS	nuclear weapon states
OAS	Organization of African States
ONUC	United Nations Operation in the Congo
ONUVEH	United Nations Observer Mission to Verify the Electoral Process in Haiti
OSCE	Organization for Security and Cooperation in Europe
PfP	Partnership for Peace
PKO	peacekeeping operation
PMC	post-ministerial conference
PSD	peaceful settlement of disputes
ROK	Republic of (South) Korea
SACEUR	Supreme Allied Commander in Europe
SAR	search and rescue
SFOR	Stabilization Force
SHAPE	Supreme Allied Headquarters of Allied Powers in Europe
START	Strategic Arms Reduction Treaty
TAC	Treaty of Amity and Cooperation
UNAVEM	United Nations Angola Verification Mission
UNCI	United Nations Commission for Indonesia
UNCIP	United Nations Commission on India and Pakistan
UNEF	United Nations Emergency Force
UNFICYP	
UNGOMAP	United Nations Good Offices Mission in Afghanistan and Pakistan
UNIIMOG	United Nations Iran–Iraq Military Observer Group
UNITAF	United Task Force
UNMOGIP	United Nations Military Observer Group in India and Pakistan
UNPROFOR	United Nations Protection Force
UNSCOB	United Nations Special Committee on the Balkans
UNTAC	United Nations Transitional Authority in Cambodia
UNTAG	United Nations Transition Assistance Group
UNTSO	United Nations Truce Supervision Organization

UNUCA	United Nations Observer Group in Central America
WAG	Washington Ambassadorial Group
WEU	Western European Union
WMD	weapons of mass destruction

INTRODUCTION

Celeste A. Wallander, Helga Haftendorn, and Robert O. Keohane

International institutions play important roles not only in economic or environmental issue-areas, but also where threats or use of military force occur. Some of these institutions are alliances, such as the North Atlantic Treaty Organization (NATO) during the cold war; but others, such as the arrangements embodied in chapters 6 and 7 of the United Nations Charter, and the Organization for Security and Cooperation in Europe (OSCE), are designed to manage conflict among their members. That is, they are security management institutions. In this volume we argue that the institutional dimensions both of alliances and security management institutions are important, and often overlooked. Institutions play a role in security relations by affecting states' cost-benefit calculations; by shaping their strategies; by inducing conformity to established conventions and norms; and even, in the long run, by altering how societies view their interests and the mandates that states have to act in world politics. Even in security affairs important phenomena such as the management and resolution of regional and local conflicts, the form and pace of alliance formation, and the development of security cooperation in different regions of the world can only be explained if we pay attention to institutions.

We seek in this volume both to illuminate contemporary security issues and further to develop institutionalist theory. On the one hand, we seek practical knowledge: better understanding of recent developments in international relations, such as NATO enlargement, the regionalization of peacekeeping, and the formation of new security architectures in Europe and Asia. On the other hand, we wish to extend the domain of institutional theory to security issues. As we see it, security studies, still dominated by realist thinking, will greatly benefit by incorporating institutionalist approaches.

We define international institutions as persistent and connected sets of rules, often affiliated with organizations, that operate across international boundaries. Institutions range from conventions (such as sovereignty) to regimes (such as the non-proliferation regime) to formal organizations (such as NATO). Security institutions are designed to protect the territorial integrity of states from the adverse use of military force; to guard states' autonomy against the political effects of the threat of such force; and to prevent the emergence of situations that could endanger states' vital interests as they define them.[1] NATO, the Western European Union (WEU), UN peacekeeping, the Organization of American States (OAS), the ASEAN Regional Forum, and the OSCE are examples of such institutions. This book documents the effects of such institutions on national policies. It also seeks to describe change in security institutions, and to explore the conditions that affect it.

Security problems come in a variety of forms. The simplest and most obvious of these are threats. Security threats are posed when a state (or group of states) has both the intention and capability to circumscribe the security of another state. Threats are the classic problem in security studies, and understanding when they arise and how states cope with them through deterrence or defence has comprised the bulk of work in the field. But not all security problems are posed by states that have the intention and capability to harm others. Security may be diminished by a state that is politically unstable (thereby posing the risk of disintegration, instability, and regional conflict) or the future of which is uncertain and problematic (creating the danger of a regime with aggressive or revisionist intentions). In a global society, new security challenges arise with the proliferation of deadly weapons (be they nuclear, bacteriological, or chemical), the denial of vital resources (such as oil or water), or the spread of extreme ideologies (e.g. Islamic fundamentalism). The potential for different security problems creates the necessity for special security strategies to cope with them. And if special strategies are needed to cope with a variety of problems, then institutions will also vary in their forms and functions in relation to the threat, risk, or challenge posed.[2] Genuine security requires not only the absence of or protection against a military threat, but also the management of a multitude of risks concerning the political, economic, and social well-being of states and their peoples.

The remainder of this Introduction proceeds as follows. In section 1 we summarize some of the essential elements of our institutionalist approach

---

[1] For a discussion of the concept of international security and security regimes, see Haftendorn (1991).

[2] Wallander and Keohane, this volume, Ch. 1.

to the study of world politics.[3] We then in section 2 briefly raise objections to this approach from a variety of viewpoints, and indicate the responses to be taken in this volume. Sections 3–5 raise the three central questions of this volume: the functions and forms of security institutions, their effects on state policies, and how they change over time. In section 6 we comment on some issues of research design, and section 7 describes the chapters that follow in this volume.

1. Institutional Theory and Security Relations

Institutional theory leads us to expect that states can cooperate to pursue common interests, since cooperative strategies under some circumstances produce more benefits than unilateral ones. Cooperation does not imply harmony: states will worry about being exploited and may under certain conditions be concerned with relative gains. But security issues often generate common interests in coping with threats such as preventing military attack, or in controlling risks such as those involved in nuclear proliferation or regional conflict and instability. Such common interests generate incentives for devising cooperative strategies. Although the potential for exploitation can never be eliminated, its likelihood and effects can be minimized by increasing information about the actions and intentions of other states, by creating incentives for good behaviour and by applying sanctions against the violation of international commitments. Cooperation is not always possible, but when it is, institutions can promote reciprocity, make members accountable for their actions, and contribute to the maintenance of cooperative security strategies.[4]

Institutions play a role in security relations because states are bedeviled by the problem of uncertainty.[5] Uncertainty means not having information about other states' intentions and likely choices. Since choosing a strategy depends not merely on what a state wants but also on what it believes other states seek, uncertainty can be a very significant problem in security relations. Governments therefore find it worthwhile to invest in information that will enable them to design strategies that are appropriate to their

---

[3] In some of the literature, this approach has been referred to as 'neo-liberal institutionalist', but we prefer 'institutionalist', for simplicity's sake but also because 'liberalism' is a complex and often misunderstood set of doctrines, arguments, and perspectives on issues ranging from co-operation in world politics to the role of the state on economic affairs and the protection to be given to civil and political rights. See also Hall and Taylor (1996).

[4] Keohane (1984). [5] Wallander (1999).

environments. One way of investing in information is to create institutions that provide it. Institutions can serve as the informational and signalling mechanisms that enable states to get more information about the interests, preference, and intentions of other states. They reduce uncertainty by providing credible information. Furthermore, successful institutions develop norms and rules that regularize the behaviour of states belonging to them, making it more predictable. Hence, if it is rational for states to invest in information, they may also invest in institutions that reduce uncertainty.

It is not only the information one receives, but the information one is able to provide to others that contributes to more efficient strategies.[6] States that can increase the credibility of their own threats and promises by conveying information about their true intentions have a bargaining advantage over those who cannot credibly do so. Therefore, information becomes an instrument of security policy whether a state wishes to avoid conflict or to exercise influence over the behaviour of others. Costly actions are more credible signals of intention than costless ones; hence, information is often conveyed through costly action, such as making alliance commitments.[7]

2. Critical Perspectives on Institutionalist Theory

The conventional wisdom on international security issues, political realism, has responded to the institutionalist challenge by reiterating its view that states, at least in their political-military relations, face very strong constraints on their behaviour, which undermine the potential for cooperation. In this view, the anarchic international environment leads states to rely on self-help strategies and to seek relative gains.[8]

Realist theory does admit that under tightly defined circumstances cooperation may be rationally chosen; for example, states can cooperate with one another when they face a dangerous military threat. Thus for realist theory, the abundance of alliances throughout history is not surprising, because alliances have been mostly *ad hoc* responses to threats and crises. States can and will cooperate to deter or defeat powerful or threatening states, but this cooperation is contingent, unstable, and the by-product of dangers posed by imbalances of power or serious threat.[9] Such cooperation under situations of potential power imbalances or threat

---

[6] For the classic discussion, see Schelling (1960).
[7] Fearon (1994b); Powell (1990); Martin (1992a).
[8] Waltz (1979); Grieco (1988).   [9] Waltz (1979); Walt (1987).

will be facilitated if there is a hegemon to create and enforce institutions which are in its interest. Hence from the realist standpoint the American alliance system during the cold war can be explained by a combination of potential power imbalance in Europe, the threat posed by the Soviet Union, and the fact of American hegemony within the non-communist camp.

In the realist view, such cooperation is temporary and will disappear quickly after the disappearance of the special conditions that created it. Hence realist theorists expected that with the end of the cold war institutions created on the basis of that era's bipolar configuration of power would not remain effective or survive. Institutionalist theory, in contrast, holds that institutions can be of general value to states in so far as they help them to cope with uncertainty. The end of the cold war has supported institutionalist hypotheses: not only have quite a few security institutions persisted, some (such as NATO) have even acquired new functions. However, there has been a great deal of variation in the effectiveness and persistence of international institutions. Hence the contributions to this volume go beyond propositions about institutional persistence to explore the dynamics of international security institutions, and variations in their effects.

Institutionalist theory has been criticized for overstating the chances for cooperation or failing to deal adequately with distributional and bargaining problems.[10] Power and interests are, of course, important; indeed, this is a proposition on which institutionalist theory has been built, rather than one that it has ignored. More critically, the emphasis in institutionalist theory on explaining cooperation has sometimes led to inadequate consideration being given to distributive and bargaining issues, and to strategies designed to alter situations by force. One of the threads running through this volume is the effort to understand both how security institutions are created in order to realize potential joint gains from cooperation, and how conflict within them is generated by distributional issues and often perpetuated by bargaining dynamics. By dealing directly and non-polemically with realist criticisms, in the context of specific security institutions, we seek to go beyond fruitless debates by linking state power with institutional dynamics.

As sketched in section 1, our brand of institutionalism relies heavily on contractual theories in economics and on the rationality assumption, albeit a 'soft' one. States are viewed, within limits, as actors whose strategies can be seen as the result of rational calculations by their leaders. Sometimes coalitional and institutional politics within countries lead these strategies to

---

[10] Krasner (1991); Walt (1997); Fearon (1998).

be self-contradictory or ineffective abroad; but the assumption of rational action helps, as a first approximation, to make sense of much state behaviour.

Historical institutionalists often object to the rationality assumption, and what they see also as the static nature of contractual models. Not only relationships among actors, but the character of the actors themselves, change over time. Without relaxing the rationality assumption and the assumption that actors' preferences are fixed, they contend, issues of institutional change cannot be adequately addressed.[11] In the view of historical institutionalists, the myopic attention of many contractual or rational-choice institutionalists to contemporary institutions, or to their activities within a short span of time, leads them to avoid important issues of institutional change. Likewise, constructivists have criticized the same premises of fixed preferences and instrumental action.[12]

We are interested both in comparative statics and in change. Over certain periods of time, among certain countries (e.g. NATO members during the cold war), the assumption of fixed basic preferences seems reasonable. Its analytical advantages are significant, since it prevents the analyst from tautologically inferring 'changed preferences' whenever behaviour changes. Where the assumption of fixed preferences is justified, institutional effects can be analysed by seeing how institutions affect the incentives facing actors, given their preferences, and therefore their instrumental strategies. However, when fundamental shocks occur, or over long periods of time, actors and their preferences do change. Under these conditions, the analyst has to explore how the fundamental interests of societies, and therefore the preferences of their agents (states or governments), may change. International institutions may also play a role in these changes, although it is important not to overemphasize their impact as compared to that of fundamental changes in technologies, geopolitical situations, or domestic politics.

3. *Function and Form of Security Institutions*

Security problems can be created by four different underlying situations: collaboration, coordination, suasion, and assurance.[13] In all four situations, uncoordinated self-help policies lead to suboptimal results, but the reasons

---

[11] Thelen *et al.* (1992).
[12] Katzenstein (1996); M. C. Williams (1997).   [13] Martin (1992*b*).

for these failures to achieve potential joint gains are different in each case. Because the reasons for failure are different, solutions which permit cooperation differ, as do the institutional features which can provide those solutions to states. The relationship between function and institutional form is important for institutional theory because it provides the basis for explaining variation in institutional form, and for hypotheses about the causes and directions of institutional change. Each chapter in this volume, though to varying degrees, will thus look at the functions and the range of tasks performed by an institution; the degree of institutionalization; and how and with what authority decisions are made.

In collaboration games such as Prisoner's Dilemma, cooperation is not self-enforcing, and cheating is a fundamental problem. Under these conditions, protecting oneself from becoming a 'sucker' implies forgoing gains from cooperation. Coordination games, in contrast, have stable equilibria, from which no participant has an incentive unilaterally to defect. Since solutions to coordination problems are self-enforcing, these may seem easier to solve than collaboration problems. However, in the typical co-ordination problem, several different modes of coordination are possible, with differential advantages for various partners. The key problem is that of choosing among multiple equilibria; although cooperation is not thwarted by dominant strategies of defection, it may never be launched, due to disagreement about coordination points.[14]

In assurance problems, mutual cooperation is the preferred outcome of each actor. However, cooperation may be obstructed by incomplete information about other states' preferences or states' fear that another state's intention to fulfil the agreement will be altered by shifts in domestic politics that change dominant interpretations of national interests. Suasion problems arise where one state's dominant strategy is to cooperate, enabling the other state to defect by effectively exploiting its partners' unconditional cooperation.

These different underlying obstacles require different solutions, and imply different institutional forms. In order to overcome collaboration problems, states need mechanisms that sustain credibility of promises and mitigate the consequences of defection (that is, cheating). To solve these problems, institutions impose costs on participants (hence preventing free-riding and discouraging potential cheaters); establish standards and monitor conformity with them; and institute rules of transparency, making cheating harder to conceal. These issues are familiar from discussions of

---

14 Schelling (1960); Fearon (1998); Raiffa (1982).

trade policy and other issues in the world political economy, where models of market failure as modelled by Prisoners' Dilemma are often (although not always) applicable. The basic means of enforcing agreements in collaboration games, in international institutions as well as in local self-governance, is reciprocity.

Solving coordination problems typically requires a focal point—an equilibrium solution presented to the parties as a result of the dominant power of one actor, historical evolution, or decisions by previously established institutions.[15] Such a focal point may need legitimation through institutional processes; but once adopted, solutions to pure coordination games are self-enforcing.

Problems of assurance require mechanisms for transparency, which show that the institution's members do not have exploitative intentions, but seek instead to maintain cooperative relations. The task of such institutions is not to enforce rules or sanction members, but to make it easier for them to reveal their benign intentions. In particular, confidence-building measures will be central to institutions with assurance functions. More ambitiously, to reassure states that their partners will not involuntarily defect from their agreements, international institutions for assurance can create transparency about domestic politics and be designed to reinforce those domestic political institutions that favour cooperation. For example, NATO was not merely a military alliance for deterrence against the Soviet Union, but was a mechanism for shaping Germany's domestic politics, and in particular its civil-military relations, to preclude hostile and nationalist interests.

Institutions play a different role in suasion problems, which have asymmetrical equilibrium outcomes that leave one actor dissatisfied. For instance, the United States had a unilateral incentive to control technology exports to the Soviet bloc during the cold war, and continues to have an incentive to prevent nuclear proliferation, regardless of the policies of other states. Smaller states therefore had incentives to try to 'free-ride', to which the United States has responded by setting up institutions to monitor their behaviour and provide a vehicle for linking these issues to others. Weaker states, forced to comply, use these multilateral institutions as excuses for their concessions. In suasion games, therefore, we should expect international institutions to be dominated by powerful states and not to be at all transparent.[16]

---

[15] Milgrom *et al.* (1990); Garrett and Weingast (1993).
[16] For this argument, see Martin (1992*b*: 777–80).

4. *The Effects of Security Institutions*

Institutions may affect any of several factors that influence outcomes in international security relations. Most simply, institutions may affect a state's strategies by changing the options available and altering their costs and benefits. A military alliance such as NATO provides for collective defence by credibly threatening joint retaliation, and in doing so it may deter aggression. The nuclear non-proliferation regime institutionalizes international monitoring in order to make the diversion of nuclear technology for weapons production more difficult and therefore to reduce incentives to acquire nuclear weapons. UN peacekeeping under chapter 6 provides additional options to inaction, unilateralism, or enforcement measures under chapter 7. Comprehensive political security institutions such as OSCE are meant to prevent the return to mistrustful and overly defensive security strategies by involving member states in an ongoing process of information exchange and transparency.

Institutions can also affect outcomes by altering the power resources available to states in their interactions. It is obvious that a highly integrated and capable alliance such as NATO is far more than the sum of its national militaries, and is a significant factor itself in the European balance of power. As a result, membership in NATO confers additional influence on its major participants: during the cold war, German power in world affairs was enhanced by close institutional affiliation to NATO.[17] More modestly, the operations of international peacekeeping forces can alter the outcomes of crises and enhance the influence of states that play a lead in the organizations controlling these forces: as a result, being a permanent member of the United Nations Security Council confers a degree of influence on countries that are otherwise middle powers, such as Britain and France, while exclusion from that status constrains a country such as Germany.

More subtly, the information that international institutions create, or allow states to convey, can serve as a source of influence. A state that develops a history of providing reliable information may thereby gain influence with its partners. More generally, states that can shape the norms governing international practice, and whose behaviour fits those norms, may command resources of 'soft power'.[18] In the long run, these resources may be of immense importance if other states accept these norms and thereby alter their preferences—their conceptions of self-interest—in ways

---

[17] Haftendorn (1996a); Tuschhoff, this volume, Ch. 5.   [18] Nye (1990).

that are favourable to the norm-creating state. The United States has successfully promoted democracy and free markets around the world; the
resulting configuration of countries is much more favourable to American
policy than would be a world of state socialism.

But power is not the whole story, even 'soft power'. Institutions can affect
prevailing ideas and norms. For instance, norms against biological weapons
production, nuclear proliferation, or the offensive use of force could lead
states to redefine their interests in terms of refusal to produce biological
weapons, maintenance of non-nuclear status, or the construction of an
entirely defensive military doctrine.

One task of this book is to demonstrate that international institutions
have significant effects on state security policies, whether by affecting the
options available, hard and soft power resources, or the norms governing
international interactions. We should, however, beware of the easy fallacy of
assuming that institutions have only positive effects. History provides many
examples of alliances being employed to aggregate power resources in the
hands of nations with aggressive intentions. The ineffectiveness of UN
peacekeeping in Somalia and Bosnia should remind us that, when there is
a mismatch between institutional capabilities and the mission to be performed, reliance on an international organization can be a recipe for
disaster. And even when the motivations for institutional action are benign
and its activities effective, cooperation in international institutions can
attenuate democratic control and thus undermine democratic legitimacy.[19]

When institutions change the costs and benefits of the options facing
states, we speak of institutions affecting state *strategies*. Under these
circumstances, underlying interests—state preferences—remain the same.
For instance, NATO's preparations for deterrence of, and defence against, a
potential Soviet attack on West Germany during the cold war through
NATO raised its costs and lowered the benefits: it did not change Soviet
security interests or preferences. The availability of the UN enabled states to
choose multilateral, rather than unilateral, action (or no action) in places as
diverse as Cambodia, Somalia, and Iraq.

Sometimes the effect of institutions goes deeper: states' fundamental
objectives are altered. The Federal Republic of Germany was constituted not
as a totally independent state with traditional sovereignty, but as a member
of international institutions that both constrained it and provided it with
legitimacy. Germany's institutional commitments became 'reflexive': its
reliance on a web of international institutions 'became so complete as to

---

[19] Scharpf (1994).

cause these institutions to become embedded in the very definition of state interests and strategies'.[20]

In comparing these types of effects, the language of 'preferences, interests and strategies' becomes confusing because these terms are used inconsistently in the literature. This issue can be clarified by thinking in terms of ends-means chains: means at a more fundamental level in the chain are ends at a less fundamental level. For instance, a people's most fundamental objectives may be 'life, liberty, and the pursuit of happiness', and they may therefore constitute governments as means to these ends, as in the US Declaration of Independence. At the next level, maintaining the resulting state structures becomes an end, to which building an effective military defence is a means. But it may be that alliances are essential to military effectiveness; that institutionalization is necessary to make alliances function smoothly; and that a reallocation of state resources is essential to institutionalize the alliances. In the ends-means chain, what was a means or a 'strategy' at a more fundamental level becomes an end or a 'preference' at the next stage.

The implication of the ends-means chain is that the distinction between 'preferences' and 'strategies' should not be reified: from one perspective, maintaining alliance institutions will be properly seen as a strategy (a means to a higher level end), while from another vantage-point, it will appear as a preference (an end in itself). What is most important is to recognize the relationship of actions at various levels to one another: to see how they are linked together in a causal chain. But to avoid confusion, labelling must be consistent. In this volume, therefore, we will only speak of preferences changing when we observe changes in principled beliefs, causal beliefs, or general world-views.[21] We will use the terminology of 'changes in strategy' when the changes in beliefs take place at lower levels on the chain: for example, when beliefs change about other actors' preferences and strategies or policy options created by institutions.

5. *Continuity and Change in Security Institutions*

We are interested not only in the effects of a given set of security institutions, but in how these institutions change and adapt. Institutions are both affected by environmental factors and themselves affect the process of institutional change. For example, purposive organizations, with bureaucracies and executive heads, are important components of security institutions. When

[20] Anderson and Goodman (1993: 60).   [21] See Goldstein and Keohane (1993).

conditions such as the security environment change, these organizations can react by changing their allocations of resources, the tasks they pursue, and the constituencies that they seek to satisfy. That is, they can adapt to change. In addition to variation in the international environment such as evidenced at the end of the cold war, other sources of change may be the persistent violation of norms by a member state, or other forms of defection. We need to know more about which features make an institution most robust against violations. As Shanks and her colleagues show, the death-rate among intergovernmental organizations is quite high (over 30 per cent between 1981 and 1992): adaptation seems to be necessary to survival. Indeed, all preliminary findings indicate that the ability of an institution to thrive, or even to survive, depends on its adaptability.[22]

Adaptation requires that organizations be sensitive not only to general changes in their environments, but specifically to the interests and foreign-policy preferences of their most important members. Hence, this volume pays a great deal of attention to reciprocal interactions between institutions and national governments, focusing on the impact of institutions on national policy and the impact of such national policy on the institutions themselves. As noted above, institutions can have effects on policy by affecting preferences, one actor's understanding of others' preferences or beliefs, or environmental constraints. Each chapter clearly identifies the points on the causal chain that are affected, how these impacts affect behaviour later on the causal chain, and how feedback operates from later to earlier points in a recursive process. Since feedback is so important, most of the chapters in this volume devote some attention both to the effects of institutions and to issues of institutional change. Indeed, the feedback process between institutions and policy makes consideration of both sets of issues essential to understand either institutional effects or institutional change. They are difficult to comprehend separately.

One way to sort out the state–institutions relationship is to begin at the state level. A state's policies will be affected by certain *exogenous* changes over which it has no control. These include changes in the international system itself, including shifts in power and in other states' policies, which affect our particular state's security problems. Some changes, in contrast, may be direct results of the state's own policies, and therefore *endogenous* to state policy. Finally, other changes will be mixtures of exogenous and endogenous factors. For instance, changes induced by past institutional developments are likely both to reflect actions of other states, over which our country had little or no control, and its own past actions. The more

---

[22] Shanks *et al.* (1995); Haftendorn (1996*a*).

powerful the country concerned, the larger the endogenous element in the institutional mix.

Since institutional change in the security domain largely reflects changes in state policies, an analysis of institutional change should begin by investigating sources of changes in state policies, as discussed above. Such an analysis then needs to be extended to institutional dynamics: how interactions between state policies yielded outcomes, through bargaining processes, that were not necessarily predictable from the set of policies themselves.

Different theoretical approaches in international relations call attention to different potential sources of change. Realists argue that changes in the power and interests of states are key sources of institutional change. Institutionalists, while accepting the importance of power and interests, point to the roles played by institutional forms, the structuring of options by institutions, and the resulting institutional effects on the capabilities of states to act collectively. Liberal pluralists emphasize domestic politics and its impact on state policy. Finally, analysts interested in the role of ideas, including social constructivists, emphasize the impact of changes in fundamental beliefs and therefore in preferences. All of these factors will be considered in this volume, as we wrestle with the complex problem of how to account for institutional change.

6. *Research Design and Methodology*

World history records only one highly institutionalized multilateral alliance with operational organizations that has lasted for more than forty years: NATO. The resulting centrality of NATO to our analysis is methodologically uncomfortable. We can neither sample from a large population of security institutions, nor even examine a relatively small set of independent security institutions that perform similar functions in different contexts—as students of comparative politics have tried to do with states. There are other security institutions in Europe, such as OSCE and WEU, but they are clearly influenced by the existence of NATO; there are security institutions elsewhere, such as those revolving around the UN Security Council and the Asian Regional Forum discussed by Iain Johnston in this volume, but they perform very different functions. In so far as our unit of analysis is the security institution, this is definitely a 'small-n' study.

It is always difficult to establish causality in a small-n situation. Researchers cannot experiment with history, but have to seek to find well-controlled comparisons to increase the number of cases available to them, or otherwise to find ways to get around the fundamental problem of causal inference.[23] This volume gives explicit attention to specifying the points in the ends-means chain that a given set of institutions affects, and attempts to carry out a comparative analysis of security institutions; but we do not pretend to have overcome the fundamental problems inherent in our subject of study. As a result, the following chapters principally engage in descriptive rather than causal inference: they seek to describe institutions and events in coherent ways that make sense of the actions we observe, without pretending to generate causal hypotheses from independent theory, much less to test those hypotheses. Hence we offer 'explanations' only in the weak sense of accounts that enable us, as observers, to understand the incentives and rationales for the actions that we see.

Some of the papers in this volume examine the impact of institutions on state policies and international outcomes. In terms of our ends-means chain, they examine how institutions affect strategies, or fundamental preferences. Other papers focus on processes of institutional change as the dependent variable. Here the emphasis is on how state policies affect institutions rather than vice versa. In either case, other factors are important: for instance, the structure of cooperation problems (involving the relative power of states and their interests), prevailing norms, and exogenous shocks may affect state policies and outcomes. In our analysis we will seek first to understand the effects of these extraneous factors; and having done so, to control for them in order to investigate what principally concerns us: the impact of institutions on state policies and outcomes, or the process of institutional change.

7. Preview of the Chapters of the Book

The book is organized according to the questions posed. Part I deals specifically with the functions and forms of security institutions. We need to clarify both the relationship between function and form and the variations in this relationship before we can formulate hypotheses about the effects of institutions and the causes and directions of institutional change. Chapter 1, written by Celeste Wallander and Robert Keohane, proceeds from the point that security institutions, like any institutions, vary both in their levels of institutionalization and in their forms. The authors construct a typology of security coalitions based on the degree to which they are

---

[23] King *et al.* (1994: 79–80).

institutionalized, whether they are organized exclusively or inclusively, and whether they are designed to cope with threats or risks. Besides establishing a relationship between function and form, Wallander and Keohane are most interested in institutional change. They argue that the tasks performed by alignments or alliances will become less valuable to members when threats are transformed into risks, but the functions that could be performed by security management institutions will become potentially more valuable. Examining three historical cases as well as the transformation of NATO after the end of the cold war, they conclude that institutionalized alliances are more likely to persist than non-institutionalized alignments, and that hybrid institutions, performing multiple functions, are more easily transformed than institutions which focus only on coping with threats.

Following an argument made by Wallander and Keohane, in Chapter 2 Louise Richardson asks whether institutions are historically contingent. The answer to this question is extremely important for judging the reach of institutional theory, and has not been explored at any depth before. Applying institutionalist concepts to the work of diplomatic historians, Richardson examines the Concert of Europe. Her findings demonstrate convincingly that an analysis of institutions prior to today's institution-rich environment can expand the database by providing evidence of institutional effect, adaptation, persistence, and demise. Her analysis of the Concert suggests that institutional form is a product of (*a*) institutional function, (*b*) technical feasibility, and (*c*) recent experience by members. Her chapter makes furthermore the case that institutions are not merely means for the maintenance of the status quo but can peacefully accommodate changes in the distribution of power.

In Chapter 3, Carsten Tams looks at a more recent case where the relationship between function and form is significant. In analysing the negotiations on establishing a European Security and Defence Identity (ESDI), he explains the ostensible difficulties Britain, France, and Germany have in reaching a substantive agreement on its institutional form, as a result of their fundamental disagreements about which functions an ESDI should perform. While France, supported by Germany, promoted collective defence as a core function of ESDI, Britain fervently opposed it. In contrast, all three countries agreed that the ESDI should serve the purpose of out-of-area intervention. Therefore, Tams expects that an ESDI, if achieved, will take the form of an institution for coping above all with out-of-area risks.

While states use institutions to further their interests, institutions also have an impact on state behaviour. Thus, Part II deals with a variety of effects security institutions may have. In contrast to theories understanding

the causes and effects of alliances exclusively in terms of 'capability aggregation', Christopher Gelpi begins his analysis in Chapter 4 from the
assumption that alliances can influence the behaviour not only of external
threats, but also of member states. In particular, they can serve as instruments of inter-allied control. Gelpi investigates the influence that alliance
commitments have had on the success of mediation attempts in international crises, and the impact that alliance ties to the mediator had on the
probability that the challenger would prevail. His findings indicate that
realist and institutionalist arguments about the impact of alliances complement each other. Alliance ties give leverage to mediators, as institutional
theory expects; but (consistent with realism) great powers are more effective mediators than neutrals.

Christian Tuschhoff and Helga Haftendorn also look at the impact an
institution has on members' preferences and strategies and the institution's
ability to change. In Chapter 5, Tuschhoff challenges the realist expectation
that inter-alliance cohesion will weaken if major changes in the balance of
power among its members occur, meaning that states must hedge both
against an ally with increasing capabilities and against an exterior enemy.
He finds that in NATO members rarely hedged against a rising power,
Germany. He argues that alliance institutions reduced uncertainty about
German political behaviour and mitigated concerns that it would use its
increased power—understood as control over actors, resources, and outcomes—for unilateral purposes. He concludes that NATO maintained its
cohesion because it allowed its members to manage Germany's increased
power while at the same time maintaining and strengthening their defence
commitments, exchanging information, and enforcing joint agreements.

In Chapter 6, Helga Haftendorn traces in the evolution of the Quad—
quadripartite cooperation and consultation procedures between the representatives of Britain, France, Germany, and the United States—from its
feeble beginning in the mid-1950s through its acquisition of an elaborate
institutional repertoire in the cold war years and to its largely secretive
existence in the present. Using the nature of the cooperation problem,
members' valuation of the institution, and the degree of commonality as
explanatory variables, she focuses on the changing institutional specificity
of this institution, its surprising persistence in spite of a radically transformed international environment, and its management of the internal
redistribution of power. Although the specificity of the Quad's form and the
portability of its rules and procedures are explained by the nature of the
cooperation problem, its tasks and members' valuation of its institutional
repertoire account for its persistence. Haftendorn also observes a redistri-

bution of power and influence within the Quad in favour of Germany parallel to Tuschhoff's regarding NATO, which she attributes at least in part to the trust that had evolved among the members of the Quad.

At its core, the issue for institutional theory is to establish that changes in states' behaviour result from institutional effects. Ingo Peters in Chapter 7 examines the effects Germany's membership in the Conference on Security and Cooperation in Europe[24] (C/OSCE) had on its foreign-policy strategies. He shows that German policy toward the C/OSCE was driven by two major policy preferences: to safeguard unification and the management of European security risks. Because of the benefits Germany derived from its C/OSCE membership, it did in turn see this organization not just as a means, but as end in itself and continued to follow multilateral strategies even after the end of the cold war when unification had been achieved and the military threat had subsided. Thus, he argues that in this instance the C/OSCE affected not only German strategies, but its fundamental security preferences.

While the preceding papers dealt predominantly with the effects security institutions had on state preferences and strategies, those of Part III concentrate on continuity and change in institutions themselves. In Chapter 8, Christopher Daase looks at an institution that has not been deliberately created but has evolved over time. Combining institutionalist and constructivist approaches, he analyses the evolution of international peacekeeping by explaining how conventions evolve without conscious human design, maintain themselves without the existence of formal enforcement mechanisms, and change without a plan for further institutional development. Drawing on invisible hand explanations of institutional change, Daase sees the adaptation of peacekeeping as an incremental transformation through continuous marginal adjustments of practice, and explains it as the cumulative causal consequences of many separate functional decisions by political actors. The emergence, stability, and transformation of peacekeeping can thus be explained as the unintended effect of intended behaviour.

Henning Riecke's contribution to this volume, Chapter 9, deals with the nuclear non-proliferation regime. Specifically, he focuses on the impact that unilateral actions—i.e. actions outside of established institutional procedures—by a powerful actor or small groups of actors have on the effectiveness of this regime. He concludes that unilateral actions by powerful states can have a positive impact on the effectiveness of the regime if they

---

[24] In Dec. 1994 the name changed to Organization for Security and Cooperation in Europe, hence its current acronym 'OSCE'.

neither violate its principled rules nor are the strongly held preferences of other relevant actors. He further assumes that a high degree of specificity of both principled and procedural rules will best ensure the effectiveness of the non-proliferation regime.

Iain Johnston, in Chapter 10, supplements institutionalist with social constructivist analysis in a study of the Asian Region Forum (ARF). He argues that the initial low level of ARF institutionalization was a result both of the lack of consensus about operative security problems and of a deliberate design to ensure China's participation. The ARF's evolution has been a story about path-dependence and mutual constitution, as the ARF itself created conditions for its evolution toward greater institutionalization and a more intrusive security agenda. He concludes that the ARF story shows that actors' interests may be changed by social interaction inside an institution, thereby showing one way institutions themselves change. In contrast to Riecke's assumptions, Johnson's findings indicate that an optimal institution may not be the one with a high degree of specificity in its institutional repertoire, but rather one that is most likely to change an actor's interests in ways that maximize the likelihood that it will voluntarily accept maximally constraining commitments. This might well be an institution without especially intrusive monitoring and sanctioning mechanisms to elicit cooperation from potential defectors.

In the concluding chapter the editors compare the findings of the empirical analyses with each other. They ask which new insights the various cases have yielded regarding the relationship between functions and form, the effects of institutions on state preferences and strategies, and on the mechanism of institutional change. They are confident that the results will not only reaffirm and sharpen institutionalist theory and its application to a wide number of security institutions, but will also contribute to the further development of the theories of international relations.

I

Function and Form of
Security Institutions

1

RISK, THREAT,
AND SECURITY INSTITUTIONS

Celeste A. Wallander and Robert O. Keohane

The post-cold war world presents challenges for both policy and theory in international relations. One important challenge to international relations theory is the anomaly of NATO's continuity after the cold war. Inspired by the Soviet threat, created under American leadership, designed to bolster the security of its members against the Soviet Union by aggregating defence capabilities, NATO ought to be either collapsing or withering away: dying with a bang or a whimper. Indeed, since the end of the cold war theorists working in the realist tradition have clearly and forcefully predicted NATO's demise, if not in 'days' then in 'years'.[1]

This prediction turned out to be wrong. More than nine years after the Berlin Wall was dismantled and seven years after the Soviet Union collapsed, NATO not only continues to exist but is growing and taking on new tasks. It is an obvious magnet for states of Central and Eastern Europe; it plays a central role in the former Yugoslavia; and it clearly remains the primary instrument of American security policy in Europe. Reports of NATO's death were exaggerated: like other established international institutions,

This research was supported by the Weatherhead Center for International Affairs of Harvard University (WCFIA); the National Council for Soviet and East European Research; and the German Marshall Fund of the United States. They are not responsible for the contents or findings of this study. We thank Lois Kaznicki for her excellent research assistance. For their insights, ideas, and critiques, we especially thank members of the WCFIA Study Group on Alliances and members of the Arbeitsstelle Transatlantische Außen- und Sicherheitspolitik of the Freie Universität, Berlin, with whom we have had many productive meetings on these issues. We also express our gratitude to participants at a panel on alliance theory at the 1995 ISA conference in Chicago and to participants at an Olin Institute National Security Group seminar at the Center for International Affairs. We are grateful to Robert Art, Peter Barschdorff, Marc Busch, John Duffield, Christopher Gelpi, Hein Goemans, Peter Gourevitch, Iain Johnston, Mark Kramer, David Lake, Jeff Legro, Lisa Martin, Andrew Moravcsik, James Morrow, Joseph S. Nye, Jr., Robert Paarlberg, Dan Reiter, Louise Richardson, Stephen Walt, and Reinhard Wolf for written comments on various versions of this paper. Special thanks go to our colleague, Helga Haftendorn, who offered astute and comprehensive comments on several drafts over several years.

[1] Mearsheimer (1990); Waltz (1993).

it remains valuable because of the uncertainty that would result if it disappeared.[2]

What went wrong with realist theory and right with NATO? In this chapter, we develop a typology of security institutions and propositions on their form, function, persistence, and change. We use contractual theories of institutions to suggest answers to a general question which the response of NATO to the end of the cold war illustrates: what happens to alliances when their precipitating threats disappear? Our framework and propositions complement the more in-depth analyses of the effects and dynamics of a variety of security institutions developed by the authors in Chapters 2–10 of this volume.

The core of our analysis is based on recognition that security institutions, like any institutions, vary both in their levels of institutionalization and in their forms. Major wars, and long struggles such as the cold war, generate alliances, which are institutionalized security coalitions designed to aggregate capabilities and coordinate strategies to cope with perceived threats. When threats disappear, the original *raison d'être* of alliances would appear to have vanished and we might expect the institutions to be discarded. But when threats disappear, other security problems remain. Hence, efforts may be made to maintain the institutionalized security coalitions, but to transform their functions to cope with the more diffuse set of security problems we characterize as risks, and thus to transform alliances into security management institutions. Such institutional transitions have been difficult to effect. After the Napoleonic Wars and this century's two World Wars, attempts were made to transform alliances or alignments into security management institutions; and only in the earliest case, that of the Concert of Europe, did this transformation work. Yet in the contemporary case of NATO, it appears that an alliance is being transformed into a security management institution. We seek to understand, through conceptual and historical analysis, what the conditions are for such a successful transformation to occur. In doing so, we both broaden institutional theory beyond its roots in political economy and deepen its explanatory power by advancing institutional hypotheses on change.

To help us understand the transformation of security institutions, we construct a new typology of security coalitions, based on three dimensions: the degree to which they are institutionalized, whether they are organized exclusively or inclusively, and whether they are designed to cope with threats or risks. We use this typology to generate two key propositions. The first proposition is a standard institutional hypothesis: highly institutional-

---

[2] This statement paraphrases a sentence in Keohane and Nye (1993: 19).

ized alliances are more likely to persist, despite changes in the environment, than non-institutionalized alignments. Our second proposition, more novel, builds on the other two dimensions of our typology. Alliances are exclusive security institutions, designed principally to deal with threats from non-members. Some alliances, however, also have to cope with risks of conflicts among members, and therefore develop an 'inclusive' aspect, oriented toward risk-management. Our key hypothesis is that these more complex alliances are more likely to be able to adapt to the ending of threats by elaborating and developing those practices designed to cope with risks rather than threats. In our terminology, the rules and practices of 'hybrid' institutions will be more 'portable' than the rules and practices of single-purpose alliances focused only on threat.

We explain our typology in section 1 of this chapter, by elaborating our distinctions between threat and risk and exclusivity versus inclusivity; and by discussing what we mean by institutionalization. In section 2 we set out our hypotheses, which we illustrate with reference to previous situations in which threats disappeared, and with reference to NATO. However, we do not pretend to test our hypotheses in this chapter. A number of the authors of subsequent chapters use our typology, or some of our hypotheses, to structure their empirical investigations. The evidence is mixed and far from comprehensive; but our concepts and arguments seem relevant to change in security institutions, and to NATO in particular.

The final section of this chapter, section 3, argues for the reframing of the problem of NATO enlargement—from one of alliance expansion to institutional change. We argue that NATO is changing from an alliance to a security management institution; that this transformation should be encouraged because it encourages stability in Europe; and that it implies the continued expansion of NATO to include all countries in the region that can reliably be counted on to support its principles and follow its rules. Eventually, NATO as a security management institution could even include a democratic Russia. Refocusing the issue as one of institutional change rather than mere expansion sheds new light both on the criticisms of NATO expansion and on the conditions that should be fulfilled for such expansion to continue.

1. A Typology of Security Institutions

Some commonly understood rules are intrinsic to all diplomatic interchange, so in that sense, all of international politics is institutionalized. But the institutionalization of security coalitions (as of other practices in international relations) varies greatly, from minimal to substantial. As we will see, it matters for a security coalition how institutionalized its practices are.

Institutionalization can be measured along three dimensions: commonality, specificity, and differentiation.[3]

(1) Commonality refers to the degree to which expectations about appropriate behaviour are shared by participants.
(2) Specificity refers to the degree to which specific and enduring rules exist, governing the practices of officials, obligations of states, and legitimate procedures for changing collective policy. Greater specificity is reflected in more detailed and demanding primary rules, specifying what members must do; and secondary rules, indicating how rules can be changed or recognized as binding, that are clear, more comprehensive, and that provide for rule-change and recognition that preclude vetoes by individual members.[4] For example, the European Union now is more institutionalized in this sense than its predecessor, the European Economic Community, was in the 1970s; and NATO, although less institutionalized than the European Union, is more institutionalized than it was in the 1950s.
(3) Functional differentiation refers to the extent to which the institution assigns different roles to different members. As Kenneth Waltz has argued, one mark of an 'anarchic' international system is that it is composed of 'like units', performing similar functions in so far as their differing capabilities permit them to do so.[5] Conversely, a mark of an institution is that it organizes and legitimizes a division of responsibility, with different participants performing different functions.

Threats and risks

The security strategies with which we are concerned in this chapter involve measures to protect the territorial integrity of states from the adverse use of military force; efforts to guard state autonomy against the political effects of potential use; and policies designed to prevent the emergence of situations that could lead to the use of force against one's territory or vital interests.[6]

---

[3] This discussion builds on, and modifies, Keohane (1989: 4–5).
[4] Hart (1961).   [5] Waltz (1979).
[6] Security can be defined much more broadly, even to the point where it becomes identical with preservation of any value, as in 'economic security' and 'environmental security'. Since definitions are not matters of right or wrong, the fact that we have defined security in a relatively limited way does not imply that we reject such definitions; but such a broadening of the concept is not necessary for our purposes. See Walt (1991), Art (1994), and Wolfers (1962) for relatively narrow definitions of security. For a good discussion of the boundaries of the concept of security and the limitations of such a restrictive definition, see Haftendorn (1991).

Where a state's leaders regard it as facing a positive probability that another state will either launch an attack or seek to threaten military force for political reasons, it faces a *threat*. Threats pertain when there are actors that have the capabilities to harm the security of others and that are perceived by their potential targets as having intentions to do so. When no such threat exists, either because states do not have the intention or the capability to harm the security of others, states may nevertheless face a security *risk*.[7]

To illustrate the distinction, consider the classic security dilemma as discussed by John Herz and Robert Jervis. Herz and Jervis explained that when states with purely defensive or status quo intentions adopt policies to provide for their own security, they can unintentionally lead other states to take countermeasures that lead toward a spiral of mutual fear and antagonism.[8] Although intentional threat is absent, states may still face serious security problems.

In modern informational terms, the essence of the security dilemma lies in uncertainty and private information. As realists have long recognized, the key problem for policy-makers is the difficulty of distinguishing revisionist states with exploitative preferences from status quo states with defensive intentions. It may be possible for security dilemmas to be avoided or ameliorated if status quo states can provide credible information to distinguish themselves from revisionists eager to exploit the unwary.[9]

Another way to understand the distinction between threats and risks is to build on an analytical distinction between collaboration and coordination first drawn by Arthur Stein and referred to in the Introduction. While collaboration problems, such as Prisoners' Dilemma, entail threats because they involve the potential for cheating and exploitation, coordination (or bargaining) problems do not entail threats. The problem in coordination situations is that the players will be unable to come to an agreement because of competitive incentives, but if they can manage to agree both are satisfied with the outcome and would not exploit the other. Lisa Martin has further elaborated the distinction and discusses assurance problems, which are akin to coordination problems in that they do not involve the threat of exploitation and cheating but instead entail the risk that states will fail to achieve or maintain mutually beneficial cooperation because of fear, mistrust, and uncertainty.[10]

Thus, security arrangements may be designed not only to cope with security threats, as are classic alliances, but also with security risks. Because

---

[7] Daase (1992: 70–2 and 74–5); Wallander (1999: ch. 3).
[8] Herz (1951); Jervis (1978).   [9] Wolfers (1962); Fearon (1994); Powell (1996).
[10] Stein (1990); Martin (1992*b*).

the means to deal with these different security problems vary, we would expect institutional forms to vary as well. Institutions meant to cope with security threats will have rules, norms, and procedures to enable the members to identify threats and retaliate effectively against them. Institutions meant to cope with security risks will have rules, norms, and procedures to enable the members to provide and obtain information and to manage disputes in order to avoid generating security dilemmas. This distinction is the first building-block in our typology.

Inclusivity and exclusivity

Another dimension along which security coalitions can vary is their inclusivity or exclusivity. Coalitions can be designed to involve all states that could pose threats or risks, or they can deliberately exclude some of them. Collective security arrangements are inclusive, since they are designed to deal with threats among members; alliances are exclusive because they deter and defend against external threats.[11]

Although in principle states are free to choose either inclusive or exclusive strategies to cope with both threats and risks, exclusive strategies seem better suited to coping with threats, while inclusive strategies appear to be better able to cope with and manage risks.[12] Threats to national security posed by states with aggressive intentions are best met by aggregating capabilities and sending strong and credible signals of resolve, as in classic balancing alliances. Collective security arrangements are often vulnerable and ineffective because aggressive states may be able to exploit their symmetrically framed rules and processes, which present opportunities for obfuscation, delay, or vetoing action.[13] On the other hand, the problems posed for national security by risks and the security dilemma tend to be exacerbated by exclusive coalitions, because the institutions associated with such coalitions do not provide for transparency and information exchange between those states that are most likely to come into armed conflict with one another. Indeed, close coordination within alliances, along with distant relationships between them, may exacerbate suspicions associated with the security dilemma.

Combining the dimensions

Our distinctions between threats and risks, and inclusive versus exclusive

---

[11] Wolfers (1962: 183).   [12] Wallander (1999: ch. 2).   [13] Betts (1992).

inclusive	collective security	**security management institutions and diplomatic conferences**
exclusive	**alliances and alignments**	out-of-area coalitions
	threat	risk

Participation Criteria:

Situation facing states

FIGURE 1.1. Variation in Security Coalitions

institutions, yield the fourfold typology of Figure 1.1.[14] For reasons sketched above, the most successful arrangements will be found in the lower-left and upper-right sections of the diagram: exclusive arrangements will be associated with threats (alliances and alignments) and inclusive coalitions will be associated with situations of risk (security management).

Figure 1.2 directs attention to the two most important and successful types of security coalitions: (i) inclusive coalitions designed to deal with risk, and (ii) exclusive coalitions designed to cope with threat—the upper

inclusive/ risk	**diplomatic conferences**	**security management institutions**
exclusive/ threat	**alignments**	**alliances**
	minimally	highly

Participation Criteria and Focus of the Arrangement:

How institutionalized are the coalitions?

FIGURE 1.2. Institutional Variation in Security Arrangements

14 We are indebted to Hein Goemans for suggesting the terms 'inclusive' and 'exclusive', which clarified distinctions we had earlier tried to make, and to Carsten Tams for developing the exclusive/risk category and term 'out-of-area' (see Ch. 3 below).

right and lower left section of Figure 1.1, respectively. Let us first consider inclusive coalitions.

Diplomatic conferences called to discuss specific issues, such as the Geneva Conference of 1954 on Korea and Indochina, are inclusive and only minimally institutionalized. The Geneva Conference included China, the Soviet Union, Britain, France, and (reluctantly) the United States, as well as the Vietminh. It developed rules, but they were not highly elaborated; the expectations of participants were not closely aligned, and the institution did not prescribe functionally differentiated roles.

We use the term 'security management institution' to denote an inclusive, risk-oriented arrangement with highly institutionalized practices. The Concert of Europe in the nineteenth century and the Organization for Security and Cooperation in Europe today provide clear examples of security management institutions.[15] The League of Nations and United Nations were designed in part as collective security institutions (inclusive, seeking to cope with threats), but they also served as security management institutions, seeking to deal with risks—as exemplified by United Nations efforts at peaceful settlement of disputes under chapter 6 of the Charter.

Alignments and alliances, unlike diplomatic conferences and security management institutions, are directed against specific threats and are exclusive in membership form. We make a clear distinction between alliances—which we define as exclusive security institutions oriented towards threat—and alignments. Alignments are minimally institutionalized: examples include the 1967 Arab coalition against Israel and the coalition supporting UN action against Iraq during the Gulf War in 1990–1, which included both Syria and the United States.[16] In its earliest years, before being institutionalized, NATO was an alignment. Alliances, in contrast, are institutionalized security coalitions directed against specific threats. Alliances have rules, norms, and procedures to enable the members to identify threats and retaliate effectively against them. Expectations about actions in the event of future contingencies are shared among members; rules of behaviour are specific; and different roles are assigned to different participants. NATO, of course, is a model alliance, highly institutionalized.[17]

The key points are that we expect successful security coalitions to develop institutionalized rules and practices (as both NATO and UN peacekeeping have done); and that these rules and practices will broadly reflect the

---

[15] On OSCE, see Ch. 7, by Ingo Peters.

[16] On the 1967 coalition, see Walt (1987: 101). The Syria–United States example was suggested by James Morrow in a seminar at Harvard University, 28 Feb. 1995.

[17] Ch. 5 by Tuschhoff shows how NATO was institutionalized in all three ways.

functions performed by the institutions. Institutions meant to cope with security threats will have rules, norms, and procedures to enable the members to identify threats and retaliate effectively against them. Institutions meant to cope with security risks will have rules, norms, and procedures to enable the members to provide and obtain information and to manage disputes in order to avoid generating security dilemmas.

Our categories are ideal types. Institutionalization is always a matter of degree and mapping actual security institutions into Figure 1.2 would yield a continuum in the horizontal dimension. The vertical dimension would also be a continuum: alliances, as we will see in the case of NATO, may seek to manage the risks of conflict among members as well as to amass resources and coordinate members' actions against external threat. That is, alliances may function in part as security management institutions.[18] Nevertheless our typology makes useful distinctions which are helpful in explaining change in security coalitions and institutions, now and in the past. In particular, it highlights the important risk–threat distinction, which is often overlooked; and it emphasizes the importance of institutionalization for the actual operation of security coalitions.[19]

2. *Institutional Hypotheses on Change and Adaptation*

Institutional theory in international relations has addressed itself principally to two questions: (i) what explains variation in degree of institutionalization and institutional form? and (ii) what are the principal effects of international institutions? An explanation for institutional change requires, in addition to these foundations, an integrated understanding of how changes in the environment create pressures for institutional change, and how characteristics of institutions themselves affect which changes actually take place. In this section, we will begin by focusing on exogenous changes, stemming from the environment; then discuss endogenous sources of change; and finally, illustrate our hypotheses by discussing institutional change after three major wars: the Napoleonic Wars, and the First and Second World Wars.

---

[18] Schroeder (1976, 1994*a*).

[19] The emphasis on threats in the realist literature has led to an emphasis on exclusive security coalitions, and realism's underemphasis of the significance of institutionalization has contributed to its lack of interest in institutional variation, which is seen as either unimportant or merely a function of underlying power relations.

Uncertainty, problem durability, and issue density

Institutions arise, according to institutional theory, largely because of uncertainty, which generates a need for information. Uncertainty means not having information about other states' intentions and likely choices. Since choosing a strategy depends not merely on what a state wants but also on what it believes other states seek, uncertainty can be a very significant problem in security relations.[20] Governments therefore find it worthwhile to invest in information that will enable them to design strategies that are appropriate to their environments. One way of investing in information is to create institutions that provide it. Institutions can serve as the informational and signalling mechanisms that enable states to get more information about the interests, preferences, intentions, and security strategies of other states. They reduce uncertainty by providing credible information.[21] Furthermore, successful institutions may regularize the behaviour of states belonging to them, making it more predictable and decreasing uncertainty. Hence, if it is rational for states to invest in information, they may also invest in institutions that reduce uncertainty.

However, it is not only the information one receives, but the information one is able to provide to others that contributes to diplomatic success. This point has two distinct aspects. First, if one country influences the way others see the world—as the United States has during recent decades—it gains what Joseph S. Nye calls 'soft power'.[22] Much of US soft power is exercised through international institutions, ranging from the International Monetary Fund (IMF) to NATO. Second, within a given perceptual framework, being able to provide credible information to others is a source of influence.[23] Since uncertainty is high in world politics, the credibility of a state's own threats and promises becomes a factor in its ability to exercise influence over the behaviour of others. Hence, having a reputation for keeping commitments can be an asset.

Often theorists in the realist tradition argue that because institutions are costly to join (that is, they constrain state strategies) they will be avoided. However, this misses the point: it is precisely *because* actions are costly that they are credible and therefore can be valuable to self-interested states.[24] Institutions *enable* state strategies because it is costly to join and abide by them—thus, they are instruments for credible signalling. The question is whether the enabling benefits of joining a security institution are worth the

---

[20] Jervis (1976).   [21] Keohane (1984); Milgrom *et al.* (1990); Shepsle (1986).
[22] Nye (1990).   [23] Schelling (1960).
[24] Powell (1990); Martin (1992*a*); Fearon (1994).

costs and constraints. Institutionalist theory holds that to understand the demand for security institutions, we will need—as with other international institutions—to understand both how they provide information to states and how they affect credibility and reputation.

Uncertainty provides a generic reason for establishing security institutions. But institutions are costly to create, and do not arise automatically simply because they could be useful. We therefore need to ask what will affect the willingness of members (or potential members) to pay the costs of creating and sustaining the institutions. The key choice for potential members is between achieving cooperation on an *ad hoc* basis and investing in institutions. *Ad hoc* cooperation entails lower investment costs but forgoes the long-term benefits of having enduring rules and practices that facilitate future cooperation at low cost. Two variables should affect the willingness of potential members to make institution-specific investments: the durability of the problems and issue density.

The durability of the problems being faced is of obvious importance, since the longer challenges are expected to last, the more sensible it is to invest in institutions to deal with them. Thus variations in states' expectations of the durability of their security problems should help to explain variations in institutionalization. States will be more willing to pay for institutions when they expect the threat they face to be durable rather than transitory. For forty years after 1949, Western leaders expected what John F. Kennedy would call 'a long twilight struggle' against the threat of Soviet communism. The establishment of NATO depended on its members' beliefs that the threats they faced were durable.

Issue density refers to 'the number and importance of issues arising within a given policy space'.[25] In dense policy spaces, issues are interdependent, and need to be dealt with in a coordinated way to avoid negative externalities from policies for one issue on other policies. In dense policy spaces, institutions may achieve 'economies of scale'. For example, the issue density in European security relations from 1946 to 1949, when NATO was created, was substantial: in addition to deterring a Soviet attack, the potential Western allies were faced with the problem of a weak and possibly revanchist divided Germany, the need ultimately to rearm Germany yet to control it, French distrust of German intentions, and devastated economies of the potential allies which virtually precluded substantial defence spending by individual states.[26] Issue density can be a function of domestic

[25] Keohane (1982: 339–40).
[26] Osgood (1962: 72–4, 96–8); Hanrieder (1989: 40–1); Kugler (1993: 41–50); Duffield (1995: 39–40).

politics, high levels of economic and military interdependence, or close connections between internal politics and the external environment.

More generally, issue density means that interactions are likely to be repeated on related issues, providing the scope for strategies of reciprocity, which can sustain cooperation in iterated games.[27] Hence issue density may increase states' confidence that their partners will not act opportunistically in such a way as to vitiate the investment in institutions.[28] Mutual confidence is likely to be reinforced by the institutionalization of these multiple relationships, for two reasons. First, past institutionalized practice will have reduced uncertainty and increased trust. Second, the existence of other valued institutions, which could be jeopardized by opportunism in one institution, will provide incentives not to behave opportunistically. We therefore expect cooperative responses to be more likely when institutionalized behaviour has characterized the issue area in the past; and when related issue areas are highly institutionalized.

Problem durability and issue density both increase the number of issues that may be affected by sets of rules and practices that comprise institutions. When problems appear more durable and issue density higher, investments in institutions will have greater benefits, because they will pertain to more issues over a longer period of time. These benefits include providing information, increasing credibility, and reducing the costs of cooperation. We expect states to be most inclined to create institutions when problem durability and issue density create incentives to do so. And as long as densely clustered sets of problems exist, institutions that enable states to cope with them are likely to persist.

This framework, adapted from institutional theory, provides the basis for understanding the conditions that should be conducive to the institutionalization of security coalitions. In the next section we focus on endogenous sources of change: features of institutions that may facilitate a shift from institutions designed to cope with threats to institutions designed to cope with risks. We introduce two novel concepts—hybridization and portability—that help to explain variations in the adaptability and continuing significance of security institutions in general, and that throw light on the transformation of NATO into a security management institution.

Adaptation and hybridization

We have seen that security coalitions may be distinguished by their pur-

---

[27] Axelrod (1984); Martin (1995: 77).   [28] On opportunism, see Williamson (1985).

poses as well as by their degree of institutionalization. In particular, they may be directed against a specific external threat or designed to deal with the more diffuse problem of risks. Alliances and alignments, which are designed to cope with threats, need effectively to aggregate the military capabilities of their members in order to pose credible deterrence threats or efficient instruments of defence. In contrast, security management institutions do not need to mount credible deterrents and effective defences against adversaries. They need to provide for transparency, consultation, and incentives for cooperative strategies among members.

The question we pose is the following: under what conditions do decreases in threat lead to the abandonment of existing alignments or alliances, or instead, to their evolution? Our first argument is that institutionalization matters: alliances are better candidates for adaptation than alignments. More highly institutionalized coalitions are more likely to persist, since the marginal costs of maintaining existing institutions are smaller than the average costs of new ones. The sunk costs of old institutions have already been paid: in economics, 'bygones are bygones'.[29] Hence, even if the old institution is not optimal for current purposes, it may be sensible to maintain it rather than to try to form a new one—especially if the costs of negotiating such an entity would be very high, or uncertainty about success is great.[30]

However, this inertial explanation is insufficient. When situations change —for example, from an international environment in which threats are the main security problem to one in which risks are the principal focus of attention—the continued relevance of institutions depends on how well they can adapt rules and procedures devised for one set of problems to the emerging issues of the day. A classic example of successful adaptation is the March of Dimes, which was founded to combat polio. After the Salk vaccine was developed, the March of Dimes was able to shift its orientation from polio to birth defects, because its organizational competence was in raising funds rather than being specific to polio. However, adaptability is by no means assured. In international relations, institutions that were built on principles contradictory to those of a new era may become worse than useless. After 1989, both the Warsaw Pact and CoCom—the institution devised by the United States and its allies to deny strategic materials to the Soviet bloc—disappeared.[31]

---

[29] For this argument, see Keohane (1984: 100–3). Stinchcombe (1968: 120–1) has a good discussion of sunk costs. The phrase, 'in economics, bygones are bygones', was the first part of a *bon mot* of Charles Kindleberger, the second half of which was, 'while in politics, they're working capital'.   [30] For this inertial institutional argument, see McCalla (1996).

[31] CoCom stands for Coordinating Committee for Export Controls. On CoCom's demise and institutional successor, the Wassenaar Accord, see Wallander (1999: ch. 7).

We use the word 'portability' to describe the ease with which the rules and practices of one institution can be adapted to other situations. Institutional repertoires are often adjustable, at least within some range. Both portability and its limits are illustrated by the attempt by the United Nations to adapt its institutional arrangements for peacekeeping to the war in Bosnia. Sufficient similarity between traditional UN missions and the issues in Bosnia existed for the UN to be able to mount a Bosnian expedition and achieve some tactical successes by negotiating cease-fires as well as providing relief to the civilian population. But coercing belligerents was not part of the UN's peacekeeping repertoire, and the mission collapsed over its inability to perform that function, which was essential to achieving an enduring cease-fire.

We argue that institutions are more likely to adapt to new conditions when their rules and practices are portable. Institutions that combine a variety of functions are more likely than narrowly focused institutions to find that some of their rules and practices are more portable: the fact that they have a variety of rules and organizational repertoires means that some of those rules and repertoires are more likely to remain relevant after sudden environmental change occurs. Specifically, institutions that combine functions related to risk *and* threat are more likely than single-purpose institutions to have more rules and repertoires that are portable after threat declines. Paul Schroeder has argued that alliances can be 'tools of management' as well as modes of aggregating power against threats.[32] We follow Schroeder's analysis in recognizing that alliances have in fact often contained measures to manage relations among members. We call institutions that combine risk-directed management functions with threat-directed power aggregation functions *hybrid institutions*. Hybrid security institutions deal both with security problems created by external threats or problems and those problem posed by risks, mistrust, and misunderstandings among members. The classic conceptualization of alliances as arrangements to aggregate power does not allow for these multiple purposes, and therefore fails to capture the reality of contemporary alliances. For instance, the highly institutionalized bilateral alliance between the United States and Japan has developed a rich set of common expectations and specific rules and a clear functional division of labour, both to guard against external threats and, increasingly, to deal with the risk that tensions on economic issues between the two countries would disrupt their security partnership.[33]

---

[32] Schroeder (1976).

[33] On the US–Japanese security dialogue, which in our terms sought further to institutionalize the relationship by establishing firmer common expectations, see Nye (1995).

On the other hand, alignments such as that of the Axis powers during the Second World War, or even the Grand Alliance of Britain, the United States, and the Soviet Union, were not highly institutionalized and were dominated by the single purpose of winning the war. The point is that security arrangements differ with respect to degree of hybridization, because some focus only on threats while others encompass issues of risk as well. We put forward the hypothesis—although we do not prove it—that hybrid institutions are generally more adaptable than non-hybrid arrangements.

The concept of portability helps us understand why member states attempt to use existing NATO practices, procedures, and rules to deal with new security problems and to overcome new obstacles to security cooperation among the allies. It also suggests that having discovered over time that some such procedures are portable, members will become more willing to invest in them in the future. We see this pattern in the reliance of NATO members on NATO infrastructure and procedures to develop, deploy, and operate multinational peace enforcement forces in Bosnia, even though those procedures and that infrastructure were created to deter and defend against the Soviet threat—quite a different matter. This development is also apparent in the resources NATO has invested in Partnership for Peace.

We turn now to a comparative analysis of alliance adaptation, illustrating the historical relevance of our concepts, and our argument, for the attempted transformations of 1815, 1919, and 1945. In section 3 we will return to the case of NATO.

Institutional adaptation when threats decline: three cases

Our argument holds that the functions performed by alignments or alliances will become less valuable to members when threats are transformed into risks, but the functions that could be performed by security management institutions will become potentially more valuable. States will therefore have incentives, when threats disappear but risks persist, to seek to transform alignments or alliances into security management institutions. In this section we briefly examine one alliance and two alignments that successfully dealt with threats to their members: the Quadruple Alliance, formed during the Napoleonic Wars and renewed in 1815; the Anglo-French alignment of the First World War (1914–9), joined by the United States in 1917; and the Grand Alliance (in our terms, an alignment) of Great Britain, the Soviet Union, and the United States of 1941–5. Each alignment or alliance was followed by attempts to establish a security institution to deal with post-war risks, but these institutions varied in members' commitment, durability, and effectiveness. Our claim is that successful transformation of alignments or alliances into security management institutions requires three conditions: (i) a change in the security environment to one of risks rather than threats; (ii) the previous construction of a genuine alliance—an institution—rather than merely an alignment; and (iii) that the previous alliance be a hybrid, possessing some rules and practices that were designed to mediate disputes and prevent the emergence of security dilemmas among them.

Napoleon and the Concert of Europe: The Concert of Europe, which was established by the victorious allies of the Napoleonic Wars along with the restored monarchy of France, is generally recognized as a case of successful security cooperation. It is commonly explained as the result of the recognition by four European great powers, Great Britain, Austria-Hungary, Prussia, and Russia, that their previous competitive behaviour had allowed France under Napoleon to conquer most of Europe and nearly destroy it in the process. In 1815, these powers did not perceive a threat from any of them, including a France with legitimate monarchical rule re-established; but they worried about the risks inherent in great power rivalry. They recognized that they had substantial long-term common interests in a stable Europe resistant to revolution—that 'problem durability' was high. They also believed that many issues would arise on which there might be incentives for one state or another to seek unilateral advantage, but that such self-serving activities could lead once again to war. Hence 'issue density' was high as well. Recognizing their common interests, these great powers were able to develop a system based on consultation, norms of reciprocity, and rules of behaviour which precluded unilateral advantage and supported mutual restraint.[34] As Louise Richardson shows in Chapter 2, this system of rules and norms (by any definition, a security institution) had a significant impact on the security relations of the great powers in the first half of the nineteenth century, and contributed to an unprecedented period of peace among them.

Our argument attributes the formation of the Concert of Europe not only to problem durability, issue density, and the common values and interests of its members, but to the previous anti-Napoleonic alliance having been a hybrid institution. The earliest anti-French coalitions were usually *ad hoc* commitments which states could and did easily escape. Faced with the threat of the French armies poised to attack, erstwhile allies defected at the crucial hour, thus contributing to Napoleon's military success. Indeed,

[34] Jervis (1986).

until 1812, the European great powers were defeated as much by their own perfidy as by French military power. Over time, however, as the futility of such behaviour became apparent to European leaders, they sought to develop more precise commitments and greater coordination in their diplomatic and military campaigns against France. As Schroeder shows, after 1812 they did a better job of managing and containing the temptation to exploit others and seek deals with France. High-level policy-makers met in virtually continuous session, and self-consciously followed rules that minimized attempts at exploiting situations for unilateral advantage. The anti-Napoleon alliances were not solely directed against the external threat; they were designed to keep an eye on allies and reduce the potential for defection or mitigate its effects.[35] That is, the post-1812 alliances were, to a significant extent, hybrid security institutions. In our framework, therefore, it is not surprising that the post-1812 alliance's basic practices served as something of a precedent when far-sighted leaders such as Metternich and Castlereagh sought to create a mechanism for managing their rivalries and uncertainties.

The First World War and Versailles: The end of the First World War brought an end to severe threats to the security of the victorious Western allies, but left risks, including Bolshevism, revival of Germany, and the spread of nationalism in the former Ottoman and Habsburg empires. The League of Nations was designed to meet these risks. However, the condition for success in developing a security management institution—the existence of a previous hybrid alliance institution—was not present in 1919.

The Entente Cordiale between Great Britain and France, which provided the core of the victorious coalition of the First World War, was a very loose association between two traditional rivals. When war broke out in 1914, 'vital questions of strategic deployment and military coordination remained unresolved . . . The stage was set for a war of attrition between the allies as each struggled for military authority and strategic control on their common front'.[36] For over three years, this struggle divided the political and military leaders of each country, as well as pitting the governments against one another. The British and French governments both sought to impose more burdens on their partners and gain more benefits for themselves, while the military and political leaders of each country contested with each other for authority over strategy and tactics. Only in November 1917 was a Supreme War Council established, at the insistence of British Prime Minister Lloyd George, and with the mandate to prepare war plans, subject

---

[35] Schroeder (1994*b*: chs. 10–12).   [36] Philpott (1996: 1).

to the approval of the governments involved; and only due to the shock of the German offensive of March 1918, and the uncoordinated British-French reaction to it, was General Ferdinand Foch made generalissimo for the western front. Even then, Foch did not have the right to issue orders to subordinate commanders, but only to have 'strategic direction' of operations. Effective unity of command eluded the allies, due to the differences among the governments concerned, and sometimes within governments, 'about the objectives for which they were fighting and the means they needed to deploy to achieve them'.[37] And the bureaucracy set up to service the Supreme War Council could not overcome fundamental differences of allied interests.[38]

Ad hoc bargaining on the basis of resources available and power positions characterized decision-making on security issues, not adherence to institutionalized rules, norms, and practices.[39] Indeed, those agreements that were made between Britain and France were subject to opportunistic reneging when circumstances changed, as indicated by the fate of the Sykes-Picot agreement on the Middle East, which Britain overturned in 1918, to the dismay of its French ally.[40] On 3 October, Lloyd George told the War Cabinet that 'Britain had won the war in the Middle East and there was no reason why France should profit from it.'[41]

The lack of institutionalization in the Entente meant that the architects of the post-war system, centred around the League of Nations, had to build their institutions from scratch. The sad story of the League, beginning with the defection of the United States and the weakness of Britain and France, is familiar. The Versailles Treaty, in which the League was embedded, failed to become legitimate, even to the victors' publics. Germany was not reintegrated into a mutually beneficial international order, unlike the treatment of France in 1815. The victors of 1918 failed to build effective post-war security institutions.

[37] French (1995: 226).

[38] Ibid. 288. See also Cruttwell (1936: 36), who claims that the function of the Supreme War Council 'in the crucial days before the March [1918] disaster was little more than that of a military debating society'.

[39] For eight months, from March to Nov. 1918, technical cooperation among ministers of operational agencies, unmediated by foreign offices, characterized the Allied Maritime Transport Council, established to coordinate shipping requirements for the allies. However, even the secretary of the AMTC, and author of its history, admitted that 'a power of decision vested in a single authority, the British Government, which could compel observation of a programme it considered reasonable, whether agreed or not, by a refusal to allot British ships except on specified conditions'. Whether such an interministerial arrangement would have continued to operate after the United States also had shipping available to allocate is unclear. See Salter (1921: 242).

[40] M. L. Dockrill and J. D. Goold (1981: 131–50).

[41] French (1995: 262), citing War Cabinet minutes.

Had the allies formed an institutionalized alliance—an effective tool of management as well as a means of aggregating power—the history of the League might well have been different. The US Senate might have been more willing to join; practices of promoting cooperation among allies might have spilt over into Anglo-American-French cooperation after 1919. It is also possible, however, that the centrifugal forces of interest and parochialism would have torn even such a League apart. All we can say with confidence is that failure to make the League of Nations into an effective security management institution is consistent with our argument, since a non-institutionalized alignment was not transformed into a security management institution.

The Second World War, the Grand Alliance, and the Cold War: During the Second World War, the Soviet Union, United Kingdom, and United States were linked by the Grand Alliance, which was closer, in our terms, to an alignment than to an alliance. Due to logistical necessity it became more institutionalized than the Entente of the First World War, but its institutionalization was limited by conflicts of interests and intense mutual suspicion. The Grand Alliance was a stark response to the demands of national survival. The previous two decades had provided little basis for amicable relations between the Anglo-American countries and the Soviet Union, and good reason for suspicion. However, after the German attack on the Soviet Union in June and the Japanese attack on Pearl Harbor in December 1941, the fates of all three countries became bound together. Survival of the Soviet Union became crucial for British security. Prime Minister Churchill said that 'if Hitler invaded Hell I would make at least a favourable reference to the Devil in the House of Commons'.[42] Although not codified in a single trilateral treaty (indeed, only the Soviet Union and United Kingdom concluded an official treaty), this alignment was based on a series of meetings and commitments in 1941 and 1942.[43]

The cornerstone of the alignment was an agreement that despite the Anglo-American war against Japan in the Pacific, defeat of Germany was the unquestionable priority. This agreement implied an Anglo-American commitment to a 'second front' in Europe. It also generated massive Western logistical aid to the Soviet Union, including shipments of thousands of aircraft and tanks and hundreds of thousands of trucks.[44] Cooperation in the field of intelligence was also extensive.[45] However, although the United States and Britain mounted joint military operations in North Africa and

[42] Quoted in Feis (1967: 7).   [43] Nadeau (1990); Feis (1967); Edmonds (1991: chs. 9–11).
[44] Ulam (1974: 329–30).   [45] Bradley F. Smith (1996).

the Normandy landings, no such joint command developed with the Soviet Union. The fact that the war was fought on separate eastern and western fronts limited joint military operations between the Soviet Union and its allies to such enterprises as the use by American and British aircraft of Soviet bases for bombing operations in Hungary and joint naval operations in the north.

While adapting their separate practices to win the war, the three countries failed utterly to agree upon norms, rules, or procedures for coping with their suspicions about one another, particularly (though not exclusively) between the Soviet Union on one side and the Anglo-American countries on the other. Most important, the allies never developed an institutional solution to the conundrum of Eastern and Central Europe: how both to ensure the independence of the small countries of the region and to reassure the Soviets about their own security. The recent history of German invasion, the intense hostility between the Soviet Union and the West since the Bolshevik Revolution, and the territorial ambitions of Stalin rendered such a solution elusive, despite efforts at the wartime conferences at Teheran (1943), Yalta (1945), and Potsdam (1945).[46]

The absence of a highly institutionalized wartime alliance surely made post-war cooperation between Russia and America more difficult than it would otherwise have been. But even had such an alliance existed, the fundamental rivalry between the Soviet Union and the West would probably have prevented extensive cooperation. By 1947 the security environment was one of threats rather than risks. Our argument is that both an absence of threat from one's former partners and a previous history of institutionalized cooperation are necessary for threat-oriented alliances to be transformed into security management institutions. Neither condition for successful transformation was present after the Second World War, and it is therefore not surprising that, despite the provisions of chapters 6 and 7 of its Charter, the United Nations did not become an effective security management institution in the aftermath of the Second World War.

3. *The Transformation of NATO*

The question of NATO's future has emerged as one of the most important and difficult issues of post-cold war European security. The North Atlantic

---

[46] Gormly (1990). For detailed discussion on specific Soviet demands of the allies at the wartime conferences, see Ulam (1974: 350–7, 367–77, 388–94).

Treaty Organization was established in 1949. In the well-known turn of phrase of its first secretary-general Lord Ismay, it was created 'to keep the Russians out, the Americans in, and the Germans down'. Its sixteen member states are Belgium, Canada, Denmark, France, Germany (since 1955), Greece (since 1952), Iceland, Italy, Luxembourg, the Netherlands, Norway, Portugal, Spain (since 1982), Turkey (since 1952), the United Kingdom, and the United States. It is a political and military collective defence arrangement: article 4 of the treaty provides for consultations among the allies whenever any members believe their territorial integrity, political independence, or security is threatened, while article 5 provides directly for military cooperation by stipulating that an armed attack against one or more of the members in Europe or North America is considered an attack against them all.

At its beginning, the North Atlantic Treaty was the foundation for an *alignment*, in our terms, between the United States and Western Europe. 'NATO I'[47] was essentially a unilateral security guarantee by the United States, reassuring Western Europe about American support against a Soviet threat, and reassuring the countries that had recently fought Germany against a revival of the German threat. Without much in the way of institutionalization, there was not much 'organization' to NATO.

This changed after the outbreak of the Korean War in June 1950. The United States deployed troops in Europe, and NATO established a supreme command under the initial leadership of General Dwight D. Eisenhower. Over the years, NATO developed extensive structures for multilateral cooperation among its members, from the summit-level North Atlantic Council to committees for many aspects of defence planning and integration.

A major cause of the institutionalization of NATO after 1951 was heightened threat: the Korean War shocked American and European leaders into a reassessment of the Soviet threat and of the necessary form of a military presence in Europe for deterrence and defence. The result was a decision by the Truman administration to commit ground forces to Europe, contradicting previous assurances by Secretary of State Dean Acheson in hearings on the treaty that the United States would not expect to station substantial numbers of troops in Europe on a permanent basis. After a 'great debate' lasting from January through March 1951, the US Senate voted 69-21 on 4 April to approve sending troops to Europe.[48] The second

---

[47] Helga Haftendorn distinguishes different stages in NATO's development as NATO I, NATO II, and NATO III. Haftendorn (1997).

[48] P. Williams (1985: 87–91).

major cause of NATO's institutionalization was the need to cope with a large set of intra-alliance problems generated by the need to make the alliance effective by including West Germany in its military structure and by 'locking in' US participation and thus reassuring its European partners. The rejection of the European Defence Community (EDC) by the French National Assembly in 1954 led directly to innovations that made NATO a hybrid institution, combining extensive security management functions with power aggregation. At London in the early fall of that year, six continental European countries plus Britain, Canada, and the United States agreed on a complex bargain involving German membership in NATO, resting on three mutually reinforcing commitments: (i) a US nuclear guarantee and promise to maintain troops in Europe; (ii) a British promise to keep troops on the continent; and (iii) a commitment by Germany to rearm in a way that was politically acceptable to its allies.[49] This bargain meant that to succeed as an alliance, NATO also had to be an effective security management institution—that is, it had to manage 'the German question'. NATO therefore developed a security management repertoire as well as an alliance repertoire, a hybrid combination that served it well when security management functions became most in demand after 1989.

The functions of NATO II centred on security cooperation among its members, integration of Germany and the United States in European defence (although for different purposes), and maintaining a substantial defence capability to deter possible Soviet military attack. Consequently, its structures emphasized intra-alliance consultation, provisions to make American military deployments sustainable given the vagaries of domestic politics, and impressive military capabilities. NATO developed rules, procedures, and processes which were meant not only to mount a credible deterrent and defence against the Soviet Union, but to bind Germany in such a way that it could no longer threaten the countries of Western Europe, which were now its partners in NATO. A major aspect of Western European security management therefore entailed creating mechanisms for intra-alliance transparency and rules meant to reinforce the democratic character of NATO member governments.

NATO was thus mixed in institutional form because its purposes were mixed. Sometimes the institutional features which served one target served the other: the deployment of allied forces on German territory both enhanced the credibility of NATO's military threat against the Soviet Union,

---

[49] Kugler (1993); Schwartz (1991).

and severely constrained any potential independent German military options. Sometimes, however, NATO's purposes brought alliance members into tension with one another or generated domestic dissension, as in the cases of the decision to permit German rearmament in order to create sufficiently capable conventional forces in the 1950s, and of the decision to enhance the credibility of NATO's nuclear deterrent in the 1970s by deploying Pershing II and cruise missiles.[50] Indeed, coalitions with mixed objectives may be generally prone to such crises.[51]

As the European context began to change in 1989, NATO acquired incentives to shed structures that had become dysfunctional and to create structures to deal with the new requirements of the changing security environment. Militarily, NATO needed to reduce its huge forces directed against the Soviet Union, which had become a major liability in pursuing security cooperation. The alliance has sought to develop smaller forces with greater flexibility and adaptability, including a Rapid Reaction Force, more truly multinational military formations, and the creation of Combined Joint Task Forces designed to make NATO's joint military assets usable for wider operations by NATO nations or by the WEU. Even before the creation of the UN-approved Implementation Force (IFOR) and Stabilization Force (SFOR), NATO played an important role in the UN operations, beginning with the April 1993 enforcement of air-exclusion zones over Bosnia. NATO operations in Bosnia since 1995, sanctioned by the United Nations, were facilitated by these organizational changes, which enabled NATO as an institution, rather than merely its members as independent states, to respond to UN calls for peacekeeping and peace enforcement.

NATO has also adapted politically to an environment in which threat is not the main security problem. Its London Declaration of July 1990 and the new Strategic Concept adopted at the Rome Summit in November 1991 declared that the countries of the former Warsaw Pact were not adversaries but rather partners for Western security, and reduced the alliance's dependence on nuclear weapons. Also at the Rome summit, NATO created the North Atlantic Cooperation Council (NACC) as a political organization, and invited all the members of the former Warsaw Pact to join. This action served two functions: it brought countries in, and extended the function of NATO to consultations, information exchange, and transparency.[52]

These decisions reflected the beliefs of European élites and decision-makers that the problem of security in Europe is different from that of the cold war. For example, the threat of deliberate aggression by either Russia or

---

[50] Risse-Kappen (1988).   [51] Richardson (1996).   [52] Wallander (1999: ch. 6).

Germany is held by leaders in either country to be very low, and German and Russian officials and politicians told one of the authors repeatedly that the new problem of security in Europe was now one of 'risks' or 'challenges' rather than 'threats' and that this entailed fundamentally different problem with fundamentally different requirements. In particular, it requires policies and instruments to increase stability and transparency; in general, it requires integration rather than deterrence.[53]

Yet NACC did not directly address the fundamental question, which was the relationship between the membership and purpose of NATO after the cold war. While the functions of NATO could be expanded and adapted to the new environment, and its activities coordinated with non-alliance members, there remained the fundamental problem: whether NATO itself should expand. Partly as a way to move towards enlargement and partly as a way to deflect political attention from the issue at the time, the alliance created the Partnership for Peace (PfP) program in 1994, and by 1996 twenty-six states including Russia had joined. The stated purpose of PfP was to improve cooperation between NATO members and prospective members, although membership in PfP did not imply eventual NATO membership. Its activities focus on transparency in defence planning and budgets; democratic control of military forces; training and readiness for UN and OSCE operations; and military coordination and training with NATO for peacekeeping, humanitarian, and search and rescue missions.

Despite the institutional innovations of NACC and PfP, the issue of NATO enlargement would not go away. NACC and PfP turned out not to be substitutes for the enlargement of NATO, whose members agreed in May 1997 to admit Hungary, Poland and the Czech Republic to membership, and which left the door open for additional accessions later.

The NATO that is expanding, however, is not the old NATO—an alliance focused on threats from the Soviet Union. NATO is in the process of changing from an alliance to a security management institution. As US Secretary of State Madeleine Albright recently wrote, 'NATO does not need an enemy. It has enduring purposes.'[54] NATO III remains an organization, but it is designed less as a alliance, and more as a security management institution. For example, the NATO–Russia agreement of May 1997 which paved the way for Russia's reluctant acquiescence to enlargement committed NATO to the position that it has 'no plans, no reason, and no intention' to forward deploy conventional military forces nor nuclear forces on the territory of any new member states. This commitment thus eliminates one

---

[53] Wallander (1999: ch. 3).   [54] *Economist* (15 Feb. 1997), 22.

of the core defining features of NATO's cold war military alliance practices and reduces its effective capability for collective defence.

The nature of the environment in Europe—risks rather than threats—goes quite far towards explaining NATO's transformation. Equally critical, however, are the continued commitments of its major member states to NATO institutions. Supporting these commitments are NATO's legitimacy as a mechanism for Western security and the deep, wide networks of officials and politicians in the NATO countries who are committed to the alliance and familiar with one another. Other potential rivals, such as the Western European Union (WEU) or the Organization for Security and Co-operation in Europe (OSCE) do not have such resources at their disposal. US commitment to NATO is vastly greater than its commitment to OSCE; and, of course, it is not a member of WEU.

More tentatively, we suggest that the hybrid nature of NATO's institutions is also important. NATO developed explicit practices to control security dilemmas among its members through its experience with Germany. These practices are portable and can be transferred at relatively low cost to new situations. Proposals for extending membership to new members or for merely extending cooperation of the alliance with non-members (i.e. Partnership for Peace) aim at the further development and institutionalization of practices meant to create transparency and cooperation among NATO members during the cold war.[55] Because NATO has already developed rules, procedures, and structures for security management among states, it is more efficient to rely upon them than to create new institutions from scratch. NATO has been able to become the leading security management institution in Europe, we suggest, not only because it was a successful alliance, but also because it was a successful hybrid security institution.[56]

Our argument has policy implications. If NATO is indeed becoming a security management institution, the implication of our argument in section 1 is that it should become inclusive rather than remaining exclusive. Responding to risks rather than threats, it should include the other countries of Europe, especially those where those security problems and instabilities lie. NATO's expansion could thus foreshadow, not the enlargement of a

[55] Some arguments on whether NATO should expand its membership and functions focus on these issues. See Asmus *et al.* (1993); Brzezinski (1995); Glaser (1993); Holbrooke (1995); Brown (1995).

[56] For this insight we are indebted to Tim Snyder of the Olin Institution, Center for International Affairs, Harvard University, in a comment at a meeting there on security institutions, 17–19 Mar. 1997. Whether NATO will continue to transform itself successfully remains to be seen, and is beyond the scope of this paper. For a comparison of NATO with OSCE, see Wallander (1999: ch. 6).

threat-oriented military alliance, but the transformation of an alliance into a security management institution.

4. Conclusions

NATO is changing from an exclusive alliance focused on threats to an inclusive security management institution concerned chiefly with risks. The contemporary debate in the United States on NATO expansion seems to miss this point. Some opponents have worried about alienating Russia, while others have criticized the alleged dilution of NATO's military capabilities as a result of the May 1997 consultation agreements with Russia. Both seem to assume that NATO will remain a military alliance, although one set of critics laments expansion of such an alliance (allegedly threatening Russia) and the other side attacks what they see as weakening of article 5 guarantees and measures to give Russia a voice in NATO decision-making.

If NATO is becoming a security management institution, the debate looks very different. NATO's military functions will decline as threats diminish; and it should gradually expand to encompass all democratic European states that are committed to maintaining peaceful, friendly relations on the basis of the territorial status quo. Those who want to encourage a peaceful transition to democracy in Russia should endorse, not oppose, this sort of transformation.

Clearly such an institutional transformation would be difficult, and could only take place over a substantial period of time. It may be quite some time before Russia becomes a stable democracy that could be a worthy partner in NATO. In the meantime, it might be necessary to restructure NATO decision-making so that it could act effectively even with twenty or twenty-five members: as in the European Union, this might require some form of qualified majority voting. In any case, NATO's expansion has to be carried out with the clear understanding that the point is not to expand the geographical scope of an exclusive military alliance—there should be no prospect of applying article 5 to Russian borders to its south or east—but to create an inclusive security management institution, limited to Europe.

For the moment, what is most important is to avoid confusion, leading statesmen or policy-influential élites in Russia, Western Europe, or the United States to believe that NATO remains an exclusive alliance focused on threats. Policies based on such a premiss will be inappropriate and self-defeating.

If the transformation of NATO is as successful as we hope, NATO will be only the second security institution—along with the Concert of Europe—to endure for a significant period of time with high levels of commitments from its members. History should therefore make us only cautiously optimistic. But NATO is differentiated by extensive institutionalization and an extraordinarily high level of commitment on the part of its members, compared both to these past alignments or alliances, and to other contemporary organizations, such as OSCE and WEU.

Having been a successful alliance, NATO is building on the practices and networks constructed in response to threat, as resources for its adaptation to the role of international security institution. Like the March of Dimes, it resists the logic that expects institutional collapse as a result of functional success. Its prospects for transformation into an inclusive security management institution seem bright, as long as policy-makers recognize that the expansion of NATO must be accompanied by its reorientation toward problems of risk rather than threat.

2

THE CONCERT OF EUROPE AND SECURITY MANAGEMENT IN THE NINETEENTH CENTURY

Louise Richardson

'Britain has declared her disposition with certain exceptions to sacrifice these conquests for the welfare of the Continent, being Desirous of providing for her own security by a common arrangement, rather than by an exclusive accumulation of strength and resources.'[1] It would be difficult to find a clearer repudiation of relative gains seeking than this British Cabinet statement of 1813. The gains spoken of were military conquests won in the course of the Napoleonic Wars. The British government, then as now ambivalent about its role in Europe, was nevertheless prepared to relinquish these gains in order 'to promote the general interest'.[2] This highlights a fascinating period in European history when the belligerents convened in Vienna, in accordance with the terms of the Peace of Paris, in order to redraw the map of Europe and share the spoils of victory. As it happened they did very much more than this. They established the Concert of Europe, which served for the next forty years very much as a contemporary international security institution.[3] In the first half of the nineteenth century the Concert of Europe brought together the leading statesmen of Europe to manage their security relations. In so doing the Concert succeeded in enabling statesmen to avoid the mistakes of earlier generations and facilitated peaceful adaptation to change in the international distribution of power.

The current realist/institutionalist debate in the field of international relations has stimulated significant scholarly debate and generated some very incisive insights. Yet, it has many flaws, not least of them the fact that it tends to be quite ahistorical in nature. It has, until recently, tended to pay

---

[1] Cabinet Memorandum, 26 Dec. 1813 in Webster (1921: 126).

[2] Ibid. 124.

[3] I am very grateful to my colleagues on the CFIA/ATASP project for their extensive verbal and written comments on earlier drafts of this paper.

very little attention to events prior to the Second World War and even less to ones before the twentieth century.[4] Instead, the empirical cases around which the debate rages have often been selected almost entirely from the institution-rich environment of the western hemisphere in the twentieth century. This chapter represents an effort to see if the debate has any relevance prior to the twentieth century. In so doing I will rely on the work of several diplomatic historians who often find themselves marginalized in their own field of history yet who have made significant contributions to political science and in particular to empirical applications of international relations theory.[5]

Much of contemporary realism, or neo-realism, and here I am thinking particularly of Waltz, is in fact quite historically bound and makes much less sense when applied outside the confines of the cold war. Part of the enormous appeal of more traditional realism, however, is precisely its ability to trace its analysis through the ages and to locate eloquent exponents of its principles at least as far back as Thucydides. In challenging realist analysis institutionalists have confined themselves to the contemporary period, which prompts the question, are institutions historically contingent? Does it make sense to think of institutions prior to the twentieth century? If it does not, then the institutionalist challenge to realism will always be limited. But if it does, then perhaps there are other long-standing forces at work which mediate interstate relations, forces that served as the functional equivalents of contemporary international institutions.

This chapter explores the possibility that the Concert of Europe was one such force. As such it attempts to expand the database, as it were. In so doing it will address the question of the historical contingency of institutional analysis. If one accepts my argument that the Concert of Europe was an international security institution, then an examination of the nineteenth century can provide useful insights on such issues as the adaptation, enlargement, persistence, and dissolution of institutions, important subjects which the twentieth-century cases most often examined have a limited capacity to test. The Concert is an extraordinarily interesting period in European history in and of itself, but aside from that, it appears to have succeeded, with a minimum of institutional architecture, in accomplishing the central goal of many contemporary and very complex institutions, namely, facilitating peaceful adaptation to changes in the international system.

---

[4] There is, of course, a large body of literature on 19th-cent. economic institutions.

[5] Here I am thinking in particular of the work of Paul Schroeder but also of John Lewis Gaddis, Gordon Craig, and others. For the results of a symposium on the relationship between history and theory, see *International Security*, 22/1 (Summer 1997).

1. The Concert as a Nineteenth-Century Security Institution

Given the working definition of security institutions adopted in this volume,[6] several nineteenth-century alliances as well as the three great Peace Congresses at Vienna, Paris, and Berlin arguably qualify. The nineteenth-century body which provides the best fit with this definition, however, is clearly the Concert of Europe.

This view of institutions is similar to the usage employed by Hedley Bull in his seminal work, *The Anarchical Society*. Bull writes: 'By an institution we do not necessarily imply an organization or administrative machinery, but rather a set of habits and practices shaped towards the realization of common goals.'[7] Bull goes on to argue that not only do these institutions serve as an expression of interstate collaboration but that they also serve *to sustain* this collaboration. In Bull's terms, the nineteenth-century European state system was not only an international system, but also an international society, in that the members were conscious of common interests and values and conceived themselves to be bound to one another by a common set of rules.[8]

The Concert of Europe was brought into being by article 6 of the Quadruple Alliance, which read, at the insistence of the British Foreign Secretary, Castlereagh:

To facilitate and to secure the execution of the present Treaty, and to consolidate the connections which at the present moment so closely unite the Four Sovereigns for the happiness of the world, the High Contracting Parties have agreed to renew their Meetings at fixed periods, either under the immediate auspices of the Sovereigns themselves, or by their respective Ministers, for the purposes of consulting upon their common interests, and for the considerations of the measures which at each of these periods shall be considered the most salutary for the repose and prosperity of Nations, and for the maintenance of the Peace of Europe.[9]

The treaty was signed on 20 November 1815 and the Concert of Europe was born. The idea of a federation or concert was not new, having been frequently discussed among publicists in the eighteenth century, but nothing had come of these discussions. A number of factors combined to ensure that the idea would not be lost again. Not least among these was the extraordinary destructiveness of the Napoleonic Wars and the inordinate difficulties experienced by the allies in forging an effective coalition against France,

---

6 See Introduction.   7 Bull (1977: 74).
8 Ibid. 13.   9 Text of the Treaty in Hertslet (1875: 375).

which demonstrated to a number of far-sighted European statesmen the need for more consistent collaboration among the great powers.

The Concert of Europe was designed, therefore, to maintain stability after the Napoleonic Wars. The Peace of Paris and the Quadruple Alliance had stipulated the terms of the peace and the Concert was designed to maintain the order established by the peace. The Concert was not, therefore, a mere club of victors combining to protect their gains, as evidenced both by the generosity of the peace and by the ease with which the defeated power, France, was integrated into the new system. Rather, the leaders of the great powers gathered at Vienna genuinely believed that along with their right to preside over Europe went the responsibility to maintain the European order. They believed that they had, in Castlereagh's words 'not only a common interest but a common duty to attend to'.[10]

At Vienna, the great powers, Austria, Britain, Prussia, Russia, and shortly France (this was the first time a formal distinction was drawn between great powers and the rest) essentially established an oligarchy to manage their security relations. The members of this small group had much in common. The revolution in France, and the use Napoleon had made of this revolution in waging a devastating war, had exposed the domestic vulnerabilities of all the great powers. There were differences on this point between the two western and more liberal powers and the three eastern and more conservative powers. Nevertheless, there was a powerful conservative consensus among the diplomats gathered at Vienna and an acute recognition of the need for their legitimacy domestically and their sovereignty internationally to be recognized and reinforced. The revolution, and the war that followed, demonstrated that domestic and international politics could not be entirely divorced. At Vienna, however, the diplomats concentrated on regulating their international or rather their European affairs, for the Concert was very much a European affair. Events occurring outside the continent were only considered in so far as they had ramifications within the European system.

Norms, rules, and procedures

In attending to their common duty, the great powers developed a set of norms to serve as a code of conduct, they established rules of behaviour to regulate the competition among them, and followed a set of procedures designed to maintain order. These norms, rules, and procedures were directed both internally and externally. The norms were addressed by the

---

10 Cited by Gordon Lauren in George (1983: 56).

powers to each other, reassuring them of their commitment to the common endeavour and disavowing any intentions of defection. The rules were designed to ensure that the interests of all would be protected, again enhancing the benefits of cooperation and increasing the costs of defection. The procedures provided mechanisms for enhancing transparency, for demonstrating continued commitment to cooperation, and reducing the incentives for defection.

The Concert's norms were: self-restraint; consultation in time of crisis; willingness to act together and (its corollary), refusal to act unilaterally; and constant assurances of one another of their pacific intent and commitment to the maintenance of stability. Alongside these norms were some explicit rules of behaviour: (i) conference diplomacy was to be used to deal with crises; (ii) territorial changes must be approved by the great powers; (iii) essential members of the system must be protected; (iv) the interests and honour of great powers must not be challenged.[11] Finally the members of the Concert adopted a number of procedures designed to create an elaborate crisis prevention system. Paul Gordon Lauren has identified no less than nine such procedures:

(1) mutual consultation and collective decision-making;
(2) creation of buffer states;
(3) establishment of neutral states and demilitarized zones;
(4) localization of regional conflicts;
(5) limitation of resources in third areas;
(6) delineation of interests and areas of involvement;
(7) intervention by multilateral action;
(8) pacific settlement of disputes;
(9) communication and provision of advance notification.[12]

While the organization of the Concert of Europe was fairly inchoate compared to the systematic organizations of many twentieth-century security institutions, the norms, rules, and procedures adopted were explicit, well-established, and complex. The creation of the buffer states of the German Federation, for example, served not only the obvious function of discouraging a French attack east, an Austrian move north, and a Prussian move west, but also by involving Austria and Prussia jointly in the management of this buffer zone served both to inhibit conflict and also to promote cooperative behaviour. So with an extremely loose institutional form the

---

[11] These rules are spelt out in Elrod (1976: 163–7).
[12] See Lauren (1983: 31–64).

Concert of Europe nevertheless managed to effect extremely complex functions.[13]

Form and function

The function of the Concert was spelt out in the Quadruple Alliance. It was to secure the peace by implementing the treaty and consolidating connections between the great powers. The founders were, in fact, quite explicit about the need, in effect, to institutionalize connections in order to enhance cooperation. The form chosen by the statesmen gathered at Vienna was simply a convening of the four (and soon five) great powers when crises arose.

This arrangement is generally perceived to be simply a reflection of the distribution of power at the time. Certainly the arrangement was not impervious to the distribution of power. For example, Spain and Portugal, who had fought the war and participated in the peace, were not included. Yet the view of the Concert as a gathering of five roughly equal powers is also misplaced. Paul Schroeder has amply demonstrated that power was not neatly distributed in this way. Rather he argues that 'the balance of power in 1815 consisted of a pentarchy composed of two superpowers, one authentic but vulnerable great power, one highly marginal and even more vulnerable great power, and one power called great by courtesy only'.[14] This suggests that in the nineteenth century there was a link between the function and the form of security institutions. Had the function been simply to maintain peace then a simpler arrangement might have been possible whereby the two superpowers, Britain and Russia, agreed either jointly or alone to commit their resources to the maintenance of peace. But the purposes or functions of the Concert were more complex and required the satisfying of the prestige as well as the territorial aspirations of the lesser great powers. Stability was best ensured by investing those with the ability to disrupt it with an interest in its maintenance. The statesmen of the time have often been criticized for their exclusion of the voice and the interests of the minor powers. However, the form of the Concert (restriction to the great powers) flowed naturally from the function (the maintenance of stability in the international order).

While they would never have cast it in these terms, the leaders of the great

---

[13] Of course one runs the risk of circularity in deriving norms, rules, and procedures from behaviour and then using them to explain behaviour. I am aware of this trap yet there seems to me to be more than enough evidence available to support the position I take that these norms were both widely understood and followed.   [14] Schroeder (1992: 688).

powers saw themselves as engaged in a game of assurance. They shared an interest in cooperation but they were not at all sure that they could trust each other to cooperate. They therefore designed a system which would provide as much transparency as possible by providing opportunities to promise cooperation and disavow defection. There were no resources to compel cooperation, only efforts to facilitate it, which in turn led to expectations of cooperation and increased costs of defection. Again, the form followed the function. As an institution designed to cope inclusively with risks, the Concert was a security management institution.[15]

The form of an institution is largely attributable to its function but it is also dependent upon the resources available. The very loose institutional structure of the Concert is a stark contrast to its twentieth-century successors and must be in part accounted for by technology. The slow speed of travel and communications were such that representatives at these continental meetings were often vested with plenipotentiary powers by their governments. This was generally acceptable due to the very senior position in their home governments occupied by these representatives. It would have required a significant restructuring of government to grant plenipotentiary powers to representatives assigned to a permanent body outside the country. As it was, the senior statesmen of the period spent a very long time away from their home governments and this gave them a certain licence in interpreting their instructions. Castlereagh, for example, was on the continent for a full eighteen months. Given that he was way out in front of his government and domestic public opinion in his degree of commitment to Europe, he needed the latitude granted by distance to complete his negotiations successfully.

Pitt had spelt out the function of any post-war institution as early as 1805 in his famous correspondence with the Tsar. He was quite explicit in listing the three functions of any arrangement: to reduce France to her former boundaries, to create viable states from those liberated from France, and 'to form, at the restoration of the peace, a general agreement and guarantee for the mutual protection and security of different powers, and for re-establishing a general system of public law in Europe'.[16] The settlement itself could be arranged through the accepted means of an international congress, but a guarantee of that settlement, as Pitt originally outlined and as later stipulated in the treaty, was a function which required a new institutional form. In the course of the congress the idea of guaranteeing the settle-

---

[15] See Ch. 1, above.

[16] Cited in Langhorne (1981/2: 76). The full document is to be found in Temperley and Penson (1966: 18).

ment evolved into the idea of managing the security system established by the settlement. The way the security system was managed was to convene together, to consult, and ultimately to constrain each other.

In establishing an organizing principle for the Concert the statesmen attempted to learn from the success of the Fourth Coalition and the failure of its predecessors. The earlier coalitions had proven incapable of forging a lasting settlement against Napoleon. Members of the coalitions were as suspicious of each other as they were of France and lost no opportunity to abandon the coalition to make a separate settlement with the enemy. In short, they behaved very much as states did, and were expected to do, in the eighteenth century.

The final coalition was distinguishable from the others in the degree to which the statesmen were in constant personal communication. Castlereagh was not alone in believing that this had been crucial to its success. In a letter to Liverpool he referred to 'the habits of confidential intercourse which a long residence with the principal actors has established'.[17] On another occasion, in which he instructed the British representatives, Castlereagh wrote:

It is impossible to have resided at allied headquarters even for the short period I have myself passed at them without perceiving how much the interests of the Confederacy are exposed to prejudice and disunion from the want of some central council of deliberation, where the authorized Ministers of the respective Powers may discuss face to face the measures in progress, and prepare a result for the consideration of their respective sovereigns, You must all be aware how deep was the distrust and alarm which existed some days ago as to supposed divergences of opinion, which it was feared were irreconcilable in themselves, and how soon these differences disappeared when the allied Ministers were ordered officially to enter upon their discussion. To such a degree did this happen, that every individual question has been decided, not only unanimously, but with cordial concurrence.[18]

In the words of his biographer, C. K. Webster, Castlereagh 'had learnt the lesson of the closing years of the war as no other had done'.[19] There was, therefore, a sense of institutional learning in attempting to adapt the methods successful in wartime for the maintenance of the peace. The existence of a shared common interest in stability was not in itself enough to prevent misunderstanding of the intentions of others. To reduce uncertainty, to ascertain the true intentions of others, it was thought necessary to meet and to do so at the most senior levels of government.

The idea of setting up a fixed, permanent structure along the lines that

---

[17] Castlereagh to Liverpool, 4 Jan. 1815, in Webster (1921: 281).
[18] Quoted in Webster (1931: 209).   [19] Ibid. 497–8.

were to become familiar in the ensuing century appears not to have occurred to any of the participants. But it is important to bear in mind that this was none the less a very significant departure from earlier diplomatic practice. Prior to 1814 international meetings had been convened but their function had been strictly confined to arranging the terms of a peace settlement. The type of conference envisioned by the Concert, in which the powers convened during peacetime to make changes to the Vienna settlement, was historically unprecedented. This is precisely what happened at the London conference of 1830 when a conference of the powers created the Kingdom of Belgium on its own authority. The form of the Concert, therefore, seems to have been determined in part by the functions it was hoped to serve but also by the recent experience of the participants as well as a sense of what was practically feasible.

2. *The Concert as a Security Management Institution*

One of the many drawbacks of such a loose institutional arrangement is that it makes it very difficult to analyse. There is, for example, no agreement whatsoever among historians as to when the Concert came to an end. Had the Concert consisted of a formal institutional arrangement it might have been closed down and its officials sent home in 1822, 1848, 1854, or as late as 1914. One could argue, for example, that the Concert ended when France ceased to be a threat. France was admitted as a member of the Concert at the Congress of Aix-la-Chapelle in 1818. More commonly it is seen to have ended with the collapse of the congress system at Verona in 1822. Alternatively it has frequently been argued that the Concert ended in 1848 when domestic revolutions upset the conservative consensus. It is equally commonly argued that the Concert ended with the Crimean War of 1854, since the Concert had been designed to prevent war between great powers. Still others, like Albrecht-Carrie and Carsten Holbraad, argue that the Concert lasted throughout the nineteenth century until the next great systemic upheaval.

The crucial question to be asked of the Concert of Europe as of any international security institution, however, is not how long it lasted but rather whether it mattered. This is where realists and institutionalists begin to disagree. Most observers of the Concert, oblivious to the nuances of the realist/institutionalist debate, could agree that it served as an arena for the exercise of influence, constrained bargaining strategies, facilitated side payments, enabled signalling, enhanced predictability, and specified obligations guiding state action. Analysts differ on the implications. Did the Concert of Europe affect state strategies and even influence the shape of state interests? An examination of the Concert of Europe suggests that it did. Rather than acting unilaterally or defecting, state leaders for a time chose to conduct their policies in accordance with the norms and procedures they had established. The Concert was more than simply a method for communicating state interests to others: membership in the Concert became a source of status for which states were prepared to pay by cooperating with other great powers. In this way they permitted their behaviour to be constrained.

As to when the Concert ended, it is most helpful to think of the Concert of Europe as operating in four distinct phases: 1815–18, 1818–22, 1822–48, and 1848–56. The first phase was one of technical cooperation, and the second was the period of the congress system. The third phase witnessed the subtle but significant management of the security relations of the great powers, and the final phase, between the revolutions of 1848 and the outbreak of the Crimean War, saw the steady erosion of the Concert. Seen in this way the Concert provides an example, rare in the twentieth century, of institutional persistence and adaptation. Despite its failure in the Crimean War, the Concert did bequeath a powerful institutional legacy to the latter half of the century, as seen at the Congress of Berlin in 1878. Moreover, another system-wide conflagration did not occur until a century after Vienna. Nevertheless, by mid-century the necessary conditions for the successful functioning of the Concert of Europe as a security management institution had evaporated.

1815–1818: technical cooperation

Cooperation between the great powers operated most smoothly, as one might expect, when activities were directed against the defeated France. Ambassadors of the great powers were based in occupied Paris and met weekly to coordinate their responses to internal developments in France. There was little disagreement between the allies in this period but there was little of major import to be resolved. Instead, the diplomats coordinated their activities, as they had eventually learnt to do in wartime, on such issues as the future laws of France, domestic opposition parties, and even the content of political speeches in the French legislature. This phase was of short duration and lasted only as long as France was occupied. Three years after the war France had paid its indemnity and the forces of occupation left, thus bringing an end to this phase of the Concert.

This change then was exogenously inspired and the Concert adapted. The form of the institution—ambassadors working together daily in close proximity in order to fulfil detailed and specific functions—was now replaced by meetings at a higher level of representation, with less technical and more international concerns.

1818–1822: the congress system

In 1818, at the congress of Aix-la-Chapelle France was admitted to the Concert. The decision to integrate France into the system derived directly from the purposes that had been discussed at Vienna. Even a weakened France was clearly a great power and stability would best be protected by the active participation of each of the great powers in managing the system. By her inclusion in the system, moreover, the allies no doubt sought to ensure her continued commitment to the cause of stability in Europe. But stability in Europe meant ratifying France's position as a defeated power. Membership of the Concert bequeathed to France great power status without her having to fight for it. In this way France did not have to engage in any unilateral or disruptive action in order to secure her place 'at the top table'. It was simply given to her in the interests of a peaceful order.

No sooner was France admitted into the Concert, however, than serious disagreements began to emerge. The disagreements tended to pit Britain against the three eastern powers (Russia, Prussia, and Austria) that, with considerable justification, saw themselves to be more threatened by domestic dissent. Nevertheless, over the next four years no fewer than four congresses were held, thereby marking the zenith of the congress system. At the congresses of Troppau in 1820 and again at Laibach in 1821 the great powers argued over the extent of the threat posed to their system by liberal revolutions. In the absence of Castlereagh, and over British objections, the Troppau Protocol established the principle that changes wrought by revolution were illegitimate and asserted the right of the Concert to intervene wherever they chose in order to repress revolutionary agitation.

This principle was soon put into practice at the Congress of Laibach when Austria sought and received approval from the Concert to intervene in Naples in the name of Europe, in order to repress a revolt against Ferdinand I. Had Austria acted unilaterally in Naples, and a few months later in Piedmont, the other powers would have responded vehemently, and probably forcibly, but by acquiring multilateral approval for its actions Austria could be seen to be acting legitimately. Britain was unalterably opposed to the developing generalized right of intervention and Castlereagh refused to attend the congresses.[20] In his famous state paper of 5 May 1820 Castlereagh wrote:

The principle of one State interfering by force in the internal affairs of another, in order to enforce obedience to the governing authority, is always a question of the greatest possible moral as well as political delicacy—to generalize such a principle and to think of reducing it to a System, or to impose it as an obligation, is a Scheme utterly impracticable and objectionable.[21]

This congress demonstrated the important point that institutions are not just about consensus. Clearly, there were very profound differences on the issue of intervention. The Concert, however, provided a venue in which these disagreements could be aired with the expectation that they would be aired peacefully. Refusing to attend a congress, while undoubtedly damaging to the Concert was certainly less provocative than dispatching a gunship or mobilizing troops.

At the final Congress of Verona in 1822 the Concert considered yet another case of domestic revolt against a legitimate monarch, this time in Spain. Tsar Alexander was more than willing to dispatch his troops to repress the Spanish revolt but the prospect of Russian troops marching across Europe was enough to give even these committed interventionists pause.[22] Instead, the Concert empowered France to act in Spain. Only eight years after the conclusion of the Napoleonic Wars, a French army of 100,000 men marched south in the name of the coalition that had defeated it. Within six months Ferdinand VII was back on his throne. All of this was too much for Britain which refused to be represented at future congresses.[23]

Britain did not actually secede from the Concert. On the contrary, the British government expressed a willingness to meet with the other powers when the peace was threatened: 'We shall be found in our place when actual danger menaces the System of Europe.'[24] Thus the Concert, even in its most formal phase, learnt the difficulty (a difficulty relearnt by the League of Nations a century later) of arriving at agreement on what constituted a threat

---

[20] Castlereagh lays out his position on intervention in the State Paper of 5 May 1820. The text is in Temperly and Penson (1966: 48–63). For an analysis of Castlereagh's views on intervention see: Hafner (1980: 71–84).

[21] State Paper, 5 May 1820, in Temperly and Penson (1966: 61).

[22] In 1826 Russia had an estimated 860,000 men in its European army, which was more than the combined forces in Europe of Austria, Britain, France, and Prussia.

[23] In Dec. 1823 Spain attempted to convene a congress to discuss the issue of her American colonies then in revolt. Canning refused to attend. He declined again the following year when Tsar Alexander summoned a Congress on Turkey, thereby effectively ending the congress system of the old type.

[24] State Paper of 5 May 1820 in Temperly and Penson (1966: 63).

to peace. In both cases procedures were established for how to behave once the peace was threatened, but not on how to come to that determination. The Concert thus failed as a collective security system.

When the formal machinery of the Concert, in the form of frequent congresses, proved unpopular with some of the members the principles underlying the Concert and the norms and rules it represented found expression in less formal mechanisms. The British government, clearly unhappy with the shorter term function the eastern powers were trying to perform, withdrew from the institutional form which the eastern powers had adopted to pursue their goal of an antiliberal crusade. The link between form (the congress system) and function (suppression of liberalism) was so close in the mind of the British leadership that they could only oppose the function by undermining the form. Had the British government not felt that the congress system facilitated the realization of their allies illiberal objectives, they would surely not have withdrawn from the congress system they had done so much to establish.

This change came about because of disagreements between the members on the issue of intervention. These differences reflected fundamentally different perspectives based on the domestic circumstances in each country. Britain had much less to fear from liberal revolutions than her eastern colleagues. When she saw the Concert being used as an instrument for the pursuit of ends she did not support, Britain sought to undermine the system by refusing to participate. Britain was determined that the Concert not be used merely as a means of conferring legitimacy on the pursuit of unilateral interests, especially illiberal ones. Britain's withdrawal did not bring about the demise of the Concert, again it adapted, assuming a less concrete form. By changing its form from the congress system the Concert denied multilateral endorsement for unilateral action against liberal re-volutions and thereby raised the costs of undertaking such action.

1822–1848: self-restraint in security relations

The third phase is, in many ways, the most interesting in the history of the Concert. The previous period had demonstrated that, while there was great power agreement on the fundamentals of the post-war system, there were significant differences between the powers on how to interpret some of these fundamentals. They agreed that the sovereignty of the great powers was inviolable, but disagreed on the extent to which the Concert could go in opposing perceived threats to that sovereignty.

It was also agreed that there should be no wars between the great powers.

In the post-congress period there was no formal machinery designed to achieve this end but the norms, rules, and procedures established by the Concert served this function. In the period between the Congress of Verona and the outbreak of the revolutions of 1848 there are many instances in which the leaders of each of the great powers appear to have exercised self-restraint in accordance with the principles of the Concert. There was no war between the great powers in this period. In stark contrast to eighteenth-century practice, they jointly regulated several crises which might easily have degenerated into war. In this way the Concert fulfilled its most important function of facilitating peaceful adaptation to change. Change is endemic in international relations and it is attended by much uncertainty. It is this uncertainty that generates fears and misperceptions, which often lead to conflict. By reducing uncertainty in this period, raising the benefits of cooperation, and raising the costs of defection, the Concert facilitated peaceful change.

In his examination of Russia and the eastern question, Matthew Anderson argues that first Alexander and then Nicholas repeatedly sacrificed their interests for the good of the Concert.[25] Tsar Alexander, for example, in spite of the almost unanimous view of domestic political opinion, declined to act in support of the Greeks against the hugely unpopular Turks. Both Metternich of Austria and Bernstorff of Prussia used the language of the Concert, the primacy of great power unity, in an effort to persuade the Tsar to forgo local gains. Early in the crisis, Alexander said: 'Nothing, without doubt, appeared more agreeable to my interests, to the interests of my peoples, to the public opinion of my country, than a religious war with Turkey.'[26] Nevertheless, citing 'the danger of my intervention for my allies', Alexander refrained from intervention.[27] In fairness, it must be pointed out that as the author of the Holy Alliance and a deeply conservative man, Alexander was also probably reluctant to align himself with any rebels, even rebels against the Turks. In this instance, both his innate conservatism and the requirements of great power unity operated in the same direction.

The success of the Concert was not tied to one leader but persisted throughout several changes of leadership in several of the member states. Alexander was succeeded by his brother Nicholas in late 1825 and the implosion of the Ottoman empire continued. Britain, meanwhile, was concerned lest Russia exploit the situation to enhance her influence in the

[25] Anderson (1979: 79–97).   [26] Quoted ibid. 83.
[27] Quoted by Daugherty, in Snyder and Jervis (1993: 86). Daugherty makes several similar arguments about the system management functions of the concert.

region. Britain and Russia then acted very much in the spirit of the nineteenth century and completely out of keeping with eighteenth-century practices. They signed a protocol in which they offered joint mediation between the Sultan and the rebels and forswore any unilateral advantages as a result of their involvement.[28] Subsequently Britain, Russia, and France signed a treaty agreeing to joint intervention and again explicitly declining any unilateral advantage: 'The Contracting Powers will not seek, in these Arrangements, any augmentation of territory, any exclusive influence, or any commercial advantage for their subjects, which those of every other nation may not equally obtain.'[29] The three powers then undertook military intervention which secured Greek independence in 1832 while limiting their own involvement in the region.[30] It is very difficult to see how this outcome can be explained without reference to the Concert and its practices. Clearly by its practice of providing reassurance to fellow members the Concert increased the costs while decreasing the benefits of defection. This is not to suggest that the Concert alone ensured this outcome, only that, given state preferences, the Concert affected the strategies states adopted to realize them.

There are other cases too in this period when the great powers self-consciously restrained themselves in accordance with the norms of the Concert. Repeatedly the powers are seen to feel constrained by the principles they have established and to broaden the definition of their interests to include the maintenance of the Concert as a compelling national interest. Belgium is a case in point. The question of independence for Belgium once again brought the great powers to the brink of war. The union of Belgium and Holland was the type of arrangement for which the Congress of Vienna has long been criticized. The populations of the area were not consulted and their historical, linguistic, religious, and economic differences were ignored in the interests of stability between the great powers. In October 1830, after several months of agitation, a provisional government declared Belgian independence.

Russia and Prussia were willing to send troops to repress the revolt of the Belgians. French public opinion favoured the Belgians, but King Louis Philippe was prepared to stay out of the conflict provided other powers did too. He was not, however, prepared to permit great power intervention so close to the French border. Britain was willing to accept Belgian independence provided that Belgium did not then become a French satellite. Con-

---

28 For the text of the protocol see: Hertslet (1875: 741–3).
29 Ibid. 771–2.
30 See Daugherty (1993), for an analysis of Greek independence along these lines.

cerned that events could deteriorate dramatically, Palmerston, acting again in accordance with the norms of the Concert, urged Russia and Prussia to postpone action until after the five powers convened for a conference on the subject in London. Palmerston managed to persuade the other powers that the separation of Belgium from Holland, however regrettable, was inevitable and that their task should then be to impose such conditions on Belgian independence as would suit the interests of peace between them. The Concert demonstrated the ability to accept change and to adapt to it in part by attempting to direct it. By meeting together transparency was enhanced, reducing (though certainly not eliminating) the possibility that clandestine deals might be done. The meeting provided Britain with the opportunity to sell its peaceful solution to the problem. As acceptance of the British proposal had the added benefit of adhering to the norms of the Concert, its acceptance was rendered more likely.

The powers then, as in the case of Greek independence, repudiated the opportunity to seek unilateral advantage, reassured each other of their commitment to peace, and guaranteed the permanent neutrality of Belgium under an independent monarch.[31] William I of Holland refused to accept this and marched on Brussels. France intervened first and then consulted her allies who retroactively authorized French action on the grounds that France was not acting in furtherance of unilateral objectives and had not had time to receive advanced authorization. France agreed to the insistence of the other powers that she withdraw as soon as the armistice was restored and that her armies stay well away from Prussian and German borders. The flexibility shown by the other members in accepting the explanation for French behaviour was a product of Concert practices. Rather than forcibly opposing French action, they sought to impose conditions on it to reduce the threat to the stability of the system. In 1831 the five great powers signed a treaty granting Belgian independence and guaranteeing it against attack. This was finally accepted by the Dutch in 1839. Again, this is clearly a case in which the practices and principles of the Concert served to constrain the actions of the participants and in so doing the Concert served the crucial function of facilitating peaceful change within the international system.

The next crisis to bring crowds to the streets demanding war occurred on the fringes of Europe. The pasha of Egypt, Mehemet Ali, sought gains commensurate with his skills in fighting the incompetent Turks. In 1832 it looked as though he was on the verge of overrunning Asia Minor. Metternich, declaring the Sultan a legitimate ruler and Mehemet a rebel,

---

[31] Ibid. 90.

sought to bring the powers together to protect Turkey. French sympathies were with Egypt and Britain equivocated so Russia stepped in to support Turkey. Peace was thereby secured temporarily and Russia and Turkey signed a treaty of mutual assistance. In 1839 the situation on the ground appeared to be repeating itself as the Egyptians repelled a Turkish attack and soon stood once again at the gates of Constantinople.

Britain, convinced that Egypt was a French satellite, was anxious to protect land routes to India from both France and Russia and proposed a general guarantee of Turkish independence. Concerned at the opposition to her treaty with Egypt, Russia agreed, as did Austria and Prussia. The four signed a convention with Turkey in 1840 in which they assured the Sultan that they would secure Constantinpole and the Straits and assured each other that they would not exploit the situation to their individual advantage.

The problem, of course, was France. Public opinion was powerfully pro-Egyptian and mobs in the streets of Paris demanded war against Britain, Prussia, and Austria. The Thiers government did not dare to oppose such vehement opinion. The king eventually did. Louis Philippe sacked Thiers and informed the other powers that France did not want to be excluded from the league of the great powers. Exclusion from the inner circle was a blow to French prestige rather than French security. By going ahead without France the other powers were able to enforce French compliance to their will. At French insistence they declared an end to the convention signed without her and all five, along with Turkey, signed the famous Straits Convention in 1841. Mehemet Ali was driven back to Egypt and the powers agreed that the straits of the Bosphorus and the Dardanelles would be closed to foreign warships in peacetime. French desire to be reintegrated into the Concert and the speed with which she was invited back suggest that the continuation of the Concert and compliance with its practices became in itself part of a state's definition of its national interest.[32] Membership of the Concert conveyed great power status and for this national governments were prepared to pay a price. In previous eras they had fought to earn and defend this status, the Concert provided the opportunity to do so peacefully. This had an impact on state strategies as national governments sought to bring their policies into line with those of their colleagues in the Concert.

Paul Schroeder describes the forces at work as follows: 'Deterrence under the Vienna system took the form of moral and legal political pressure, the threat that reckless or unlawful behavior would cost the offending state its

---

[32] For details on the Near Eastern crises see Schroeder (1994: esp. ch. 16). See also Daugherty (1993), for an application of Concert practices to this crisis.

status and voice within the system leading to isolation from it and the attendant loss of systemic awards and benefits.'[33] Clearly, it was these forces which deterred France from action in support of the Belgians and Egyptians, and Russia from supporting the Greeks in the three cases described above.

There were also many other instances in this period in which the great powers resisted their own public opinion and opted instead to act with their allies. On several occasions, for example, Austria passed up potential gains in Italy in order not to be seen to be engaging in self-aggrandizement. Liberal opinion in both Britain and France strongly endorsed support for the rebels in Poland in 1830 and in Piedmont in 1848 yet both governments resisted. According to Matthew Anderson, it was Russia's genuine eagerness 'to co-operate with the other powers and to do nothing to weaken their unity' that prompted Tsar Nicholas to make the Münchengrätz agreement in 1833 and to withdraw his garrisons from the Danubian principalities without receiving the promised indemnity in the following year.[34]

Time and again throughout the years 1815 to 1848, in each of the capitals of the five great powers, the Concert of Europe can be seen to have functioned as an international security institution. It served not only to provide a context for the exercise of state policy but influenced the formation of state strategies[35] and facilitated peaceful adaptation to political change. It was never to be so effective again. This time again the change was exogeneously inspired by events in the national capitals. But the same forces that compelled the changes undermined the ability of the Concert to adapt successfully.

1848–1853: erosion

The powerful consensus that united the three conservative eastern powers and the two liberal western powers was shattered by the revolutions of 1848 which paralysed Austria and Prussia, transformed France into a radical republic and deeply frightened, in the words of Palmerston, 'the only two Powers in Europe—that remain standing upright'.[36] Remarkably, however, the revolutions of 1848 were not accompanied by warfare. No state took advantage of the fact that a neighbour was suffused by violence to attempt

---

[33] Schroeder, June 1992, 699–700.

[34] Anderson (1979: 92).

[35] I readily concede that a convincing demonstration of this point would require a much closer examination of the primary sources on the decision-making processes in each of the five capitals. I doubt that the conclusion would be different.   [36] Cited by Craig (1960: 260).

militarily to gain advantage. No anti-revolutionary leader sought to garner support by leading a campaign against an external enemy. The norms of cooperation and self-restraint were, even then, deeply embedded.

In the ensuing years of revolution Britain and Russia worked, both separately and on occasion together, to ensure that the internal upheavals did not spill over into general war. Britain was largely responsible for averting a major French intervention in Italy, and an attempt by Prussian liberals to liberate Poland, and thereby risk war with Russia. With Palmerston's blessing, the Tsar suppressed the Hungarian revolution and acted as the guardian of the balance in East and Central Europe.

The revolutions may not have led to immediate warfare but they did undermine the Concert in a number of ways. By bringing to power new governments, and a new generation of leaders, who were not necessarily committed to the international order, the revolutions undermined the confidence of the members of the Concert that the other leaders would adhere to its norms. The trauma of 1848–50 had the effect of calling into question all the values of the past and in international affairs this meant calling into question the norms of self-restraint and moderation. Cavour had replaced Castlereagh on the international scene. The revolutions, moreover, demonstrated the peril of ignoring domestic opinion which would increasingly play a constraining role in foreign policy. Far from repressing the wave of nationalism, many governments now sought to ride it in order to ensure their own survival. A strategy of moderation through the Concert was becoming increasingly incompatible with these newly articulated state preferences.

The revolutions left a legacy of distrust among the powers. Britain and Russia were wary of France, while Austria was resentful of her dependence on Russia. The deterioration in Austro-Prussian relations was evident in the Diet of the German Confederation. Prior to the revolutions the two states always consulted beforehand and came to the Diet with agreed positions. After 1848 they never consulted and instead waged a diplomatic war of advantage at the Diet. The norms and rules of self-restraint were evaporating. The Concert became a less appealing venue for resolving difficulties. The more national leaders thought so, the less impact the Concerts could in turn have on their state strategies.

As it happened, when the event occurred which the Concert was designed to prevent, war between great powers, it occurred between the two powers least affected by the revolutions. While the Crimean War marked the effective end of the Concert, the fact that such a war could break out at all was a testament to the erosion of the principles of the Concert set in progress by the revolutions of 1848. This war of devastating brutality was, as has often been said, an unnecessary war. Indeed, it was precisely the type of war that the Concert was designed to prevent and could have prevented had its practices been followed. The war was essentially caused by misperception on the part of the Tsar and the combination of a divided government and an aroused public in Britain. The war was made much worse by rampant incompetence on both sides. The Tsar believed, wrongly, that his honourable and limited motives would be clear to Aberdeen whom he had previously met. Aberdeen was prepared to allow the Concert to impose a settlement but Palmerston, with whom he shared power, was not, and so the two countries stumbled, slowly, into a very bloody war. The Crimean War of 1854 marked a watershed in the nineteenth century. It was preceded by four decades of peace and followed by four wars in rapid succession which transformed the map of Europe drawn at Vienna.

The Concert was not thereby eradicated. Its institutional legacy could still be seen in operation in the limitation of the war (in spite of Britain and France's efforts to widen it), in the efforts made at the wartime conference in Vienna to negotiate a settlement, and in the ultimately successful efforts to persuade Britain to make peace sooner that she would have preferred.

The conference which met in Paris to end the war and order the peace had all the ostensible trappings of the Concert, but the substance was largely gone. The peace treaty accorded the powers acting in Concert a right of intervention in international disputes as well as numerous specific mandates. The conference, moreover, self-consciously invited the Ottoman empire to join the ranks of the great powers as a member of the Concert. Finally, the conference invited Cavour to make his case before the Concert. In spite of this auspicious showing, however, the necessary condition for the successful functioning of the Concert, acceptance of the underlying status quo, no longer obtained.

France, Russia, and Prussia were now revisionist powers. The internal upheavals they had experienced caused them to re-examine their preferences. They now preferred defection to cooperation. Louis Napoleon had hoped to overthrow the Vienna settlement even before the war but his military success in the Crimean War, relative to the other belligerents, had emboldened his plans. Russia, naturally, was deeply unhappy at the terms of the peace: even though the terms were reasonable enough, they still spelt defeat. Prussia was shaken by the efforts of Austria to drag her into war and worried that her great-power status was in doubt, as evidenced by the delay in her inclusion in the deliberations in Paris. Austria and Britain remained defenders of the Vienna settlement but Austria, weakened by military expenditures and isolated by her role in the war, was unable, and Britain, smarting from her appalling performance in the war and with a public deeply opposed to continental commitments, was unwilling, to defend the status quo.

The Concert did not abruptly end but it gradually became irrelevant and played no role in the wars of Italian and German unification and the crises in the Balkans which dominated the latter part of the nineteenth century. On the rare occasions when the Concert met in conference it was now to discuss matters of secondary importance. The one notable exception to this trend was the Congress of Berlin in 1878, but this was to remain an exception.

Institutional adaptation in the Concert

The institution of the Concert adapted when it no longer needed ambassadors taking care of the administration of France. It changed its form to regular meetings at a higher level of representation in the form of congresses. It then adapted when a major player, Britain, decided to undermine this form by refusing to participate in the congress system out of opposition to the plans of other members. The Concert at that point became a more *ad hoc* but still effective meeting of major players. But once some of the major players were transformed by domestic events it was badly weakened and finally it could not adapt when two of its members went to war against each other.

The demise of the Concert demonstrates the obvious point that a security management institution is just that: it manages state security in a world in which that security is determined by a great many factors, both domestic and international. The successful functioning of the Concert, and any other security management institution, requires the acceptance of certain fundamentals. Once there is agreement on the fundamentals, the experience of collaboration can in turn affect the manner in which a state behaves, but absent that underlying agreement, the institution is impotent. Cast in terms of the realist/institutionalist debate, this finding supports the institutionalist claim that while a realist analysis can be most helpful in understanding the parameters within which a state operates, an understanding of specific state behaviour requires the insight of institutionalist analysis.[37]

---

[37] A thorough understanding of state behaviour in international affairs also, of course, requires an examination of the domestic context of state behaviour but that is not the subject of this paper.

3. The Concert and Related Institutional Forms

Conducting international relations and managing security relations may have been less complex in the nineteenth century than it is today, but it was still complex. For this reason the Concert was far from being the only means of conducting foreign policy. In fact the Concert was part of an interlocking system including congresses and alliances.

Nineteenth-century congresses

The Concert of Europe, as I have argued above, consisted of the shared norms, rules, and practices adopted by the great powers in the nineteenth century. The mechanism, or form, which the powers developed to operationalize, as it were, these norms and procedures was meetings of the great powers in congresses and conferences. The statesmen of the time drew a distinction between a congress which was attended by heads of state and their foreign ministers and conferences which were attended by ambassadors accredited to the host government.[38] Conferences were generally designed, moreover, to focus on specific issues, whereas congresses, after Verona, had a broader focus. By carefully choosing the location for a congress the European leadership sought to acknowledge, ratify, and legitimate changes in the balance of power. The choice of Paris in 1856, for example, served to rehabilitate Napoleon and demonstrate that France was restored to great-power status. The choice of Berlin over twenty years later was a reflection of the new role of Germany in the centre of Europe. Berlin also marked the emergence of Italy on (almost) equal terms with the great powers.

Each of the congresses assumed the form of a gathering of the great powers treated as equals. Elaborate care was taken with preparations to ensure that the proprieties were appropriately observed. Lesser powers were also included but there was never any doubt as to where power resided. Eight powers had signed the Peace of Paris which convoked the Congress of Vienna. The representatives of the four most powerful countries, Austria, Britain, Prussia, and Russia, drew up a complicated plan whereby they alone would conduct the real work of the congress, Spain and Portugal were given some perfunctory tasks, and the others ignored. In fact the congress never officially opened and never met in plenary session. As a practical matter, the critical decisions were made in what today might be called 'four-plus-one'

---

[38] This point is made by Hinsley (1963: 213).

talks between the four and France. By his presence at the congress, however, and his extraordinary diplomatic skill, Tallyrand was able to win concessions that would probably not have been possible had France not been represented. This is an example of how the form of the institution produced outcomes that would not have occurred in a different setting. True, these outcomes were relatively minor amendments to the overall settlement, but wars have been fought on precisely these kinds of issues.

All three of these congresses shared the general function of establishing a durable peace. Each of the participants, however, brought expectations that the congress would also fulfil more specific functions. In Berlin, for example, Britain wanted the congress to preserve as much of Turkey as possible, to prevent Russia from entering Constantinople, and to dismantle the Three Emperors' League. Russia, on the other hand, wanted the congress to preserve as many of the gains embodied in the Treaty of San Stefano as possible. Both sides compromised, but Russia conceded more than Britain. It is hard to see Russian concessions, however, as produced by the persuasion of the assembled diplomats. The main reason Russia conceded was that Britain was prepared to go to war to wrest these concessions: Russia was in no shape for war, and her leaders knew it. Absent an international forum it is certainly possible that Britain and Russia might have gone to war, as many in Britain wished.

It is important to bear in mind that the consequences of these congresses were not necessarily benign. While the Congress of Berlin did help to avert further warfare it also had the perverse consequence of poisoning relations between Germany and Russia. Élite opinion in Russia, with some justification, perceived the congress as a defeat. Due in part to the machinations of the Russian chancellor, Gorchakov, who had attended the congress and who sought to avoid responsibility for the concessions Russia made, the myth was accepted that Bismarck had betrayed Russia. This widely held view, which was quite false, was to have serious ramifications for the diplomatic relations between the two countries. Prussia's treatment in Paris is another case in point. In the early days of the Concert, the members had stressed the importance of upholding the prestige of each of their number. The delayed invitation to the talks in Paris caused Prussia to fear that her status as a great power was in question and, along with other factors, encouraged her to adopt an aggressive foreign policy.

The Congress of Berlin also serves to demonstrate the persistence of the institutional legacy of the Concert.[39] It represents a case in which the com-

---

[39] See Christopher Daase's distinction between institutional precedent and prototype in Ch. 8.

munity of powers in Europe was sufficiently powerful to oblige a victorious belligerent, Russia, to submit its victory, as embodied in the Treaty of San Stefano, to the judgement, and ultimately the revision, of a congress of non-belligerent powers. In so doing it reaffirmed the principle that significant territorial changes within Europe were matters of European concern and could not be effected without the sanction of Europe.

Statesmen attending these congresses self-consciously perceived themselves to be participating in an ongoing convention, or in other words, an iterated game. A norm evolved, for example, that congresses should further the development of international law. At the Paris Congress, Count Walewski, the French Foreign Minister and president of the congress, reminded the body that the Congress of Westphalia had consecrated liberty of conscience and that the Congress of Vienna had both abolished the slave trade and established free navigation of rivers, in order to win support for his proposals which were enshrined in the Declaration of Paris and set out a maritime law in time of war. Bismarck, the president of the Congress of Berlin, was much less interested in such matters but even this Congress did agree to make a contribution and did so by providing greater emphasis and stronger guarantees for the principle of religious liberty than previously existed.[40]

One of the points most often made by institutionalist analysis is that international institutions facilitate coordination by providing opportunities for side payments. The most casual glance at nineteenth-century congresses reveals that this was a central element. The arrangements were quite explicit. Full meetings were held only once every few days in order to allow ample opportunity for private negotiations. Envoys arrived early to cut deals in advance. When Clarendon, for example, arrived in Paris a week before the opening of the congress in 1856 in order to conduct some pre-congress negotiations, he was furious to discover that his rivals the Russians were already there before him. Moreover, the prospect of the meeting served then, as it does now, to provide incentives to concerned parties to try to resolve their differences in advance. Before the Congress of Berlin, for example, the protagonists fenced diplomatically for months and signed three secret conventions prior to the congress.

---

[40] This was at least in part a result of pressure applied by the antecedents of contemporary lobby groups such as the 'Alliance israelite' who travelled to Berlin to plead the case of their kinsmen in the Balkans before the assembled notables. Here we see the congresses, by virtue of the notables gathered together, acquiring the unintended function of a court of appeal. This might suggest that it is worth drawing a distinction between the defining functions which determine the form of the institution and the unanticipated functions which follow from this form.

It is quite clear then that these congresses, part of the institutional form of the Concert of Europe, provided an arena for the exercise of influence, they reduced uncertainty by facilitating signalling of intentions and enhancing the flow of information. All of these roles are consistent with both realist and institutionalist analysis. However, there is little evidence that congresses did more than this: they did not affect state strategies in the way that I have argued the norms, rules, and procedures of the Concert did. The congresses at Paris and Berlin demonstrate the power of the institutional legacy, in that the form of the institution persisted long after agreement on its functions had evaporated. However, the form alone remained no more than a mechanical remnant without the infusion of the shared norms.

Alliances and the Concert: an interlocking system

It is impossible to consider security management in the nineteenth century without giving some thought to the nature of the alliances in the period. The literature on alliances is enormous and this is not the place for a thorough analysis either of alliances in general or even of the nineteenth-century variants.[41] I will simply make a few points about the relationship between alliances, congresses, and the Concert in this period. Alliances, the Concert and the congresses were all part of an interlocking system through which the powers tried to regulate their relations. It is often very difficult to separate one from the other as the same statesmen were involved in all cases. Castlereagh, however, believed that the Concert could only function effectively if it was based on the firm foundation of the Quadruple Alliance. The Quadruple Alliance therefore explicitly set out concrete terms outlining the territorial settlement. The more nebulous Concert was, for him, the means of preserving the alliance. The alliances and the Concert, then, were in no sense rivals but rather complemented each other. The Concert was seen as a means of providing flexibility to the alliance by, for example, permitting amendments to be openly discussed and ratified by the group and thereby reducing the incentive for secret bilateral deals.

Unlike congresses, of which there were only three (one launching the Concert, one marking its end, and one as a belated reminder of a happier past), there were a great many alliances in the nineteenth century. These alliances initially reflected the underlying principles of the Concert, soon demonstrated the tensions within the membership of the Concert, and

---

[41] For two brief and very different analyses of 19th-cent. European alliances see Schroeder, in Knorr (1976: 227–62) and McGowan and Rood (1975: 859–70).

ultimately demonstrated the end of the Concert system. The changes that took place in the Concert can perhaps most concretely be seen in the changes in the nature of alliances in this period.

It need hardly be argued that an alliance is an international security institution, indeed it is almost one by definition. Alliances, however, have generally been seen in pure power-political terms as an instrumental means of capability aggregation. The statesmen at Vienna deliberately tried to move away from this type of ruinous alliance, which had prevailed in the eighteenth century, to create a more permanent system. The signatories of the Quadruple Alliance agreed that it would stay in effect for twenty years. Tallyrand wrote: 'We flattered ourselves . . . that the congress would crown its labours, by substituting for these fleeting alliances (the result of necessities and momentary calculations) a permanent system of universal guarantees and general equilibrium.'[42]

The generosity of the terms offered to France, even after the interlude of the Hundred Days, demonstrates the desire to create a lasting arrangement, one that France restored to strength would not want to overturn.

The Concert, as mentioned earlier, was brought into existence by an article in the Quadruple Alliance. The interplay between the alliances, the Concert and the congresses was constant thereafter. An example of this occurred at the first congress. While the signatories were meeting at the Congress at Vienna, relations deteriorated significantly between Russia and Prussia on the one hand and Austria and Britain on the other. At one point in December it appeared as though both sides might go to war on the issue of Saxony. In a brazen move demonstrating both his ability to exploit the procedures of the congress to enhance his position and the desire of his government to end their isolation from the big four, Tallyrand proposed a secret alliance between France, Britain, and Austria, in which they agreed to resist Russo-Prussian action. Initially reluctant, Castlereagh signed the tripartite treaty in January 1815. In the hotbed of the congress the secret was soon known to everyone and the Polish/Saxony crisis dissolved immediately.

The other great alliance signed in 1815 was the Holy Alliance of Austria, Prussia, and Russia. This was the brainchild of Tsar Alexander, who remained its most committed supporter. The idea was a radical one. The alliance proposed that the signatories should see themselves acting as the agents of God in the protection of religion, justice, and the great-power way, wherever it was threatened. Castlereagh expressed his reaction in a letter to Liverpool: 'Foreseeing the awkwardness of this piece of sublime mysticism

---

[42] Quoted in Holsti (1991: 114).

and nonsense . . . I examined with Prince Metternich every practical expedient to stop it . . . The fact is that the Emperor's mind is not completely sound . . . [Metternich] thinks good may come from indulging the Emperor.'[43] Austria and Prussia, sharing the Tsar's conservatism if not his mysticism, and anxious to retain his friendship, signed the alliance. The Prince Regent sent the Tsar a letter expressing support for the views expressed in the alliance, which was as far as the British government was prepared to commit itself. The two alliances of this period, therefore, give tangible expression to the two views of the role of the Concert that were to divide Britain from the eastern powers in the debates of the congress period. Each of the two perceptions of the appropriate function for the Concert, therefore, found expression in a different institutional form, the two alliances. The Concert, for its part, was sufficiently flexible to embrace these two orientations under its rubric, though of course it created tensions, the very tensions that caused the shift from phase two to phase three of the Concert.

This second phase of the Concert, marked by the convening of five congresses from Vienna to Verona, witnessed the constant competition between Russia and Britain, as Russia sought to bring the Concert into line with the Holy Alliance while Britain sought to restrict it to the Quadruple Alliance. The Russian view supported by Prussia and Austria prevailed at the congresses and thus it was in the name of the Holy Alliance that Austria marched into Italy to suppress the uprisings in Naples and Piedmont. Castlereagh became increasingly disenchanted. He wrote:

In this Alliance as in all other human Arrangements, nothing is more likely to impair or even to destroy its real utility, than any attempt to push its duties and obligations beyond the Sphere which its original Conception and understood Principles will warrant. It was an union for the Reconquest and liberation of a great proportion of the Continent of Europe from the Military Domination of France, and having subdued the Conqueror it took the State of Possession as established by the Peace under the Protection of the Alliance:—It was never however intended as an Union for the Government of the World, or for the Superintendence of the Internal Affairs of other States.[44]

The Concert, the alliances, and the congresses were therefore operating simultaneously, largely with the same membership, all seeking means of regulating their interactions while protecting their interests. Alliances were essentially a complementary part of the institutional form and therefore a critical component of the Concert and difficult to analyse separately.

---

[43] Castlereagh to Liverpool, 25 Sept. 1815 in Webster (1921: 382–4).
[44] State Paper, 5 May 1820, in Temperley and Penson (1966: 54).

Just as the Concert was eroded in the course of the century so did the nature of the alliances change. Indeed, as the alliances gave concrete expression to the somewhat inchoate norms of the Concert, one can chart the changes in the Concert by looking at the changing alliances. Prior to the Crimean War the alliances were flexible arrangements and managed to circumvent the ideological divide between the three conservative eastern powers and the two western liberal ones. In the years prior to the war the alliances were usually defensive in nature. They were generally designed to protect members from internal difficulties or from the encroachment of foreign influence. After the war, however, alliances were more likely to be aggressive in intent. They were designed with a war plan in mind and intended to secure either the assistance or the neutrality of other members.[45]

Early in the century too, alliances were far more likely to be used as 'tools of management' rather than 'weapons of power':[46] as security management institutions rather than mechanisms for capability aggregation.[47] The Quadruple Alliance was quite clearly an effort by the victors to restrain each other, and while explicitly directed against France it was implicitly directed against Russia, a member. The management aspect of the alliance is demonstrated by the speed with which France was invited to join. Even the mystical Holy Alliance had more material aspects; it served as a means for the three conservative powers to manage their many rivalries in Germany, the Near East, and Italy. This was not only true of the large multi-member alliances but true of bilateral alliances of the period too, the Russia-Turkish alliance of Unkiar Skelessi being a case in point. Russia did not enhance her security nor did she add to her power, but she did gain some control over Turkey with this alliance. Later in the century, alliances and especially the many alliances orchestrated by Bismarck, appeared to serve far more the military and security needs and less the management aspirations of the members. Bismarck skilfully managed to extract both functions from his alliances but for his successors alliances were classic capability aggregation mechanisms. As the consensus underlying the Concert eroded, therefore, the nature of the alliances changed.

The alliances, like the congresses, were tangible manifestations of the operation and ultimately the failure of the Concert of Europe. They were all part of an interlocking system for the management of security relations between the great powers. They operated most effectively when the most powerful governments shared a consensus on the legitimacy of the

---

[45] Craig makes this point (1960: 271).
[46] See Schroeder in Knorr (1976: 227–62).   [47] See Chris Gelpi in Ch. 4.

prevailing order. They were all, therefore, largely driven by the states which were their members, by the culture and ideas which prevailed there, and by events in the domestic capitals of these states. Nevertheless, the Concert managed in turn to influence the shaping of strategies and preferences over policies, in the capitals of Europe, especially in the early nineteenth century.

4. *Conclusion*

An analysis of institutions prior to today's institution-rich environment can expand the database by providing examples of institutional adaptation, persistence, and demise. More substantively, institutions are not merely mechanisms for the maintenance of the status quo but can peacefully accommodate change in the international distribution of power. The strongest evidence in support of this claim is provided by the integration of France into the international system in 1818 and the creation of the Kingdom of Belgium in 1831. Third, institutions are not merely transmission belts for the conveyance of state interests, but rather, the existence of the institution can have an impact on the strategies adopted by states. The Concert served to reduce uncertainty by generating expectations of behaviour and by providing opportunities for reassurance and for discussion of differences. Moreover, membership in the Concert and the status that went along with it became a prize in itself. States were prepared to pay the price of increased constraints in order to attain the benefits of membership. In short the Concert increased the benefits of cooperation while increasing the costs of defection. Finally, this analysis of the Concert also suggests that institutional form is a product of (*a*) institutional function, (*b*) technical feasibility, and (*c*) recent experience of members.

There are many factors which account for the success of the Concert. Some could be replicated today, many could not. This was a style of co-operation which democracies might find difficult to handle. The Concert could thrive in part because of the flexibility and the authority of the plenipotentiaries. The norms of the Concert did however survive many changes in leadership in the member states. The spread of democracy undermined the Concert by constraining the flexibility of the national leaders and by increasing uncertainty. Nevertheless, it is at least interesting to note that this nineteenth-century precursor to twentieth-century security management institutions experienced many similar pressures. The Concert, for example, survived the end of the unifying threat from France by integrating France into the system. The obvious twentieth-century corollary is, of course, the defeat of Russia in the cold war. The threat from France, however, was soon replaced as institutional glue by the threat from domestic revolution. No comparable candidate for a shared threat has yet presented itself to twentieth-century institutions. There are also echoes of today's debates on NATO enlargement in the nineteenth-century Concert. At the Paris Peace Congress the Ottoman empire was ceremoniously invited to join. In doing do the Concert members explicitly acknowledged the progress the Turks had made in adhering to Western standards of behaviour and hoped that membership in the Concert would encourage these developments. Of course it did not, but as I have argued above, the Concert was essentially defunct by that stage anyway. Nevertheless, the Concert did persist for at least forty years and in that time it adapted peacefully to many changes in the international distribution of power, the very types of changes that in preceding centuries had led to war.

I do not for a moment wish to argue that the Concert was the only factor driving interstate relations in nineteenth-century Europe. Realpolitik, domestic politics, culture, ideas, and even individuals were also powerful impetuses for state behaviour. I simply wish to make the relatively modest point that the Concert of Europe did, for a time, in the instances outlined above and quite probably in others, constrain the behaviour of the five great powers. Beyond this, through the acceptance of its norms, rules, and practices, the Concert shaped the strategies of states in such a way as to enable them to include participation in the Concert as part of the definition of their national interests.

Table 2.1. *Nineteenth-Century Congresses*

Location	Date	Subject
Vienna	1815	Peace Treaty, Quadruple Alliance, Concert
Aix-la-Chapelle	1818	France
Troppau	1820	Revolutions, Naples
Laibach	1821	Naples revolution
Verona	1822	Italy, Spain, Eastern Question
Paris	1856	Peace Treaty
Berlin	1878	Eastern Question

Source: F. H. Hinsley, *Power and the Pursuit of Peace* (Cambridge: Cambridge University Press, 1964), 214.

Table 2.2. *Nineteenth-Century Peace Conferences*

Location	Date	Subject
London	1830–2	Belgium
Rome	1831–2	Reform of the Papal States
London	1838–9	Belgium
Vienna	1839	Eastern Question
London	1840–1	Eastern Question
London	1850–2	Schleswig-Holstein
Vienna	1853	Eastern Question
Vienna	1855	Eastern Question
Paris	1858	Principalities
Paris	1860–1	Syria
London	1864	Schleswig-Holstein
London	1867	Luxembourg
Paris	1869	Crete
London	1871	Black Sea
Constantinople	1876–7	Eastern Question
Madrid	1880	Morocco
Berlin	1884–5	Africa

Source: F. H. Hinsley, *Power and the Pursuit of Peace* (Cambridge: Cambridge University Press, 1963), 214. Hinsley's list does not include ambassadorial and other conferences which did not consist of the great powers. He also excludes technical meetings on issues such as armaments.

Appendix: 19th Century Alliances 1815–1899

1815	Quadruple Alliance (Austria, Britain, Prussia, Russia against France)
1815	The Holy Alliance (Austria, Prussia, Russia)
1818	Quintuple Alliance (modified the Quadruple Alliance by adding France)
1833	Russo-Turkish Alliance (Treaty of Unkiar Skelessi)
1847	Austria-Moderna alliance
1848	Austria-Parma alliance
1851	Austro-Prussian alliance
1851	Holy Alliance restored (Austria, Prussia, Russia)
1854	Franco-British Alliance
1854	Austro-Prussian offensive and defensive alliance and military convention
1854	Franco-Austrian Alliance
1854/55	Triple Alliance (Austria, Britain, France)
1859	Franco-Sardinian alliance
1863	Renewal of the Triple Alliance
1864	Austro-Prussian alliance
1866	Prussia-Wurtemburg alliance
1866	Prussia-Baden alliance
1866	Prussia-North German States alliance
1866	Prussia-Hesse-Darmstadt alliance
1866	Prussia, Mecklenburg-Schwerin, Mecklenburg-Strelitz alliance
1866	Italo-Prussian alliance
1866	Franco-Austrian alliance
1872	Dreikaiserbund (Germany, Austria, Russia)
1878	Anglo-Turkish defensive alliance re the Asiatic provinces
1878	Austro-British alliance
1879	Dual Alliance (Austria, Germany)
1881	Dreikaiserbund (renewal)
1881	Austro-Serbian alliance
1882	Triple Alliance (Austria, Germany, Italy) secret defensive alliance
1883	Austro-German-Rumanian Alliance (Romania joins the Triple Alliance)
1884	Austro-German-Russian Alliance (renewal of Dreikaiserbund)
1887	Russo-German Reinsurance Treaty (defensive alliance)
1887	Triple Alliance renewed
1888	Austro-German alliance
1894	Franco-Russian alliance
1897	Austro-Russian entente

3

THE FUNCTIONS OF A EUROPEAN SECURITY AND DEFENCE IDENTITY AND ITS INSTITUTIONAL FORM

Carsten Tams

1. Introduction

The concept of a European security and defence identity (ESDI) reflects the belief of some European states that they must cooperate more closely in providing for their own defence and security. ESDI has been pursued in several ways.[1] The creation of the European Political Cooperation (EPC) process and the revitalization of the West European Union (WEU) during the 1980s were first steps, followed by the creation of the Common Foreign and Security Policy (CFSP) by EU member states in the Treaty on the European Union in 1991.[2] The treaty links the EU and the WEU by stipulating that the EU can request the WEU 'to elaborate and implement decisions and actions of the Union which have defense implications.'[3] The next year, the WEU was empowered to deploy military forces in humanitarian, rescue, peacekeeping, and crisis management missions.[4] France, Germany, and Great Britain have been active in this process, and ESDI has become a standard formula in their discourse about European security. An analysis of their respective policies reveals, however, that Britain strongly opposes some of the Franco-German proposals for institutional change.

Why do different states have different preferences regarding the design of

I would like to thank Helga Haftendorn, Michael Kreft, Ingo Peters, and Celeste A. Wallander for helpful written comments and suggestions on an earlier draft of this article.

[1] On ESDI see Hellmann (1996); Plantin (1993); Schmidt (1995); and Yost (1991).
[2] Treaty on the European Union, art. J.   [3] Ibid., art. J4.2.
[4] Petersberg Declaration, Western European Union, Council of Ministers, Bonn, 19 June 1992, *European Yearbook 1992*, WEU 13.

an institution? State preferences for institutional form vary with preferences for institutional functions. Security cooperation among states involves four main functions: collective defence, collective security, security management, and out-of-area intervention. Each of these functions involves different cooperation problems, with each type of problem requiring different institutional mechanisms. Disagreement among states on the institutional form of ESDI is a result of disagreement over the functions ESDI should perform.

The evidence for this hypothesis is twofold. First, France, Germany, and Great Britain agree on only one function of ESDI: out-of-area intervention. Each of these states advocates institutional mechanisms that solve problems related to functions in which that state is most interested. In particular, they all suggest decision-making procedures which do not constrain their choice of whether to deploy armed forces in a crisis; and they agree on the need for mechanisms which enhance the convergence of interests among them, such as joint planning and analysis. Second, the contested issue is collective defence as a function of ESDI: France, supported by Germany, promotes it; Britain fervently opposes it. States cooperating for collective defence face the problem of abandonment. It is the issue of collective defence that leads to substantial conflicts over the institutional form of ESDI. Because creating new institutional mechanisms is costly, Britain opposes the relatively high degree of integration advocated by France and Germany. In particular, Britain strongly objects to the integration of the WEU into the European Union.

This chapter first outlines the four basic functions security cooperation can serve, the cooperation problems involved for each, and the institutional mechanisms which can solve these problems. Then, it analyses the security functions assigned to the ESDI by France, Germany, and Britain. This enables us to identify the mechanisms each state's policy requires for ESDI to carry out its functions effectively. The third section analyses the negotiations over these issues as a test of my hypothesis that the function of cooperation determines its institutional form.

2. The Functions of Security Cooperation

Walt has defined security studies as 'the study of the threat, use, and control of military force'. According to Axelrod and Keohane, cooperation takes place 'in situations that contain a mixture of conflicting and complementary interests. In such situations, cooperation occurs when actors adjust their behavior to the actual or anticipated preferences of others.' 'Security cooperation' refers, then, to policy adjustment between two or more states with regard to the threat, use, and control of military force.[5]

A framework for distinguishing the functions of security cooperation

In order to account for the variety of forms security cooperation can take, we may ask what kind of security challenge is involved: threat or risk? Which strategies do states choose in dealing with inclusive or exclusive challenges?[6]

The concept of threat is commonly employed to describe a situation in which three elements come together. First, the threat must emanate from an identifiable actor; second, this actor must have or be perceived to have an aggressive intention; and finally, this actor must have the ability to carry out its intention.[7] From the West's point of view, the cold war was based on threat: the Soviet Union and its allies were actors; their ideology was perceived as aggressive; and their conventional superiority gave them the military potential to inflict severe damage.[8] The Atlantic Alliance was the institutional form that West European states chose for dealing with this threat.

Now, after the cold war, West European states increasingly focus on security challenges of a different nature.[9] Nuclear proliferation, migration flows, and inter-ethnic wars on the periphery are not threats as classically defined; they pertain to national security in the wider sense. These security risks all lack at least one of the three constituent components of a threat, and they involve a relatively high degree of uncertainty. This is reflected in the NATO Communiqué of December 1990:

The risks that the Allies now face in Europe arise less from the likelihood of de-liberate aggression against Allied territory by former adversaries than from the *unforeseeable* strategic consequences of instabilities that *might* emerge in a period of rapid and widespread political and economic transformation. [...] Nor can we exclude the possibility that risks to the Allies' security may arise from *elsewhere*. [...] The proliferation of weapons of mass destruction and the spread of destabilizing military technology have implications for Allied security and illustrate that in an ever more interdependent world, we face new security risks and challenges of a global nature.[10]

---

[5] Walt (1991: 212); Axelrod and Keohane (1985: 226); Wallander, Haftendorn, and Keohane, the Introduction, above. See also Lynn-Jones and Nye (1988: 6–7).

[6] This framework has been suggested by Wallander and Keohane. See Ch. 1.

[7] Daase (1992: 71–2); similarly Walt (1987: 21–8).   [8] Daase (1992: 77).

[9] For a more extensive elaboration see Greco (1995/6).

[10] North Atlantic Council Ministerial Communiqué, Dec. 1990, *NATO Review*, 38/6: 22–4. Emphasis added.

This uncertainty implies that the assessment of risks is more dependent on subjective perception than the assessment of threats.

With the cold war over, the international system is less polarized and security policies are less determined. The choices a state makes, the risks it identifies, and the actions it takes rest to a greater degree on its sympathies, ideological predilections, and fears.[11] This new-found freedom also means more uncertainty and contains a higher potential for disagreement over risks and responses. Accordingly, risks lend themselves to dispute more than threats do. States find it more difficult to agree on what to cooperate for than to agree on what to cooperate against. When coping with risks, states will find it more difficult to build and maintain cooperative relations, since their interests are more likely to diverge on specific issues.[12] The institutional form a state chooses for its cooperation therefore depends partly on whether cooperation addresses clear and present threats or ambiguous risks.

States have the option of dealing with these security challenges through either inclusive or exclusive strategies. This framework yields four different types of security cooperation: collective defence, collective security, security management, and out-of-area intervention. Each function raises specific problems, and specific institutional mechanisms are required to solve these problems.

Collective defence, collective security, and security management

The purpose of collective defence is to protect the members of an alliance against threats from non-members. States aggregate their defensive capabilities and thereby hope either to establish an effective deterrent or, if deterrence fails, to provide an effective defence.[13] With other collaboration problems, collective defence arrangements confront their members with the possibility of being abandoned or entrapped by an ally.[14] Compared to functions where risks are involved, however, states cooperating to ward off threats are relatively more concerned about abandonment. Alliances

---

[11] Wolfers has made an equivalent argument concerning the extension of the meaning of aggression (1962: 188–9).

[12] Daase therefore assumes that conditions of risk lead to a 'particularization of security policy' (1992: 75).

[13] Wolfers (1962: 182).

[14] Snyder (1984: 466–8). Snyder distinguishes primary and secondary alliance dilemma. The primary dilemma is the choice whether to ally or not to ally. The secondary dilemma arises once that decision has been made. Concerns of abandonment and entrapment arise at this second stage. The question this article poses is how states conceive the institutional form of cooperation, given what they hope this cooperation will achieve. Thus, the decision to cooperate has already been made. Only the secondary dilemma is, therefore, of concern here.

therefore have to provide mechanisms that enhance the credibility of members' commitment and reduce the transaction costs of decision-making.

In both collective security and collective defence arrangements, countries commit themselves to assist one another against attack. Collective security, however, is inclusive: the members commit themselves to come to the aid of one member if it is attacked or threatened by another member.[15] Collaboration games in collective security cooperation differ from those in collective defence in the number of players involved, because collective security arrangements tend to include many states, including the future aggressor. The functions performed are the same, but the institutional requirements will be more demanding.[16]

Security management institutions are inclusive coalitions that respond to risks.[17] Many institutions exist which serve the purpose of security management: Jervis describes the European Concert as an institution that views mutual cooperation as a prerequisite for a state's individual stability;[18] the main function of the WEU has been to control Germany's rearmament; and the Quad is yet another, albeit scarcely known, institution whose function was to prevent West Germany from pursuing a unilateral foreign policy.[19]

Two obstacles to cooperation are uncertainty and competitive bargaining. Coping with threats poses problems of collaboration; coping with risk poses problems of assurance and coordination. Solving assurance problems requires mechanisms that allow member states to exchange information about one another's preferences. Solving coordination problems requires negotiating forums and bargaining structures. Neither requires centralized enforcement mechanisms, so security management institutions will have different forms from those of collective defence and collective security institutions.[20]

Out-of-area intervention

Not all risks can be dealt with efficiently by inclusive strategies. Some risks are 'multi-faceted in nature and multi-directional, which makes them hard to predict and assess'.[21] Such risks include the proliferation of weapons of mass destruction, civil wars, disruption of the flow of vital resources, acts of terrorism and sabotage, and ecological disasters. These risks can occur at

---

[15] Wolfers (1962: 182); Gärtner (1996: 361).   [16] Martin (1993: 96–8).
[17] See Ch. 1 above.   [18] Jervis (1983).
[19] On the Quad see Ch. 6.   [20] See Ch. 1.
[21] 'The Alliance's New Strategic Concept, November 1991', *NATO Review* 39/6: 25–32, at 26.

any time or place, so it would be very costly to set up permanent, global institutions to deal with them.

If a state perceives any such risk as significantly affecting its national security, but lacks the ability to counter on its own, it will seek cooperation with other states. Often such coalitions are formed *ad hoc* because of significant policy disagreements in other areas. Yet building coalitions, setting up mechanisms for political consultation, assembling the required military resources, and setting up C^3I structures on an *ad hoc* basis consume resources that can be very scarce in crisis situations. Swift action can be decisive in a conflict-prevention operation. Therefore, states might wish to set up permanent mechanisms that allow them to intervene at an early stage of a crisis. Security institutions such as NATO and WEU increasingly take on functions of out-of-area operations.[22]

What are the problems that states confront in out-of-area interventions? States cooperating in such interventions seek to address risks. Risks are more ambiguous than threats, so it may be more difficult for states to define common security interests or to agree on the source of the security challenge and the objective of collective action. (One recent example is the EU member states' incapacity to agree on a common policy in the Yugoslav crisis.[23]) Given the high potential for diverging interests, 'each partner will worry about being trapped into "pulling the other's chestnuts out of the fire"'.[24] The cooperation problem facing states that seek long-term cooperation in out-of-area intervention is a suasion game. 'Suasion problems have equilibrium outcomes that leave one actor dissatisfied. While player A's dominant strategy is to cooperate, player B's dominant strategy is to defect.'[25] The dilemma facing the state that desires cooperation is to persuade or coerce others to cooperate.

If power is distributed asymmetrically, suasion problems are more easily solved. Issue linkages and side payments create incentives to cooperation. Under an asymmetrical distribution of power, decision and agenda-setting control 'will likely be maintained by the hegemonic state, with face-saving arrangements to isolate others from domestic pressure'.[26] A hegemon may

---

[22] Communiqué of the Ministerial meeting of the North Atlantic Council in Oslo, 4 June 1992, *NATO Review*, 40/3: 30–2; Communiqué issued by the Ministerial meeting of the North Atlantic Council, Brussels, 17 Dec. 1992, *NATO Review*, 40/6: 28–31; Petersberg Declaration, Western European Union, Council of Ministers, Bonn, 19 June 1992, *European Yearbook 1992*, WEU 13. On NATO and its role in out-of-area missions see Winrow (1994).

[23] The most prominent examples are the dispute over recognition of Croatia and Slovenia, pushed by Germany, as well as the question of a military intervention. See Stark (1992); Edwards (1997).

[24] Snyder (1984: 474).   [25] Martin (1993: 103).   [26] Ibid. 105.

also rely on institutions to solve suasion problems, but formal organizations should become more important as disparities in power decrease.

If power is relatively diffused, it is unlikely that one state will yield discretion in decision-making or agenda-setting to another state or subgroup of states, given the asymmetry of interests in suasion games. In institutions which are set up to facilitate cooperation in out-of-area intervention, assistance will not be provided automatically as in alliances, and states will preserve discretion respecting their decision to participate in any mission. Reluctance to give away discretionary powers will increase as the costs of enforcement rise—for example, when they imply the use of armed force. Coalitions for action therefore have to be established case by case.

If decisions must be unanimous, joint action will be difficult to achieve. Given the asymmetry of interests in these matters, the principle of unanimity would give any state the power to keep all other states from acting together: the institution would prevent cooperation instead of enabling it. This problem can be remedied in two ways. The obvious solution is to relax the requirement of full unanimity. But then assets may be used for purposes that run counter to the national interest of one of the members. The other solution is to enhance the convergence of interests among member states. This can be done through extensive consultation and joint planning, although this can prove a lengthy process, dooming an institution to ineffectiveness. Furthermore, the effectiveness of this solution will decline as the number of players increases. In sum, joint decision-making in suasion games is difficult. If a hegemon with strong coercive power is absent, formal organizations will play a central role in providing additional scope for issue linkages. They will contain very specific and differentiated mechanisms that facilitate joint action while respecting members' concern over entrapment, leaving intact their discretionary power to join or not join a coalition.

Some common assets are required to increase the effectiveness of action. Crisis management and conflict prevention call for a variety of measures, both political and military. The toolbox of an alliance such as NATO contains several such elements. The problem is that crisis management requires military forces different from those required by collective defence. This is reflected in NATO's London Declaration: 'NATO will field smaller and restructured active forces. These forces will be highly mobile and versatile, so that Allied leaders will have maximum flexibility in deciding how to respond to a crisis.'[27] The requirement of maximum flexibility also applies

---

[27] 'London Declaration on a Transformed North Atlantic Alliance', July 1990, *NATO Review*, 38/4: 32–3, at 33.

to C³I structures. Highly integrated structures or functional interdependence of national forces would be counterproductive, since not all member states are likely to participate in every mission. Common assets will include particularly those military capabilities which are too expensive for individual members and which are not highly vulnerable.

3. State Policies on ESDI

France

In the early 1990s, France's foreign policy pursued three fundamental aims: to control newly unified Germany's increased power; to maintain independence in foreign diplomacy; and to preserve France's international influence. The 'German question' was of major concern to French politicians once it became apparent that German unity could not be prevented. How would German unification affect the balance of power in Europe? The French political élite expected that Germany would evolve into the predominant power in Europe.[28] They believed that economically and demographically Germany would gain twice the strength of France and that, over the medium term, Germany would acquire the military instruments corresponding to its responsibilities as a great power.[29] This rise in Germany's power nurtured several, partially contradictory fears: that Germany would challenge France's claims to leadership within the European Community; or that it would pursue its own national interests with greater vigour, imposing its interests on its partners. France also feared a second Rapallo: i.e. that Germany would lose interest in *Westbindung* and turn to the East.[30] In adapting to the post-cold war era, France was above all concerned about its relative power position *vis-à-vis* Germany. If it could not extend its own power correspondingly, it had to contain Germany's.

The second imperative of French foreign policy was to keep, and if possible extend, its international influence. Like de Gaulle, Mitterrand believed that *la Grande Nation* had a distinctive role to play in world affairs. France has traditionally displayed a strong interest in the Middle East and in North, West, and Central Africa. The *Livre blanc sur la défense* described at length the strategic challenges France faces on its southern flank, which include domestic and interstate rivalries, the proliferation of weapons of mass destruction and medium-range missiles, and non-military risks such

---

[28] Gordon (1995: 87).   [29] *Livre blanc* (1994: 25).   [30] Hoffmann (1993: 135).

as international terrorism of Islamic provenance and international organized crime.[31] Accordingly, France undertook enormous efforts to influence international politics. Successive presidents burdened France with the high costs of acquiring and maintaining the status of a nuclear power. In the early 1990s, France sent more blue helmets to international trouble spots than any other country.[32] France rivals the US in its determination to exert influence in regions that it considers to be of strategic interest. In fact, France strongly resents the overwhelming predominance of the United States in international politics, which is expected to continue for the next twenty years. France's intervention in Rwanda in 1994 was interpreted as a demonstration of its intention to maintain its sphere of influence against Anglo-Saxon challenges.[33] On the other side, France expects that Europe will become less important for the US, leading eventually to further reductions in its military presence. France's call for a stronger European voice in security and defence matters thus stems both from a long-standing resentment of the international predominance of the US, and from recent structural changes in Europe.

France was confronted by a dilemma, since limiting Germany's power and maintaining its own international role are incompatible with its third aim, the maintenance of France's 'dogma of strategic independence'.[34] Integration seems to be the only available strategy to control Germany's sudden rise in power. As Hoffmann put it: 'In the world of 1990–1991 independence for France could not but license full independence for Germany', which meant 'a risk of German predominance in the federation'.[35] The discrepancy between France's international ambitions and its capabilities became apparent when it was largely ignored by the US in the political settlement of the Gulf crisis of 1991.

Once Mitterrand recognized that the status quo in Europe could not be maintained, he favoured the acceleration and deepening of European integration among the Twelve as the best French policy in the transformed international environment. France endows the Political Union with full competence in defence and security matters.[36] The promotion of a politically and strategically more autonomous Western Europe—according to Bozo, the most permanent feature of French international policy since the Second World War[37]—was an integral part of this strategy. ESDI could fulfil several functions in this strategy. First, it could provide for security

[31] *Livre blanc* (1994: 21–45).
[32] International Institute of Strategic Studies (1993: 44–5).   [33] Philippi (1997: 236).
[34] Bozo (1992: 211).   [35] Hoffmann (1993: 132).
[36] Yost (1991: 327).   [37] Bozo (1992: 205).

management. A deepening of integration in the foreign and security policy field could assure France of Germany's benevolent intentions. Second, ESDI was assigned the function of providing a framework for cooperation in out-of-area intervention. France increasingly seeks to contain political instabilities on its southern flank by cooperating with other countries.[38] France realized that it could only hope to influence world political affairs if it played the European card.[39] Through the aggregation of dispersed resources, ESDI could contribute to the emergence of a world in which the European Union takes an important place between North America and East Asia.[40]

Finally, France was the country that more than any other assigned to ESDI the function of collective defence. Menon points out that 'by the 1990s French officials were referring to European defense cooperation in more far reaching terms than ever before'.[41] For the French Foreign Secretary Dumas, it was 'inconceivable to leave security aspects at the margin of this process: defense is both an object of cooperation and an element of sovereignty with which the federal entity, which is our long-term objective, will or should be endowed'.[42] The policy-makers in Paris recognized that only through NATO could the strategic preponderance of Russia in Europe be balanced. Nevertheless, Mitterrand remained ambivalent with regard to NATO until the end. He resisted most of the new NATO initiatives and interpreted NATO reform as a disguised attempt to hinder the Europeans from acquiring their strategic independence through ESDI.[43] Resentment of American dominance and fear of American disengagement led to the conviction that Europeans must eventually take their defence into their own hands.[44]

Germany

In the early 1990s, German security policy had three fundamental aims: to stabilize its eastern periphery, to extend its room for manœuvre in security matters, and to prevent a renationalization of foreign policy by West European states. Germany's principal security risks lay on its eastern border.

---

[38] Philippi (1997: 223).

[39] This view was held by the majority of the French political class. See Randzio-Plath (1992: 30).

[40] *Frankfurter Allgemeine Zeitung* (31 Aug. 1996); see also Schrader (1993: 35), and *Livre blanc* (1994: 45).

[41] Menon (1995: 22); also Cornish (1996: 755).

[42] Dumas's intervention before the Ministerial Council of the WEU, 10 Dec. 1990, cited in Yost (1991: 334).

[43] *Le Monde* (10–11 Nov. 1991, 23 Mar. 1991, 6 June 1992); *Libération* (6 Dec. 1991).

[44] Grant (1996: 59).

Structural economic deficits, social tensions, and nationalist tendencies in Central and East European countries (CEECs) impeded the latter's transformation into functioning democracies and market economies. With the dissolution of the Soviet Union, tensions between ethnic groups within newly independent countries came to the surface. The conflict in former Yugoslavia has nurtured fears that similar rivalries in the region between the Baltic states and the Black Sea could escalate into armed conflict.[45] As long as Russia's domestic stability and its foreign policy remain unpredictable and the CEECs are not embedded in viable European structures, the greatest risks to Germany's security come from its eastern periphery.[46]

A second challenge for Germany's security policy is to increase its contribution to international security. Reunification increased Germany's weight in international affairs. The Federal Republic numbered 63 million citizens on 2 October 1990; the next day, there were 16 million more. In the long run, reunification was also expected to increase Germany's economic power. With the coming into force of the 2+4 treaty on 15 March 1991, Germany rid itself of the legal constraints imposed on it after the Second World War by the Allies and regained 'full sovereignty over its internal and external affairs'.[47] The realm of *Bundeswehr* deployment was successively extended on the political and legal front. The Federal Minister of Defence, Rühe, pushed for participation by the German army in out-of-area missions, such as AWACS surveillance of the no-fly zone in Bosnia or the UNOSOM I and II missions in Somalia. At the same time, a legal dispute over out-of-area missions took place before the Federal Constitutional Court. On 12 July 1994, the Court repudiated an interpretation of the Basic Law according to which the German army could not participate in missions other than collective defence in NATO. Given the increase in Germany's power, large parts of the German public and many of Germany's international partners were increasingly dissatisfied with Germany's chequebook diplomacy[48] and urged the government to make a more equitable contribution to international peace and security. That expectations regarding Germany's international role had significantly increased became

---

[45] For Germany's security priorities in the 1990s see Bundesministerium der Verteidigung (1994: 27–9).

[46] Klaus Kinkel, Statement of Federal Minister for Foreign Affairs, Berlin, 21 June 1994, in Auswärtiges Amt (1995: 1065).

[47] *Vertrag über die abschließenden Regelungen in bezug auf Deutschland* ('2+4 Treaty'), art. 7.2.

[48] Within Germany, this view was particularly strong among CDU/CSU members. See CDU-Bundesgeschäftsstelle (1992a: 5); see also the resolution of the third party convention of the CDU, Düsseldorf, 25–8 Oct., CDU-Bundesgeschäftsstelle (1992b: 9–11).

obvious when President Bush offered Germany a 'partner in leadership' role.[49]

At the same time, Germany sought to reassure domestic groups and other countries that it would not return to unilateralism or aspire to European hegemony. In some European capitals, German unification raised questions about the stability of Europe. Uncertainty about the reliability of a more powerful Germany led Prime Minister Thatcher and President Mitterrand to try to slow down the process of unification.[50] Strong political factions in Germany also had reservations. Some suspected that the 'return to normality'[51] was really an attempt to revive German militarism.[52] The German government for its part was concerned about a possible renationalization of foreign policy by its international partners, a prospect which recalled the seesaw politics that traditionally left Germany at a disadvantage because of its *Mittellage*, or central geographical position in Europe.[53]

These challenges to Germany's security policy confront its policy-makers with a dilemma. They have to walk a narrow line between new expectations and old resentments. On one side, its international partners and the situation on its eastern periphery demand that Germany take a more active role in securing international peace and stability. On the other side, there are fears of a new German assertiveness.

European integration is the centrepiece of Germany's response to this dilemma. European integration is considered the best instrument for ensuring that the power shifts on the continent will not threaten its stability. The present cooperative relations between Germany and its European partners should be sustained and developed through further European integration. When German unification was still contingent on the goodwill of the Four Powers, Germany had a particular interest in proving its reliability through a commitment to international institutions. As late as November 1989, the key players in German politics omitted no occasion to stress that reunification must be embedded in a process of further European integration. Germany, as Chancellor Kohl confirmed at the European Council meeting in Rome, promised not to use its newly regained sovereignty in

---

[49] 'Bush Declares Berlin Wall "Must Come Down"', Bush speech in Mainz, Germany, 31 May 1989: US Information Service, *Information and Texts*, 70 (1 June 1989), 2.

[50] Wolffsohn (1992: 151); Langghut (1991: 137); Richardson (1993: 150).

[51] Speech by German Secretary of Defence Volker Rühe in Mainz, 7 Oct. 1993, quoted in Leimbacher (1995: 49).

[52] These fears were particularly pronounced among the political left. See the resolution *In Frieden leben* of the SPD convention, Bremen, 31 May 1991.

[53] Nötzold (1993: 38).

a retrograde fashion.[54] In a speech in Cambridge, Kohl called for further progress in European integration as a means of ensuring that united Germany remained tightly integrated into European structures.[55] These pleas for European integration signalled to its neighbours that fears of a renationalization of Germany's foreign policy were unfounded. United Germany would stick to the same principles that were fundamental to the foreign policy of the Federal Republic: multilateralism, European integration, and a European culture of security.[56] Closer European cooperation in security and defence clearly fulfilled a security management function.

Furthermore, a reinforced ESDI could help Germany overcome its foreign-policy dilemma by providing a multilateral framework for out-of-area intervention. Tightly integrated security cooperation can help Germany bind its European partners in the effort to stabilize its eastern periphery. Through the aggregation of capabilities of various kinds, policies can be made more effective. Through embedding its foreign and security policy in a cooperative framework, Germany can diffuse fears of German unilateralism and overcome domestic resistance against a more assertive stance in security policy, in particular with regard to the participation of its army in out-of-area missions. A reinforced ESDI can, furthermore, prevent the renationalization of the foreign policies of Germany's European partners.

Germany is ambivalent about whether to advocate collective defence as a function to ESDI. There are two reasons for this ambivalence. First, NATO remains indispensable as the only efficient defence alliance as well as the central cornerstone of transatlantic cooperation.[57] Second, Germany's closest partner, France, remains reluctant to alter its position regarding the Alliance.[58] Some therefore consider that the Franco-German proposals for closer European defence cooperation 'stem primarily from French initiatives, and that Germany's support is in fact rather ambiguous and based on a desire to maintain positive relations with France'.[59] To deal with this dilemma, Germany has chosen a two-track strategy. It supports France's position on closer defence cooperation among Europeans.[60] At the same time, Germany hopes that the multilateralization of France's defence policy will bring it closer to the Alliance.

---

[54] Presse- und Informationsamt (1990*c*: 1405).
[55] Presse- und Informationsamt (1990*b*: 336).   [56] Nötzold (1993: 37).
[57] Presse- und Informationsamt (1990*a*: 310); Bundesministerium der Verteidigung (1994: 42).
[58] Hoffmann (1993: 139).   [59] Yost (1991: 334).
[60] For example, Federal Minister for Defence Rühe supported France in its struggle with the US over the NATO command of CINCSOUTH.

Great Britain

The end of the cold war was greeted happily in Great Britain, now 'more remote from military threat than at any time in its history'.[61] British Defence Secretary Malcolm Rifkind—faithful to the British culture of moderation—said in March 1993: 'It is undeniable that the direct threat posed to the United Kingdom and its allies is lower than it has been for many years.'[62] Under these conditions, Britain sees no need to reinforce its defence co-operation. On the contrary, one of its top priorities is to retain a maximum of independence in its foreign policy.[63] Traditionally, Britain resents supranational forms of cooperation as they exist within the EU and are represented by the EC Commission.[64] This scepticism is behind Britain's reluctance to provide the EU with a competence in the military field. Britain worries that the supranational rules and procedures that characterize co-operation within the EU could spread and undermine the authority of the nation-state in security matters. Britain therefore has sought to slow the momentum of European integration. A key element in its strategy was to support further EU enlargement.[65] In a Union that includes Austria, Finland, and Sweden, which have a long tradition of neutrality, it would become more difficult to deepen cooperation in defence.

Britain, like France, regarded the prospect of German unification with unease. It seemed to threaten one of the traditional aims of British foreign policy: to keep any one power from dominating Europe. Furthermore, Britain feared that the US could turn from Britain to Germany as its closest European ally, a fear that seemed to be confirmed by Bush's strong endorsement of Kohl's unification policy and his offer in 1989 of a 'partnership in leadership'.[66] Finally, worries about Germany's reliability as an alliance partner caused serious headaches among the political class in London.[67]

A third priority of British foreign policy is to maintain its impact on world affairs. Britain defines its interests and responsibilities in the security field as spanning the globe. However, the changes on the European continent seemed likely to erode further Britain's influence in both the European and the global arenas. Increasingly, Britain's global ambitions overextend its national capabilities. Britain's slowness to expand its net of diplomatic missions to the states resulting from the break-up of the Soviet Union is a case in point.[68] The changed international environment also confronted

---

[61] Wallace (1992: 434); see also Clarke (1995: 48).

[62] Malcolm Rifkind, 'Defense in the 90's', speech in London, 30 Mar. 1993, quoted by Garnham (1994: 126).

[63] Hill (1996: 70).   [64] Richardson (1993: 165).   [65] Ibid. 158.

[66] Ibid. 130.   [67] Edwards and Sanders (1994: 431).   [68] Hill (1996: 88).

Britain with the necessity of engaging in a costly modernization of its armed forces if it was to contribute significantly to the maintenance of international peace and stability, even while domestic calls for a peace dividend further increased the budgetary constraints on military reform.[69]

There are signs that Britain's international influence is decaying. The role of driving force behind the development of EPC, held by Britain in the early 1970s, has been taken over since the mid-1980s by France and Germany. Meantime, Britain's insistence on its independence has largely isolated it within the Community;[70] and its privileged relationship with the US is diminishing, since the latter looks increasingly to Germany and France as its key European interlocutors.[71] The traditional triangle of foreign-policy priorities—balance of power, international influence, and national independence—became increasingly contradictory with the end of the cold war.[72] Neither the balance of power on the continent nor Britain's international influence could be maintained on the basis of an independent policy. Britain simply lacked the required resources.

Britain saw NATO as the prime instrument for pursuing its fundamental security goals. For one thing, Britain saw Germany's continued commitment to NATO as a *conditio sine qua non* for reunification and as the appropriate instrument for containing Germany's power. For another, NATO was the forum through which Britain hoped to maintain its international influence in security affairs and its privileged relationship with the US. To convince its allies that NATO still had a purpose, Britain strongly promoted NATO reform. NATO's functions should be expanded to areas other than defence; the political dimension of cooperation within NATO should be enhanced;[73] its activities should expand beyond Europe.[74] However, there have been signs that Britain is opening up to the idea of a more independent stance by Europeans in security affairs. The crisis in Yugoslavia has shown that, as in the past, European security will remain fragile, the vanished Soviet threat notwithstanding.[75] In the new strategic environment, crisis management operations falling short of territorial defence will gain in importance and will require new instruments.[76] At the same time, even the British begin to have their doubts that the US will always be at Europe's side when it comes to maintaining security on the continent. The unilateral decision of the Clinton administration in November 1994 not to contribute any longer to the enforcement of the UN arms embargo on Bosnia cast

[69] Richardson (1993: 153).

[70] Hill (1996: 79).

[71] *The Economist* (26 Feb. 1994), 17–18.

[72] Hill (1996).

[73] Richardson (1993: 159).

[74] Bailes (1995: 86–9).

[75] Rifkind (1993: 20).

[76] FCO (1996: 20); Goulden (1996: 21).

doubts on the reliability of the US as Europe's ally.[77] Commentators in Britain, which contributed ground forces to UNPROFOR, interpreted this incident as 'the beginning of a rift that fatally weakened [the] alliance'.[78] The British government began to acknowledge that 'it would be unreasonable to expect the United States and Canada to participate in every such mission in future'.[79] There 'may be circumstances where European nations will need to be ready and able to take the lead, or to act on their own',[80] Britain therefore supported stronger European cooperation in out-of-area intervention. In the view of the British government, the WEU provides the best framework for the development of this cooperation.[81]

Having analysed the security functions that Britain, France, and Germany assign to ESDI, what conclusions can we draw about their likely input to the negotiations? In sum, France, Germany, and Great Britain only agree on one function of ESDI: out-of-area intervention. Cooperation in out-of-area intervention requires a solution to suasion problems, which contain a high potential for diverging interests. Cooperation requires highly differentiated decision-making procedures that enable joint action while taking account of member states' acute concerns about entrapment. Institutions for out-of-area intervention should also contain some pooling of military resources indispensable for rapid reaction to international crises; however, military cooperation will fall short of integration, since the latter leads to functional interdependence, which is antithetical to the need for high flexibility in coalition-building.

France and Germany both assign to ESDI the functions of security management and collective defence. Britain believes that these functions are best fulfilled by NATO. Security management raises assurance problems, which can be solved through mechanisms that provide for the signalling of intentions. Integration is one possible mechanism for exchanging information when none of the cooperation partners sees benefits from defecting, i.e. returning to unilateral policies. Assurance games, however, do not justify highly centralized or supranational mechanisms at the decision-making or implementation stage. The negotiations over stronger European cooperation in out-of-area intervention will suffice to signal benevolent intentions and reduce fears of defection. This difference over ESDI's functions between France and Germany on one side and Britain on the other should not, therefore, lead to substantial conflicts over ESDI's institutional form.

[77] Assembly of Western European Union (1995).
[78] *The Economist* (19 Nov. 1994), 18.
[79] FCO (1996: 21 and 34).
[80] Ibid. 34.
[81] Ibid. 21 and 34.

Cooperation in collective defence raises collaboration problems that require a relatively high degree of integration to reduce members' fear of abandonment. We should therefore expect France and Germany to advocate additional institutional mechanisms that promote integration. Moreover, France's and Germany's interest in strengthening European defence cooperation should moderate their enthusiasm for enlarging the union, since an increase in the number of member states will raise the transaction costs of decision-making. Because creating new institutional mechanisms is costly, Britain may be expected to oppose institutional mechanisms other than those required for cooperation in out-of-area intervention.

The next section analyses the negotiations over the institutional form of ESDI. This will provide evidence for or against the hypothesis that there is a link between a state's view of the purpose of cooperation and its view of the institutional form required.

4. Negotiating the Institutional Form of ESDI

Disagreement on collective defence

Dissent over the issue of collective defence led to substantive disagreements between France (supported by Germany) and Britain. According to the French and the Germans, the WEU should be developed step by step into the defence component of the EU. Ultimately this should be achieved by integrating the WEU and the defence commitment of article 5 of the Brussels Treaty into the EU. A clear organic relationship between the political union and the WEU should be established, as well as clear targets for further steps towards WEU's integration into the EU. By 'organic relationship', they understand the formal subordination of the WEU to the EU. The Union should have a *Leitlinienkompetenz* (authority to set guidelines) *vis-à-vis* the WEU. The WEU would elaborate and execute the decisions of the Union in the sphere of security and defense in conformity with the guidelines set by the latter.[82]

In their attempt to integrate the WEU into the union, however, France and Germany had to take into account that some of the latter's member states did not belong to the former. The case is particularly acute with regard to those EU member states that have a long-standing tradition of neutrality, such as Ireland, Austria, Sweden, and Finland. This has not

---

[82] See Weidenfeld (1994: 130).

sidetracked France's and Germany's plans for collective defence cooperation within the EU. The problem, they hope, can be solved if the neutral
states eventually become members of the WEU. In the short term, 'the
relations between the WEU and those states of the Community, which are
not at the same time members of the WEU, should gradually be reinforced
with view to their future membership'.[83] In view of the likely northern
enlargement of the EU, France and Germany offered observer status at the
WEU to members of the Union that are not part of NATO.[84]

What would be the benefit of integrating the WEU into the EU? Integration would not entail any new commitment to collective defence. The
commitment of article 5 of the Brussels Treaty would merely be integrated
into the Treaty of the European Union. What would be new is that the EU
would provide a distinctly different framework for collective defence
cooperation than the WEU does. The EU, not the WEU, is perceived as the
organization that binds together the nations of Western Europe, and therefore seems better suited to accommodate the fears of abandonment that are
typical of collective defence cooperation. Military integration through
multinational units and cross-stationing agreements (deployments of military formations on a reciprocal basis on allied territory) is another means
of dealing with the problem of abandonment within alliances. France and
Germany have engaged in close military cooperation, in particular through
the creation of the EUROCORPS. In March 1996, Alain Juppé, then French
Prime Minister, called for a European army numbering 350,000, independent of US control and answering to the European Union.[85] It has been noted
that military cooperation through the EUROCORPS falls short of integration, since each country retains full control over its troops.[86] Since de Gaulle
decided in 1966 to withdraw France from the alliance's integrated military
structure, French presidents have resisted any kind of military integration.
In order to build a European defence facility, France would have to compromise the autonomy and independence 'that they have made the bedrock
of their national defense consensus'.[87] This might explain why 'the core
concept has remained a vague notion of a defense dimension in the treaty
for EC political union, with (particularly since December 1990) the aim of
making the WEU the instrument of the European Council'.[88] Defence
cooperation remains a long-term policy goal. As Yost notes: 'Mitterrand's
public comments, before and after the critical changes of late 1989, have

---

83 Ibid. 122.
85 Cornish (1996: 756).
87 Yost (1991: 346).

84 Finland, Austria, and Sweden joined the EU in 1995.
86 Sauder (1995: 292–8); also *Le Monde* (21 May 1992).
88 Ibid. 334.

almost always been oriented towards the long term and have acknowledged the realities of NATO today and for the foreseeable future. Indeed, he has sometimes stated that a common defense cannot be attained without prior achievement of EC political union.'[89] The main dilemma of French security policy is to choose between European defence cooperation and autonomy in defence issues. Against this background, the steps France takes towards closer multilateral military cooperation have to be judged in a different light. For the first time since 1966, France participates in a standing multinational force. This is a significant shift.

Britain strongly objects to the integration of the WEU into the union. This would instantly provide the EU with a competence in defence matters. The British government 'believes that defense of the territory of NATO Member States should remain a matter for NATO [...] NATO is the bedrock of our common defense against threats to our territorial integrity and that of our Allies.'[90] Britain suspects that integrating the WEU into the EU will erode the intergovernmental procedures that currently apply to cooperation in defence issues. This is why Britain successfully opposed the French and German proposal to apply majority rule to issues with defence implications. The 'separate, intergovernmental treaty base [of WEU] ensures that decisions on defense policy are taken by consensus and remain where they belong—with sovereign nation states'.[91] Only if WEU is maintained as an autonomous organization will it be possible to assure that the Commission, the European Parliament or the European Court of Justice have any role in defence decision-making. Britain categorically refuses the idea of a *Leitlinienkompetenz* for the union over the WEU, arguing that WEU should merely take into account the decisions made by the European Council.

Consensus on out-of-area intervention

In contrast, the creation of an institutional framework for out-of-area intervention was favoured by all three governments under consideration. Negotiations over the institutional form of ESDI therefore concentrated very much on this issue.

Full integration of security affairs into the EC/EU: France and Germany favoured the development of ESDI within the EC/EU. The EPC only provided for cooperation in the political and economical dimensions of security. Military aspects were deliberately left out.[92] Furthermore, meetings

---

[89] Yost (1991: 344).   [90] FCO (1996: 34).
[91] Ibid. 21.   [92] Single European Act, art. 30(6)(*a*).

of foreign ministers were held in a separate forum. France and Germany argued that in the future cooperation should cover all aspects of security, including those having military implications, and that policy coordination in external affairs should take place within the same forum as in the other policy areas, that is, within the Council of Ministers.[93]

At first, Britain was very reluctant to upgrade the EC's role in defence and security affairs.[94] During the negotiations leading to the Maastricht Treaty, Britain's proposals on the improvement of EPC were very limited in scope and assumed that any improvement would take place only gradually. The formal separation between EPC and EC should be maintained. An extension of the competencies of EPC to areas other than the political and economical dimensions of security was not considered. Decisions should continue to be made unanimously. To improve procedures, Britain suggested that a committee of representatives be created in the framework of the Political Committee. *In extremis*, however, Britain agreed to the Maastricht Treaty, which replaced EPC with CFSP. According to the new provisions, ministerial meetings for EPC affairs have been abolished; decisions are made within the Council of Ministers. CFSP covers 'all questions related to the security of the union, including the eventual framing of a common defense policy, which might in time lead to a common defense'.[95]

Decision-making procedures: Since the signing of the Maastricht Treaty, Britain has been actively engaged in the discussions on the improvement of CFSP. Britain, France, and Germany agree that the efficiency of CFSP can be improved. They also agree that decision-making power and operational control should remain in the hands of national governments. How to increase the efficiency of CFSP remains a controversial issue. France and Germany believe that the rule of unanimity has to be relaxed. Decisions on the fundamental orientations and principles of CFSP by the European Council, composed of presidents and heads of state, should continue to

---

[93] In its description of the French and the German position concerning the development of ESDI, this section relies on numerous proposals of both countries. The four joint proposals (from Apr. 1990 to Oct. 1991) issued during the run-up to the signing of the Maastricht Treaty can be found in Weidenfeld (1994). For the joint Franco-German proposal to the Intergovernmental Conference see Kohl and Chirac (1995); Presse- und Informationsamt (1996); Kinkel and de Charette (1996).

[94] My description of the British position concerning the development of ESDI draws mostly on FCO (1996) as well as on the joint British-Italian declaration of 4 Oct. 1991, printed Weidenfeld (1994: 125–7).

[95] Treaty on the European Union, art. J4.1. The revised treaty contains a similar provision in art. 17.1.

require unanimity, but the European Council should be able to specify that implementation decisions can be taken by a majority. Within the Council of Ministers (General Affairs), composed of the foreign ministers, decisions should generally be taken unanimously. Abstentions, however, should not block a decision. Only decisions on the principles and orientations of CFSP should continue to require unanimity.[96]

In the second round of negotiations, France and Germany continued to request further steps away from unanimity. Enlargement and the demand for unanimity were perceived as incompatible. In a union with fifteen or more member states, Kohl and Chirac argued, the principle of unanimity would lead to stasis. They proposed that majority voting should become the rule for implementation decisions by the Council of Ministers and that this practice should also be extended to security and defence matters. This would ensure that Europe did not lose its ability to act when not all partners were participating militarily in an undertaking. In the European Council, the consensus rule should be applied, though in a relaxed form. As an alternative to majority voting, they suggested 'constructive abstention', which would not preclude decision-making in cases where unanimity continues to be required.[97] They also suggested introducing a 'solidarity clause' into the TEU with two components: first, that a minority should not block a majority from acting jointly; and second, that the majority should respect the legitimate interests of individual member states.

Britain argues that 'decision-making has not been a major problem'. In Britain's view, enough flexibility is provided by the Maastricht Treaty, in which member states have already agreed 'that they should try not to stand in the way of a given policy which has majority support'. Britain is not ready to 'accept a commitment to be constrained by collective decisions which we do not support'.[98] France and Germany agree that the deployment of armed forces should not be automatic. Britain argues for flexibility when the use of armed force is required

because the missions they [i.e. the armed forces of European countries] undertake will not be concerned in the main with territorial defense, the coalitions of those involved will vary from mission to mission. Individual nations will decide on a case-by-case basis whether they wish to contribute forces to particular operations [. . .] Future structures must be able to accommodate this 'variable geometry.'

[96] A similar procedure was finally introduced into the treaty. See Treaty on the European Union, art. J3.2.

[97] See Treaty on the European Union (consolidated), art. 23, which further relaxes the principle of strict unanimity.

[98] FCO (1996: 17–20).

Designing arrangements that can do so will strengthen rather than weaken the flexibility with which we will be able to respond to the challenges we face.[99]

France and Germany stress that a majority decision should not oblige any member state against its will to provide national forces for military or policing tasks. The dispatch of troops would continue to require the approval of the dispatching state.

Britain does not agree with France and Germany about whether states that engage in collective action not supported by all member states should be able to draw on common assets. According to the French and German view, member states which are overruled by a majority decision ought to support the decision politically and financially. The operational expenses of CFSP actions should be financed through the Community budget. Objecting to these arguments, Foreign Secretary Rifkind said: 'Policies using Community institutions and the EC budget should only be undertaken by less than the full membership when this is agreed by all. Policies agreed by some against the objections of others should not carry the imprimatur of the European Union, or use EC institutions or resources.'[100] This formulation has to be read carefully: it does not exclude the use of common assets if a policy was decided by a majority with other member states abstaining. This suggests that Britain might be willing to accept the idea of positive abstention, as proposed by France and Germany.

Enhancement of convergence of interests through joint planning and analysis: Instead of extending majority voting procedures, Britain believes that the effectiveness of CFSP can best be improved through the practice of common analysis and common policy. The decision-making process can be improved through an increase in the frequency of meetings of the Political Committee, which prepares ministerial decisions. Another improvement would be to strengthen the role of the Council Secretariat, in particular its 'CFSP Unit', formerly the EPC Secretariat. This could be done through the creation of a 'Planning Unit' inside the Council Secretariat. Thus strengthened, the Council Secretariat could produce analyses and options papers for the Political Committee or the Council. This is equivalent to the French-German proposal to create a unit for planning and analysis. Britain also supports the French proposal to create the post of President of the European Council,[101] which would give a face and a voice to CFSP,

[99] Ibid. 36.
[100] Speech by the Foreign Secretary, Malcolm Rifkind, House of Commons, 21 Mar. 1996, IGC White Paper Debate, *Verbatim*, 10 (21 Mar. 1996).
[101] Lellouche (1996: 242). See also FCO (1996: 19).

enhancing its visibility and continuity. The President's main function would be to represent the union externally. He would be elected by the European Council for a period of three years and could rely on the CFSP general secretariat. Britain also suggested the creation of

a new WEU body at Head of State and Government level involving Full Members, Associate Members and Observers. This new body would provide a reinforced decision making process for matters relating to European defense. [...] The essential intergovernmental nature of decision making on defense would be preserved. [...] In order to improve links between the WEU and the European Union, it could meet back-to-back with Heads of State and Government meeting in the European Council.[102]

Implementation level: There has been a strong consensus on the operational strengthening of WEU. Britain, France, and Germany agree that EU decisions with military implications should be implemented by the WEU. Britain suggested moving the ministerial organs of WEU from London to Brussels in order to provide for better coordination of the activities of WEU, NATO, and the EU. From the British perspective, 'the immediate and practical requirement is to strengthen the WEU's planning capabilities; to improve its provision for offering politico-military advice to Ministers in crisis; and to develop its practical arrangements, such as a Situation Center and improved intelligence-handling capabilities'.[103] Similar proposals for the operational strengthening of the WEU have been made by France and Germany. They include the creation of a military planning and coordination staff inside WEU, cooperation in armament with the aim of setting up a European armament agency, and regular meetings by the chiefs of general staff.

All three countries also agree that the WEU must be able to draw on military forces, but while Chirac at first favoured creating rapid reaction forces on the model of EUROCORPS, EUROFOR, and EUROMARFOR, the British insisted that new WEU capabilities would have to be compatible with, not in competition with, those of NATO. In order to equip the WEU for its new missions, WEU should use NATO assets and facilities as provided for by the Combined Joint Task Force (CJTF) concept, agreed to by Alliance Heads of Government in January 1994, which 'provides a vehicle through which NATO can make available separable but not separate elements of NATO's command structure for European-led missions'.[104]

---

[102] FCO (1996: 36).   [103] Ibid. 37.   [104] Ibid.

5. *Conclusion*

A review of British, French, and German positions and proposals on reinforced security cooperation among EU countries supports the hypothesis that their respective preferences concerning institutional form are determined by their views on which cooperative functions should be assigned to ESDI.

In its current design, ESDI falls short of an institution for collective defence. Among Britain, France, and Germany there is fundamental disagreement over whether they should engage in developing collective defence cooperation separate from NATO. This disagreement over its functions is at the root of disagreements about more integrated structures for ESDI, which would be required to accommodate states' fears of abandonment. As long as these states disagree on European collective defence, ESDI will not contain highly integrated structures. The 'D' in ESDI should not, therefore, be taken at face value.

In contrast, France, Germany, and Britain agree on out-of-area intervention and this agreement is reflected in their preferences regarding institutional design. Decision-making procedures in this area are highly specific, respecting member states' concerns about entrapment. All three countries agree that whether a country supplies troops in an operation is to be decided by the dispatching state exclusively, so the coalitions involved in specific missions will vary from case to case. The CJTF concept accommodates the requirement of flexible coalition-building. These countries also agree on the need to enhance the capacity of the EU and the WEU for joint planning and analysis, aiming at a greater convergence of member states' interests.

The concept of cooperation problems helps explain the obstacles to different types of security cooperation and the institutional mechanisms chosen for solving them. The same concept also points to the constraints states face when seeking cooperation with others. This sheds new light on the debate about European states' security cooperation. The problematic efficacy of European security cooperation is partly due to the numbers, of course: the security policy of a single entity will be more effective than that of a decentralized system of cooperating states. But this chapter has demonstrated that another important aspect of European cooperation in developing an ESDI is explained by the complicated relationship between cooperation problems and institutional form and function. As long as out-of-area intervention is pursued not by a single entity but cooperatively, by a number of sovereign states, a high potential for diverging interests must be taken into account when designing the required institutional mechanism.

II

Effects of Security Institutions

4

ALLIANCES AS INSTRUMENTS OF INTRA ALLIED CONTROL

Christopher Gelpi

Although realist theories of international relations have frequently denied that international institutions have any independent influence on state behaviour, one set of security institutions that realist scholars have paid attention to is alliances.[1] The theoretical core of this literature asserts that alliances form as a response to external threats or imbalances of power.[2] That is, alliances are believed to influence the behaviour of states *outside* the alliance. This framework for understanding the causes and effects of alliances has become known as the 'capability aggregation model'. Institutionalist theories, on the other hand, have tended to focus on the influence of institutions on the behaviour of the members themselves.[3] As a result, institutionalists have often overlooked the most significant institutions which address security issues: alliances. To some extent this volume represents an effort to redress this imbalance. Consistent with the arguments presented by Wallander and Keohane, in this work I hope to integrate institutionalist and realist perspectives on alliances. I do so by examining the functions that alliances can perform between alliance partners while continuing to acknowledge the important role that alliances play as tools of power and coercion. Specifically, I develop and test an argument which suggests that alliances can be used as instruments of intra-allied control. That is, in the terminology of Wallander and Keohane, I develop and test the proposition that 'alliances' can function additionally as security management institutions.

Empirically, I investigate this claim by examining two sets of relationships. First, I examine the influence that alliance commitments have had on

---

[1] For a critique of the impact of international institutions see Mearsheimer (1994/5). For a realist analysis of alliances see Walt (1987).

[2] Walt (1987); Waltz (1979).

[3] Keohane (1984); Krasner (1983).

the success of 117 mediation attempts in international crises between 1918 and 1988.[4] Briefly, my findings indicate that realist and institutionalist arguments about the influence of alliances complement one another as causes of successful mediation. Second, I examine the impact that alliance ties to the mediator have on the probability that the challenger will prevail in those same 117 international crises. This analysis reveals direct evidence that alliance ties can be used to restrain alliance partners in international crises. Realists are right to emphasize the role of power and military capabilities in making credible alliance commitments effective in altering state behaviour. Moreover, realists are right to argue that alliances can be used as tools of capability aggregation and deterrence. But my results indicate that alliances can also perform additional functions not addressed by their theoretical approach—those of security management. Finally, my research undermines several assertions that have become conventional wisdom in the literature on international mediation. Specifically, my findings call into question the belief that the most effective mediators are weak neutral parties that refrain from engaging in coercive tactics.

This paper proceeds in six parts. First, I review some of the existing literature on military alliances and discuss some relevant works on international mediation. Second, I outline the contributions that I hope my research will make to these literatures and my reasons for focusing on cases of mediation for measuring intra-allied control. Next, I present two complementary institutionalist arguments about the sources of intra-alliance control. Both of these arguments emerge from the literature on signalling and international commitments. Fourth, I derive several hypotheses about determinants of successful mediation and the winners and losers of these mediated disputes. These hypotheses will be drawn from the institutionalist arguments mentioned above as well as from a realist perspective on alliances and a more traditional view of mediation. It is important to note that I do not view the realist and institutionalist hypotheses as competitors, but rather as complementary explanations of mediation success. In addition, I will also discuss several control variables which will be included in my analysis. Fifth, I discuss the data and measurements which I use to test these hypotheses. Finally, I present the results of my statistical analyses and discuss their implications for the realist and institutionalist literatures on alliances.

---

[4] I define mediation rather broadly as any attempts by third parties to produce a negotiated settlement. Such efforts could involve anything from offering 'good offices' through official attempts at mediation or arbitration to direct forcible intervention.

1. *Alliances and the Capability Aggregation Model*

The debate between realism and institutionalism began over issues of political economy. Consequently, some progress has been made toward integrating realist and institutionalist perspectives in this area.[5] In the area of security affairs, however, realist scholars have yet to begin such an integration. The realist literature on alliances has almost exclusively viewed these institutions through the lens of what has come to be known as the 'capability aggregation' model.[6] That is, realist analyses have begun from the presumption that the sole purpose of forming an alliance is so that the alliance partners can pool their military capabilities against some external foe. Within this framework, scholars have attempted to use alliance formation to predict the initiation, escalation, and outcome of wars. A number of recent works, for example, have used game-theoretic models to analyse the deterrent capacity of military alliances.[7] The assumption underlying these models is that allies will contribute to the defence of their partner in case of war, and thus threaten to impose costs on their partner's opponent. Other recent works have used similar game-theoretic models to describe intervention in ongoing wars and to predict war outcomes.[8] Once again, the assumption driving these analyses is that allies pool their resources in order to defeat an enemy outside the alliance. Finally, numerous empirical studies have relied on the 'capability aggregation' model to build measures of the military capabilities available to a state in the event of a conflict.[9]

However, an emerging body of literature suggests that alliances may perform a variety of functions that range well beyond the scope of the capability aggregation model. Most of these arguments concern the effect of alliances on the relationship *between* allies rather than as a deterrent against aggression by some third party. In his analysis of nineteenth-century European diplomatic history, for example, Paul Schroeder has argued that alliances were often used as a tool for controlling one's *alliance partner*.[10] In particular, he suggests that Bismarck was extremely competent at heading off threats to German interests by strategically aligning with and then constraining the sources of threat. Similarly, James Morrow has argued that alliances may involve an exchange of resources between allies rather than an

---

[5] For an example of realist literature that attempts to integrate institutionalist perspectives see Grieco (1996).   [6] Morrow (1991).

[7] A. Smith (1996*a*); Papayouanou (1995).

[8] A. Smith (1996*b*); Gartner and Siverson (1996); Bennett and Stam (1996).

[9] Huth *et al.* (1993); Bueno de Mesquita (1981).

[10] Schroeder (1994*b*, 1977).

effort at pooling capabilities.[11] In particular, he suggests that weaker states may trade foreign policy autonomy for the security that can be provided by a powerful ally. As the price for such protection, these smaller states allow their patrons to control some aspects of their foreign or domestic policies to meet their patron's interests.[12] While the style of Morrow's analysis differs radically from Schroeder's, they share a common expectation that powerful states will use alliances to shape the behaviour of their allies.

Finally, explicitly institutionalist scholars have also begun to incorporate alliances into their theoretical and empirical analyses. For example, in Chapter 1 Celeste Wallander and Robert Keohane have offered an institutionalist view of NATO's persistence in the absence of an external threat. The authors develop a general framework for their analysis in which alliances can vary across at least two important dimensions: the level of institutionalization of the alliance commitment, and the extent to which the sources of threat are incorporated into the alliance. Thus an institutionalist approach to alliances explicitly draws attention to the intra-alliance functions of these institutions. In doing so, this approach unifies the study of alliances and collective security organizations through a single typology of security institutions. As with the work of Schroeder and Morrow, this has led to the expectation that alliances can serve as instruments of *intra*-alliance influence and control in *addition* to their role as instruments of deterrence.

2. Alliances and Mediation

The aim of this work will be to investigate the hypothesis that allies can use their alliance to constrain one another's behaviour. While such an analysis might appear simple on its face, some significant research-design issues complicate this process. In general, arguments about the influence of international institutions suffer from potentially severe problems of spuriousness. Any states which share membership in an international institution will also share a number of common interests which drew them into membership. Thus, when we observe state behaviour that appears to reflect the causal influence of institutional constraints it is often not clear whether we should attribute such behaviour to the effect of the institution or to the

---

[11] Morrow (1991).

[12] The precise terminology that Morrow uses is an exchange of 'autonomy' for 'security'. In attempting to formalize his analysis, Morrow operationalizes 'autonomy' in a somewhat different manner than I discuss here. My discussion is consistent with his informal use of the term 'autonomy'.

prior common interests.[13] For example, the observation that allies are less likely to become involved in militarized disputes with one another would not demonstrate that alliances constrain conflict between allies, since the lack of conflict could be attributed to the common interests which inspired the formation of the alliance. One way of avoiding this spuriousness problem is to analyse the influence of international institutions on situations in which the members' interests conflict.[14] Thus if we wish to know whether alliances constrain behaviour between allies, then we should look to interactions between allied states in situations where their interests are not congruent. One such set of circumstances is the situation in which the mediator in an international crisis is allied to one of the disputants. In such cases the two allies have at least partially conflicting interests because a mediator in an international crisis generally views its central task as finding a peaceful settlement to the crisis that is acceptable to both parties. If the disputant's ally shared and supported the disputant's interests entirely, it would have intervened in direct support of the disputant rather than as a mediator. It is possible, of course, that an ally could feign impartiality in an effort to deceive the third party into accepting a settlement. Third-party disputants should be aware of this possibility, however, and so they will only accept the mediation efforts of states when they believe they share some interests. Thus the fact that the mediation efforts of an allied state are acceptable to *both* disputants suggests that an allied mediator has a mixture of congruent and conflicting interests with both parties. For this reason, I plan to investigate whether mediators which are allied to one of the disputants in a crisis are more effective in persuading the parties to settle.

3. Hypotheses on Mediation Success

Although the central focus of this work is on the role of alliances in mediation, a substantial literature exists on international mediation in its own right. In fact, my work challenges a number of assertions which have become conventional wisdom concerning the mediation of international crises. Thus in evaluating my arguments about the influence of alliances I will begin by outlining some of the central hypotheses which emerge from the literature on international mediation. These hypotheses will serve as a basis of comparison for the hypotheses drawn from the realist and institutionalist frameworks. Much of the literature on international mediation

---

[13] Mearsheimer (1994/5).   [14] Gelpi (1997).

and dispute resolution emerges from two complementary theoretical perspectives. The first perspective views mediation as a legal process which can bring justice and order to international disputes. According to this view, conflicts are a result of breakdowns in the legal order and peace can best be restored by extending the legal process of dispute resolution to international conflicts. A second perspective on international mediation suggests that international conflict is a result of misperceptions and an erosion of trust between the disputing parties. According to this view, mediation which can resolve conflicts by facilitating communication and trust between the parties will be the most effective. These approaches to conflict resolution hold a number of interpretations for the kinds of mediators who will be successful in resolving international conflicts.

First, the mediation literature suggests that neutral mediators will be the most successful.[15] Stulberg, for example, insists that mediators must be '(1) Neutral. A mediator must have not personal preference that the dispute be resolved one way or another. . . . (2) Impartial. A mediator must treat all parties in comparable ways, both procedurally and substantively. . . . (3) Objective. A mediator must be able to transcend the rhetoric and emotion of the parties.'[16] The legalistic approach to mediation approves of neutral mediators because of their ability to act as an impartial judge. In this way the mediator can steer the parties towards a settlement that is both legitimate and fair. The trust-oriented approach emphasizes the need for neutral mediators because of their ability to gain the trust of the disputants by acting as an unbiased source of information. States that are allied to one of the disputants, however, are unlikely to be viewed as neutral or impartial by either party. Thus the mediation literature suggests that allies will be ineffective mediators.

HYPOTHESIS 1: The more unequal the mediator's alliance ties to the disputants, the lower the probability that mediation will be successful.

A second common assertion in the mediation literature is that weak states (or even weaker non-state actors) will be the most effective mediators.[17] Bercovitch and Houston, for example, find that 'both the leaders and representatives of large states fare rather worse than expected' as international mediators.[18] From a legal perspective, small states should be good mediators precisely because of their weakness. Perhaps the biggest threat to

---

[15] Young (1967); Northedge and Donelan (1971); Stulberg (1987); Brouillet (1988); Carnevale and Pruitt (1992).

[16] Stulberg (1987: 37).

[17] Young (1967); Ott (1972); Slim (1992); Bercovitch and Houston (1996).

[18] Bercovitch and Houston (1996: 27).

peaceful conflict resolution, according to this view, is the illegal and illegitimate use of force. Small state mediators cannot credibly threaten force to resolve a dispute and thus are more likely to act according to legal precedent. Similarly, the trust-oriented approach to mediation views coercion as counterproductive because it undermines trust and communication between the disputing parties and the mediator. Thus small states should be more effective in facilitating trust and communication because they do not threaten either party.

HYPOTHESIS 2: The greater the mediator's military capability, the *lower* the probability that mediation will be successful.

A third common assertion in the mediation literature is that coercive tactics by the mediator will reduce the probability of mediation success. Fisher, Schneider, Borgwardt and Ganson, for example, claim that 'a foreign policy that concentrates on raising costs to our adversary is likely to prove both ineffective with regard to our adversary and costly for us'.[19] Similarly, Brouillet writes that the mediator's mission 'should be an endeavour to achieve a *rapprochement*.[20] He [*sic*] should emphasize the points of agreement that gradually emerge during the reconciliation process.' Once again the legalistic view of mediation frowns upon coercive tactics because they are a violation of the legal process which can facilitate a just and peaceful settlement. The trust-oriented approach, on the other hand, emphasizes the loss of trust and increase in suspicion and misperception which results from coercive tactics. But while the mediation literature frowns on coercive tactics, these theorists do argue that so-called 'directive' strategies are more effective in mediating settlements than simple consultation and facilitation of communication.[21] Princen, for example, suggests that active involvement by the mediator in crisis diplomacy contributes to mediation success, but the use of coercive tactics by the mediator will be counterproductive and will lead to missed opportunities for peaceful settlements.[22] Dixon also finds that mediation, arbitration, and the facilitation of communication contribute to the peaceful settlement of disputes, while direct intervention by the mediator does not.[23] These works suggest the existence of a curvilinear relationship between the coerciveness of the mediator's strategy and mediation success. Moderate pressure to settle combined with a facilitation of open communication are likely to be effective mediation tools. Direct

[19] Fisher *et al.* (1997: 195).
[20] Brouillet (1988: 171).
[21] Bercovitch (1986); Fisher and Keashley (1991); Bercovitch and Houston (1996); Keashley and Fisher (1996).
[22] Princen (1991, 1992).
[23] Dixon (1997).

attempts by the mediator to coerce the disputants and impose a settlement, however, are not.

HYPOTHESIS 3: A curvilinear relationship exists between the coerciveness of the mediator's strategy and mediation success. Moderately coercive strategies will be successful. Neither extremely weak nor highly coercive strategies will be successful.

It is important to recognize that these three hypotheses do not reflect the entirety of the literature on international mediation. Carnevale and Arad, for example, suggest that biased mediators may also be able to exert influence.[24] Similarly, Touval and Zartman conclude that biased mediators may be effective because of their ability to generate leverage over the disputants.[25] None of these works, however, suggest that biased mediators will actually be *more* effective than neutrals. Touval and Princen also suggest that large states, such as the United States, may be effective mediators because of their ability to manipulate 'carrots and sticks' that persuade the disputants to settle.[26] Despite these exceptions, I believe that the hypotheses 1–3 reflect the expectations of the majority of the literature on international mediation. Moreover, they reflect the legalistic and trust-based frameworks that—explicitly or implicitly—underpin much of the work on mediation.

4. Alliances and an Institutionalist View of Mediation

An institutionalist approach to alliances and mediation begins with the observation that alliances represent costly signals of intent. An alliance represents a promise to intervene with military force on behalf of an alliance partner under specified conditions. Both the size of the promised military aid and the nature of the conditions may vary among alliances, but this promise or commitment of military aid remains the core substance of an alliance. Such military support is obviously valuable to states, since allied military aid can greatly increase a state's chances of winning a war.[27] But the very *promise* of such aid itself can be valuable because it can act as a persuasive signal with regard to at least two important issues. First, alliances— as indicated by the capability aggregation model—can persuade potential aggressors that each alliance partner will intervene on the other's behalf in the event of war.[28] This knowledge, in turn, can deter the initiation of wars

---

[24] Carnevale and Arad (1996).   [25] Touval (1975); Touval and Zartman (1985).
[26] Touval (1982); Princen (1992).   [27] Gartner and Siverson (1996); Choi (1997).
[28] A. Smith (1996a, 1996b); Papayouanou (1995).

in the first place. Alliances have these deterrent effects because they represent costly signals of intent.[29] States which join alliances suffer a number of costs, and the stronger the alliance commitment made by the parties, the more costly the commitment is to them. Some of the more prominent alliance costs include: (i) transaction costs in negotiating the agreement, (ii) reputational costs if they fail to honour their commitment, (iii) any costs from institutionalization of the alliance, (iv) costs of vulnerability because of specialization in defense functions, and (v) costs from altering other policies as a condition of the alliance agreement. The conclusion of stronger alliances is more costly because such commitments require investing one's reputation more strongly, greater institutionalization, specialization, and so on. The critical link which turns alliances into *persuasive* signals, however, is that such commitments are *more* costly for states which do not intend to honour them.[30] Clearly, states which intend to honour their alliance commitments do not risk reputational costs by joining an alliance, nor are the costs of specialization or institutionalization as high since such states will gain a benefit from these investments if they are ever called upon to honour their commitment. Thus the conclusion of an alliance should represent a persuasive signal—both to the allies and to third parties—that the allies are more likely to intervene on one another's behalf in the case of armed conflict.

A second important piece of information that alliances can convey—both to the alliance partners and to others—is that the members of the alliance share substantial common security interests. As I stated above, two of the costs involved in concluding an alliance are the transaction costs involved in reaching an agreement and the substantive policy constraints that an alliance places on state behaviour. States which share substantial common interests will need to make fewer concessions in order to reach an agreement. Moreover, such states are likely to face fewer transaction costs, given the modest conflicts of interest that must be bridged. As a result, the conclusion of an alliance should represent a persuasive signal that the allied states share common interests.[31]

Alliances as leverage for mediators

If alliances represent persuasive signals that states share common security interests and will defend one another with military force, how will such

---

[29] Fearon (1994*b*).

[30] For the logic of signalling and adverse selection games, see Rasmussen, 1989.

[31] Bueno de Mesquita (1981).

information affect the success of allied states as mediators of disputes with third parties? As I discussed earlier, the conventional wisdom concerning mediation suggests that allied states should be poor mediators. Given the information that is revealed by their alliance bond, allied mediators are unlikely to be viewed as neutral. Contrary to this conventional wisdom, however, I shall argue that an institutionalist perspective on alliances suggests that allied mediators should be more effective at helping the disputants reach an agreement because of their ability to coerce concessions out of both parties. First, as I discussed above, an alliance pledge is valuable to a disputant both because it can be helpful in case of a future war and because it can deter such a war from occurring. Given that the allied mediator has made such a valuable pledge to one of the disputants, it can use the threat of withdrawing this pledge as leverage for extracting concessions with regard to the dispute at hand. These threats of abandonment may be credible to the allied disputant, despite the costs that the mediator has invested in the alliance, because the mediator's interests *with regard to the issue in the dispute* differ from those of the disputant. If that conflict of interest outweighs any future benefit that the mediator might gain from the alliance, it would become willing to abandon the alliance.

Moreover, a disputant should be more likely to be willing to make any concessions when these requests come from a mediator which it trusts because they share an alliance tie. The greater the level of trust between the allies, the more diffuse their sense of reciprocity will become. Thus as the mediator and disputant become more closely allied, the disputant becomes more likely to grant current concessions on the issue at stake in the crisis in exchange for future benefits of allied support.

The mediator's ability to extract concessions from its allied disputant is common knowledge to the disputants, so one might expect that the third-party disputant would respond to this information by escalating its demands in order to gain a better settlement. Such an escalation might erase any effect that the allied mediator's leverage might have on the dispute. Two aspects of the mediator's alliance with the disputant make such escalatory behaviour by the third party unlikely. First, as I discussed above, the alliance bond between mediator and disputant demonstrate to the third party that the other two states share substantial security interests. Thus the third party will know that the mediator is unlikely to be willing to push its ally *too* far toward conceding. Second, if the third party does push the allied disputant too far, the mediator is likely to intervene militarily on behalf of its ally.[32]

---

[32] Smith (1996*b*).

The prospect of fighting a war against the allied disputant *and* the mediator will deter it from escalating its demands too extensively.

Thus strong alliance bonds between the mediator and one of the disputants should allow the mediator to hold coercive leverage over *both* the disputing parties. On the one hand it can use the promise of future military support to restrain its ally. On the other hand, it can use the threat of intervening to deter its ally's opponent. Perhaps the most prominent example of such a tactic operating in practice is Kissinger's deft mediation between Israel and Egypt following the October War of 1973. Precisely this combination of demands and assurances to both US allies in Israel and (then) adversaries in Egypt resulted in the resolution of one of the most virulent and long-standing disputes of the twentieth century.

HYPOTHESIS 4: The more unequal the mediator's alliance ties to the disputants, the higher the probability that mediation will be successful.

5. *A Realist View of Mediation*

While an institutionalist perspective on mediation suggests that biased allied mediators should be especially effective, a realist perspective suggests that militarily powerful states will be the most effective mediators. As with the institutionalist approach, a realist model would expect that the use of credible threats and promises will be the key to successful mediation. However, realism would predict that the credibility of those threats and promises will *not* depend on the institutionalization of those commitments in an alliance. After all, realism argues that institutionalized alliance ties are simply a reflection of common interests between states. By examining cases of allied mediation, however, I have selected cases in which the mediator and the disputants have disparate interests. A realist would not expect an alliance tie to continue to influence state behaviour in these circumstances. Instead, realism would expect the effectiveness of the mediator's threats and promises to depend on its military capability. Powerful states can make more effective threats and promises to the disputants both because their intervention would be less costly for them to undertake and because they have the capacity to determine the outcome of the crisis. Once again, this expectation runs directly contrary to the conventional wisdom in the mediation literature which argues that *small* states should be more effective mediators precisely because they are *not* threatening to anyone.

HYPOTHESIS 5: The greater the mediator's military capability, the higher the probability that mediation will be successful.

6. Integrating the Institutionalist and Realist Perspectives

It seems possible that institutionalized alliance ties and the military power of the mediator may interact to make *powerful allies* especially effective mediators. Both the institutionalist and realist perspectives on alliances and mediation emphasize the role of effective threats in successful mediation. The institutionalist approach focuses on institutional ties as a source of influence. The realist approach, on the other hand, emphasizes having the military capability to force the disputants to comply with the mediator's wishes. It seems possible, however, that mediators will be especially successful if they can use institutional ties as a mechanism for exercising their military capabilities. Absent the military capability to make their threats of intervention and abandonment intimidating to the disputants, mediators may find the institutional ties which make such threats credible have little impact on mediation success. At the same time, however, the mediator's military capability may have little impact on mediation success absent the ability to demonstrate that it is *willing* to intervene.

Thus *powerful allied mediators* may be particularly capable of persuading the disputants in an international crisis to settle. Third-party states are more likely to be deterred by the threat of a powerful mediator which is allied to its opponent for at least two reasons. First, the intervention of a powerful state is more likely to result in the defeat of the third party. Second, more powerful states are more likely to intervene because of the possibility that they will prevail and will suffer fewer battlefield costs in doing so. Similarly, allied disputants are more likely to be swayed by a powerful ally's threat to abandon the alliance. First, abandonment by a powerful ally is more costly to the allied disputant because of the greater protection that such an ally can provide. Second, the threat to abandon the alliance is more credible when it comes from a powerful ally because the alliance contributes less to its security. This logic suggests an interaction between strength of alliance bond and relative strength of the allied mediator in determining the success of mediation.

HYPOTHESIS 6: The inequality of the alliance bonds between mediator and disputants interacts with the military strength of the mediator. The stronger the mediator, the stronger the effect of the alliance bias on the success of mediation.

7. *Institutionalist/Realist View of Coercion and Mediation Success*

Drawing on the mediation literature, hypothesis 3 predicted a curvilinear relationship between coercive actions by the mediator and mediation success. In general, this literature argues that mediation is unlikely to succeed if the mediator makes no effort to alter the demands of the disputants. At the same time, however, this literature claims that the use of explicitly coercive tactics will undermine successful mediation by exacerbating the conflict, undermining trust among the parties, and violating norms of legitimate international practice. On the other hand, my synthesis of realist and institutionalist perspectives on mediation suggest that coercive tactics *will* be effective in mediating disputes. My argument suggests that mediators will be successful when they have the capacity to make credible threats against both their own ally and the third-party disputant. The interaction of military capabilities and alliance bias is one source of such credibility. The use of coercive mediation tactics is another way in which the mediator can credibly demonstrate that it is willing and able to enforce a compromise solution to the crisis.

HYPOTHESIS 7: The more coercive the mediator's strategy the higher the probability that mediation will be successful.

8. *Control Variables*

In addition to addressing the influence of alliance ties, military power, and coercion on the success of mediation, I will include a number of control variables in my analysis. These variables emerge from the literature on crisis bargaining and mediation. I have given particular attention to addressing the most plausible and prominent alternative explanations of successful mediation.

Disputants share an alliance tie

In addition to making mediators more successful, shared alliance ties between the disputants themselves should also make them more likely to settle. One of the principal obstacles to the peaceful settlement of international crises is the frequent inability of the participants to make credible commitments to abide by the negotiated solution.[33] The mechanism of an

---

[33] Fearon (1995).

institutionalized alliance tie between the disputants, however, gives them the ability to make credible commitments to abandon the alliance if the settlement is not upheld. Much like the alliance ties between the mediator and the disputants, I expect that this ability to threaten punishment credibly will help to resolve such commitment problems. Thus I expect that states which share an alliance will be more likely to resolve their dispute through a formal or informal settlement.

Relative military strength of disputants

In general, the mediation literature suggests that such efforts are more likely to be successful when the disputants are relatively equal to one another in terms of military strength.[34] Severe imbalances will lead one of the disputants to prefer to impose its will—by force if necessary—rather than accept the compromises that are involved in accepting a mediated settlement.

Level of violence used by the disputants

As the level of violence in the crisis escalates, both parties suffer increasing costs. These costs make it more difficult to offer concessions in order to reach a settlement because the disputants must justify the costs of international conflict to their domestic constituents by prevailing on the issue at stake in the crisis.[35] Thus domestic audiences may force both states to make unacceptable demands of their opponent, making it impossible to resolve the matter through negotiation.[36]

9. Further Implications

My argument concerning alliances as tools of management led to the prediction that allied mediators would be more successful than neutral parties. It is possible, however, that allies might be successful mediators not because they constrain allies but because they bully the non-allied state. This alternative explanation would have devastating implications for my

---

[34] Butterworth and Scranton (1976); Bercovitch *et al.* (1991).

[35] Bercovitch *et al.* (1991).

[36] This control variable is important in other studies of mediation. Unfortunately, my measurements are unable to distinguish violence which occurs prior to the failure of mediation in a crisis from violence subsequent to that failure. This raises an obvious potential problem of reciprocal causation. I reanalysed my data with this variable excluded. As described in n. 39, my results are robust to this respecification.

approach. The central implication of my theoretical approach is that states use alliances for control functions that range well beyond the traditional capability aggregation model. If allies are more successful mediators because they bully the non-allied states, however, then this finding is entirely consistent with the capability aggression approach.

In order to test more directly the mechanism by which biased mediators are successful I perform a secondary analysis. In this analysis, I use the extent of the mediator's alliance ties both to the challenger and defender to predict which state will prevail in the dispute. If my argument about alliances as tools of constraint is correct, then we would expect that challengers should be *less* likely to prevail in a dispute if they share alliance ties with the mediator as the mediator reins in its ally. Conversely, alliance ties between the mediator and the defender should actually make the challenger *more* likely to prevail. If the capability aggregation model explains mediation success, on the other hand, then we would expect that challengers will be *more* likely to prevail if they share an alliance tie with the mediator as the mediator supports its ally and uses its capability to impose its will on the defender. Conversely, this approach would suggest that alliance ties between the mediator and the defender will make the challenger less likely to prevail.

HYPOTHESIS 8: The stronger the mediator's alliance ties to the challenger, the lower the probability that the challenger will prevail in the dispute.

HYPOTHESIS 9: The stronger the mediator's alliance ties to the challenger, the higher the probability that the challenger will prevail in the dispute.

HYPOTHESIS 10: The stronger the mediator's alliance ties to the defender, the higher the probability that the challenger will prevail in the dispute.

HYPOTHESIS 11: The stronger the mediator's alliance ties to the defender, the lower the probability that the challenger will prevail in the dispute.

10. Data and Measurements

I test my hypotheses on a set of all mediation attempts by state leaders in international military crises between 1918 and 1988. My dataset is an adaptation of the revised International Crisis Behavior (ICB) dataset. Specifically, I made five alterations to the ICB dataset of 390 crises which occurred between 1918 and 1988. First, I removed crises which occurred within the context of a full-scale war because I believe these cases differ fundamentally from crises which occur in a peaceful context. Once full-scale armed conflict is under way I believe that the further decisions about the settlement of the crisis become largely a function of military strategy and tactics rather than diplomatic factors such as crisis mediation (deletion of 11 cases). Second, I removed crises in which I failed to find evidence of either verbal threats or threats of force accompanied by military deployments (deletion of 17 cases). In the absence of such threatening actions I was not convinced that these cases qualified as international military crises. Third, I aggregated cases in which several crises erupted within ongoing guerrilla campaigns over several years (deletion of 22 cases). Since the use of force was nearly constant throughout these persistent conflicts, I concluded that the recurrent flare-ups were essentially intra-war crises. Fourth, I added several cases by disaggregating disputes which contained multiple conflictual dyads (addition of 12 cases). For example, the single case identified by the ICB dataset as the 'Yom Kippur War' was disaggregated into two cases: Israel versus Egypt and Israel versus Syria. For each of the remaining crises I have identified a primary challenger and defender. The challenger is defined as the first state to take or threaten militarized action with regard to the issue at stake in the crisis. The defender, on the other hand, is defined as the primary state against which the challenger's militarized act or threat is aimed.

Finally, from this revised set of international crises, I identified all of the attempts by state leaders to mediate in these crises. I define a mediator as any third-party state actor which attempts to intervene in order to produce a negotiated settlement in the crisis. It is important to note that I distinguish intervening *on behalf* of one of the disputants from an attempt to produce a negotiated settlement. Thus states are not included as mediators if they exclusively support the claims of one of the disputants in the crisis. In a number of cases more than one third-party state attempted to mediate the crisis. If these mediation efforts were distinct and unrelated to one another, then I coded them as separate cases in the dataset. If several states acted jointly to mediate a crisis, I coded the mediation behaviour of the entire group (i.e. joint military capabilities, alliance of any mediator to disputants) as a single case. Through this process I identified 117 mediation attempts by third-party states in international crises between 1918 and 1988. Fifty-two of these mediation attempts were successful in producing a negotiated settlement to the crisis, while sixty-five were not. In the subsequent analysis I will attempt to explain the success or failure of each of these attempts.

Clearly this population of 117 mediation attempts does not represent a randomly selected set of international interactions, nor is it even a randomly selected set of international crises. Instead, three different parties must make choices that select international crises into my dataset. First, the mediator must offer its services to the disputants, and then each of the disputants must accept that offer. This process raises the issue of selection effects with regard to the generalizability of my findings. On the one hand, I am explicitly and consciously using selection effects in order to add validity to my findings. That is, I select cases where allies choose to intervene as mediators rather than in direct support of their ally in order to separate the impact of alliances as indicators of common interests from their impact as institutional signals of commitment. This selection implies that my findings regarding alliances should be generalized *only* to cases of mediation, and not to the impact of alliances on international crises or international behaviour in general. Thus I do not wish to claim that alliances are *always* used as tools of constraint. I merely wish to demonstrate that they *can* and *have* been used in this way.

On the other hand, the selection process that generated these mediation cases also implies that such cases may not be representative of all situations in which allies attempt to constrain one another's behaviour. In particular, if state leaders are aware of the constraining impact of alliance ties, then this should influence their decisions to accept an asymmetrically allied state as a mediator. That is, leaders should only accept a mediator more closely allied to their state than to their opponent if they are already quite powerful and likely to prevail in the crisis. Under these circumstances allowing a state with asymmetrically close alliance ties to serve as mediator might restrain the leader to accept some compromise outcome which still achieves a number of its goals. Leaders of weak states, on the other hand, should be generally likely to avoid accepting allies as mediators because doing so would result in outright defeat. This selection process implies that by examining cases of crisis mediation for evidence of alliance constraints, I tend to select cases in which mediators are attempting to restrain their allies from imposing their will on weaker third-party states. Empirical evidence from my dataset also supports this contention.[37] As a result, my analysis will tend to *underestimate* the general impact of alliances as tools of constraint by selecting out hard cases for testing my argument.

---

[37] I regressed the strength of the mediator's alliance ties to the challenger and defender on the balance of relative military strength of the disputants. The stronger the mediator's ties to the challenger the higher the proportion of dyadic capabilities that were controlled by the challenger (b=0.06; p<.02). Thus for each one level increase in the strength of the challenger's alliance ties to the mediator, the challenger possessed a 6% larger share of the dyadic capabilities. In crises with an unbiased mediator, the ratio of military capabilities between the challenger and defender was almost precisely an even 1:1. However, when the mediator shared a defence pact with the challenger and was unallied to the defender, the challenger averaged better than a 2:1 advantage. Alliance ties between the mediator and defender have a nearly identical impact but in the opposite direction (b=−0.06; p<.01).

Mediation success

This is the dependent variable for my primary analysis. I coded this variable on the basis of the outcome of the dispute as coded in the ICB dataset. The ICB dataset identifies crisis outcomes as formal or semi-formal settlements, tacit settlements, imposed outcomes, and stalemates. Crises with outcomes imposed by one of the disputants or which resulted in stalemates were coded as mediation failures (value of 0). Then I reviewed each of the cases which result in a negotiated agreement—formal, semi-formal, or tacit—to determine whether the efforts of the mediator contributed to that settlement. If so, the mediation effort was coded as successful (value of 1). If the mediator's actions did not contribute to the settlement, its efforts were coded as unsuccessful (value of 0).

Inequality of alliance ties between mediator and disputants

In coding this variable I relied on the Correlates of War (COW) data set on alliances as updated in 1993. Thus I use a four-point ordinal scale to identify the strength of an alliance: no alliance, entente, neutrality pact, and defence pact. I began by determining the strength of the mediator's alliance ties to each of the disputants. If the mediator is not allied to a disputant I assign their relationship a value of 0. If a mediator shares an entente with a disputant I assign a value of 1. If the mediator and a disputant share a neutrality pact I assign a value of 2. I code neutrality pacts as stronger than ententes because an entente only includes a commitment to consult in the event of a crisis. It does not include any specific commitment to use force on behalf of the ally, nor does an entente bar a state from using force against its ally. A neutrality pact, on the other hand, does include a specific commitment *not* to use force against one's ally. Finally, if the mediator shares a defence pact with a disputant I assign a value of 3. Then I determined the mediator's alliance bias by calculating the difference between the strength of the mediator's alliance ties to the challenger and the defender. For example, if the mediator shares a defence pact with one disputant and an entente with the other then I assign a value of 2.

Strength of mediator

This is a dummy variable which identifies great-power mediators. If any of the states involved in a particular mediation attempt were great powers, then I assign a value of 1 for this variable. Otherwise a value of 0 is coded. I identify great powers on the basis of the Correlates of War (COW) dataset on military capabilities. From 1918 to 1945 I identify Britain, France, Germany, Italy, the Soviet Union, Japan, and the United States as great powers. From 1946 to 1988 I identify Britain, France, the People's Republic of China, the Soviet Union, and the United States as great powers.

Interaction of inequality of alliance tie and strength of mediator

This variable is composed of the inequality of the mediator's alliance ties to the disputants multiplied by the strength of the mediator. Including this interaction as a separate variable in the analysis will allow me to identify the impact that the mediator's great-power status has on the relationship between the mediator's alliance bias and the success of its mediation efforts.

Strength of mediation efforts

I use a seven-point ordinal scale to code the strength of the mediator's efforts. The first category includes cases in which the mediator simply discusses the possibility of a diplomatic solution to the crisis with the disputants. The second category includes cases in which the mediator engaged in fact-finding or provided its 'good offices' to facilitate negotiation. The third category includes cases in which the mediator warned the disputants against the use of force, condemned the outbreak of violence, or called upon the disputants for a peaceful settlement. It is important to emphasize that none of these exhortations were supported by any threat of more direct intervention. The fourth category includes cases in which the mediator engages in formal mediation or attempts to arbitrate or adjudicate the dispute. The fifth category identifies cases in which the mediator threatened or actually undertook economic sanctions against the disputants in an effort to force them to settle. The sixth category includes cases of indirect military intervention by the mediator, such as providing weapons to one or more of the disputants or offering the use of its military bases or hardware to support military operations. Finally, the seventh category includes cases in which the mediator actually threatens or undertakes directly military intervention in the crisis with its own regular armed forces. If the mediator used more than one strategy in mediating the dispute, then I coded the strongest strategy. The information for coding this variable was drawn from the detailed case summaries provided by the ICB dataset and the bibliographies it provides for each crisis.

Military equality of the disputants

I code a state's military capability as the average of three elements: number of troops, military expenditures, and military expenditures per soldier.[38] The variable was created in four steps. First, the raw data was converted to a percentage relative to the global total of the element (e.g. a states' troops in 1919/global total number of troops in 1919). Second, when necessary, the totals were discounted to reflect the distance between the state and the location of the conflict.[39] Third, for each element, the state's capabilities were calculated as a percentage of the combined capabilities of both actors according to the following formula: defender's capabilities/(challenger's capabilities + defender's capabilities). Finally, I averaged the three elements (troops, expenditures, expenditures per soldier). The resulting variable ranges from 0, in which case the challenger controls all capabilities in the dyad, to 1, in which case the defender controls all the capabilities.

In order to transform this variable into a measure of the military equality of the disputants, I subtracted .50 from this value and took the absolute value of this difference. The result is a measure of military equality in which 0 reflects a perfectly balanced dyad, while a score of .5 indicates that either the challenger or defender controls all the capabilities in the dyad.

Disputants share an alliance tie

This is a dummy variable which takes on a value of 1 when the two disputants in the international crisis share a defence pact, neutrality pact, or an entente. Otherwise the variable is coded 0.

Level of violence used by the disputants

This is a dummy variable which takes on a value of 1 if one of the primary disputants commits more than 1,000 troops into combat. Otherwise I assign a value of 0.

Challenger prevails in dispute

This is the dependent variable in my secondary analysis which tests hypo-

[38] The source of the troop and expenditure data was the COW dataset entitled 'National Capabilities of States, 1816–1990'.

[39] The method used to discount power projection capability can be found in Bueno de Mesquita (1981: 103).

theses 8 to 11. This variable is drawn from the ICB dataset and is coded on a four-point scale: loss, stalemate, compromise, and victory. Losses involve cases in which the crisis ended on terms which the challenger considered worse than the *status quo ante*. Stalemates involve cases in which the crisis has no clear resolution or in which the challenger's perception of the status quo is unchanged. Compromises include cases in which the challenger is able to achieve some of its goals, but is not entirely successful in revising the status quo. Finally, victories represent cases in which the challenger was able to prevail on the issues at stake in the crisis.

Strength of mediator's alliance ties to the challenger

As was the case with alliance variables described above, this variable was generated with the COW data on alliances. The value assigned for this variable is the strongest alliance tie between any of the mediators and the challenging state in the dispute.

Strength of mediator's alliance ties to the defender

This variable is created with COW data on alliances. I assign the value of the strongest alliance tie between any of the mediators and the defending state in the dispute.

Relative military strength of the disputants

This variable is coded with the same data as the 'military equality of the disputants' variable discussed above. In this case, however, I simply leave the measure as reflecting the challenger's capabilities divided by the sum of the challenger and defender capabilities. Thus this variable reflects the proportion of the military capabilities in the dyad that is controlled by the challenger.

Tables 4.1 and 4.2 summarize some of the general characteristics of the dataset. Table 4.1 describes my dataset according to two variables: the inequality of alliance ties and the identity of the mediator. I divide the mediators into three categories: the United States, major powers other than the United States, and minor powers. Clearly the United States is the most frequent mediator of disputes, comprising one-third of the cases. However, a substantial number of other states also engage in mediation, including a number of other great powers. In fact, the dataset is nearly evenly divided among the three categories. Moreover, there appears to be little difference in

Table 4.1. *Cross-Tabulation of Mediator Bias by Identity of Mediator*

Identity of Mediator	Inequality of Alliance Ties				
	None	One Level	Two Levels	Three Levels	TOTAL
Minor Power	36	0	2	5	43
	84%	0%	5%	12%	
Non-US Great Power	24	7	1	3	35
	69%	20%	3%	9%	
United States	30	8	0	6	39
	77%	8%	0%	15%	
TOTAL	90	10	3	14	117
	77%	9%	3%	12%	

the readiness of various mediators to intervene when they have unequal alliance ties to the disputants.

Table 4.2 displays the extent of mediator bias in the two principal historical periods covered by my dataset: the inter-war period (1918–45) and the cold war (1946–88). Dividing the number of mediation attempts by the number of years in each period reveals that mediation was attempted 1.3 times per year during the inter-war period and 1.9 times per year during the cold war. Thus while mediation was somewhat more frequent during the cold war, this tool of diplomacy was often used long before the onset of a bipolar international system. Moreover, mediators were just as likely to have unequal alliance ties during the inter-war period as they were during the cold war.

Table 4.2. *Cross-Tabulation of Mediator Bias by Historical Period*

Historical Period	Inequality of Alliance Ties				
	None	One Level	Two Levels	Three Levels	TOTAL
Inter-War (1918–1945)	28	3	2	3	36
	78%	8%	6%	8%	
Cold War (1945–1988)	62	7	1	11	81
	77%	9%	1%	14%	
TOTAL	90	10	3	14	117
	77%	9%	3%	12%	

11. Data Analysis

I test hypotheses 1–7 through logit analysis, which is analogous to linear regression but is an appropriate statistical tool for dichotomous dependent variables. The results of this analysis are presented in Table 4.3 and Figure 4.1.[40] In brief, the results support a synthesis of the realist and institutionalist views of mediation success at the expense of the traditional mediation literature.

Hypotheses 1–3, which are all drawn from the mediation literature, are *not* supported by my analysis. Hypothesis 1 predicts a negative relationship

Table 4.3. *Logit Analysis Predicting Mediation Success: Institutionalist Variables, Realist Variables, and Control Variables*

Explanatory Variables	Coefficient	Standard Error	Significance Level
Institutionalist and Realist Variables			
inequality of mediator alliance tie	−0.15	0.36	—
mediator bias × great power mediator	0.90	0.51	< .08*
great power mediator	0.94	0.53	< .08*
mediator strategy	0.81	0.20	< .01
Control Variables			
disputants share alliance	1.07	0.58	< .05
crisis involves major violence	−1.11	0.48	< .02
parity of disputants	1.72	1.85	—
Constant	−4.26	1.06	< .01

   * Denotes two-tailed test for statistical significance. All other significance tests are one-tailed.

Number of observations = 117
Number of observations correctly predicted = 87
Percentage correctly predicted = 74%
Initial log likelihood = −160.8
Log likelihood at convergence = −117.5
Proportional reduction in error = 34.6%

---

[40] Auxiliary regressions reveal that multicolinearity does not present a problem in this analysis. Because of the interaction between the great-power status of the mediator and the mediator's alliance bias, colinearity levels among these variables is slightly higher but not disturbingly so. Auxiliary r^2 for these variables range from .23 to .68. Auxiliary r^2 for the remaining variables are quite low, ranging from .03 to .23.

| Observed | Predicted Outcome | | Percentage |
Outcome	Failure	Success	Correct
Failure	50	15	77
Success	15	37	71
		Overall	74

FIGURE 4.1. Logit Model's Prediction of Mediation Success

between alliance bias and success in mediation. The coefficient for this variable is slightly negative but does not approach statistical significance. In other words, the effect of this variable cannot be distinguished from 0. Hypothesis 2 predicts a negative relationship between great-power status and success in mediation. Instead, the coefficient for great-power status is *positive* and significant at p<.08 with a 2-tailed test of significance. Hypothesis 3 expects a curvilinear relationship between the coerciveness of the mediator's strategy and success. The coefficient on the mediator's strategy is positive but the relationship is linear. Thus increases in the coerciveness of the mediator's strategy above active mediation to the use of sanctions or threats of force actually *improve* the probability of mediation success. The results in Table 4.1 reflect the linear nature of this effect. In other analyses, I tested for curvilinearity by including the square of the mediation strategy variable. Its coefficient was small and not statistically significant (p<.23). Furthermore, a likelihood ratio test revealed that the data were not more likely to have been generated by a curvilinear relationship (Chi-squared= 1.6 with 1 d.f.; not significant).

The institutionalist explanation *alone* also does not perform well. Hypothesis 4 predicts a positive relationship between alliance bias and success. As described above, the coefficient for this variable is slightly negative but not significant. Thus, in general, institutionalized alliance ties do *not* provide leverage in international mediation.

A synthesis of the institutional and realist paradigms, however, performs well in explaining mediation success. Consistent with hypothesis 6, alliance ties do generate leverage in *interaction* with the mediator's status as a great power. The coefficient for this interaction term is positive and statistically significant at p<.08 with a 2-tailed test. Moreover, as we shall see below, this coefficient is substantively quite large. Consistent with hypothesis 5, I find that great powers are also generally more successful mediators independent of the interaction between great powers and alliance ties. As described above, this coefficient is positive and significant at p<.08. However, as we shall see below, this independent impact of great-power status is not nearly as large as its interactive impact with alliance ties. Finally, consistent with hypothesis 7 drawn from both realist and institutionalist paradigms, we have seen that mediator coercion has a positive linear impact on mediation success. As it turns out, this impact is substantively quite large especially with regard to the use of highly coercive tactics.

Two of the control variables perform as expected. Alliance ties between the disputants and the outbreak of violence in the crisis have their predicted coefficients and are statistically significant at the .05 and .025 levels respectively. The positive coefficient on alliance ties between the disputants indicates that disputants are more amenable to mediation when they share an alliance tie with one another because of their added capability to cope with commitment problems. The negative coefficient on the outbreak of major violence, on the other hand, indicates that such crises are more difficult to mediate.[41]

More surprisingly, the coefficient for the military equality of the disputants is *positive*. This coefficient indicates that mediation attempts are more likely to be successful in crises between *unequal* disputants. This counterintuitive finding is not a result of multicollinearity, nor is it sensitive to the particular set of control variables included in the model. While it is true that this coefficient does not achieve statistical significance, its estimated substantive impact is also considerable. Thus I do not believe that this unexpected coefficient should simply be dismissed as a statistical anomaly. One possible interpretation of this coefficient is that it is easier to resolve disputes peacefully and on mutually acceptable terms when the outcome of any potential military confrontation is known with greater certainty. This explanation would be consistent with previous work by Fearon, and is further supported by other results from my analysis.[42] In particular, I find a strong correlation between dispute *imbalance* and compromise outcomes (r=.34, p<.001).

Although the results in Table 4.1 indicate the direction of the effects of the variables and the statistical significance of the coefficients, it is difficult

---

[41] In order to ensure that this simultaneous causation did not seriously bias my results (see n. 34), I re-estimated the equation in Table 4.3 with this variable excluded. The coefficients for great-power mediator and the interaction between great-power mediator and the inequality of alliance ties are slightly reduced in this re-estimation and their level of statistical significance shrinks marginally as well. The substantive interpretation of the results, however, remains essentially unchanged.   [42] Fearon (1995).

to infer the substantive impact of the variables from their logit coefficients. I calculate the substantive impact of the interaction of the inequality of the mediator's alliance ties and its great-power status in Table 4.4. In the first part of this table, I estimate the marginal impact of the inequality of the mediator's alliance ties separately for great-power and minor power mediators. As I described above, the mediator's alliance bias actually has a slightly negative effect on the success of minor-power mediators. Specifically, as a minor-power mediator shifts from having equally strong alliance ties to both disputants to having ties to one party at one level stronger than their ties to the other, the probability of successful mediation declines by 2 per cent. A further increase in the inequality of the mediator's alliance ties from one level to two levels reduces the likelihood of successful mediation by another 2 per cent. Finally, minor-power mediators which share a defence pact with one of the disputants and have no alliance with the other (a difference of three levels) are an additional 1 per cent less likely to be successful. Thus it seems clear that biased mediators' threats of intervention and abandonment cannot be influential if they lack the military capability to back up such threats.

When the mediator is a great power, however, the inequality of its alliance ties to the disputants has a powerful impact on mediation success. Specifically, Table 4.4 indicates that a great power which has alliance ties that are one level stronger to one disputant than to the other is 18 per cent more likely to be successful in mediating an international crisis than is a great power with equal ties to both parties. Similarly, a great power with ties that are two levels stronger to one disputant than to the other is 18 per cent more likely to be successful than a great power with alliance ties that are only unequal by one level. Finally, great powers which share a defence pact with one of the disputants and have no alliance with its opponent are an additional 14 per cent more likely to be successful in their mediation efforts. The overall impact of alliance ties on the success of great-power mediators is quite striking. Specifically, great powers with equal ties to both parties are successful in mediating international crises only 31 per cent of the time. Great powers which share a defence pact with one of the disputants and have no alliance with the other, on the other hand, are successful 81 per cent of the time. Thus it appears that alliance ties do help powerful mediators make persuasive threats of abandonment against their allies and persuasive threats of intervention against the unallied disputant.

The middle section of Table 4.4 holds the allied status of the mediator constant and describes the impact of its great-power status at each level of alliance inequality. As the table indicates, when the mediator's alliance ties

Table 4.4. *Marginal Effects of Institutionalist and Realist Variables*

**Effect of Inequality of Mediator's Alliance
Ties Controlling for Mediator's Great Power Status**

Change in Inequality of Mediator's Alliance Ties	Change in Probability of Mediation Success
Mediator is Not a Great Power	
None to one level	−2%
One level to two levels	−2%
Two levels to three levels	−1%
Mediator is a Great Power	
None to one level	+18%
One level to two levels	+18%
Two levels to three levels	+14%

**Effect of Mediator's Great Power Status
Controlling for Inequality of Mediator's Alliance Ties**

Change in Mediator's Great Power Status	Change in Probability of Mediation Success
Mediator Alliance Ties Equal:	
Minor Power to Great Power	+16%
Mediator's Alliance Ties Unequal by One Level:	
Minor Power to Great Power	+35%
Mediator's Alliance Ties Unequal by Two Levels:	
Minor Power to Great Power	+55%
Mediator's Alliance Ties Unequal by Three Levels:	
Minor Power to Great Power	+71%

Effect of the Strength of the Mediator's Strategy

Discussion to Mediation/Arbitration	+27%
Mediation/Arbitration to Military Intervention	+53%

Note: Marginal effects were calculated by generating predicted values from the logit model while changing the values of selected variables and holding the others at their means or modes. The predicted values were transformed into probabilities that the outcome would fall into each category by summing the area underneath the logistic distribution up to the predicted value.

to the disputants are equal, its status as a great power has only a modest influence on its mediation success. In this situation, great-power mediators are only 16 per cent more likely to be successful than minor powers. As the mediator's alliance ties to the disputants become more unequal, however, the coercive leverage that it gains from its military capabilities increases as well. When the mediator's alliance ties are unequal by one level, it is more than 35 per cent more likely to be successful if it is a great power than if it is a minor power. When the mediator's alliance ties are unequal by two levels, its likelihood of success increases by 55 per cent if it is a great power rather than a minor power. And finally, great-power mediators which share a defence pact with one of the disputants and have no alliance with its opponent are a striking 71 per cent more likely to be successful in settling the crisis than are minor powers with a similar alliance ties. Minor-power mediators in this situation are successful in their mediation efforts only 10 per cent of the time. Great powers, on the other hand, are successful 81 per cent of the time. These results seem to indicate that while alliance inequality helps mediators to make credible threats, those threats are not likely to influence state behaviour in international crises if they are not backed up with substantial military capabilities.

Finally, the strength of the mediation efforts also has a powerful impact on mediation success. As expected by much of the mediation literature, strategies of active involvement by the mediator, such as mediation and arbitration, are more successful in producing settlements than are passive strategies such as discussing the issue with the disputants or offering one's 'good offices'. Specifically, Table 4.4 indicates that increasing the strength of the mediation efforts from a simple discussion of the issues to active mediation or arbitration increases the probability of success by 27 per cent. Contrary to the conventional wisdom in the mediation literature, however, I find that *continued* increases in the coerciveness of the mediator's strategy further improve its chances of mediation success. For example, an increase in the coerciveness of the mediator's efforts from mediation to direct military intervention improves its chances for success by an additional 53 per cent. In fact, mediators which intervened in the crises militarily were successful in facilitating a settlement 83 per cent of the time. The fact that such highly coercive tactics have such a substantial impact on mediation success constitutes particularly strong evidence *against* the conventional views of the mediation literature.

Two of my control variables also had a statistically significant impact on mediation success. The marginal effects of these variables are displayed in Table 4.5. First, in addition to helping mediators to make credible threats

Table 4.5. *Marginal Effects of Control Variables*

Change in Value of Independent Variable	Change in Probability of Mediation Success
Disputants Share an Alliance Tie: No to Yes	+16%
Crisis Involves Major Violence: No to Yes	−17%

Note: Marginal effects were calculated by generating predicted values from the logit model while changing the values of selected variables and holding the others at their means or modes. The predicted values were transformed into probabilities of mediation success by summing the area underneath the logistic distribution up to the predicted value.

that coerce the disputants into settling, I find that alliance ties between the disputants themselves also contribute to successful mediation. Since allied disputants can credibly threaten to punish their ally by abandoning the alliance if the settlement is violated, they should be more capable of solving the commitment problems which can be a barrier to a successful mediation. In fact, I find that mediation is 16 per cent more likely to succeed if the disputants share an alliance tie.

Second, while military intervention by the mediator facilitated the settlement of crises, the outbreak of violence between the disputants had precisely the opposite effect. Consistent with the findings of previous studies of mediation, my results indicate that mediation is 17 per cent less likely to succeed in crises in which at least one of the disputants commits at least 1,000 troops into battle.[43]

My evidence of a strong relationship between alliance inequality and mediation success provides solid support for the proposition that alliances can be used as instruments of intra-allied control. Moreover, this finding indicates that alliances perform security management functions (as described by Wallander and Keohane) as well as their well-known and documented capability aggregation functions. However, up to this point, my analysis has not directly tested the mechanism of control which generates mediation success. Thus a realist might contend that biased great-power mediators are more successful, not because they constrain their own ally but because they bully the non-allied disputant into settling. Such an interpretation would suggest that alliances act purely as methods of capability aggregation.

Hypotheses 8–11 make predictions which more directly test the mechanism of intra-allied control. Each of the hypotheses concerns the relationship

[43] Bercovitch *et al.* (1991).

Table 4.6. *Ordered Probit Analysis Predicting Challenger Victory*

Explanatory Variables	Coefficient	Standard Error	Significance Level
Strength of mediator's alliance to the challenger	−0.20	0.11	< .06*
Strength of mediator's alliance to the defender	0.18	0.11	< .10*
Relative military capabilities	0.64	0.20	< .08
First Threshold	0.20	0.28	ancillary parameters
Second Threshold	0.76	0.29	
Third Threshold	1.43	0.30	

* Denotes two-tailed test for statistical significance. Other significance tests are one-tailed.

Number of observations = 117
Initial log likelihood = −150.0
Log likelihood at convergence = −146.6

between the mediator's alliance ties and the likelihood that the challenger will prevail with regard to the substantive issue at stake in the dispute. I also include the relative military capabilities of the disputants as a control variable in the analysis. Since challenger victory is coded on a four-point ordinal scale, I test these hypotheses through the use of ordered probit analysis. This method is analogous to linear regression but is appropriate for ordinally ranked dependent variables. The results of this analysis are presented in Table 4.6.[44]

These results support my argument concerning intra-allied control and mediation success and are *not* consistent with the capability aggregation approach. Consistent with hypothesis 8, but contrary to hypothesis 10, the coefficient for the strength of the mediator's alliance to the challenger is negative and significant at the .06 level. This coefficient indicates that the challenger is actually less likely to prevail in a dispute if it shares an alliance with the mediator. Conversely, the coefficient for an alliance tie between the mediator and the defender is positive. Consistent with hypothesis 9 and contrary to hypothesis 11, this finding indicates that the challenger is more likely to prevail if the mediator is allied to the defender. Finally, as we would expect, the coefficient on relative military capabilities indicates that a chal-

---

[44] Auxiliary regressions reveal that multicolinearity does not present a problem in this analysis. Auxiliary r^2 for the alliance variables are approximately .45. Auxiliary r^2 for relative military capabilities is .07.

lenger which controls a higher proportion of the military capability in the dispute dyad is more likely to prevail.

The marginal impact of alliance ties on substantive dispute outcomes is also fairly strong. As Table 4.7 indicates, each increase in the strength of the mediator's alliance ties to the challenger actually increases the probability that the challenger will *lose* the dispute by 8 per cent. On the other hand, the probability of a challenger victory or a compromise *decreases* by 3–4 per cent with each increase in the value of this variable. These effects may appear rather modest until their impact is summed across the range of the variable. For example, the probability that the challenger will suffer a defeat in a dispute in which it shares no alliance with the mediator is 45 per cent. If the challenger shares a defence pact with the mediator, however, the probability that it will be defeated is 68 per cent. Moreover, the probability that the challenger will win a dispute involving an unallied mediator is 14 per cent, while the probability of winning when bargaining with a mediator that shares a defence pact is only 5 per cent.

Alliance ties between the mediator and defender have a similar substantive impact. In this case, each increase in the strength of the alliance ties between the mediator and the defender improves the probability that the

Table 4.7. *Marginal Effects of Alliance Ties on Challenger Victory*

Change in Strength of Mediator's Alliance Tie	Change in Probability of Challenger			
	Loss	Stalemate	Compromise	Victory
Strength of Alliance Tie to Challenger				
No Alliance to Entente	+8%	–1%	–3%	–4%
Entente to Neutrality Pact	+8%	–2%	–3%	–3%
Neutrality Pact to Defense Pact	+8%	–2%	–3%	–3%
Strength of Alliance Tie to Defender				
No Alliance to Entente	–7%	0%	+2%	+5%
Entente to Neutrality Pact	–7%	0%	+2%	+5%
Neutrality Pact to Defense Pact	–6%	–1%	+1%	+6%

Note: Marginal effects were calculated by generating predicted values from the probit model while changing the values of selected variables and holding the others at their means or modes. The predicted values were transformed into probabilities that the outcome would fall into each category by summing the area underneath the cumulative normal distribution between the predicted value and each of the category thresholds.

challenger will prevail in the dispute by 5–6 per cent. Conversely, each increase in the strength of the mediator's alliance with the defender decreases the probability that the challenger will *lose* the dispute by 6–7 per cent. Summing across the range of this variable indicates that the probability of a challenger victory increases from 14 to 29 per cent as the mediator shifts from having no alliances with the defender to sharing a defence pact. Similarly, this same change in the mediator's alliance ties to the defender decreases the probability of defeat for the challenger from 45 to 25 per cent.

These findings provide yet further support for the argument that alliances *can* be used as security management institutions that constrain behaviour *within* the alliance. The capability aggregation model of alliances simply cannot account for the fact that great-power allied mediators use their coercive leverage to negotiate settlements that limit and constrain their own allies. Understanding this phenomenon requires a new paradigm—one in which alliances can function both as methods of capability aggregation and tools of security management. By building on the work of Schroeder, Morrow, and Wallander and Keohane, I have tried to begin filling in the implications of such an approach.[45]

In doing so, however, I want to emphasize that I am not suggesting that alliances act as instruments of control *instead* of as tools of capability aggregation. Thus I do *not* wish to claim that the intervention of an ally in a dispute is always or even generally bad for its alliance partner. I concur with recent research which indicates that alliances can act to aggregate capability and therefore can improve the probability that a state will prevail in an international dispute or war.[46] None the less, I do want to indicate that when allied states choose to intervene as *mediators* rather than in full support of their ally that these allied mediators generally act to constrain their own ally so as to produce a peaceful settlement of the dispute. Thus the very same alliance that is used for capability aggression in one context can be used as a tool of management in another.

12. Conclusions

The realist literature on alliances has tended to view these institutions purely as mechanisms for aggregating military capability. Consequently, these works have focused on the external functions of alliances. That is,

---

[45] Schroeder (1994, 1977); Morrow (1991).
[46] Choi (1997); Gartner and Siverson (1996); A. Smith (1996*b*).

alliances have been viewed as tools for guarding against *external* threats and imbalances of power.[47] More recently, however, the institutionalist literature has begun to place alliances within the broader theoretical context of security institutions.[48] In doing so, these scholars have begun to draw attention to the functions that alliances can perform *among* alliance partners.

In this work I have begun building on a framework which integrates institutionalist and realist perspectives on alliances. Expanding upon the literature on institutional ties and credible commitments, I have constructed an argument concerning alliances as instruments of *intra-allied* control. My findings indicate that the functions of alliances reach well beyond the capability aggregation model to a variety of tasks described by a theory of alliances as security management institutions. At the same time, however, my findings also validate realist expectations that alliances will be used as mechanisms for exercising military power and control.

Specifically, my analysis has focused on 117 mediation attempts in international crises between 1918 and 1988. By studying cases of mediation I am able to distinguish the influence of *institutionalized* alliances as separate from the influence of the common interests that states which are *aligned* with one another share. My examination of these cases indicates that the *interaction* between the mediator's alliance ties and its military capacity has a dramatic impact on mediation success. Thus I find that the most successful mediators in international crises are great powers which are allied to one of the disputants and choose to use coercive mediation tactics to persuade the disputants to settle. Moreover, I also find that biased mediators are successful because they erode the position of their own ally in forging a settlement to the dispute. This finding does *not* indicate that allied intervention is *generally* detrimental to a state's performance in a crisis. However, when an ally chooses to intervene as a *mediator*, then its coercive leverage will be used in ways that cannot be understood through the traditional capability aggregation paradigm. While these findings fit well with a synthesis of institutionalist and realist theories of alliances, they run directly contrary to much of the conventional wisdom concerning international mediation. I hope that my work may also push this literature one step further toward viewing mediation as a process of bargaining rather than one of adjudication.

---

[47] Waltz (1979); Walt (1987).   [48] Wallander and Keohane (1995).

5

ALLIANCE COHESION AND PEACEFUL CHANGE IN NATO

Christian Tuschhoff

Nearly a decade after German unification and the demise of the Soviet Union, it has become commonplace to note that NATO has not disappeared as a result of these fundamental changes in the European balance of power, notwithstanding the predictions of neo-realist scholars.[1] Less attention has been paid, however, to the failure of neo-realist theory to account for NATO's cohesion during the cold war despite the rise of German power in the 1950s and 1960s. Alliances have often broken apart because the balance of power within them altered, but this pattern of alignment and realignment changed after the Second World War. Although the balance of power shifted from core NATO members France and Great Britain to a newer member, the Federal Republic of Germany (FRG), NATO not only persisted but its cohesion grew and its mutual defence commitments were strengthened.[2]

The explanation for NATO's enhanced cohesion is that its features as a security institution allowed the members to manage the changing intra-alliance balance of power caused by Germany's re-emergence in the post-war period as a sovereign state with a powerful economy and substantial military forces. Although its allies did hedge against rising German power, as realist theory would predict,[3] they did so multilaterally and by developing NATO's institutional features, not by unilateral balancing. Through multi-lateral command and control systems, transparency, mechanisms to facilit-

This article derives from a larger study on Germany, NATO, and nuclear weapons 1949–67 that is based upon detailed archival and document research. Given the limited space I could only use few examples to illustrate the basic argument. I gratefully acknowledge comments by Peter Brecke, Marc Busch, Helga Haftendorn, Gunther Hellmann, Robert Keohane, Robin Moriarty, Dan Reiter, Thomas Risse, Celeste Wallander, and Reinhard Wolf on earlier drafts.

[1] McCalla (1996); Mearsheimer (1990); Waltz (1993).
[2] For a theoretical discussion of such a peaceful change see Efinger *et al.* (1990).
[3] Hellman and Wolf (1993: 9).

ate concessions, the integration of otherwise diverse national personnel, and the enforcement of national commitments, NATO's procedures enabled Germany's allies to accept and manage Germany's rising power and increased role in alliance policies and practices. These procedures reassured the other allies that the rise of German power did not mean an increased German threat, on the one hand, and reassured Germany that its national security interests and policy preferences would play a role in alliance policy, on the other.

Without NATO's institutions in place, France, Britain, and the other allies would not have agreed to German rearmament. With them, the allies were content to steer German armed forces away from national and toward collective defence.[4] Without those institutions, Germany would have developed a national defence posture independent of NATO and would not have postponed unification for thirty-five years. With them, the FRG was able to adopt a national security and defence policy that did not threaten its new allies and to achieve unification with the agreement of the four Second World War victors. Even the Soviet Union eventually accepted that a united Germany *in* NATO posed less of a threat than a non-aligned Germany in the centre of Europe.[5] Clearly, NATO as a security institution played a vital role in keeping the peace during the cold war, and not merely in the way commonly thought. It did so not only by deterring East–West conflict but also by peacefully managing the shifting Western balance of power.

This chapter has two parts. First, I demonstrate that German power relative to its alliance partners grew in the 1950s and 1960s. I then analyse the role of NATO rules and procedures in coping with Germany's relative gains and maintaining alliance cohesion.

1. The Changing Balance of Power among Allies

The balance of power within a group of states or institutions is usually measured by three indicators: control over actors, control over resources, and control over outcomes.[6] In an alliance, control over actors means that one ally can influence another to perform an action that it otherwise would not have carried out. Control over actors is low if allies only issue soft promises of collective defence; it is high when promises are backed by military arrangements necessary to implement collective defence. A change

---

[4] Meier-Dörnberg (1983, 1990); Mager (1990); Dockrill (1991).
[5] Zelikow and Rice (1995).   [6] Hart (1976).

in the level of control over actors occurs when allies add or subtract military commitments to collective defence. Control over resources in an alliance is measured by the assets that allies allocate, individually or collectively, for common defence purposes. A change in the balance of power occurs if one ally takes control over resources it did not control before or if resource allocation requires a multilateral rather than a unilateral decision. A member increases its control over outcomes if its stated preferences or goals become the preferences or goals of the entire alliance. A change in the levels of control over outcomes occurs when the alliance shifts its preferences or goals in favour of one or more member states.

Historical analysis shows that Germany increased its control on all three dimensions, and therefore that German power within the alliance grew.[7]

Control over actors

The Federal Republic's control over its allies increased dramatically within the first ten years of its NATO membership. It forced its allies to substantiate in military terms their declaratory article 5 commitments to the FRG by moving NATO's first line of defence from the Rhine eastward to the Elbe and establishing the strategy of 'forward defence'. 'Forward defence' meant that the territory of the FRG was no longer considered the main NATO– Soviet battlefield. The Federal Republic also succeeded in reducing the number of targets on German territory that would come under nuclear attack in case of war.[8] These improvements to Germany's defence and security situation required detailed changes in allied military planning, strategy and tactics, force deployments, weaponry and equipment, roles and missions, nuclear targeting, training, and the like. They affected all foreign troops stationed in Germany as much as the German army. They clearly indicated an increased allied commitment to the collective defence of the FRG.

In the 1960s, during the negotiations on implementing 'flexible response',[9] the United States made additional commitments of nuclear deterrence and defence beyond the original intentions of the Kennedy and Johnson administrations, particularly the acceptance of 'deliberate escalation' as a crucial element of NATO strategy.[10] This is another indication of Germany's

---

[7] On the case of the Netherlands see Megens [1994].

[8] Nuclear History Program (n.d.); Strauß (1989: 377).

[9] Freedman (1989); Stromseth (1988); Haftendorn (1996b); Pedlow [1997].

[10] It is crucial to understand that inserting 'deliberate escalation' into the MC 14/3 Document (Pedlow [1997]: 345–70) is an insufficient indicator of strategy change. More important are the

increased control over actors: the change favoured the Europeans, and Germany played a leading role as the main proponent of maintaining a strong coupling of nuclear and conventional forces in alliance military strategy.

Control over resources

Many scholars view NATO as an asymmetrical alliance, in which the United States is a security producer and the European allies are security consumers, and bilateral US–European relations as asymmetrical because the United States controls more resources than each West European country. While this view is basically correct, the asymmetry was by no means as pronounced as most scholars believed. The United States depended for at least some resources on its European allies. For example, Europeans (and Germany in particular) controlled the territory that would have become the most likely battlefield in a major war between the two opposing alliances.[11] German territory became crucial for allied troop deployments, particularly after France withdrew from NATO's military organization in 1966 and asked its allies to remove their armed forces from French territory. For Germany, the crucial change of control over resources came in 1955, when the three western powers surrendered most of their occupation rights and the Federal Republic became a sovereign state. Only then could the FRG use its territory as an asset in negotiations with its allies. Control over territory proved to be an important resource to determine how the allies deployed their forces in accordance with German defence interests.

The Paris and Bonn Treaties allowed the FRG to build armed forces, another important resource over which it gained control. These resources were further expanded, when the allies received delivery systems capable to launch nuclear weapons.[12] Initially, the allies constrained the use of German armed forces as a resource by preventing the German army from producing weapons of mass destruction and several categories of conventional

detailed military arrangements, i.e. institutions, that would have enforced this strategy in a crisis or war. Institutions such as the assignment of roles and missions to the nuclear capable aircraft of the German air force, the involvement of German officers in NATO's nuclear planning and the like convinced Germany and other non-nuclear Europeans that the allied nuclear umbrella over its territory was a credible deterrent to the Soviets and that the allies would honour their nuclear defence commitments. Daalder (1991).

[11] Some other countries, such as Norway or France after 1966, did not allow foreign troop deployments on their soil. This fact highlights the importance of control over territory within an alliance.

[12] Mellisen (1993); Nuti (1989, 1994); Mahncke (1972); Tuschhoff (1990, 1994).

weapons. But in the 1980s Germany succeeded in eliminating the limitations on conventional weapons in negotiations with the allies, and thus gained control over a wider range of military resources. Moreover, by making decisions on deployment, armament, training, roles, and missions of the growing German armed forces that provided the bulk of NATO forces in Central Europe, the Federal Republic increased its control over how NATO pursued its collective defence goals.

However, the treaties also constrained the use of these two resources—territory and armed forces—in several ways. First, the three western powers retained important rights of troop deployment in Germany; only changes of strength and deployment required the Federal Republic's permission.[13] Second, the restrictions on nuclear weapons remained in place and were incorporated into the 2+4 treaty in 1990.[14] Moreover, Germany had to agree not to develop a national chain of command for its armed forces, thus ensuring that the *Bundeswehr* could only be employed for collective defence purposes under NATO's chain of command.[15]

Finally, the building of German armed forces allowed the FRG to influence NATO's military strategy. For instance, Germany rejected US demands to re-equip its nuclear-capable delivery aircraft for dual roles, i.e. nuclear and conventional missions. Originally, the German air force and NATO had envisioned ten squadrons with a single nuclear role. When the first seven squadrons became operational in 1966, the American Secretary of Defense, Robert McNamara, declined to make more nuclear warheads available for the remaining three squadrons until after the Germans assigned a dual role to the first seven squadrons. The Federal Republic refused to budge to such American blackmail and instead accepted a primary conventional role for the three squadrons.[16] Maintaining the primacy of nuclear roles for the German air force was a deliberate decision that served two important purposes. First, it denied NATO the conventionalization of its military strategy; and second, Germany maintained the military hardware to claim participation in the nuclear decision-making of the alliance.

---

[13] Bartsch and Sauder (1994); Haftendorn and Riecke (1996). In the 2+4 Treaty of 1990 the victorious powers of the Second World War finally surrendered their residual occupational rights and responsibilities. See also Brand (1993); Zelikow and Rice (1995).

[14] Rademacher and Rentmeister (1990); Gerhold (1992); Brand (1993); Zelikow and Rice (1995).

[15] After unification the German armed forces developed their own national command and control system, which parallels NATO's chain of command. For the first time since the Second World War, German armed forces are assigned to both multilateral *and* national command authorities and can be employed outside the NATO command and control system. See Young (1996); Tuschhoff (1993a and b).

[16] Nuclear History Program (n.d.).

Control over outcomes

For measuring power relations within an alliance, the most important outcomes are agreements implementing the indivisibility of security. Usually these agreements take the form of a common military strategy. The military strategy of an alliance consists of two components. The first component is the military doctrine as outlined in alliance documents.[17] The second component consists of force deployments, weapons procurements, and command and control arrangements and the like to implement the strategy.[18] The military strategy of an alliance does not depend primarily on the political documents but rather on the military capabilities that each member assigns to its collective defence. Military strategy gives a good indication of allied commitments. To the extent that allies are able to change alliance strategy to better reflect their national preferences they gain control over outcomes.

Comparing NATO's earlier strategy of 'massive retaliation' to its later strategy of 'flexible response' is instructive. The former completely corresponded to the United States' preferences, while the latter failed to respond to some of the most important new goals of 'The McNamara Strategy'.[19] NATO's 'flexible response' entailed an element of 'deliberate escalation', which the Kennedy and Johnson administrations had attempted to avoid. In the strategy eventually adopted, NATO reserved the right of nuclear first use if a conventional attack engaged at least three NATO divisions and could not be effectively repulsed. This outcome reflected European—and most prominently German—preferences. It rejected optimistic American threat assessments and US demands to improve conventional European capabilities, and it increased foreign troop deployments. As a result, the United States had to accept a greater risk of nuclear escalation than it would have preferred. Robert E. Osgood coined the phrase of 'NATO—The Entangling Alliance'[20] to indicate that the US military commitment to European security exceeded its original preference. Europeans made a deliberate decision to risk American non-compliance with deliberate nuclear escalation rather than improve NATO's conventional defence capability until a conventional defence against a conventional attack was possible. This risk was acceptable because of the credible US nuclear commitment to European security. Without that commitment the non-nuclear NATO members would most

---

[17] Haftendorn (1996); Stromseth (1988). NATO recently released the text of its basic strategy documents (Pedlow 1997). For further documents see Nuclear History Program (n.d.)
[18] Rosenberg (1986).   [19] Kaufmann (1964).   [20] Osgood (1962).

likely have developed a national nuclear capability. To make the American commitment both credible and enforceable the European allies relied on institutions that explain the continued cohesiveness of and peaceful change in the alliance.

2. Explaining Cohesion and Peaceful Change

How did NATO cope with these changes? How did institutions contribute to maintaining the cohesion of the alliance? The changes in the distribution of power—increased allied commitments to the defence of the Federal Republic, the reinforcement of the indivisibility of defence, and the strengthening of alliance cohesion—cannot be explained without crediting alliance institutions. Institutions thus helped NATO and its member states to monitor and enforce national commitments to collective defence.

The integrated defence planning system of NATO[21] linked national and international planning procedures, thus forcing states to make and stick to commitments beyond their national preferences. The planning procedures fed NATO force goals into national defence planning and set priorities that national governments could not ignore, since they had in turn to report their national goals to NATO. Planning cycles enforced deadlines for national responses to NATO force requirements. Governments also had to report and justify any shortcomings. The distribution of these data and of comments by the NATO international staff created an extraordinary transparency on national commitments and on the implementation of collective defence. Governments understood that they risked the solidarity of their allies if they did not contribute their fair share to NATO's military capabilities. This exchange of national defence data made it very difficult to cheat, because the data on national capabilities and defence plans had to meet a standardized NATO format. This made it easy to detect a negligent ally.

The international planning process set timetables that national governments had to meet, and these alliance timetables served as a strait-jacket for national military planners, since governments, parliaments, and bureaucracies had to stick to a sequence of decisions or risk missing NATO's deadlines. NATO's defence planning system established a number of different decision-making cycles—on force goals (five years), ministerial guidance (three years), and annual review questionnaires (one year)—

---

[21] Baldauf (1984); also NATO Information Service (1989: 219–26). For a similar argument on how intergovernmental European Union institutions change national preferences by applying the so-called 'community method' see Lewis (1998); Hayes-Renshaw and Wallace (1997).

to which national governments had to respond. The shorter the cycle, the firmer the commitment of national defence plans to NATO goals.[22] National governments could not opt out of this process and had to justify any deviation from NATO goals. Given the monitoring ability of NATO and all the allies, such justifications had to be very solid. The NATO defence planning system thus forced national governments to make firm commitments and reasonable contributions to collective defence that met their allies' expectations. It prevented governments from free-riding, inaction, or cheating. Allies were accountable to the same standards. The defence planning system also provided a useful tool for monitoring allied behaviour. Governments and states came under tight scrutiny and could easily lose their peers' trust if they missed NATO force goals. Their defence planning could no longer follow the logic of national interests and preferences but had to conform to the logic of jointly established force goals of NATO collective defence planning.

Participation and representation

The Eisenhower administration used NATO force planning for setting goals for European defence institutions and to monitor compliance. 'Massive retaliation' was implemented without noticeable European or German resistance in NATO. At that time few German officers held high command posts in NATO because the FRG in the 1950s did not contribute many troops to collective defence missions. Furthermore, US officers effectively guarded all secret nuclear information on the operational consequences of nuclear weapons.[23]

When German military contributions to the collective defence increased, its influence on the making of strategy grew considerably.[24] German representation and participation in NATO's military organization was an

---

[22] The strong link between national and multilateral defence planning processes that strengthens and enforces national commitments to collective defence is similar to the relationship between big modern companies and suppliers. In both cases, planning systems based on a number of cycles varying in length increase mutual predictability, enforce commitments, and monitor behaviour. Coriat (1997).

[23] Nuclear History Program (1989/90a).

[24] The Federal Republic used control over its military resources to influence NATO strategy. The American effort to implement a strategy of 'flexible response' failed because the European allies individually and collectively were unwilling to substantially increase their conventional forces and to disassociate NATO forces that had a conventional *and* a nuclear role (Nuclear History Program, n.d.). Europeans agreed only to raise the nuclear threshold, but forced the United States to maintain and strengthen its commitment to escalate to a nuclear war level if the threshold was crossed.

important first step towards assuming more control over collective defence commitments. German officers gained increased access to NATO head-quarters and command posts when Germany assigned more armed forces to the alliance. When they participated in the detailed exchange of crucial military information, they quickly learnt about the deficits of NATO defence planning in regard to German security.[25] By feeding their own planning papers to SACEUR, the supreme NATO commander in Europe, and an American four-star general, German officers were influencing allied military planning and subtly nudging it in a direction more conducive to Germany's defence interests.[26] When their nuclear aircraft entered service, German officers started to participate in the organization for nuclear planning of the Supreme Headquarters of Allied Powers in Europe (SHAPE). Figure 5.1 shows SHAPE's nuclear planning organization of 1963 by position, country, service, and rank of the officer involved. NATO's planning for nuclear targeting required the cooperation of all national units equipped with nuclear delivery systems to coordinate targeting and employment of nuclear weapons. As soon as German commanders of strike aircraft units participated in the targeting conferences of NATO's tactical air forces, they received full information about NATO's entire nuclear strike plan.[27] NATO military institutions thus provided Germany with access to crucial information with which they could monitor allied military planning. This access was a crucial first step towards changing the allies' strategic preferences.

Modification of loyalty

Alliance institutions created more complex loyalties within individuals who worked for NATO. American officers serving in NATO headquarters, including SACEUR, often sided with the European allies rather than with their national government. As NATO officers they served as a source of impartial military expertise. The complex multinational loyalty of NATO officers made possible more equitable solutions to the problem of control over allied military resources than were available in non-integrated alliances. Military integration is an international institution operating in an alliance;

---

[25] Kelleher (1975); Nuclear History Program (n.d., 1989/90b); Strauß (1989: 377).

[26] Tuschhoff (1993b, 1994). The Chairman of the Joint Chiefs of Staff, General Lyman L. Lemnitzer, observed in late 1961: '[T]he Germans were the source of three important initiatives for this meeting. In actual fact, they proposed yet a fourth (...) [W]e may expect increasing effort by the Germans to be accepted fully into all aspects of NATO military activity.' (FRUS, 1994: 351).

[27] The high number of nuclear targets and the redundancy of their planned destruction surprised German officers. For some targets NATO planned five different missions. Nuclear History Program (1989/90b).

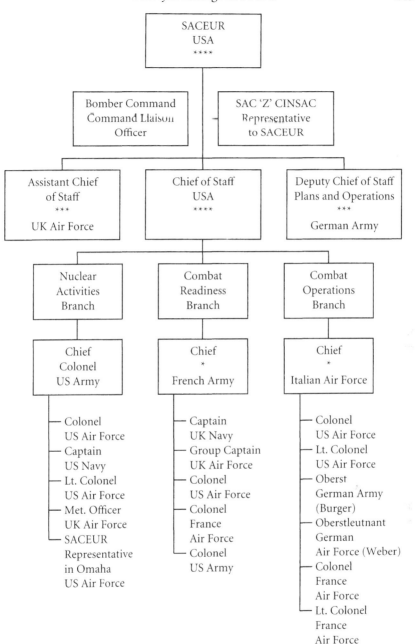

FIGURE 5.1. SHAPE Organization for Nuclear Planning 1963
(Nuclear History Program)

it provides a much larger set of options for solving the complicated problems of control over resources. The impartiality of NATO commanders also made national concessions easier, because they helped governments save face. NATO members would rather concede to an impartial allied commander than to another ally.[28] National governments realized that these officers were not just loyal representatives of their countries of origin but military experts deeply committed to the collective defence of the alliance.[29] This reputation gave recommendations and demands from NATO headquarters an air of objectivity that made them hard to reject.

The expertise of NATO commanders also became a convenient negotiating tool. The Europeans frequently used the expertise of SACEUR as a supporting argument when they negotiated with the US government. The administration in Washington could not easily dismiss a recommendation or demand by SACEUR, who was not only an American but also served as the supreme commander of US forces in Europe. NATO's secretary-general often acted as a mediator between nuclear and non-nuclear members of the alliance and catalyzed converging expectations.[30]

NATO held frequent military exercises to test its military capabilities and plans. Allied bilateral or multilateral study groups scrutinized the feasibility of new plans. The Europeans used these institutions to bring home to the American military that a conventionalization of European armed forces was impossible because NATO would lose the battle even if it increased conventional forces to levels proposed by the US.[31] The results of multilateral exercises and study groups convinced NATO members—particularly, in this case, the Americans—that their national preferences had to be adjusted. Since all proposals on the adaptation of military strategy were discussed in several NATO institutions, no single government was able to control the outcome of this rather technically and bureaucratically involved process. This decision-making method gave all allies an equal voice over time, as their proposals were tested against the same standards of feasibility.

---

[28] I am grateful to Ernest May for bringing this argument to my attention.

[29] Nuclear History Program (n.d.). NATO's secretary-general, Dirk Stikker pointed out that SACEUR, General Lauris Norstad, 'was regarded as an international commander with a completely independent status' (FRUS, 1994: 318).

[30] One example is Dirk Stikker's intervention in Washington that facilitated the approval of the Athens Guidelines (FRUS, 1994: 357–64). He based his proposal of 'Control of Nuclear Weapons' of 23 Jan. 1962, that became known as NDP 62/2, on a German initiative (Nuclear History Program, n.d.). President Kennedy concluded from his conversation with Stikker 'that the Germans might well have a "natural concern" as to the circumstances under which the United States would decide (. . .) to use nuclear weapons' (FRUS, 1994: 363). In response to the President's enquiry Stikker responded that Germany would be satisfied with a 'voice' in the nuclear decision-making process and would not use its 'exit' option. Ibid.   [31] Nuclear History Program (n.d.).

Institutional mechanisms

Alliance institutions helped national governments monitor the compliance of their allies with their defence commitments. NATO's system of information exchange reduced mutual uncertainty and increased the predictability of behaviour in case of attack. These institutions reinforced the principle of indivisible security. Taken together, the three functions of NATO institutions—monitoring, information exchange, and enforcement—helped maintain the cohesion of NATO when the underlying balance of power shifted.

Monitoring: In an alliance member states face two problems of uncertainty that they find hard to resolve without the support of multilateral institutions. First, an ally can build military strength for collective defence purposes that other allies perceive as threatening to their own security because current allies may turn into future enemies. Second, a state may enjoy the protection of collective defence without contributing a fair share to the common defence burden but decide to 'free ride'. NATO institutions addressed both problems of uncertainty effectively, despite continuous political debates on 'the German threat' and 'burden sharing'.

NATO's defence planning system required members to disclose their current military capabilities and their future force goals as well as their financial and industrial capacities. NATO's standardized questionnaires and answer formats ensured the comprehensiveness of disclosure and made the members' information readily comparable. The alliance supplied all members with pertinent information on the military strength and capability of all partners along with an independent assessment by NATO experts, thus providing evidence whether or not states met their collective military commitments without threatening one another. All the allies could monitor one another's actions and military preparedness because NATO not only collected but also distributed to all members the answers to its annual review questionnaire.[32] The standardized format increased mutual transparency. The disclosed data allowed members to assess the current and future military capabilities of their allies and determine the impact on their own security. The institution of NATO's defence planning system reduced the uncertainty of military threat.

The standard operating procedures of the integrated military planning system were also crucial to the monitoring and enforcement of force goals.

---

[32] Baldauf (1984); also NATO Information Service (1989: 219–26).

Agreements on NATO's ministerial guidance and national force goals set the standards against which actions could be measured in order to detect a free-rider. In this respect the financial and industrial capacity data became important measures. Furthermore, NATO staff and national defence experts compared the data to both national and NATO force goals to assess whether the member states met their goals and commitments. In case of a discrepancy the member was asked to explain the difference and correct its failure. This information helped to assess whether the collective defence burden was fairly shared among all members. Thus, the institution of the NATO defence planning system reduced uncertainty of free-riding.

The change in the balance of power would have been unthinkable without the facilitating role of NATO institutions, which allowed member states to monitor their partners' compliance with force goals and allied commitments. This monitoring constrained state behaviour because unilateral actions would have been detected and counteracted immediately. Multinational cooperation in NATO's military organization also eliminated the possibility that the United States could unilaterally reduce its commitment to extended deterrence without European detection. In consequence, the United States shied away from using a reduction in its commitment to extended deterrence as a way of forcing the Europeans to improve their conventional defences, even though such a move would have served the American interest in modifying the new NATO strategy.[33] Even when the Europeans did not meet the American demand for improved conventional defence capabilities, the US did not abrogate its commitment, since unilateral action would have been counterproductive. Instead, the US government decided to consult with its allies in order to find a solution to their disagreements over NATO military strategy.

Monitoring of behaviour also helped governments build a reputation for faithfully adhering to joint commitments. It was especially important for Germany, which hoped to exercise great control eventually over NATO's military capacity, that it had achieved a reputation as a reliable and trustworthy partner.[34] It was important for Germany to prove that it was

[33] The Kennedy and Johnson administrations frequently linked their promise to maintain and improve extended deterrence to the precondition that the European allies improve their conventional defence capabilities e.g. the May 1961 Ottawa speech of President Kennedy. Schwartz (1983: 87–9).

[34] These efforts first failed when the newly appointed German Defence Minister, Franz Josef Strauß, was forced to admit at a NATO Council meeting on 29 Oct. 1956 that he would miss the target of building a 500,000 troops army by 1958 (Greiner, 1993). This was not a revelation to the other allies due to NATO's information exchange system. Strauß reorganized the German defence planning system to meet both national and NATO targets. Subsequently, the FRG fulfilled most of

committed to collective defence and would live up to allied expectations. It continuously signalled to NATO and its partners that it met and would continue to meet collective defence requirements, and it used the monitoring channels of the alliance to reassure its members that its growing military capabilities were not directed against any of them.

The system of integrated planning created standardized formats of information exchange and provided transparency, which made it impossible for the allies to keep military secrets from one another and reassured them of their partners' peaceful intentions. The role of institutions in confidence-building and reassurance can hardly be overestimated. It was the institutionally constructed accountability of Germany's intentions and the predictability of its foreign and defence policy that allowed NATO members to concede to the Federal Republic a larger degree of control over resources.[35] The asymmetry of capabilities between Germany and its allies was reduced over time. Without NATO institutions, its partners would hardly have agreed to a gradual reduction and eventual elimination of constraining measures against a re-emerging Germany. The most important hedge that remained in place until 1990 was Germany's membership and participation in the integrated military organization of NATO.[36]

Exchange of information: German participation in NATO planning, policy-making, and information exchange were the two most important instruments allowing the Federal Republic to catch up with its allies. The exchange of information affected the options of all the allies. In particular, the United States maintained its commitment to extended nuclear deterrence in exchange for a commitment from its non-nuclear partners in Europe not to develop a national nuclear capability.[37] Such a tacit bargain required ongoing mutual reassurance. Without NATO's information exchange system, this reassurance would have been impossible.

Nuclear and non-nuclear NATO partners exchanged reassuring information continuously when they planned and exercised the targeting and

---

NATO's force goals and delivered on its commitments to collective defence although it often missed NATO's timetable (Nuclear History Program, n.d.). The FRG thus earned a reputation in Washington of being the most reliable and dependable ally in Europe.

[35] The allies lifted arms control limitations on German forces and defence industry only after NATO commanders had certified that these measures were militarily required and posed no threat to the other allies because Germany had become a reliable ally (Rademacher and Rentmeister, 1990; Gerhold, 1992).

[36] On the constraining *and* enabling effects of NATO institutions such as the command and control system and the alarm system see below.

[37] Haftendorn (1996*b*).

employment of nuclear forces.[38] Participation in these standard operating procedures informed the Europeans about US nuclear policies and the American commitment to nuclear deterrence and defence. Since this commitment was essential to the European decision not to become nuclear, close monitoring of and control over American decisions was crucial. The cooperative relationship between nuclear and non-nuclear members in NATO continued because alliance procedures for nuclear planning, targeting, and decision-making satisfied the needs of both. They reassured the non-nuclear states of the continued commitment of the nuclear powers to deterrence and defence, and their access to NATO planning and decision-making processes in turn served to influence the nuclear powers. Alliance institutions thus reduced uncertainty and improved accountability.

The exchange of secret information on nuclear weapons also changed the relative influence of allies on military strategy. After the United States released and delivered major weapons systems—most importantly nuclear-capable delivery systems—to its European allies, it partially lost control over these resources.[39] It could no longer unilaterally determine the roles and missions of European forces. The Europeans claimed the right to employ their forces—including nuclear-capable delivery systems—in accordance with their defence interests.[40] They had therefore to participate in the strategy-making process of the alliance. 'Flexible response' became the first NATO military strategy that reflected both American and European interests. The Europeans also forced the United States to maintain a sizeable stock of nuclear weapons in Europe and not to reduce it without prior European consent. The United States briefed its European allies regularly on the status of its nuclear stocks and on the availability of nuclear weapons for European delivery means.[41]

The NATO members also exchanged threat assessment data through alliance channels and analysed them thoroughly. This exchange of data and estimates was complemented by information from national intelligence agencies. NATO's information-gathering exchange system deeply penet-

---

[38] Nuclear History Program (1989/90*b*).

[39] For instance, the US government linked proliferation of nuclear capable delivery systems such as the Sergeant and Pershing missiles to Germany to 'increased efforts' of the Germans to strengthen their conventional defence capabilities (Nuclear History Program, n.d.). Contrary to these American preconditions the German government decided to make participating and strengthening NATO's nuclear deterrence capability its first priority, to which the improvement of conventional defence had to be subordinated (*Akten*, 1994: 514–15). However, the United States never carried out the threat to enforce these linkages despite the German non-compliance with its conditions.

[40] See section on control over resources above.

[41] Nuclear History Program (n.d.).

rated national governments and made conflicting data available to all allies. Through this system, NATO created an enormous amount of transparency among its members. When Robert McNamara presented the US threat assessment to NATO defence ministers at Athens in 1962, the Europeans analysed the American data and compared them with their own intelligence estimates. They concluded that McNamara's evaluation was overly optimistic and did not take into account some important Warsaw Pact capabilities. Most significantly, McNamara's count had left out, in his comparison of NATO and Warsaw Pact strength, the East European armed forces. On the basis of their own estimates, the Europeans demonstrated that the Pentagon's data and analysis did not conform with military realities. Moreover, through NATO channels, the Europeans received alternate US assessments of Warsaw Pact military capabilities by the US Defense Intelligence Agency (DIA).[42] After correcting McNamara's figures, the analysis showed that NATO was not capable of defending against a major conventional attack without using nuclear weapons. The alliance was also unlikely to develop such a capability even if the Europeans met the force goals that McNamara proposed. As a consequence, the Secretary of Defense had to adapt his idea of a 'flexible response' strategy. In this instance, NATO helped its members arrive at a common analysis of conflicting national threat assessments that provided the basis for realistic conclusions and policy recommendations.

Facilitating concessions: Institutions help governments to make concessions or accept compromises if the alliance, rather than other governments, can play the role of moderator. Giving in to an international organization is more palatable for several reasons. First, a government may trust an international organization more than it trusts another ally. Second, a member can monitor compliance with the decisions taken. Third, international organizations provide legitimacy for the monitoring of concessions. And fourth, governments have a chance to renegotiate their concessions later on.

NATO's military commanders and their supporting staff played a crucial role in negotiating and renegotiating complicated military arrangements of combined allied and German control over resources. When the German government assigned its armed forces to the operational command of SACEUR and his subordinate commanders, it was confident that in case of an attack on Germany he would loyally defend it even though he was an American national. The German government would in all likelihood not have accepted exclusive operational command by a (non-NATO) American

---

[42] Ibid.

commander over the German armed forces. Successive SACEURs fully justified this German trust. They worked hard on military arrangements that safeguarded Germany's security, such as forward defence and the 'layer cake' force deployment structure that substantiated the collective defence of Germany.[43]

Once the Federal Republic had regained control over its territory and its armed forces in 1955, several institutions put the use of these German resources under certain constraints. For the German government, it was much easier to accept restrictions administered by NATO or the West European Union (WEU), which it considered legitimate international organizations, than those imposed by other countries. Germany participated in the decision-making processes of both organizations and even had veto power in both. The German government also hoped that these controls would be lifted once the FRG had proved its credibility and reliability as an ally. It would eventually emerge as a normal, sovereign state, trusted by its allies, and gain full control over its resources. NATO offered the institutional means to fulfil this German aspiration. These understandings between Germany and the other allies would not have been possible without the involvement of NATO commanders, who provided impartial assessment and military expertise.[44]

Over time the Federal Republic proved to be a reliable and accountable ally—trusted to control its own resources without becoming a threat again. Thus, with few exceptions, allied constraints on German resources were lifted and control over resources returned to the federal government. NATO commanders again played a crucial role in eliminating conventional arms restrictions on the *Bundeswehr* by arguing that these changes served collective defence purposes.[45] Again, the allies found it easier to accept an impartial recommendation than a German demand. Statements and recommendations by NATO commanders possessed a higher degree of legitimacy and credibility than national ones.

Enforcement of national commitments: Finally, NATO institutions helped its members enforce mutual defence commitments and secure the principle of indivisible defence. The Federal Republic's demand that NATO implement a strategy of forward defence and that allied territory should be defended up to the Elbe rather than the Rhine was implemented in 1964. The deploy-

---

[43] For further explanation of the 'layer cake' see section on enforcement of national commitments below.

[44] Meier-Dörnberg (1983; 1990).

[45] Rademacher and Rentmeister (1990).

ment of allied forces changed to a 'layer cake' pattern. The various national forces were deployed and assigned small parts of the German territory to defend alongside one another. It ensured that any attack on the Federal Republic would affect all allied forces deployed and almost automatically trigger a collective response. The layer cake pattern 'wrote the principle of indivisibility of defense among allies in the German terrain', as one retired German general put it. This institution effectively enforced national commitments to the indivisibility of conventional defence and served to reassure the Federal Republic. By agreeing to the new force deployment pattern, Germany's allies assumed more responsibilities and risks for the defence of Germany's territorial integrity than before.

Also, all allied forces deployed in the layer cake pattern had comparable military strength in terms of troops, armament, equipment, training, command, and control. The integration of nuclear weapons into the forces of non-nuclear allies played an important role in providing similar strength to all allies. Facing a united front of NATO forces from different countries denied the Warsaw Treaty Organization the option of concentrating an attack on the weakest NATO member and increased the deterrence value of the alliance. The integration of nuclear-capable delivery means into the armed forces of non-nuclear allies also reassured them of their nuclear guardians' unconditional commitment.

Furthermore, NATO's alert system served as a major reassurance that allies would honour their commitments in case of an attack. It consisted of several alarm plans such as simple alert, reinforced alert, counter surprise, state orange, or state scarlet. The latter two served to survive a surprise air raid and entailed only defensive measures. SACEUR was authorized to issue these alerts when an attack met their contingencies. Simple alert and reinforced alert required the consensus of national governments because they implied the full mobilization of national armed forces and put them under the operational command of SACEUR. However, several NATO members including the FRG authorized SACEUR to issue simple alert in case of an emergency that required immediate action. Thus, the supreme commander of allied forces in Europe had considerable discretion to mobilize national forces without government approval and to put them under his command. Such pre-delegated authority ensured the effectiveness of NATO's defence and severely restricted national obstructions to its collective defence.[46] The transfer of national sovereignty to a military commander emphasized both the role of SACEUR as supreme commander and the trust of national

---

[46] Trebesch (1988). See also Kelleher (1987); Carnovale (1993).

governments in his military prudence and impartial political judgement. In short, the principle of the indivisibility of defence was implemented by military arrangements rather than merely by a political promise. The principle of indivisibility of defence thus improved the cohesion of the alliance.

Consultative procedures on the employment of NATO-assigned nuclear weapons further reinforced collective commitments. These procedures predetermined the allies' reaction, depending on the type of attack, and restricted their range of choices in a crisis.[47] Several stages in the development of nuclear consultation procedures among NATO allies can be identified: the Athens guidelines of 1962, the provisional nuclear guidelines of 1969,[48] and the general nuclear guidelines of 1982. All three sets of consultation and employment guidelines were standard operating procedures that limited the range of choices of nuclear and non-nuclear allies, because crucial decisions as to the contingencies and conditions of nuclear weapons employment had already been made in peacetime.[49] These procedures coupled requirements for allied consultation, *predetermined* types of military responses and conditions for nuclear employment, to the nature of an attack. The guidelines were not merely a set of recommended rules, but important decision-making procedures. They circumscribed the questions addressed and the range of options available. The NATO guidelines structured, simplified, and accelerated decision-making on whether or not to employ nuclear weapons in case of an attack. NATO members could monitor the compliance of their allies by analysing their peacetime military deployment and their behaviour in military exercises.

This argument can be further illustrated by a closer look at the Athens Guidelines of 1962. With these guidelines, the United States for the first time subjected itself to a standard operating procedure that dramatically reduced its range of options in a crisis. The guidelines reassured the Europeans about the American response to Soviet aggression and increased the United States' predictability and reliability.[50] The political significance of the guidelines was that they represented a predetermined step-by-step decision-making procedure that constrained the options available to all allies in case of an attack. NATO would choose the type of aggression, the

[47] A recent newspaper article even stated that 'Germany has had practical joint control with the United States over the American nuclear weapons stationed on its soil.' Craig R. Whitney: 'France, Germany to Open Talks on European Nuclear Defense', *New York Times* (25 Jan. 1997).

[48] Daalder (1991: 72–9).

[49] See also section on exchange of information above.

[50] The text of the Athens Guidelines can be found in Nuclear History Program (n.d.) and in FRUS (1994: 347, 385–93).

required form of consultation, the type and extent of its response. During each step, allies were required to choose among preselected options that were not open to reconsideration. The guidelines were a classic standard operating procedure for decision-makers to follow when making their choice on how to respond to an attack. They were no longer required to define the situation and the sequence of their decisions but could follow a checklist. The checklist entailed the predetermined commitment on how the allies would respond to various attacks. As such, the guidelines led to converging expectations. They facilitated a further reduction of uncertainty when decision-makers practised them during major NATO exercises.

All three elements—the agreement on standard operating procedures, the compatibility of military deployments with mutual defence commitments, and the monitoring of allied behaviour in military exercises—increased mutual transparency and confidence that allies would honour their agreements. Without these institutions the national commitments to collective defence would not have been enforceable and credible. In all likelihood Germany would have made very different choices when setting up its defence. It would have insisted on a national defence posture unconstrained by NATO, sought a national nuclear deterrence capability similar to France, and resisted arms control limitations of its military and defence industry. NATO's institutional mechanisms to enforce the commitment of the United States to extended deterrence were also the main reason why the FRG was never seriously interested in accepting or even further exploring the French offer to bring Germany under the nuclear umbrella of the *force de frappe*.[51] All French proposals stopped short of offering the institutional mechanisms to enforce such a French extended deterrence.

3. Conclusion

All three indicators—control over actors, resources, and outcomes—point to the same result: the balance of power within NATO gradually shifted in the 1960s from the United States towards the European allies and the Federal Republic of Germany. Germany turned its military capability into political influence and achieved a position from which it could block allied initiatives if these were thought detrimental to German security interests. NATO policies became a matter of intra-alliance bargaining and co-determination. This redistribution of capabilities, responsibilities, risks,

---

[51] *Akten* (1995: 768, 775); Carstens (1993: 255, 272); Osterheld (1992: 98–100).

burdens, and costs produced a peaceful change of relations among allies. In practice—though not in formal status—the difference between nuclear and non-nuclear powers narrowed.

How did the alliance cope with this dramatic change in the balance of power? Organizational structures and standard operating procedures within alliance institutions contributed significantly to the necessary readjustment. NATO offered its members an opportunity to participate in joint military and political decision-making. Without this opportunity, vital interests of alliance members would have been neglected. Representation in NATO staff and headquarters facilitated the adaptation of the alliance's military strategy and force deployments. Presence in allied headquarters produced a change in individual officers from national loyalties to more complex alliance loyalties. Conflicts were settled on the impartial advice of NATO's military commanders, whose proposals had a higher degree of legitimacy than suggestions and demands from national governments would have had. The devotion of NATO officers to collective defence also made it easier for governments to sell concessions to their domestic audience as being in the interest of NATO rather than of another member. The reputation for impartiality of NATO commanders became an important device for changing members' preferences from national to collective defence interests and international agreements.

Alliance institutions also reduced the uncertainty among members in other ways. Allies were able to establish positive reputations through co-operation with other members and within NATO's institutions. Standard operating procedures penetrated national decision-making procedures and created transparency among allies. The ability to reassure other states that no member was a security threat to others removed the necessity to hedge unilaterally against such contingencies. Trust and reassurance allowed for a redistribution of power without any ally exiting from the alliance. Non-nuclear powers refrained from developing a national nuclear capability because NATO institutions allowed nuclear sharing arrangements and assured co-determination on collective defence needs between non-nuclear and nuclear states. NATO procedures established an unprecedented system of information exchange beyond the control of national governments. Despite continuing differences in control over resources, members gained more equal opportunities to influence NATO processes as their levels of information converged.

NATO institutions allowed its members to monitor closely the extent of other members' compliance with alliance policies and the implementation of collective defence. In this way, alliance institutions served as a means to enforce the principle of the indivisibility of defence, upon which the alliance was based. Institutional support for its enforcement strengthened the cohesiveness of the alliance. The implementation and enforcement of NATO policy was institutionally reinforced as standard operating procedures and forced states to respond to alliance requests within a definite time frame. National defence planning procedures had to be adjusted to meet NATO deadlines. NATO's standard operating procedures thus compelled states to work towards collective defence goals and circumscribed their national room for manoeuvre in military matters.

Most importantly, institutional mechanisms such as the 'layer cake' pattern deployment of allied forces in Germany, consultation and decision-making procedures to employ NATO's nuclear weapons, and NATO's alert system enforced the alliance principle of indivisibility of security. These institutions guaranteed that national commitments to collective defence were enforceable and thus credible. States could trust their allies.

NATO partners chose multilateral, cooperative strategies instead of unilateral, confrontational ones in reacting to changes in the internal dynamics of NATO. Alliance institutions constrained national options and opened up international ones that would have been less available or practicable in their absence. NATO retained its cohesion because its institutions allowed its members to maintain and increase their mutual defence commitments, monitor compliance, exchange information, and enforce agreements.

6

THE 'QUAD': DYNAMICS OF INSTITUTIONAL CHANGE

Helga Haftendorn

1. Three Puzzles

Few institutions in international affairs have started with an explicit concern that they not be formally institutionalized. When the 'Interallied Working Group on Questions Relating to the So-called GDR, Berlin and the Transit Routes' first met on 14 December 1955, at the suggestion of the United States, no one in the six-year-old Federal Republic of Germany wanted any hint of a prolongation of the occupation regime which had ended only a few months before. The three western powers (France, Britain, and the United States) wished to consult with Bonn about technical issues concerning Berlin and intra-German relations, and they wished to do so on a very low administrative level whenever the latter's cooperation was necessary. They were loath, however, to involve the Federal Republic in any issue they considered their allied prerogative, such as contingency planning for Berlin. This is a first puzzle: why did the Quad[1] evolve from this feeble

Research for this paper was supported by the Max Planck and the Alexander von Humboldt Societies. Its factual basis draws on a project on allied rights and responsibilities that was supported by the German Science Foundation (DFG). For constructive criticism and helpful suggestions I wish to thank the members of the ATASP-CFIA group on security institutions, especially Robert O. Keohane, Carsten Tams, and Celeste A. Wallander. I owe special thanks to Christina Moritz and Carsten Tams for their expert research assistance.

[1] In this paper, the term 'Quad' in a general sense denotes the various formalized quadripartite activities, such as the Interallied Working Group, the Washington Ambassadorial Group, the Bonn Group, the foreign ministers' 'German Dinners', and the political directors' meetings. Understood in a restricted sense, the term 'Quad' refers to the regular meetings among the political directors in the foreign ministries of France, Great Britain, the United States, and the Federal Republic of Germany. Quad meetings on all of these levels provided a venue for the exchange of information, informal talks, consultation, and negotiation, but not for joint decision-making. Decisions were taken by appropriate national government officials and bodies or at the NATO Council.

beginning into an institution with elaborate rules and a multi-levelled structure that existed—though with changes in its function and form—for more than thirty-five years?

When Germany was unified in 1990 and the allied rights and responsibilities[2] were terminated, the legal and the political justifications for the Quad ended. The legal basis for this allied participation in (intra) German affairs was the special rights and responsibilities the three powers had retained in the General Treaty, which was in force from 1955 to 1990. In this treaty the allies[3] agreed to consult with the Federal Republic about the execution of these rights. Its political mandate was to coordinate allied and German policies regarding Berlin and Germany as a whole. Formally, the last meeting of the Quad took place on 25 September 1990. In practice, however, the four-nation consultations continued on various levels and at different places with little loss in effectiveness, though on a low level of institutionalization. This is a second puzzle. How and why can an institution persist that has lost its legal basis, (official) political function, and even its recognized form? What made it so indispensable that the members thought it wise to maintain it, albeit clouded in secrecy?

Of even more interest is a third puzzle. When the inter-allied consultations started in December 1955, they were convened to control West Germany after military occupation had ended and to manage the German question as long as the division of Germany and Europe continued. Co-ordination of practical matters arising from the division and the special status of Berlin was the purpose of these consultations. Over time, the Quad evolved into an unofficial steering group within the Western Alliance with German participation, which gave the Federal Republic a prominent role alongside the United States, Great Britain, and France in security matters. Why and under what conditions did an institution that was created as an instrument of control afford Germany—the object of that control—a

---

[2] In the 'Convention on Relations Between the Three Powers and the Federal Republic of Germany, May 26, 1952, As Amended by Schedule I of the Protocol of Termination of the Occupation Regime in Germany, Signed at Paris, October 23, 1954', the allies had retained rights and responsibilities relating to Berlin and Germany as a whole, including the reunification of Germany and a peace settlement, and, in a more circumscribed way, to the stationing of armed forces in Germany. For the text see US Department of State (1985: 425–30). Further Four Power rights, relating to the continued allied occupation of Berlin, Germany's borders, and the question of German reunification, were shared with the Soviet Union (ibid. 54–65).

[3] In conformity with the word's usage in Germany, referring to the Allied High Commission in Germany during occupation rule, I mean by 'allies' the three nations—France, United Kingdom, United States—with special rights and responsibilities concerning Berlin and Germany as a whole. The term 'Four Powers' is reserved to denominate those three above nations plus the Soviet Union, the fourth main victor of the Second World War.

considerable say in quadripartite activities? How was this shift in power[4] effected?

In this paper, I will review a number of concepts and hypotheses which have been developed in the Introduction and in Chapter 1.[5] These will be applied to a little-known post-Second World War security institution, the Quad. Security institutions, like all other institutions, comprise persistent and connected sets of rules that prescribe action for participants and influence expectations about future cooperative behaviour. They have the specific task of protecting the territory and the integrity of a member state against the use of military force and against the political effects of such use.[6] The most explicit security institutions are alliances directed against an external threat. During the Berlin crisis of 1959–61 the Quad functioned as an alliance when it dealt with the Soviet threat against Berlin, but throughout its existence the Quad was a security management institution focused on specific endogenous risks.[7] Its main functions were the containment of Germany, the management of *détente*, and the development of an equitable international framework for Germany's reunification in 1990. The Quad's norms and procedures enabled the four governments to obtain and provide information as well as to manage disputes arising from the German question through mutual consultation.

The Quad's ability to adjust its functions over time has been remarkable. Equally remarkable has been the adaptation of its institutional design or form. We may define 'form' as a set of norms, rules, and procedures that constitute an institution. They regularize members' behaviour and control its effects.[8] Norms are standards of behaviour, defined in terms of rights and obligations. Rules are specific prescriptions or proscriptions.[9] Decision-making procedures are established practices for making and implementing collective choices. Also of importance are membership and size, level and frequency of meetings, mandate, and authority. Depending on the specificity of norms, rules, and procedures[10] an institution may be highly institutionalized or may operate on a low level of authority and frequency.

After a look at the multifaceted history of the Quad, I will try to solve the

---

[4] 'Power' can be understood in a number of ways. I am primarily interested in control over policy outcomes, less so in control over resources and control over actors. See Hart (1976).

[5] See Wallander, Haftendorn, and Keohane, above, Introduction; Wallander and Keohane, above, Ch. 1.   [6] See Introduction, p. 2.

[7] For this distinction see Wallander and Keohane, Ch. 1.

[8] See Keohane and Nye (1977: 19).

[9] See Krasner (1983*a*: 2). In the German usage, the term 'norms' corresponds to rules regulating behaviour (*Verhaltensregeln*), while 'rules' refer to procedural rules (*Verfahrensregeln*).

[10] See Wallander and Keohane, above, Ch. 1.

three puzzles outlined above. First, the Quad's remarkable process of institutionalization, linking the specificity of its norms, rules, and procedures with the changing nature of the cooperation problem, will be explored. Next, the Quad's persistence in the absence of much functional differentiation—indeed, after its original functions had become obsolete—will be explained. Neither of the explanations given by Keohane and Wallander—issue density or problem durability and hybridization[11]—fits this case very well. Instead, I assume that the Quad owes its perplexing persistence and adaptability to the high degree in which its procedures and practices were valued by its members. Finally, the redistribution of power within the Quad will be analysed. Realist references to the increased power of the Federal Republic give partial answers at most. I believe that Germany's increased role in alliance affairs corresponded to the degree of commonality[12] achieved within the Quad, especially the degree to which the German government conformed to its partners' expectations of appropriate behaviour. Using in this way the nature of the cooperation problem, members' valuation and the degree of commonality as explanatory variables, I hope to gain some clues on the Quad's dynamics of change, particularly regarding its institutional specificity, its persistence and portability, and its internal redistribution of power.

2. The History of the Quad: Institutional Adaptation and Change

Its highly secretive nature has made the Quad one of the most understudied contemporary institutions.[13] It is therefore appropriate to start with its remarkable history.

---

[11] Ibid.

[12] Commonality refers to the degree to which expectations about appropriate behaviour are shared by members. See Wallander and Keohane, Ch. 1.

[13] This is underscored by a difficult archival situation. None of the foreign offices involved, to the best of my knowledge, has kept a central file on the Quad's activities. Relevant documents were filed under the issues they dealt with, such as 'Berlin', 'FRG-GDR-relations', 'Germany', or others. The thirty-year rule for the opening of official documents and their highly classified nature have also been impediments. Due to the emphasis on routine business and its low administrative level, few of these documents have been published in the *Akten zur Auswärtigen Politik der Bundesrepublik Deutschland* (Bonn), *British Foreign Policy Overseas* (London), and *Foreign Relations of the United States* (Washington) series. I have relied mostly on the collections of the Kennedy and Johnson Presidential Libraries as well as on the archives of the German Foreign Office in Bonn. In addition I conducted about sixty off-the-record interviews with Quad members and policy-makers in the four countries concerned. I also had the good fortune to obtain access to a number of private papers including diaries, timetables, and Quad agendas, on the condition of strict confidentiality. For a detailed documentation of sources see Haftendorn (1996a: 37–80).

Low-level technical discussions and
ad hoc *political consultations in the 1950s*

When an American diplomat in December 1955 approached a high-level official at the Foreign Office in Bonn and suggested creating a permanent body to coordinate intra-German and Berlin affairs between the three powers with special rights and responsibilities, on the one hand, and the Federal government on the other, he had taken into account the fact that the allies had the rights but the Germans controlled the resources. It was practical problems, such as preparing for an airlift in case of another Berlin crisis, regulating interzonal traffic, or the composition of an all-German Olympic team, that the three embassy representatives and the German desk officer discussed in the new 'Interallied Working Group on Questions Relating to the so-called GDR, Berlin and the Transit Routes'. To exchange information and to diminish uncertainty about who was doing what, they agreed to meet every other week at the level of desk officers and political counsellors, with their venue rotating between the Foreign Office and the three allied embassies in Bonn.

Both Germans and allies, however, had a hidden agenda. The Federal Republic wished to use this group as a stepping stone to being regularly included in allied consultations on the German question. It therefore argued for elevating it to the level of the Foreign Office's state secretary and the allied ambassadors in Bonn. For precisely the same reason, the allies objected to a high-level group. Given the Federal Republic's sensitivities regarding any infringements of its sovereignty, the less visible the group was, the more effect it had as an instrument of control. It gave the three powers a means to circumscribe Bonn's actions in Berlin and monitor its relations with its twin under Soviet tutelage, the German Democratic Republic (GDR). They wished to ensure that Germany posed no further risk. The quadripartite consultations were to serve as a hedge against a rise of German revisionism kindled by the division of the country, the occupation of its former capital, Berlin, and the loss of its eastern provinces.

Concerning other issues, such as German reunification and the freedom of Berlin, the allies and West Germany shared both rights and interests. When these questions were discussed at international conferences, such as the Berlin and Geneva Four Power conferences in the 1950s, both sides found it opportune to consult beforehand at the ministerial level, on an *ad hoc* basis. They thus took into account Germany's objection to anything that looked like a prolongation of the occupation regime, as well as the allies' concern that neither their rights nor their competencies should be infringed upon. They were very insistent that all consultations, other than those in the Interallied Working Group in Bonn on technical matters, not be formalized. When in early 1957 the Adenauer government continued to lobby for convening a quadripartite working group on the political level to fend off the opposition's charge that the government was not active enough in bringing about reunification, the three powers consented to more visible activities. But it was left open whether this new group was a permanent arrangement, as the Germans contended, or an *ad hoc* arrangement, as the allies insisted. For the latter, it was a palliative, designed to help the German chancellor win the next Bundestag elections. The group, consisting of the political directors from the four countries' foreign offices, was to prepare a new proposal on German reunification. Relying largely on German drafts, it produced the 'Berlin Declaration' of July 1957.[14] After serving its tactical purpose, no further meetings were held until a year later, when the Soviets put the status of Berlin into question.

These rather informal consultation processes on the political level changed when the threat to Berlin became imminent. In an immediate German reaction to Khrushchev's ultimatum of 27 November 1958, Adenauer called for a foreign ministers' conference in which the three powers and the FRG would coordinate their reactions to the Soviet challenge. With this proposal the Germans wanted to be fully included in allied consultations on Germany and Berlin. Without committing themselves to a meeting of foreign ministers, France, Britain, and the US agreed to meetings of the quadripartite working group formed the year before and commissioned it to coordinate the Western responses and to prepare a Four Power conference with the Soviets, planned for the summer. This mandate was agreed upon at a meeting between the allied foreign ministers and their German colleague on the day before the NATO ministerial conference in December 1958. Though the allies knew they could not disregard Germany's concerns, given its pivotal role in the containment of the Soviet Union, they made clear that it was their prerogative to deal with Moscow and to do it on their own terms. The FRG participated in the 1959 Geneva Foreign Ministers Conference, but as a junior partner and alongside the GDR. Bonn's input was channelled through the regular meetings of the quadripartite coordination group and the numerous meetings of the four Western foreign ministers. Plagued by far-reaching dissension between the Anglo-Saxon powers on the one side and the West Germans and the French on the other, on both

14 See 'Declaration on German Reunification by France, the Federal Republic of Germany, the United Kingdom, and the United States, Signed at Berlin, July 29, 1957', in US Department of State (1985: 510–12).

the substance and procedure of the Western negotiating position, the consultations proved of little value and were not continued once the Four Power conference was over.

The institutionalization of quadripartite consultations under the pressure of the Berlin crisis

While a resurgence of militarism and revanchism was, under the conditions of the post-war period and the elaborate precautions the Four Powers had taken to integrate the two parts of Germany into their respective security systems, a distant risk at most, the November 1958 Khrushchev ultimatum directed against the status of Berlin and the ensuing Berlin crisis had the potential to erupt into a military conflict. When in November 1959 the pressure on Berlin mounted, the four Western governments resumed quadripartite consultations to overcome their differences. For this purpose, the heads of state and of government at a meeting in December 1959—again on the eve of the NATO Council session—agreed to establish a new quadripartite working group. Made up of the Washington ambassadors of France, Britain, and Germany and the US Assistant Secretary of State for European Affairs, it was mandated to prepare new Western proposals for yet another Four Power conference. Under the leadership of the United States, which was the only power with credible means to deter the Soviet Union from abrogating Western rights in Berlin, this group met in Washington and became known as the Washington Ambassadorial Group (WAG). The advantage of this arrangement was its direct link with the US administration. A number of subgroups were formed to deal with issues that had been proposed for East–West negotiations.

Military contingency planning, especially safeguarding access to Berlin, was dealt with by the three powers separately from the ambassadorial group, by the 'Live Oak' staff in Paris, which was attached not to SACEUR but to CINCEUR. Live Oak was a tripartite and later a quadripartite body, not a NATO staff group, although its planning involved forces assigned to the alliance. Initially the German ambassador did not participate but was briefed separately, because the British and French feared that their special status would be infringed on and that planning would become too complicated.

In the WAG, however, it proved impossible to agree on political measures that were acceptable to all four governments and negotiable with the Soviets. Meanwhile, military contingency planning and related measures to ward off communist action directed at the status of Berlin gained in importance. The Germans, however, did not participate. To alleviate Bonn's increasing frustration about its exclusion from military planning in which its national survival was at stake, two steps were taken. After some more bickering on the part of the British and the French, a new Contingency Coordinating Group (CCG) was formed in Washington in which the Germans participated. It was further agreed that the ambassadors of the three powers in Bonn should consult with the German government on practical measures for safeguarding allied access to Berlin and assuring the city's ability to survive. For this purpose, the still existing Interallied Working Group in Bonn, which had changed its name to 'Interallied Consultations' was transformed into a high-level group, the so-called 'Bonn Working Group', or 'Bonn Group'. The Washington and Bonn Group consultations were complemented by regular dinner meetings of the four foreign ministers on the eve of NATO ministerial meetings and by encounters between the political directors of the four foreign ministries, either preparing the foreign minister's talks or convening *ad hoc* for policy coordination.

If Quad meetings were closely orchestrated with those of NATO, why was there a need for separate consultations at all? The reason given was that the Atlantic Alliance had no official mandate to deal with the German question, though this always figured prominently on its agenda. In practice, the Quad repertoire gave France, Great Britain, and the US, the most powerful nations within the alliance, a small and secret body more conducive to military contingency planning than the more unwieldy NATO institutions. The 'special rights and responsibilities concerning Berlin and Germany as a whole' provided a cover for legitimizing the tripartite (and later quadripartite) planning process during the one crisis in post-war Europe in which both East and West operated on the brink of nuclear war. Nevertheless, it was highly resented by the other allies. They argued that the NATO treaty required them to align in the case of a military attack, so they were entitled to a share in contingency planning. They further harboured the suspicion—even more so after the FRG was included in the planning and consultation process—that the most powerful Western nations intended to establish a kind of 'directoire', or steering committee, within the alliance as France had proposed a few years earlier.[15] As a result, relations between the Quad

---

[15] In an attempt to reform the Atlantic Alliance and to give France a position equal to the two Anglo-Saxon countries and commensurate with its claimed special status in world affairs, President Charles de Gaulle proposed in 1958 the establishment of a three-nation 'directoire' within NATO. This was rejected by the other members of the Alliance, foremost by the US. See 'Letter From President de Gaulle to President Eisenhower, September 17, 1958', in FRUS, 1958–1960, vii/2, Western Europe. 81–2.

members and the other NATO allies were occasionally quite touchy, though the three powers and the Federal Republic were concerned that NATO cohesion not be impaired.

The Soviet threat was a major incentive for further institutionalizing quadripartite consultations. By 1961 an elaborate network of institutions and specified rules were available for consultation and cooperation among the four states. But although these groups facilitated agreement on technical matters relating to the defence of Berlin, they were not very helpful in overcoming policy differences. Bonn, on the one hand, resisted any concessions to the Soviets that would amount to a *status quo minus* (such as an international access authority). The Kennedy administration on the other hand, aware of the risks of nuclear stalemate, searched for a less dangerous *modus vivendi* and was prepared to give up legal positions that had lost their usefulness. The Macmillan government went even further in its argument for accommodation, while President de Gaulle both objected to American preponderance and sought not to alienate Adenauer, with whom he was establishing a close personal and political relationship. As a result, the West could agree neither on the substance of a new proposal nor on whether to negotiate at all with the Soviet Union. Given the distribution of power among the four states, the US dominated the consultations. Its preponderance was further enhanced by the fact that the most important Quad groups met in Washington. While the US representatives had all the information they needed and could draw on the staff of the various Washington departments, the British, French, and German ambassadors had nothing comparable at their disposal and were bound by instructions received from their capitals.

As a reaction to this situation, the United States, with British support, began to de-emphasize the Quad process and turned increasingly to bi-lateral exchanges with the Soviets, the subject shifting from Berlin to arms control. France disapproved of these bilateral American initiatives without being able to stop them and began to boycott the WAG, which the bilateral talks had reduced to an information-sharing body.[16] The German govern-ment watched the bilateral American–Soviet dealings with uneasiness, if not alarm. When Adenauer himself tried through a press leak to block a Soviet–American agreement, this breach of confidence was attributed to his Washington ambassador and the WAG was further devalued.

---

[16] During the Cuban missile crisis the US used the WAG to keep its allies abreast of developments in the Caribbean. This was justified by the concern that the Cuban crisis might be a prelude to another Berlin crisis, but in fact it set a precedent for future consultations among the four nations on a number of international issues not related to Berlin and Germany.

Why did the US not discontinue its participation in Quad activities altogether when they constrained its bilateral relations with Moscow? Washington still saw a need to prevent German or Franco-German moves to obstruct US efforts to reach a solution on Berlin. Washington thought this purpose would best be served by an institution that already existed and that the Germans valued. To ensure German cooperation, the Quad's activities shifted from the WAG—except on military contingency planning—to the Bonn Group. The latter's workload had already increased when the GDR, with Soviet support, had sealed off its borders to West Berlin and West Germany. With German prodding, the Bonn Group further gained in importance and visibility. Its main task was operational planning for various contingencies on the Berlin access routes. When the Berlin crisis calmed down, the group concerned itself with the interpretation of allied rights and responsibilities and with fending off assumed German incursions into them (especially a demonstrative presence of German officials and organizations in Berlin). The WAG, for its part, was limited to an oversight function regarding Live Oak, but was reactivated when serious incidents on the access routes to Berlin or in the flight corridors occurred which could signify the beginning of a new Berlin crisis. If a threat was imminent, the US, as the most powerful nation, reasserted its control and the other partners obliged; in less tense situations a more balanced relationship evolved which afforded the Germans a greater share in the consultation process but was also more conducive to dissent and discord.

The Bonn Group and the management of Ostpolitik and détente

The late 1960s and early 1970s were marked in Europe by the search for a political *modus vivendi*. Both the Berlin and the Cuban Missile crises had demonstrated the risks of nuclear brinkmanship. This reorientation was less the result of a change of long-term preferences than a resort to new strategies. US motives owed much to the Vietnam War. Washington was interested in *détente* and partial cooperation with the Soviet Union until its resource-draining and highly unpopular war in Southeast Asia had ended. For France and Britain, though for different reasons, a relaxation of East–West tensions also had great appeal. The FRG, however, was concerned that it was expected to pay the costs of *détente* by recognizing the status quo in Europe and giving up its quest for reunification. Conversely, when the new social-liberal government headed by Willy Brandt wished to advance the national question with a new attempt at direct diplomacy, there was concern that Bonn might infringe on allied rights and responsibilities. Instead of trying to stem the tide against any deterioration of the status quo as it had done before, Bonn now sought a territorial *modus vivendi* in treaties with Moscow, Warsaw, Prague, and East Berlin. On the political level it hoped for change through *rapprochement*. Allies and Germans were thus pursuing parallel albeit competing interests.

How far and in what way were the quadripartite institutions used for policy coordination? To be sure, some policy coordination took place in NATO which, with the Harmel Report, had assumed a role of its own in an intensifying East–West dialogue. Until then, *détente* had basically been a bilateral affair between the US, or Britain, or France, or some of the smaller NATO allies, and the Soviet Union. Much to the concern of the three powers, the Brandt government followed this bilateral pattern in its negotiations with Moscow and Warsaw. Bonn soon realized, however, that a precondition for a lasting *modus vivendi*, indeed its cornerstone, was an agreement on Berlin, over which the Four Powers and not the Germans held the rights. Bonn therefore turned to the US, France, and Britain for assistance. As a result, the three powers started talks with the Soviet Union which, after prolonged and difficult negotiations, resulted in the 1971 Berlin Agreement. Although the three negotiated with Moscow on behalf of the Germans, neither the FRG nor the GDR sat at the negotiating table. This necessitated close and frank consultations between Bonn and the allies, which took place in the Bonn Group. During the Berlin negotiations it met weekly, even daily, for as many as ten–twelve hours. It delegated the preparation of position papers to deputies and experts. These meetings were further complemented by talks between the US State Secretary and the allied ambassadors as well as among the political directors of the four countries. Only in rare situations did the United States—usually President Nixon's national security advisor Henry Kissinger—intervene via a private back channel to break a deadlock in the formal negotiations with the Soviet Union. Even in this case, a link to the Bonn Group was provided through Brandt's aide, Egon Bahr, who was kept abreast by Kissinger and who in turn informed a German member. As all Bonn Group members had either the confidence and support of their administrations or a broad mandate they could fill as they saw fit, its output was largely accepted by the four governments.

The quadripartite consultations also served to monitor German *Ostpolitik*. Through mutual linkages the Eastern treaties were contingent on the results of the Berlin negotiations. The successful conclusion of both was also a precondition for Western agreement to a Conference on Security and Cooperation in Europe (CSCE), which the Soviets and several other European states wished to convene. Hence the crucial importance of the Quad consultations. Had they not been effective—had they either failed to reach an agreement or failed to protect the interests of those concerned—the *détente* process would have been halted and the cohesion of the West seriously impaired.

The quadripartite consultations were very frank, intensive, and constructive. Besides the intensity of their contacts and the confidentiality of their discussions, the members of the Bonn Group attributed their success to the close personal relationships that emerged. They were convinced that they could shape history instead of merely papering over fundamental political differences or formulating sterile protests that would not much impress the Soviets. Because of the trust that was built up in the group, the intercourse between the allies and their German counterparts acquired a new quality. From being an object of control, the FRG became a full and coequal partner. Most observers see this episode as a turning-point in the relationship within the Quad.[17]

After this high point of Quad consultations, normalcy was frustrating. The West, especially the Bonn government, had hoped that with the Berlin Agreement the city and its status would be respected and not again become a bone of contention. They were soon taught otherwise when the Soviet Union protested against extending various German federal laws to Berlin, including the law by which the Federal Republic became a member of the United Nations as well as the Basic Treaty with the GDR.[18] Soviet protests increased when Bonn established a Federal Environmental Agency in Berlin and extended to the city its election law for members of the European Parliament. Germans and allies differed on how to react. Bonn wanted to interpret the Berlin Agreement extensively, while the three powers, aware of some of the treaties' ambiguities, were determined not to tolerate any infringements on the new access and transit regulations but called for restraint on issues they considered to be of minor importance, such as a Federal presence in West Berlin or the city's links with the Federal Republic. The Bonn Group was used for mediation of these conflicting interests.

---

17 The point has been made during interviews with this author and former US counselor John C. Kornblum, former British counselor Christopher Audland, and former German *Legationsrat* Hans Otto Bräutigam, now Brandenburg Minister of Justice. All were members of the Bonn Group or assistants to members.

18 Since West Berlin was not a constituent part of the FRG and was not to be governed by it (as East Berlin was also not supposed to be governed by the GDR) but remained under allied occupation, each piece of Federal legislation was adopted through a special Berlin legislative process, provided it did not refer to those areas, such as security, that remained a prerogative of the Four Powers. In the Berlin Agreement it had been agreed that there was no change in the city's status, but that its ties with the FRG would be maintained and developed.

Among the three powers, the Americans, not wishing to disrupt their relations with the Soviets nor burden those with Bonn, were the most pragmatic in quadripartite dealings. The French, for their part, displayed the greatest sensitivity, objecting to any incursions into their special status regarding Berlin and Germany as a whole. Though the FRG had won enhanced international respect for its *Ostpolitik* and its increased economic weight, its room for manœuvre was still severely circumscribed in all questions relating to Berlin and Germany as a whole. The constraining factors were both allied rights and Germany's inability to improve Berlin's status substantially on its own. Bonn had to accept a gentlemen's agreement in which it committed itself to inform the allies early about all Federal activities in Berlin and to consult with the Bonn Group confidentially and speedily. It further agreed to instruct all government agencies as well as the parliamentary bodies accordingly. In return, the three powers promised the federal government full and constant consultation on all questions relating to Berlin. They further sanctioned the contested Federal Environmental Agency, though they extracted in return a German promise that no new Federal agencies would be installed in Berlin.

During the 1970s the Bonn Group continued to serve the purpose of safeguarding allied rights and responsibilities regarding Germany as a whole and Berlin from any infringements originating from either Soviet or German desires to change the status quo. In the early 1980s East–West relations deteriorated after the Soviet Union invaded Afghanistan and NATO sought to offset Soviet SS-20 missiles with its own two-track decision on deployment of Intermediate-range Nuclear Forces (INF). They deteriorated even further after a bomb attack on the 'La Belle' disco, a favourite hangout of US soldiers in West Berlin, in which Arab terrorists, aided by the East German Stasi,[19] were suspected. Now the allies' position changed. US diplomats became extremely strict in insisting that all agreements be faithfully adhered to and no incursions into allied rights and responsibilities by GDR authorities be tolerated. It was now the FRG which argued for flexibility in order to safeguard *Ostpolitik* against the new frost in East–West relations.

The Bonn Group was also used to mediate economic conflicts when they had some bearing on Berlin and intra-German relations. This was the case with the Yamal pipeline deal, in which Berlin was to be included and which the US violently opposed. After it became evident in quadripartite consultations that the German position was shared by both the British and the

---

[19] The GDR's 'State Security Service' (*Staatssicherheitsdienst*).

French, a compromise was found that left the deal as it stood and provided a face-saving device for the Reagan administration. Bonn was less successful in reaching an agreement in which Lufthansa, the German airline, could use the air corridors serving Berlin. In this case London and Paris joined Washington in guarding the privileges of allied airlines. Both the pipeline and the Lufthansa issues were exceptions; in general, the Bonn Group consultations were not only frank but amicable and conducive to a consensus. The same was true of the regular political directors' meetings.

Quadripartite consultations, however, continued with their usual frequency—weekly in the Bonn Group, twice a year on the level of political directors and foreign ministers—even when there was no acute threat and little disagreement about how to deal with Berlin. Besides conferring on questions relating to Germany as a whole, the foreign ministers took up other issues of interest to their countries. This practice had evolved from the so-called 'German Dinners' that preceded the bi-annual NATO ministerial sessions. At the recommendation of the US Secretary of State, the four nations used these meetings to discuss a wide range of issues. Kissinger initially wanted to use the confidentiality and restrictiveness of the foreign minister's dinners to explain his policy on Vietnam and shore up his partners' support. The Germans and the French, however, were initially reluctant to expand the Quad's original function of coordinating policies regarding Germany as a whole and Berlin. Bonn was pleased to be confided in but wary of the other NATO partners' envy and distrust, while Paris did not want to be drawn into a policy debate in which it would find few like-minded partners. A compromise was found: the official part of the meeting continued to be devoted to German questions, while after dinner the ministers would withdraw to the library to discuss whatever they chose.

Over time, Quad consultations on the political directors' level were intensified, covering a wide range of topics, with nuclear and arms control issues at the core. A precedent was set in 1971 when the directors first met to discuss the possible consequences for international security of the then-anticipated death of Yugoslav President Tito. Secrecy was necessary in order to shield these meetings from the suspicion of NATO members that a quadripartite *directoire* had been established. Most spectacular, however, was the meeting of the four heads of state and of government in January 1979 in Guadeloupe, at which the NATO two-track decision of December 1979 was devised. Because of the apprehensions this event caused among their alliance partners, it was never repeated. But it marked the tremendous increase in importance of the FRG and gave Germany an opportunity to participate directly in allied decision-making.

The 2+4 process and the suspension of allied rights and responsibilities

When the Berlin Wall fell, the German question was back on the agenda. From the beginning, the Soviet Union and the three Western powers made it clear that they intended to control the process of unification, while the two German states claimed full participation in allied decision-making. They further wished to see all allied rights and responsibilities terminated once unification was accomplished. An ingenious 2+4 process was invented to negotiate an agreement on the international aspects of German unification, including stationed forces, arms limitations, and the German–Polish frontier. In this process the two German states conferred on an equal basis with the Four Powers (although the GDR soon lost prestige and influence, partly as a result of its decision to merge with the FRG and partly through a clumsy negotiating strategy of its inexperienced diplomats). On the Western side, the 2+4 talks were prepared by regular Quad meetings on the political directors' level. An important goal of these consultations, besides preparing the Western negotiating position, was to bring over the French and above all the British. From the beginning, the Germans and the Americans took the lead, while both France's President François Mitterrand and Britain's Premier Margaret Thatcher harboured deep doubts about German reunification. If the political directors were unable to reach a break-through, they could always call on their foreign ministers to try their hand, often forming bilateral tactical alliances with one of their colleagues.

Surprisingly, the Bonn Group, in spite of its proven effectiveness during the negotiations on the Berlin Agreement, was not involved in the 2+4 process. Until its very last meeting on 25 September 1990, it met weekly but dealt only with routine matters. Perhaps the centrality of the issue of German unification necessitated the involvement of heads of state and of government, plenty of bilateral meetings among them and their closest advisors, and a high-speed diplomatic process. Consultations were required among high-level diplomats, trusted by their governments and well-acquainted with each other. Often there was no time for lengthy instructions. The political directors operated on a broad mandate formulated at the highest levels and, because of their experience, knew when they could compromise and when they had to stay the course.

Allied rights and responsibilities were suspended on 3 October 1990, when German unification took place. They legally ceased to exist when the 2+4 Agreement was ratified and went into effect on 15 March 1991. Correspondingly, the Bonn Group as well as the Washington Ambassadorial

Group (which had, since the late 1960s, been reduced to overseeing Live Oak operations) ended their activities. Quad consultations continued, although they had lost both their legal basis and their initial political function. They were now used to coordinate policies among the four nations on NATO reform, arms control, Bosnia, and other issues of common interest. But the consultations were less institutionalized, and meetings took place *ad hoc*, whenever one or another nation felt a need for it. Their level varied according to the issue: ministers of defence and their aides, political directors from the four foreign ministries, or the four countries' ambassadors at strategic posts, such as New York or Moscow. The lack of standard operating procedures allowed flexibility but also made quadripartite consultations an instrument of individual member states' preferences and strategies. Often it was the US, especially if a dynamic personality (such as Richard Holbrooke or John Kornblum) occupied the office of Assistant Secretary of State for European Affairs, who used the Quad process for furthering American interests.

What has this overview revealed? We have seen a close correlation between the demand for cooperation among the Quad states and the specific forms found. However, at this point neither the causes of this correlation nor the changes in the rules and procedures of Quad practices can be fully explained. Given the Quad members' reluctance to formalize their relationship, it took a special effort to build as elaborate an institutional network as the four states did. If the Quad had been primarily a reaction to an outside threat, as realist theory would assume, then it would have been more logical to turn to NATO for consultation. Furthermore, Quad activities would have been suspended either when the threat had abated or when the Quad had lost its usefulness for policy coordination among the four members. If containment of Germany was the allies' dominant concern, why did the elaboration of new norms, rules, and procedures coincide with the Berlin crisis, when the Soviet threat was much more dominant? Why was the Quad not de-institutionalized when the Berlin problem lost its urgency?

Even more puzzling is the fact that Quad consultations continued, though on a less institutionalized level, when with Germany's unification their legal justification and their primary political function had ended. A reference to the 'stickiness' of institutions is not much help. If this were all there was to it, then the Bonn Group might have continued but not the meetings of political directors, which were devoid of standard operating procedures and of organizational self-interest. Nor was the Quad a typical hybrid institution with a high degree of functional differentiation. Its primary function was to cooperate in managing the German question. To this was added the task of consulting on related issues of common interest. The Wallander-Keohane criterion for adaptability is therefore not fully met.[20]

Another enigma is Germany's gain in relative influence, which should have been contrary to the preferences of the other three nations, since it circumscribed their room for political manœuvre. One likely explanation is the FRG's increased economic and military weight. Indeed, the turning-point broadly coincided with the reassertion of German monetary strength as evidenced by the May 1971 decision to let the deutschmark float against the dollar. However, on issues related to the German question, the FRG's room for manœuvre was still severely circumscribed. The constraining factors were allied rights concerning Germany as a whole and the FRG's inability to improve Berlin's status on its own. The 2+4 talks are the most visible case in point. Additional explanations for the redistribution of power among the members of the Quad must therefore be sought.

3. Solving Our First Puzzle: Institutional Change and the Cooperation Problem

Can the nature of the specific cooperation problems the four states were faced with, constituted by their policies and preferences, their threat perception and the power distribution among them, provide some clues about what kind of institutional framework might prevent defection or at least make it more difficult? In the literature on cooperation problems,[21] two main types are distinguished: collaboration problems and coordination problems. The first term characterizes situations in which states choose to cooperate despite conflicting interests, the second refers to situations where common interests dominate. Both situations have equilibria. In collaboration situations such as the Prisoner's Dilemma the preferred course, or equilibrium, is mutual defection or non-cooperation. Coordination problems, however, have cooperative equilibria, i.e. stable outcomes which all states like and which entail cooperation. The problem is that there are multiple outcomes, and states have to agree which to select.

In a seminal article,[22] Glenn Snyder related the problem of desertion to alliance cohesion. He identified abandonment and entrapment as the Scylla

---

[20] See Wallander and Keohane, Ch. 1.

[21] For a recent elaboration see Martin (1992*b*). She distinguishes between collaboration problems, coordination problems, suasion problems, and assurance problems.

[22] Snyder (1984).

and Charybdis of intra-alliance relations. In a crisis situation, when interests diverge widely, each ally fears abandonment as its partners weigh the costs of cooperation and consider defecting. Partners wish to avoid entrapment, or being dragged into a conflict over an ally's interest that they do not share. In a crisis, when collaboration is essential in spite of divergent interests, a high degree of institutionalization is necessary in order to prevent defection and shore up credibility. In a less critical situation, especially when states have parallel preferences, less institutionalized forms of consultation suffice.

The establishment of quadripartite consultation in 1955 can be easily explained by the four states' interests and preferences arising from the new distribution of power after the termination of occupation rule in Germany and the latter's admission to NATO and WEU. The initial low administrative level or *ad hoc* basis of Quad served the purpose, from an allied point of view, of involving Germany, ensuring her cooperation, and at the same time controlling her dealings in sensitive issues relating to Berlin (such as Bonn's contention that Berlin was a *Land*, state, of the FRG) and Germany as a whole (such as intra-German relations). It also took care of German concerns that no reconstitution of the occupation regime take place, and at the same time gave Bonn a modest role in those affairs (such as negotiations with the Soviet Union) that the allies considered their prerogative.

The institutional design found corresponded to the new power relationship among the four states. The three victor powers of the Second World War set the rules by which a defeated and newly sovereign West Germany had to abide. Since the latter was highly dependent on cooperation with the US, France, and Britain, it accepted these rules. When the Adenauer government, for domestic reasons, lobbied for a new initiative regarding German reunification and a more prominent quadripartite consultation process, the allies acquiesced in this demand for tactical reasons. The defeat of Adenauer and the election of an SPD government could have endangered the continued integration of the FRG into Western institutions, such as NATO and the nascent European Communities. Since there were few conflicts of interest among the three allied powers, their own *ad hoc* trilateral coordinating processes, with occasional German participation, were fully adequate to the situation.

This changed, however, when East–West relations deteriorated at the end of the 1950s. No longer were the interests of the four states congruent, nor were the consultation processes adequate to the evolving collaboration problem. First, given the severity of the crisis and the wide divergence of interests, the fear of abandonment and of entrapment increased. In this situation, a strong, hegemonic US leadership and resolve were essential to maintain the credibility of the West's commitment to Berlin and to prevent defection. Second, the involvement of high-level government represent-atives and highly formalized rules were necessary to reassure and restrain partners. Third, the Germans had to be brought in fully to prevent both their frustration about perceived abandonment and their potential de-fection. Because of British and French objections, this happened only haltingly. Since Berlin contingency planning called for military and other expertise as well as secretiveness, specific forums were created that met these requirements. The result was a highly specified network of institutions that responded both to the power relationship among the four partners and the collaboration problem with which they were confronted.

Although all four states had a common interest in meeting the Soviet threat, they had different policy preferences. The United States had four goals: to contain the Soviet Union; to prevent the outbreak of a general nuclear war, which it could not win under conditions of nuclear near-parity with the Soviets; to remain the uncontested leader of the Western alliance system; and to keep the FRG tied to the West and its own influence undiminished in Germany—a country vital for the containment of the Soviet Union. These four ends called for the defence of Western rights regarding the access and survivability of West Berlin (not of all Berlin, as Bonn demanded), but in a way by which a military conflict as well as a weakening of the Western alliance might be avoided. The British were less concerned about safeguarding allied rights and responsibilities in Berlin and even more afraid of a military conflict. They therefore argued for mil-itary disengagement in Europe, though this meant alienating the Germans. The Suez experience was still fresh in their minds. It had taught them to use military power only as a last resort and to take pains to keep the British–American special relationship intact. The French, for their part, had learnt a quite different lesson from Suez: not to rely on American support in a crisis in which their interests diverged. When de Gaulle came to power he did two things: he worked towards national autonomy in defence matters and he looked for an alternative partner to the US, which he found in Adenauer's Germany. France's interests in Berlin, of which the foremost was preserving its special status, were best served by supporting Bonn in opposition to Washington. The FRG was the weakest and most vulnerable of the four countries. Given its high stakes in the Berlin crisis on the one hand, and its large political and economic dependence on the US on the other, the Bonn government very much feared abandonment by its allies but had no ability to threaten a change of alliances. In exchange for a larger and more equal role in the allied consultations, it adapted its policies gradually to those of the US, while the British were soon integrated into the American negotiating strategy, and the French were forced to cooperate when the threat was still very acute. When the threat subsided, Paris ignored quadripartite consultations and boycotted the Washington Ambassadorial Group. By this time, however, these actions were only a nuisance and did not challenge US leadership or undermine American dealings with the Soviets.

During both periods there was a close correlation between the nature of the cooperation problem and the function and form of quadripartite consultations. Before the Berlin crisis set in, the problem was to agree on a strategy regarding Germany and Berlin from which all would profit equally. None had any incentive to abandon the general consensus that neither European security nor German adherence to the West should be risked for the sake of reunification. An institutional repertoire with little formalization and specialization sufficed to deal with policy coordination. This changed dramatically under the impact of the Soviet threat. Whereas Britain and the US had much to fear and little to gain from a deterioration of the military situation, the German government was most concerned that its political interests not be abandoned. The French shared this concern. West Germany was their strategic glacis: any political or military changes would affect France immediately. Not only did the preferences of the four states diverge during this crisis; their strategies conflicted as well. The foremost goal for the US and Britain was to avoid entanglement in a military conflict they could not control. Germany feared abandonment but had no alternative course of action available. France wished to keep intact her policy of autonomy, which was built on the assumption of eventual abandonment. To deal with the resulting collaboration problem and to prevent defection, a complex set of institutions with specific rules was required. Collaboration was further assisted by the existence of a hegemon whose power was resented but not contested. The cohesion among the four states as well as among the NATO countries was thus preserved as long as a common threat was perceived by all partners.

The onset of *détente* was a significant change in the international environment. As a result, the coherence of quadripartite cooperation weakened, rules and procedures became less specific, and the centre of activity shifted from Washington to Bonn. The first two changes were to be expected: collaboration gave way to coordination when states seemingly had similar policy preferences. But how can the move to Bonn be explained, or the gradual increase in the complexity of the consultation processes without a corresponding rise in the threat? Two contradictory lines of interpretation offer themselves. One refers to the increasing political influence of the FRG resulting from its economic reconstruction, while its partners were inclined to treat the Quad consultations with benign neglect. The immediate threat was gone by late 1963, and there was not much that the allies could do about the still delicate situation in and around Berlin except for restraining the Germans. Moreover, the German question and the Berlin question, though still open, had lost their central importance for all powers except the FRG. For the US, Vietnam and arms control were much more pressing. It could afford to cede influence in the quadripartite procedures, allowing Bonn a more prominent role as long as it was kept informed of Germany's interests and the latter did not interfere with allied rights and responsibilities. With a mere coordination problem at hand, the format did not matter much.

An alternative explanation of the evolution of quadripartite consultations looks at the *détente* process during the 1960s as a collaboration problem, with conflicting interests among the four states. The US and Britain saw *détente* primarily as a way to defuse the military confrontation with the Soviet Union. With a test ban and a non-proliferation agreement as their means, they were prepared to accept a *modus vivendi* regarding the political situation in Europe. For the FRG, however, all East–West agreements ran counter to its vital interest in avoiding any steps which would either weaken its claim to reunification or make it more difficult. In Bonn's view, with the arms control agreements the West relinquished an important bargaining chip, which could have been exchanged for Soviet concessions on the German question. In addition, GDR participation in these agreements enhanced its aspirations for recognition and weakened the Bonn government's claim to be the sole legitimate representative of the German people. In sharp contrast to the Berlin crisis, this time the FRG seemed to have an option available other than adapting. Washington was concerned that Bonn might follow de Gaulle's example and loosen her integration into NATO. If West Germany withdrew from military integration, the Western Alliance lost a crucial member and risked obsolescence. It scarcely mattered whether the risk of German defection was real or perceived. The US and Britain had an overriding interest in keeping quadripartite consultations intact, highly institutionalized, and with the FRG included, even if this required giving her an important voice in it.

Plausibility argues for this second explanation. In the first case, the four powers would not have needed the institutional specificity of the Bonn Group and its expansion. In the second case, however, it made sense to move Quad consultations to Bonn in order to engage and control Germany in an allied setting. I call this the *engagement effect*[23] of institutions, which serves to prevent defection.

The severity of the collaboration problem was lessened when in 1969/70 the new German government, with Willy Brandt as chancellor, changed the country's preferences regarding reunification. After an agonizing re-appraisal, Brandt took account of the fact that the FRG risked international isolation if it stuck to its previous policies, without being able to further unification. Instead of opposing its partners' *détente* policies, the Brandt government, with *Ostpolitik* as its instrument, sought to increase coopera-tion and to negotiate a *modus vivendi* on the territorial status quo with West Germany's eastern neighbours, the Soviet Union, and even the GDR. 'Change through *rapprochement*' was its new motto. Bonn knew that *Ost-politik* had no chance of domestic ratification if it was not complemented by an improvement in the situation of Berlin. For this, however, the Federal Republic needed the support of the allies.

It obtained this support for three reasons. First, German *Ostpolitik* com-plemented the allies' *détente* policies nicely, provided Germany did not go too far and exceed their common understanding. Second, the Four Power negotiations on Berlin gave the allies a way to control the course and speed of German *Ostpolitik* and ensure its compatibility with their own interests and preferences. Third, the FRG had acquired considerable economic weight and made a substantial military contribution; it thus had become a valuable partner whose interests had to be taken into account. For the three Western powers the Bonn Group served as a means of controlling the speed and direction of German *Ostpolitik*. It did this much better than consulta-tions on a low administrative level or on an *ad hoc* basis would have done. Though the core collaboration problem had been defused, the elaborate institutional network of the Quad was retained.

Though a number of questions cannot yet be answered, some general observations regarding institutional change can be made. Most important is the correlation between the nature of the cooperation problem and the degree of institutionalization. A trend towards institutional specialization can be observed when states are faced with a security dilemma. With an acute Soviet threat challenging the Western powers' vital interests, the need for collaboration among them is imperative even though their preferences might diverge, generating a high risk of defection. In order not to endanger the credibility of their common policy, therefore, states accept the con-straints of a highly specified institutional framework. They adjust their

---

[23] See below, p. 191.

strategies to a common course. Conversely, the need for strong institutions with elaborate norms, rules, and procedures declines in the absence of an external threat, according to realist theory.

Two developments in the history of the Quad, however, do not fit this explanation. The fading of the acute threat in the mid-1960s posed a collaboration problem that was not the result of an external threat. In order to prevent German defection after France had left the integrated structures of NATO, the specification of the Quad was changed. With the move of the centre of activity in quadripartite interactions from Washington to Bonn, the German government was given a strong incentive for continued co-operation. Substantial institutional specification thus coincided with a low external threat but high internal risk of defection. The other development is the proliferation and salience of the Bonn Group during the Berlin negotiations. The only explanation for this high degree of institutional specificity in the absence of an outside threat is the risk that Germany might defect from Western *détente* policy as stipulated by the US.

4. Solving Our Second Puzzle: Institutional Persistence

What accounts for the perplexing persistence of the Quad? Institutionalist writers see institutions primarily as a response to uncertainty and a means to reduce transaction costs.[24] When the Interallied Consultations were instituted in 1955, their initial function was to manage the risks inherent in the German situation. Since institutions are costly to create, their repertoires of norms, rules, and procedures have to be agreed on and abided by, thus constraining states' policies and preferences. It was in the allied interest to consult on a low administrative level without elaborate rules. Only when the German issue became increasingly complex and the need for cooperation vital, e.g. during the Soviet threat to Berlin, were the three powers prepared to invest in a more elaborate institution. The Quad's main function became to cooperate in meeting an external threat by sharing information, improving the accountability of each partner's policies, and approving of joint plans for meeting this threat politically and militarily. The Berlin crisis was basically about who was to control the centre of Europe and dominate Germany, the Soviets or the West. The FRG was the prize in this contest and therefore had to be included in the process. It was a country whose

---

[24] See Keohane (1989c: 1–20); on transaction costs more specifically, ibid. 101–31.

reliability remained in doubt. But by integrating it into the practices of the WAG and later into allied military contingency planning, its cooperation could be achieved. The cost for all partners was providing as well as receiving credible information. After the external threat had abated, there was still a risk that one partner, most likely Germany, would defect from the multilateral management of the German question. A network of consultations was used to guard against this

The changes in the Quad's institutional repertoire largely conformed to its functions. The greatest variation was in the place and the frequency of meetings, which ranged from *ad hoc* to bi-weekly and from weekly to daily. There was also, as I have noted, variation in the level on which they were conducted. *Ad hoc* meetings took place wherever it was most convenient. The frequency of Quad meetings increased with the growing complexity and urgency of the issues as did the specificity of the institutional design. The place of routine meetings was indicative of the importance which members attributed to the Quad's activities and the influence they wished to exert. The establishment of an ambassadorial group in Washington with close ties to the State Department was no accident. Nor was the transfer of activities to the Bonn Group in the mid-1960s, when it became important to keep Germany committed to the allied framework. The most salient consultations—in the sense that their result circumscribed their member governments' freedom of action—were taken on the level of political directors, not ambassadors or desk officers. Even though major decisions were made by the foreign ministers or the heads of state or of government, they largely relied on the political directors' paperwork for their preparation. The outcome of lower-level consultations pretty much depended on which country's representative operated on precise instructions from a high government level or was given a very broad mandate to accommodate a variety of positions.

The demand for consultation regarding questions relating to Berlin and Germany as a whole continued after the Berlin crisis had withered away. Since it would have been more costly to create a new institution, the allies and the Federal Republic found it useful to continue the practices of the quadripartite consultations, though the focus of activity now shifted to Bonn. This process was not always harmonious. After the onset of *détente*, serious distributional issues emerged over which country was to reap the benefits and which was to pay the costs of a relaxation of East–West tensions. The experience of regularly consulting, however, not only generated an organizational routine which proved robust against conflicts of interest but also produced a familiarity among the group's members that made their foreign-policy actions accountable to each other. As a result, their expectations about appropriate behaviour largely converged.

This commonality was a special asset during the consultations on the Berlin Agreement of 1970/1 (as well as during the 2 + 4 talks). The closeness among the group's members and their understanding of their partners' views and interests made agreement possible among the four states even when their preferences differed. Usually a compromise was sought and achieved without much outside interference, though there was a visible preponderance of the US voice. The most vulnerable and dependent member on all issues relating to the German question was the FRG; it could only prevail if it cooperated closely with at least one other member, usually with the US. With the convergence of expectations about appropriate behaviour, being forced to give in seldom created ill feelings among the Quad's members or had a negative effect on future consultations.

When after the conclusion of the Berlin Agreement the four powers dealt with a less complex set of problems, they did not need quite so elaborate a set of rules and procedures. In view of the durability of the German question and of the Quad's positive impact on joint policy coordination, they found it opportune not to return to the low, technical level and *ad hoc* practices of the Quad's beginning. Instead of being concerned about its likely costs in terms of political room for manœuvre, they valued the familiarity and confidentiality of the Quad's processes. Being aware of their partners' preferences reduced the costs of their foreign-policy strategies. One explanation of the group's institutional persistence thus refers to the high degree of its members' valuation.

This high valuation of Quad practices also explains why the group's members continued their meetings when, after the end of the cold war, German unification and the termination of allied rights and responsibilities, no apparent reason remained for maintaining this routine. In their view, the Quad had provided a conveniently small, confidential, homogeneous forum for preparing joint decisions on issues of common interest. They therefore wished to continue it, though in a much less institutionalized form and with a high degree of secrecy.[25] The nearly complete devolution of formalized institutional features suggests that the mandate of an institution and its primary function—in the Quad's case, to manage jointly the German problem—is of crucial importance. If an institution has

---

[25] There are no written references to Quad practices after 1990; this author has therefore relied on interviews with several Quad members from the four countries concerned, such as former US Assistant Secretary of State Kornblum and his German counterpart Ischinger. I have further consulted Vera Klauer (1997).

accomplished its main mandate—even if it has been fulfilling other functions as well—and is not able to significantly transform existing practices, it will collapse. If it continues, it does so on a much lower level of institutionalization, since its members are reluctant to incur the costs associated with adaptation. They prefer a situation which puts less constraint on their room for manœuvre.

Their valuation of the Quad's repertoire induced its members to adapt it to other institutions. The most obvious of these adaptations was the increasing practice of quadripartite consultations within NATO. Over the years, the so-called 'German Dinners' among the four foreign ministers on the eve of NATO Council meetings were complemented by a variety of other meetings between representatives of the four countries. The informality and unaccountability of their procedures made them ideal for developing joint policy positions to be presented at larger multilateral gatherings, such as those of NATO, the CSCE, or the Economic Summits (G7). Britain, France, Germany, and the US also continued their habit of prior consultations on important alliance matters, even when the need for policy coordination regarding the German question had elapsed.

A constraining factor on the portability of the Quad's practices was its membership and the limited range of problems it was designed to deal with. Created to provide for consultation on the German question, its members were reluctant to deal with issues not related to their core mandate. But shifting to the routine, or desk-officers, level would have necessitated a change of personnel with well-entrenched interests. To enable consultations on a broader spectrum of problems, the Bonn Group was complemented by quadripartite meetings of political directors that, over time, gained in importance. These officers had the necessary expertise and were well placed to consult on those security-related issues which were of interest to the four nations. Another reason for not changing form was the external environment of the Quad. All four states were also members of the Atlantic Alliance, whose other members watched the Quad's activities distrustfully, anxious that they should not collide with NATO's business, and even more so that no informal quadripartite directory evolve from these consultations among the alliance's most powerful members. Quad consultations on issues other than Germany and Berlin were therefore clouded by secrecy; and the one prominent exception, the Guadeloupe summit meeting of January 1979, was never repeated. It is evident, however, that functional differentiation very much contributed to the usefulness of Quad practices beyond the narrow focus of German affairs.

The Quad concept of a small, multifunctional group also served as a blueprint for the Contact Group on Bosnia. When the conflict in the former Yugoslavia necessitated close and frank exchanges among the four nations and with the Russians, the forum was founded on the model of the Bonn Group. It was created on an American initiative when the Bosnian-Croat alliance broke up and NATO air strikes were contemplated. While this group's official function was, in collaboration with Moscow, to enforce a cease-fire, its implicit task was to engage Russia. Like Germany in 1955, Russia was 'the new kid on the bloc' that should be induced to cooperate by being offered a sharing of information. The resemblances between the Contact Group and the Quad are striking, not least in its rules and procedures and its membership. Though the motives for its creation have been interpreted differently,[26] this likeness must be more than coincidence. The Contact Group's primary security function resembles that of the original Bonn Group: to cooperate in containing the risk of defection by sharing information, reducing uncertainty, and improving the accountability of the members' policies. Furthermore, the group is not made up of the standing members of the UN Security Council, as might have been expected, but of the Quad members plus Russia. These five have been quite reluctant to include Italy as an additional member.

The Quad was most effective when a large body of common interests existed among its members. This was the case at the height of the Berlin crisis, during the Four Power negotiations on a Berlin agreement, and during the 2+4 talks. It failed, however, to produce a common strategy for negotiating with the Soviets on a *modus vivendi* for Berlin, since Bonn had not yet resigned itself to accepting the status quo in Europe. Likewise, the reluctance of the three Western powers to negotiate about a change of the status quo prevented agreement on a new plan for German reunification, for which the Federal government lobbied in the 1950s and 1960s. When the Quad members had largely identical interests and preferences, they mainly confined their consultations to an exchange of information.

But did the Quad really make a difference in the outcome of multilateral policies among its four members? Though the Quad was not unique in making an impact, its procedures had a special advantage compared with those of larger, more unwieldy institutions such as NATO, WEU, and EU. This finding is underscored by the observation that, if especially contentious issues were at stake, such as Berlin contingency planning or the removal of the US embargo on the European-Soviet Yamal pipeline deal, the four states chose to consult in the Quad and not in a NATO or EU context. Is there not,

---

[26] See Klauer (1997).

however, a danger of overestimating the Quad's impact by focusing on the sheer volume of its meetings, the persistence of the institution as such, and the portability of its institutional repertoire to other environments and purposes? If one looks for an output in terms of multilateral decisions to be jointly implemented, it is easy to argue that the Quad's effects were small. Decisions were mostly taken either nationally or in other multilateral institutions such as NATO, while the Quad concentrated on the exchange of information and on recommendations to national governments. This, however, neglects a byproduct of the Quad's procedures. Among its four members, it produced mutual familiarity and a commonality of expectations. The Quad's institutional routine provided its members with valuable information on their partners' policy preferences in other areas, which reduced the transaction costs of their foreign-policy strategies. Even when their interests diverged, they could work towards achieving a compromise solution, since no member needed to be concerned much about betrayal. The Quad's activities thus facilitated relations among the four powers. It further increased the effectiveness of *other* institutions, such as NATO, since it provided four of NATO's most important members an institutional opportunity to coordinate their policies beforehand. They were thus ready to accept the associated loss in political room for manœuvre.

This vindicates one of the most important assumptions of institutionalism: that institutions have an impact on state behaviour and can change their actors' preferences, whether they do so through their output or through the side effects of their procedures. They induce decision-makers to exchange freedom of action in foreign affairs for cooperation with other actors and increased accountability of their partners' behaviour. An institution will persist if it provides an institutional repertoire which is highly valued by its members and if this repertoire can be easily adapted to new challenges.

5. Solving Our Third Puzzle: Redistribution of Power in Favour of Germany

Why and how did an institution that had been created to control Germany —to prevent Germany from posing a new risk that could destabilize the post-war European system—eventually give the FRG an ability to control the outcomes of alliance affairs? The correlation between an external threat and internal influence is of limited explanatory value. Another possible explanation is the diffusion of the risk Germany posed compared with the rising communist threat. For the containment of the Soviet Union, the West needed the FRG's support, which it was prepared to pay by ceding influence. This explanation also has its shortcomings. Although the Berlin crisis had faded, both *Ostpolitik* and later the opening of the Berlin Wall brought the German question back onto the agenda. The durability of the German issue until 1990 thus limits the validity of this answer.

But what were the sources of German power? The most obvious is the shift in capabilities among the members of the group, especially the increased economic and military weight of the FRG while the US was entangled in a resource-consuming war in Vietnam, France had withdrawn from the integrated structure of NATO, and Britain's military contribution was declining because of its economic problems. While the FRG was able to use its economic clout to further its foreign- and economic-policy interests, even in opposition to US preferences, the division of Germany and its reliance on the US nuclear umbrella made it still very dependent on allied support and assistance. In the 1970s it could affect the terms of the international monetary and trade regimes—such as by unilaterally floating the deutschmark—but could only indirectly influence the negotiations of the Four Powers on Berlin. In relation to the German question, the FRG's room for manœuvre was severely circumscribed. The constraining factors were allied rights concerning Germany as a whole and the FRG's inability to improve Berlin's status on its own. In contrast to the 1950s and 1960s, through the Quad Germany could now participate in the West's deliberations. But when Bonn tried to implement the Berlin Agreement liberally, its partners forced it to accept a gentleman's agreement under which it promised restraint. Furthermore, it could not prevent its partners denying Lufthansa permission to serve Berlin or refusing to connect Berlin with the gas pipeline system extending from Russia to Western Europe. By referring to allied rights and responsibilities the Western powers could block German initiatives that went against their own economic interests. During the 2+4 negotiations on the international aspects of German unification, the FRG sat at the negotiating table on equal terms with its partners. It still needed their diplomatic support (especially that of the US), but in the course of events it became less an object than an actor.

Another and even more interesting explanation can be found if we examine the institutional impact of Quad practices on the behaviour of its members and on the distribution of influence among them. Institutions facilitate cooperation in complex situations in which state interests diverge and members lack complete information about their partners' preferences. Continued cooperation is contingent on each member's conforming with the rules, norms, and procedures of the institution. As a result, its freedom of action is circumscribed. The *engagement effect* of institutions, which serves to prevent defection, is most pronounced under the conditions of complex interdependence. It was quite pronounced in a situation in which the allies held the rights but the Germans controlled the resources. In each case in which the Federal Republic's cooperation was uncertain, the other Quad members tried to induce it to cooperate by giving it an increased say in alliance affairs. Engaging Bonn in the proceedings of the Quad and affording it a say in outcomes was the best way to assure cooperation. The first occasion arose in 1961 with the Berlin crisis, another during the negotiations on the Berlin Agreement, still others during the period of *détente* and during the 2+4 talks. Bonn, for its part, accepted the quadripartite system because its inherent constraints bound not only Germany but also its allies to the common consensus.

While the engagement effect of institutions serves to prevent defection, institutions also have a *confidence-building effect*. With the FRG's continuing adherence to shared norms, rules, and procedures, her accountability increased and the lingering distrust of German defection—i.e. either another revisionist turn in Germany policy or the revival of a Rapallo-type cooperation with the Soviet Union—declined. The Quad was particularly well suited to address these two concerns because of its mandate. (Concern about a new German militarism was taken care of by NATO.) As a result, the FRG's control over policy outcomes increased in relation to the commonality of the Quad's norms, rules, and procedures.

The turning-point was the experience of Quad practices during the Berlin negotiations. There were small changes, such as a greater German role in preparing the agenda for Quad meetings. More important was the extension of quadripartite practices to issues not related to Germany and Berlin. Since that year, the political directors of the four foreign ministries met regularly to discuss various aspects of international affairs, such as arms control and military security. Secrecy was necessary, given the sensitive nature of the subjects discussed and the suspicion of NATO members that a quadripartite *directoire* had been established. In addition, the four foreign ministers, meeting traditionally for their 'German Dinner' on the eve of the NATO Council of Ministers, expanded their deliberations to unrelated issues, such as the situation in Southwest Asia, the Mediterranean, and China. Formerly, the three Western powers, or the US and Britain, had met from time to time to discuss foreign-policy issues without, however, inviting the FRG to participate unless issues concerning to Germany as a whole or Berlin were at stake. From now on, the four states met regularly on various levels about a whole gamut of issues. Perhaps the most visible of these meetings was at Guadeloupe in January 1979. These consultations gave Germany—originally the object of allied control—a role and voice equal to those of its partners in international affairs.

6. Conclusions

The *first puzzle* addressed in this paper had to do with the evolution of the Quad's repertoire and the development of its institutional design. A correlation was established between the nature of the cooperation problem and the degree of its institutionalization. When states operate in a situation defined as a collaboration problem, a high degree of institutionalization will follow in order to prevent defection, which is most likely in the presence of an acute external threat or widely varying preferences. In order not to endanger the credibility of their common interests and strategies, members accept the constraints of a highly specified institutional framework. Conversely, the need for specific norms, rules, and procedures declines when the external threat decreases and a coordination problem prevails. In the Quad case, however, this did not lead to the devolution of its institutional repertoire as long as its basic function, to manage cooperation on the German problem, continued to be fulfilled.

The high degree of the Quad's institutional specificity was thus less contingent on the existence of an explicit collaboration problem than on a situation in which a risk existed that members might defect from agreed-upon policies. During the negotiations on the Berlin Agreement in the early 1970s, a high workload and not—as in two other cases[27]—the members' diverging interests made for new subgroups and an increasing the frequency of meetings. The Quad owed much of its usefulness to the fact that it offered a choice of specialized venues for quadripartite consultations—the Washington Ambassadorial Group, the Bonn Group, the meetings of political directors—whether a collaboration or a coordination problem prevailed. Its effectiveness depended on the flexibility of its procedures and on the informality and unaccountability of its meetings.

This also explains why the Quad's members chose to develop this institution separate from NATO rather than adapt the alliance to meet the challenges of the Berlin crisis. Since the three nations with special rights and

---

[27] Cases in point are the creation of the Nuclear Planning Group and the Harmel Exercise; see Haftendorn (1996*b*: 161–73, 320–74).

responsibilities regarding Berlin and Germany as a whole had already formed the practice of consulting with the FRG, they decided to use this practice and develop its institutional specificity rather than adapt NATO to the particularities of the German question. Their motive was to keep trans-action costs as low as possible. The Quad provided a degree of closeness—of secretiveness and familiarity among the members—that NATO, with its broader membership and greater variety of functions, did not. Further-more, the Quad's institutional repertoire could be more easily adapted to the changing needs of the four states concerned. Their decision, however, gave rise to competition between NATO and the Quad which required both cooperation and division of labour between them, which was not always transacted smoothly and effectively.[28]

The *second puzzle* was the persistence and adaptability of the Quad. The specificity of the Quad's institutional repertoire was limited, with changes primarily a matter of place, frequency, and administrative/political level. As the Quad fulfilled the purpose of reducing uncertainty relating to the German question, it was rational to adapt its institutional form to include meetings of political directors or heads of state and of government. Members were careful, however, not to duplicate NATO's activities unless the Quad's design promised advantages over the more unwieldy NATO system. After the Berlin situation had lost its urgency, they expanded their consultations to other issues of common interest. On the whole, though, the Quad's institutional variation was constrained by its members' strategy of using it primarily for consultation on issues related to allied rights and responsibilities regarding Berlin and Germany as a whole. In the case of the Quad, this specific design conformed best to its members' preferences. It was highly valued by all, since it made their partners' foreign-policy strategies greatly accountable. As a result, decision-makers came to prefer cooperation in a quadripartite context to complete freedom of action in foreign affairs. One of the most important assumptions of institutional-ism—that institutions have an impact on state behaviour and can change their actors' preferences—is thus vindicated.

Quadripartite practices were not only used to discuss issues unrelated to the German problem but were also employed in other institutional settings, such as NATO and the G7. At these venues the four states met informally for policy coordination in preparation for alliance meetings or economic summits. The portability of the Quad repertoire can be explained by its

---

[28] Further research is required to explore how issues are dealt with institutionally in a dense policy space in which two or more institutions compete for fulfilling similar functions.

flexibility and by the high degree of valuation by its members. They were inclined to continue the habit of consulting regularly in a quadripartite framework even though they had other forums available, such as NATO for security matters and the G7 for political and economic issues. In these cases Quad practices were transferred to new issues and different venues; in another instance, Quad rules and procedures served as the blueprint for a new institution, the Contact Group on Bosnia. In both cases, the portability of Quad procedures was limited to their basic function of providing for co-operation in situations of complex interdependence. Only the basics of its institutional repertoire were transported: limited membership, confidentiality of proceedings, and as a result, a high degree of accountability and trust.

The *third puzzle* was the increase in German influence. The most obvious answers—the external threat and changes in members' relative capabilities —were found to be of some explanatory power. Closer analysis of the institutional impact of the Quad's activities did reveal that a by-product of its consultation processes was a redistribution of power among its members. Remarkably, this rearrangement occurred in an issue area where the FRG's freedom of action was severely circumscribed and extended to military affairs, which were not among the issues the Quad ordinarily dealt with. One explanation refers to the engagement effect of institutions, which serves to prevent defection. This was most pronounced under the conditions of complex interdependence. But institutions also have a confidence-building effect. When the FRG adhered to shared norms, rules, and procedures, its accountability increased. As a result, in tandem with the commonality of Quad's norms, rules, and procedures, the FRG's control over policy outcomes increased.

The Quad's impact on international relations was threefold. First, the Quad provided for a smooth handling of the German question among the four states primarily concerned. Given the potential divisiveness of the issue, this was no minor achievement. Second, the Quad gave the most powerful members of NATO a selective and highly confidential forum they could use for consultation on the specific issues of Germany and Berlin and could extend to other issues of common concern. Contrary to their and other NATO members' intentions, it also served as a kind of steering committee for the alliance as a whole, which was most valuable in crisis situations. The Quad even persisted when the reason for its creation, the German question, had been resolved. Third, the effect of the Quad's activities was a redistribution of power that helped overcome historic legacies and gave Germany a role in international affairs commensurate with its capabilities.

7

THE OSCE AND GERMAN POLICY: A STUDY IN *HOW* INSTITUTIONS MATTER

Ingo Peters

1. Introduction

Germany's immediate aim is to rid itself of the burden of being Europe's battle-field. . . . Its medium-range interest is to rid itself of foreign soldiers, which would turn it from an instrument of alliance policy into an entirely independent entity of its own. But its long-range goal is reunification or, to paraphrase U.S. Secretary of State James Baker in another context, dreams of a Greater Germany. That dream is—there is no need to be diplomatic—everybody's nightmare. The problem is that a united Germany, or even a confederated Germany, would be the hegemonic power in an independent Europe.[1]

With the end of the East–West conflict, Germany's future foreign and security policy re-emerged as one of the core issues of international security affairs. In the same vein as Krauthammer's undiplomatic prediction, neo-realists have argued that unipolarity will not last because other great powers will emerge.[2] Germany, as one of the 'eligible states', will develop: (i) a high level of military capability; (ii) a broad concept of security that embraces a concern with regional and/or global power balances; (iii) a greater as-sertiveness than lesser powers in defining and defending its interests.[3] Germany's great-power aspirations are evidenced, in this view, by Kohl's unilateral initiatives during the process of unification, Germany's policy during the Gulf War of 1990/1, its unilateral recognition of Slovenia and Croatia in 1992, and its dominant role in EC/EU integration since 1990.[4]

The author gratefully acknowledges support from the German Science Foundation, Bonn, 1992–95 (grant # HA 778/9-1 and 9-2) for the empirical research in this study.

[1] Krauthammer (1989).   [2] Mearsheimer (1990: 7); Layne (1993: 8–16).
[3] Layne (1993: 8 n. 12).   [4] Ibid. 37–8; see also Horsley (1992).

Mearsheimer predicts that united Germany will no longer accept NATO as an instrument of its allies for controlling Germany.[5] This policy prediction has its roots in his more general claim that while states sometimes operate through institutions, these merely 'reflect state calculations of self-interest based primarily on the international distribution of power'.[6] In sum, Germany will de-emphasize its traditional multilateralism and instead favour unilateral strategies.

On the contrary, Germany has maintained its reliance on multilateralism and has not turned towards unilateral strategies. Germany has not loosened its ties to NATO and the EU in order to gain unilateral freedom of action, nor has it given up on ambitious plans for institutionalizing the CSCE. German policies and actions since 1990 have been consistent with Foreign Minister Genscher's publicly stated 1989 version of official policy: to institutionalize the CSCE in a manner that would engage the other governments in a 'dense institutional network based on common security interests, so as not to allow any single state to defect without violating its own national security interests'.[7]

Why has Germany pursued a pro-institutional policy? Germany's OSCE policy reflects the impact of that institution on Germany's preferences and strategies. As posited by *institutionalism*,[8] institutions are not mere instruments of states but are an independent factor explaining state preferences and policy strategies. Institutional embeddedness has influenced the definition of state preferences because it had made multilateralism a 'causal belief' for Germany. It has become a factor believed to be causally combined with Germany's other fundamental foreign-policy preferences. To evaluate whether institutions affect Germany's fundamental preferences and not merely strategies, the researcher must show that policies and proposals are not directly and instrumentally linked to the pursuit of simple national interests, but instead are based upon these complex and interlinked causal beliefs. My hypothesis is that Germany's post-cold war pro-OSCE policies are the result of its institutional embeddedness and causal beliefs, and cannot be explained in light of simple national interests. Accordingly, in order to provide evidence of an institution's impact on state preferences, it

---

[5] Mearsheimer (1990: 6 n. 1).

[6] Mearsheimer (1994/5: 13).

[7] Genscher (19 Oct. 1989: 49–50; translation by the author); the original text reads as follows: 'Kooperative Sicherheitspolitik strebt eine breite Vertrauens- und Kooperationsstruktur zwischen Staaten und Bündnissen an, die über den Bereich von Abrüstung und Rüstungskontrolle hinausgeht. Es geht um die Schaffung einer engmaschigen Interessenverflechtung, aus der sich kein Staat und keine Seite ohne Verletzung vitaler Eigeninteressen lösen kann.'

[8] See Keohane (1989c); Kupchan and Kupchan (1995).

has to be shown that a political actor's choice of institutionalized cooperation rests on the assumption that a policy interdependence exists requiring
institutionalized collective action. This cooperative rationale 'causes' a
corresponding policy. The institution's impact on state strategy and its
non-institutional character become evident by showing that the state's
institutionalization policy is aiming at specific institutional characteristics
which do not directly or solely relate to a national interest defined in terms
of a narrow self-interest aiming at maximizing one's own power and gains
but rather serve collectively defined purposes of the institution.

Until 1990, West Germany's major foreign-policy goals were to maintain
peace and security, sustain economic growth and well-being, and achieve
national reunification without resorting to force. Integration into Western
institutions and reliance on allied security guarantees were its dominant
foreign-policy strategies for achieving these goals. Multilateral institutions
mitigated the political, economic, and military vulnerability resulting from
its location on the borderline between East and West.[9]

With the end of the East–West conflict in 1989, unification and the management of European security risks joined peace/security and prosperity as
German policy priorities. Consequently German strategies favoured CSCE/
OSCE institutionalization, and Germany took the lead in that area. Furthermore, so strongly intertwined were German security preferences and
strategies on the OSCE that the institution became not just a means but an
end in itself. When the OSCE became a necessary means for German ends,
ends and means became indistinguishable, and OSCE institutionalization
became a German preference in its own right.

This conclusion is supported by evidence that Germany not only pursued multilateralism, but also that it consistently took the lead in promoting
the OSCE. Furthermore, Germany supported the OSCE not at the expense
of NATO and the EU, but as part of a comprehensive policy of multilateral
integration. As it did so, the OSCE became more and more a fundamental
goal of German policy.

That institutions have an impact not only on states' strategies but also on
states' interests and preferences might seem to be a constructivist argument.
It is, however, part and parcel of neo-liberal institutionalism.[10] Institutions influence the definition of states' interests and preferences when they

---

[9] See Haftendorn (1989: 35–6).

[10] e.g. Keohane (1989*c*: 6) writes: 'Yet it would be misleading to limit the significance of institutions to their effects on incentives. Institutions may also affect the understandings that leaders
of states have of the roles they should play and their assumptions about others' motivations and
perceived self- interests.'

function as a 'causal belief',[11] i.e. are taken to be an indispensable prerequisite for achieving one's preferences. Institutions are then no longer mere political instruments but have become part of a state's set of preferences.[12]

Section 2 of this chapter explains and analyses Germany's policy on the OSCE from 1989 to 1994.[13] It details German objectives, official German policies, and the outcomes in terms of actual CSCE institutionalization that the government accepted. In this section, I pay particular attention to evaluating evidence that the German government sought CSCE institutionalization, not only as a means to other goals but also as an objective in its own right. Section 3 addresses the place of Germany's CSCE policy in relation to Germany's policy on the two other crucial European institutions for cooperation and integration (NATO and the EU), in order to address the potential counterargument that CSCE institutionalization was a way for Germany to weaken integration in these other forums. I show that this was not the case, further supporting institutionalist hypotheses on the effects of institutions on German strategies and preferences.

2. Germany's Policy on the Institutional Evolution of the CSCE 1989–1994

Enhancing the CSCE for coping with collective risks:
multilateral institutions as a state preference

The peaceful revolutions in Eastern Europe and the demise of the Soviet empire brought the fundamental political conflict between East and West to an end, and with it the immediate threat of East–West military confrontation. However, Europe faced new security challenges. New risks arose from

---

[11] See Introduction.

[12] In this study the institution's impact is evaluated relative to other factors' effects (power and interests, ideas and culture, or history and learning, etc.). This relative effect of a single variable on state preferences and strategy may be defined as 'the extent that their [the variable's] operation accounts for the variance in individual and collective behavior observable across spatial or temporal settings' (Young, 1992: 163). Following from these epistemological considerations, the findings of this study will not live up to positivistic demands for 'hard tests' of the defined causal mechanism regarding the institutional impact on state preferences and policy strategies. The author more modestly aims at a convincingly plausible argument.

[13] This study is limited to the institutional evolution of the CSCE from 1989 to 1994. After the Budapest summit of Dec. 1994, only minor changes have affected the (now so-called) OSCE. In addition, developments since 1994 have not changed German policies. Since 1994, NATO enlargement undoubtedly has become the focus of the European security debate and determines, if it does not impede, the evolution of other multilateral institutions.

socially and politically unstable new democracies in East and Central Europe. Ethnic and minority conflicts within states and across borders, as well as old and new territorial claims and secessionist movements, ranked high on the new European security agenda. These major changes to the international landscape challenged the security not only of single countries but also of the whole of Europe. The German government characterized these new risks as problems that could not successfully be addressed by unilateral measures but instead required multilateral responses. According to Genscher, a 'modernization of thinking and policies' was required, and security could only be achieved through cooperation.[14] 'Security partnership', 'stability partnership', and 'all-European peace order' were recurring phrases in Chancellor Kohl's as well as Foreign Minister Genscher's foreign policy statements, and 'cooperative security' became the catchword of German foreign policy in the months after the fall of the Berlin Wall in November 1989.

The central vehicle for Bonn's all-European cooperative security strategy was the CSCE. Its comprehensive membership allowed for the use of an all-European framework providing both orientation for the new democracies and a basis for multilateral efforts in support of political transformation and stabilization. The Helsinki Final Act of 1975 and the documents adopted by the thirty-five CSCE states in 1989/90 contained norms and rules that defined the guidelines for legitimate state policy in international and domestic affairs alike. Through adoption of these politically binding documents, the governments had approved of democracy as the only legitimate form of government and accepted the principles of market economy and human and minority rights according to Western standards. Bonn considered these principles, norms, and rules to be the foundation for all-European cooperation after the East–West conflict.

However, in order to make a meaningful contribution to European stability during the social, economic, and political transformation of Central and East Europe and in the Soviet Union, the CSCE had to be strengthened. A CSCE summit was proposed for the near future at which decisions on an enhancement of the CSCE would be taken and would become the 'starting point for a new chapter in European history'.[15] Public statements from the German government in favour of strengthening the CSCE were numerous and ambitious; Kohl and Genscher seemingly competed with each other on who could give a stronger speech on CSCE

---

[14] See Genscher (19 Oct. 1989: 48–50).
[15] Genscher (23 Mar. 1990: 313).

reforms.[16] According to their judgement, the normative basis of the CSCE needed to be refined and supplemented and the implementation of CSCE principles, norms, and rules had to be improved. Instead of being confined to its old function as a body for consultations and coordination of policies across the 'iron curtain', the CSCE should now be the basis for establishing a new kind of international cooperation.[17] It should take on new assignments, including operational measures for multilateral attempts to manage and possibly dissolve emerging risks and conflicts and to foster democratization. New assignments, moreover, required institutional under-pinnings, i.e. new political structures including effective decision-making procedures, functional organs, and instruments for multilateral action. Thus, in order to make reforms at the political level, the German government publicly proposed a council of foreign ministers and regular summits for fostering confidence among participating states and mitigating or preventing conflicts with the potential to escalate. Accordingly, various agencies, forums, and institutes were suggested in order to facilitate multi-lateral measures and programmes on the operational level. Among others, institutes for crisis prevention and peaceful settlement of disputes were dis-cussed, as well as for verification of arms control agreements, monitoring democratic standards during elections, enhancing minority rights, and cooperatively managing environmental problems.

These ambitious public statements by the leading figures of the coalition government in Bonn were matched by concrete proposals advanced at the negotiation table.[18] Hence, Germany was doubtless a pace-maker and 'general activist'[19] regarding the enhancement of the CSCE. Germany's preferences for institutionalizing the CSCE and enhancing its political meaning were met by a mixed reaction from the other CSCE states. Negotiations in the EU and NATO finally predetermined the outcome on the all-European level, the CSCE document adopted by the participating states in Paris on 20 November 1990: the Paris Charter for a New Europe.[20] Regarding institutionalization, on the political level a network of regular

---

[16] See e.g. Kohl (28 Nov. 1989: 119–20); Genscher (1 Jan. 1990); Kohl (3 Feb. 1990); Genscher (13 Feb. 1990); Kohl (19 Mar. 1990); Genscher (23 Mar., 11 Apr. 1990); Kohl (21 May 1990); Genscher (1 Aug. 1990).

[17] See Genscher (6 Apr. 1990: 104).

[18] The details of Germany's substantial proposals will be addressed in the section on 'Ger-many's continuing engagement . . .' below.

[19] Germany already fell in this category in the earlier days of the CSCE: see Holsti (1984: 141–2).

[20] Conference on Security and Cooperation in Europe, Charter of Paris for a New Europe, 21 Nov. 1990. For the details on institutions, see Supplementary Document to give effect to certain provisions contained in the Charter of Paris for a New Europe.

high-level meetings—summits, councils of foreign ministers, follow-up meetings (later review conferences)—was instituted. Periodic meetings of high-ranking government officials and diplomats (Committee of Senior Officials, or CSO) were established to prepare council meetings and implement common decisions. On a functional level, permanent organs were created to provide a small international bureaucracy as a continuous organizational framework for CSCE activities. These working units give administrative support to the political level (the secretariat in Prague) and are also specialized agencies charged with assignments in various policy areas (Bureau of Free Elections in Warsaw, Conflict Prevention Center in Vienna). Instruments for implementing agreed-on measures include 'mechanisms' and 'missions', implemented through either the political forums or the organs. Mechanisms provide prearranged procedures for consultation and decision-making in conflicts or crisis situations. For example, the purpose of the mechanism for 'unusual military activities'[21] is to deal with acute threat perceptions. The 'human rights mechanism' can help tackle critical concerns about violations of human rights. These mechanisms facilitate fact-finding or observer missions to gain or verify information, thus serving as a basis for political decisions on the national or international level.

The German government's analysis and definition of the country's new security situation conveys a strong awareness of the policy interdependence in European security affairs, the necessity of tackling the new risks by collective action, and the facilitating role of multilateral institutions (in this case the CSCE) in cooperative problem-solving. Cooperation through this multilateral institution was the chosen strategy for coping with the new security challenges and for achieving the overriding goals of peaceful change and continuation of the country's economic well-being. A close look reveals the interconnectedness of goals and strategy, to the extent that institutionalized multilateralism became virtually an end in itself, and can, for practical purposes, be numbered among the goals of German foreign policy.

Germany's CSCE policy as an instrument of its Deutschlandpolitik

The institutional decisions adopted at the Paris summit were rather modest considering the German perception of security risks and, consequently, the desirability of institutional enhancement of the CSCE. The decisions were

---

21 See CSCE, Vienna Document 1990 on Confidence and Security-building Measures, para. 17.

also modest considering the broad range of institutions Bonn had advocated beforehand, especially when it came to the competencies and the
instruments of the Conflict Prevention Center (CPC). With this institutional
character the CSCE obviously could not meet the new security challenges.
Nevertheless, Chancellor Kohl considered the Paris summit a 'historic
event', praised the Charter as the 'Magna Carta of freedom',[22] and described
the establishment of the CPC as an achievement in accordance with essential German aims. This positive evaluation of the Paris summit was chiefly
due to its relevance for the German government's *Deutschlandpolitik*, i.e. its
overriding interest in unification.

Following the revolutions in Eastern Europe, and especially between the
fall of the Berlin Wall on 9 November 1989, and formal unification on
3 October 1990, West German foreign policy was preoccupied with the
unification question. The central forum for international bargaining on
German unification was the 2+4 process,[23] but the CSCE had an important
role to play in providing Europe-wide legitimacy and thus safeguarding
unification against international suspicion and possibly opposition. Chancellor Kohl stated that 'the future architecture of Germany must fit into the
future architecture of Europe'.[24] and declared the CSCE to be at the core
(*Herzstück*) of that architecture. The meaning of the CSCE for German
unification was made obvious by the early plan to present the documents of
the 2+4 negotiations on the international aspects of German unification to
the CSCE summit in Paris.[25] The multi-layered negotiations in which
unification became embedded demanded transparency at an Europe-wide
level in order to reassure Germany's neighbours—above all those who were
not taking part in the 2+4 negotiations—that unification was not directed
against anyone. At the same time, however, unification was to occur without
any formal peace treaty between Germany and the allies of the Second
World War or the other neighbouring states in order to avoid any demands
for reparations by Germany's former victims and enemies.

The CSCE was a West German instrument for unification *vis-à-vis*
Moscow especially. In response to Kohl's ten-point plan 'for overcoming the
division of Germany and Europe',[26] Soviet President Gorbachev proposed
an early CSCE summit in the second half of 1990[27] and demanded that

---

[22] Kohl (22 Nov. 1990: 1407; translation by I.P.).   [23] See Pond (1993: 173–92).
[24] Kohl (28 Nov. 1989: 119–20; translation by I.P.). See also Teltschik (1991: 59–60, 163–4);
Weilemann (1990).
[25] Genscher (20 Sept. 1990: 1185).   [26] Kohl (28 Nov. 1989: 119–20).
[27] See *Frankfurter Allgemeine Zeitung* (*FAZ*) (1 Dec. 1989): 'Rom hegt keine Bedenken wegen
eines "deutschen Revanchismus"'. At the Vienna CSCE follow-up meeting, the next such meeting
had been scheduled to start at 24 Mar. 1992 in Helsinki. See Concluding Final Document of the

Germany and its Western partners be ready to strengthen the CSCE as an all-European security institution. German commitment to the CSCE was a prerequisite for Soviet approval of German national unity, and was also necessary to satisfy the legitimate security interests and concerns of all other states. Germany responded positively, in order to overcome Moscow's opposition to German unification and especially to German and Western plans that a united Germany should be a member of NATO.[28] Consequently Germany lobbied among its neighbours and within Western organizations, in favour of enhancing the CSCE substantially.[29] Its EC partners agreed on 20 January 1990 to have a special CSCE summit in autumn 1990, and NATO followed suit on 7 February 1990.[30] By supporting a meaningful build-up of the CSCE, Bonn did justice to Moscow's wish to 'synchronize' the 2+4 process with the CSCE process.[31] Finally, during a meeting between Kohl and Gorbachev in the Caucasus in July 1990, the Soviet government officially accepted unification and withdrew its opposition to united Germany's being a member of NATO.[32]

Accordingly, at the CSCE summit in Paris in November 1990, all the European states welcomed German unification 'with great satisfaction' and approved the 2+4 treaty. The CSCE states 'sincerely welcome the fact that the German people have united to become one state in accordance with the principles of the Final Act of the Conference on Security and Cooperation in Europe'.[33] Germany successfully used the CSCE to further its national unification by gaining Europe-wide legitimacy for and Soviet consent to both unification and Germany's membership in NATO. The rather modest

CSCE Follow-up Meeting in Vienna of 15 Jan. 1989, 'Follow-up to the Conference'. Shevardnadze (1989: 150).

[28] See *FAZ* (6 Dec. 1989): 'Genscher in Moskau: Signale der Stabilisierung'; *Süddeutsche Zeitung* (*SZ*) (12 June 1990): 'Gespräche länger als geplant'; see also Genscher (28 June 1990). Genscher formulated as further preconditions for Soviet consent: (1) progress with regard to conventional arms control, (2) a qualitatively new relationship between the existing military alliances in East and West, (3) the recognition of all state borders in Europe, and (4) an intensified economic collaboration with the Soviet Union.

[29] See the government's overview on the Chancellor's international consultations regarding German unification from Jan. to Mar. 1990: 'Einbettung der deutschen Einigung in den europäischen Einigungsprozeß', *Bulletin*, 40 (27 Mar. 1990), 314.

[30] See Auswärtiges Amt (1991). 19; *SZ* (30 Apr. 1990): 'EG treibt KSZE-Gipfel voran'; 'European Council in Dublin. Special Meeting of the Heads of State or Government of the EC on 28 April 1990', *Bulletin*, 51 (4 May 1990), 401–4.

[31] See Rotfeld (1991: 595); Albrecht (1992: 75–6).

[32] See Kohl (17 July 1990: 803). There he stated: 'Das geeinte Deutschland kann in Ausübung seiner vollen und uneingeschränkten Souveränität frei und selbst entscheiden, ob und welchem Bündnis es angehören will. Dies entspricht dem Geist und dem Text der KSZE-Schlußakte.'

[33] Charter of Paris for a New Europe of 21 Nov. 1990: 1411.

results of the Paris summit and document regarding the role of the CSCE as a stabilizer for all-European security doubtless ranked second on the German foreign-policy agenda. However, with the Soviets' consent at the Caucasus meeting in July, and German unification finalized in October, Germany was enthusiastic about the CSCE because of its usefulness in achieving Germany's paramount goal. In addition, Germany had to compromise on its more ambitious plans regarding the institutionalization of the CSCE because of the reluctance of its NATO allies and EU partners. In order to maintain the Western consensus and the support of its Western partners for unification—especially the United States, which is traditionally sceptical of the CSCE—Bonn had to give ground on more rapid and extensive institutionalization of the CSCE.

Germany's continuing engagement in favour of a 'cooperative security institution'

After achieving unification Germany did not turn its back on the CSCE but renewed its support for it as a politically meaningful cooperative security institution and a multilateral instrument for collectively defined purposes. In order to become a politically meaningful institution as the German government wished, the CSCE had to be able to contribute significantly and visibly to the management of new security challenges. Hence, apart from the traditional functions of the CSCE as a body for all-European consultation and negotiation on common political principles and norms, the CSCE should be assigned concrete operational competencies regarding conflict prevention, political crisis management, and peaceful settlement of disputes. Instead of being just a talking shop and the 'toothless watchdog' of international political principles and norms, it should be equipped with operational instruments for actively fostering compliance and bringing these principles, norms, and rules to bear on the political practice of the participating states. In Germany's view, however, the role of the CSCE in conflict prevention and crisis management should be confined to the political realm, and military crisis management should be excluded. As Foreign Minister Klaus Kinkel repeatedly stated after he succeeded Genscher in May 1992, the CSCE should contribute to European security by 'preventing fires, but not putting them out' ('Brandverhüter, nicht als Feuerwehr').[34]

Consequently, the baseline of German institutionalization policy remained its comprehensive proposal for a Conflict Prevention Centre, made

[34] Klaus Kinkel on the occasion of the adoption of the bill on the CSCE Court for Conciliation and Arbitration, *Stichworte zur Sicherheitspolitik*, 2 (1994), 4 (translation by I.P.); Kinkel (1992).

in July 1990.[35] Referring to principle 5 of the Helsinki Final Act of 1975 on the peaceful settlement of disputes, Bonn proposed to give the CSCE the capacity to accomplish 'conflict prevention through cooperation'. While political control and supervision would be exercised by a council of foreign ministers, a conflict prevention centre would be assigned operational tasks concerning political conflict management. 'The center should be capable of coping with all crises and conflicts running counter to CSCE principles', be they military or non-military. The German government favoured giving the centre a role in political conflict management because 'the resolution of political conflicts would prevent military conflicts, while the early settlement of potential military conflicts would prevent escalation and facilitate political settlements'.[36] Moreover, Bonn advanced the idea that a committee of permanent representatives of all participating states would oversee an executive secretary, who would be entitled to take initiatives and advance his/her own proposals for timely conflict management. Only these characteristics, the Germans argued, would enable the CSCE to be permanently ready for consultations and action in crisis situations, even at short notice.

This proposal revealed the basic features that characterized German policy on the institutional evolution of the CSCE in the following years. The centre was conceived as an intergovernmental body, not a supranational institution implying any transfer of sovereignty from the states to the organization. Two further features of the German conception of the CSCE structure were its intention to establish permanent and politically meaningful institutions. Although no permanent political body was agreed on at Paris, the creation of a permanent CSCE institution remained one of Germany's aims in the aftermath of the Paris summit. This became obvious when Bonn proposed to strengthen the centre by making it the location of the new round of arms control negotiations which, according to the Paris document, was to be prepared and later conducted within the framework of the CSCE.[37] A decision to this end, Germany felt, would be significant because the centre would not have merely taken on a new assignment. This would moreover mean a general enhancement of the institution since it would become a quasi-permanent body for at least as long as the arms control negotiations lasted. This German aim of a permanent body for the CSCE surfaced again when the German delegation in Vienna, preceding the

[35] Proposal of the Federal Republic of Germany on a 'Konfliktverhütungszentrum der KSZE', presented at the Preparatory Committee in Vienna on 26 July 1990 (translation by I.P.).

[36] See Proposal of the Federal Republic of Germany of 26 July 1990, para. 6 and 10, pp. 3–4 (translation by I.P.).

[37] See Charter of Paris for a New Europe of 21 Nov. 1990: 10.

Prague Council meeting in January 1992, presented so-called 'illustrative models' in September and December 1991 addressing the question of what a CPC should look like. The models suggested institutionalizing a comprehensive and continuous security dialogue within the CPC or regular consultations of the Consultative Committee. This was also the case in the French-German paper of November 1991 on the structure of future security negotiations within the framework of the CSCE, which contained a proposal for a 'permanent committee' for coordinating the work of a new forum that later became formalized as the Forum for Security Cooperation.[38]

Germany had to recognize that its own preference for strengthening the CPC was not shared by all of the other participating states, including its Western partners. This did not mean, however, that Germany gave up on its plans for a permanent political forum. This core element of German institutionalization policy became more important and was more readily accepted by formerly reluctant governments in view of the violently escalating conflicts in the CSCE area, i.e. in the former Yugoslavia and the Caucasus. These conflicts revealed the weak points of the CSCE institutions. Although the Council and the CSO were charged with taking political decisions, these bodies only convened periodically and hence were not in a position to engage *ad hoc* and instantly in crisis situations. Moreover, the numerous fact-finding or observation missions sent to the trouble spots, along with other diplomatic activities of the CSCE, required continuous political control and coordination. Consequently, at the Stockholm council meeting, governments finally decided that the CSCE structures should undergo a structural reform.[39]

Before and during the negotiations on reform in Vienna, several proposals were discussed relating to a possible executive body for transforming the common decisions of the CSCE states into collective action and supervising measures taken and daily activities. In view of the increasingly visible crisis in Yugoslavia, German Foreign Minister Genscher repeatedly presented his idea of a 'European security council'[40] before the Prague Council

---

[38] German Delegation to the CSCE, Illustrative Model. Recommendations concerning the Conflict Prevention Center, Vienna, 16 Sept. 1991; German Delegation to the CSCE, Illustrative Model, Programme for Immediate Action for Arms Control, Security Cooperation and Conflict Prevention, presented at the Consultative Committee in Vienna, 19 Dec. 1991.

[39] Third Meeting of the CSCE Council of Foreign Ministers. Summary of Conclusions. Decision on Peaceful Settlement of Disputes, Stockholm, 15 Dec. 1992, s. 7, 'Evolution of CSCE Structures and Institutions', pp. 19–21.

[40] See Genscher 10 Sept. 1991, 797; *FAZ* (26 Apr. 1991): 'Die NATO sucht ein System gegenseitiger Sicherheit für ganz Europa'; *FAZ* (19 June 1991): 'Das neue Europa auf der Suche nach gemeinsamer Sicherheit'.

meeting in January 1992—an idea which had already earlier irritated the Western partners in connection with Germany's comprehensive CPC proposal (see below). Bonn and Paris, with the support of their EC partners, also proposed to establish a steering committee[41] as the political executive body of the CSCE. Despite some criticism, mainly from smaller states,[42] who saw such a committee as an instrument for preserving the predominance of the bigger powers, these ideas finally became part of CSCE decisions taken at the Helsinki follow-up meeting and the Stockholm council meeting of December 1992.[43] Accordingly, the chairperson of the Council of Foreign Ministers was upgraded to the post of Chairman in Office and formed together with the preceding and the succeeding Chairmen the CSCE troika, with such enhanced competencies as nominating *ad hoc* steering committees for political oversight and support of CSCE missions to acute trouble spots.

Moreover, Bonn's original proposal for an executive secretariat resurfaced in autumn 1992 as part of Belgian and British proposals for establishing the post of secretary-general. Bonn and its EC partners gave this idea priority in discussions about the structural reform of the CSCE. At the Stockholm council meeting in December 1992 this position was officially created. The first person nominated for this post was German Ambassador Wilhelm Höynck who took office as the first CSCE secretary-general in April 1993.[44] In Stockholm, Bonn could register three other successes.[45] First, the secretariat was built up through a departmental substructure and an increase in personnel and became the central institution for supporting the Chairperson in Office. Second, the Secretariat (apart from its documentation branch) was concentrated in Vienna; the Bureau for Democratic Institutions and Human Rights (BDIHR) and the High Commissioner for National Minorities (HCNM) remained in Warsaw and The Hague respectively. Third, the CPC, which became one of the Secretariat's departments, was strengthened in its capabilities through the creation of an operational

---

41 See *SZ* (1–2 Feb. 1992): 'KSZE: Bei Krisen schneller eingreifen'.

42 See *Neue Zürcher Zeitung* (2–3 Feb. 1992): 'Die KSZE an ihren Grenzen'; *SZ* (18 Feb. 1992): 'Belgien kritisiert KSZE-Initiative Bonns'; Heraclides (1993: 77–80).

43 CSCE, Helsinki Document 1992, The Challenges of Change, Helsinki Summit Declaration 10 July 1992, Helsinki Decisions, s. I, esp. paras. 12–22. Third Meeting of the CSCE Council of Foreign Ministers, Summary of Conclusions, Decision on Peaceful Settlement of Disputes, Stockholm, 15 Dec. 1992, s. 7 'Evolution of CSCE Structures and Institutions', pp. 19–21.

44 *FAZ* (20 Oct. 1992): 'Bonn bereitet sich auf eine Zwischenbilanz vor'; Heraclides (1993: 181–3); CSCE, 19. CSO Meeting in Prague, 4 Feb. 1993, *Journal*, 3, TOP 12 and 21. CSCE, CSO Meeting in Prague, 27 April 93, *Journal*, 2, Appendix; *FAZ* (5 Feb. 1993): 'KSZE will Embargo durchsetzen'.

45 See CSCE, Stockholm Document, 15 Dec. 1992: 19–21.

section with additional personnel. At the Rome council meeting in December 1993 the decision was taken to establish a Permanent Committee,[46]
renamed the Permanent Council at the Budapest review conference in
December 1994,[47] which became the central CSCE's consultative and
decision-making forum and was composed of the participating states'
representatives to the CSCE in Vienna. These decisions were very much in
line with Germany's long-standing wish for the CSCE to have a permanent
capacity for consultation and political decision-making. They also meant a
significant improvement in intergovernmental cooperation.[48] Instead of
mere harmonization of views through consultations, the new capacity of
the CSCE made coordination among participating governments the necessary basis for operational cooperation in collective actions.

Another of Bonn's institutional aims was to improve the operational
capabilities of the new CSCE organs by creating instruments for conflict
management. Bonn favoured establishing 'mechanisms', i.e. routine procedures for political consultation and decision-making on conflict prevention and crisis management. Hence, an emergency mechanism for acute
crisis situations, another for the peaceful settlement of disputes (including
obligatory procedures, i.e. without veto power by the states in question),
and a mechanism for the human dimension were proposed. These proposals were finally adopted at the Berlin council meeting in June 1991, the
meeting on peaceful settlement of disputes in La Valletta in January 1991,
and the Moscow meeting on the human dimension in September 1991.[49]
Although not always as robust as Bonn wished, these decisions were nevertheless a success for German policy.

Other instruments Bonn proposed included fact-finding missions in
crisis situations upon invitation by concerned states but following the
orders of the CSCE as a whole. In August 1991, Foreign Minister Genscher
had already proposed peacekeeping, i.e. the deployment of CSCE blue
helmets analogous to UN blue helmets, as an instrument for conflict prevention and crisis management. In the same vein, Germany's policy on
confidence- and security-building measures (CSBM) aimed at adjusting
existing measures to the new security challenges in order to avoid or reduce
subregional instability and the risks of misperception or miscalculation by

---

[46] Fourth Meeting of the CSCE Council of Foreign Minister in Rome, 30 Nov.–1 Dec. 1993
(Rome Document), Conclusions, s. VII, para. 3 and 7.1.

[47] CSCE Budapest Document 1994, 'Towards a Genuine Partnership in a New Era', 5–6 Dec.
1994, Budapest Summit Declaration, paras. 16–18.

[48] See P. Taylor (1990: 13–14).

[49] See Peters (1994: 169–73).

political actors. These negotiations and the resulting measures Bonn conceived as instruments for fostering cooperation in military security policy with the new democracies in Central and Eastern Europe.[50]

Of course, the German government did not favour making the CSCE a supranational institution; Bonn preferred an international structure under the auspices of the foreign ministers. This preference was made clear by Germany's support for the establishment of the post of Chairman in Office, which was clearly located on the intergovernmental level. Nevertheless, attainment of a politically meaningful and effective CSCE implied, in the German conception, that the CSCE's organs gain some operational autonomy at the political level. Bonn favoured organs with the authority and resources to initiate mechanisms and missions without prior consultation or formal decisions taken by the Council or the CSO. Accordingly Bonn proposed, during the January 1991 negotiations in La Valletta on the peaceful settlement of disputes (PSD), to assign to the CPC the power to initiate the PSD mechanism.[51] This proposal was not approved by all participants and did not enter the final document. Likewise, Germany proposed in September 1991 to allow the CPC the ability to initiate observer or fact-finding missions, and the Kinkel-Kooijmans[52] package proposed in May 1994 favoured allowing the secretary-general to initiate such missions. These proposals failed to receive the support of all participating states; while the sending of missions was adopted, the power of initiation remained with the political bodies, i.e. the Council of Foreign Ministers (now the Council of Ministers) and the CSO (now the High Council). At the Council meeting in Rome[53] (December 1993) and the Budapest review conference[54] (December 1994), however, the Permanent Council was also assigned the right to initiate missions with regard to the CHD mechanism and later to the emergency mechanism.

Operational capabilities, however, could only become politically effective if decisions were taken to apply available instruments. In times of crisis or acute conflict, CSCE decisions may easily be blocked because they require a consensus of all participating states. It is not surprising, therefore, that Germany repeatedly demanded a rule allowing decisions to be taken on the

---

[50] See *FAZ* (3 Aug. 1991): 'Genscher will Truppen-Einsatz nur unter Zustimmung Jugoslawiens erörtern'; *FAZ* (5 Aug. 1991): 'Genscher für "KSZE-Blauhelme"'; *SZ* (5 Sept. 1991): 'Genscher will KSZE-Friedenstruppen'. Peters (1993*a*).

[51] See Peters (1994: 169–73).

[52] See Kinkel 17 May 1994, 411–12; 'Joint German-Dutch agenda for preparing the CSCE summit in Budapest', *Bulletin*, 46 (20 May 1994), 412–14.

[53] See Rome Document, 1 Dec. 1993, chapter iv, para. 5, and appendix A.

[54] See Budapest Document 1994, Decisions, chapter i, para. 18.

basis of a 'consensus minus one' or 'consensus minus conflicting parties'.[55] Parties to a conflict or governments violating CSCE principles should not be allowed a veto preventing consultations, decisions, or operational measures. Hence Germany pleaded for a decision-making procedure that is also the basis for a collective security system. In the CSCE case, however, collective actions were much more restrained, i.e. confined to measures taken in response to conflicts or to crises with the potential to escalate but short of granting military assistance against an aggressor.[56]

In a moderate victory for Bonn, the consensus-minus-one arrangement became part of the emergency mechanism adopted at the Berlin council in June 1991: a consensus was no longer required for *initiating* the mechanism, i.e. for convening consultations.[57] Nevertheless, consensus remained a prerequisite for any decision on measures to be taken in response to a crisis. Another example of Bonn's policy in favour of weakening the consensus rule was the Kinkel-Kooijmans initiative of May 1994, which proposed allowing the CSCE to refer a conflict to the UN Security Council for action, including possible peacemaking activities in accordance with chapter 7 of the UN Charter.[58] This proposal failed at the Budapest summit, which also rejected a proposal to give the Chairperson in Office the power to act on the basis of a majority vote in well-defined, pre-agreed administrative matters.

German support for partial departures from the consensus rule aimed at strengthening CSCE's commitment to the basic principle of international law that no state is entitled to interfere in the domestic affairs of another state. Consequently, the CSCE's ability should be enhanced to take action against any participants violating CSCE principles. The most far-reaching success Bonn and its NATO partners attained on this score was at the Prague council meeting in January 1992, where it was agreed that in cases of gross and uncorrected violations of CSCE principles, political sanctions outside the concerned state can be applied (even against the violating state's will) in order to uphold the common standards.[59] Regarding violations of CSCE standards relating to human rights, democracy, and the rule of law, the traditional principle of international law concerning non-interference with

---

[55] Peters (1994: 167–76).

[56] See McKenzie (1994: 26–31); Peters (1995*a*).

[57] See First Meeting of the CSCE Council of Foreign Ministers in Berlin, 20 June 1991, Summary of Conclusions, appendix 2. On the operational mode of the mechanism see Vetschera (1994: 109–10), 114–16; Ropers and Schlotter (1992: 16–22).

[58] Joint German-Dutch agenda 20 May 1994, pp. 412–13.

[59] See Second Meeting of the CSCE Council of Foreign Ministers in Prague, 30/31 Jan. 1992, Prague Document on Further Development of CSCE Institutions and Structures, chapter iv, para. 16.

domestic affairs was mitigated by consensus decisions taken at the Moscow conference on the human dimension[60] and the meetings on minority problems in Geneva[61] and Copenhagen.[62] Consequently, every single state's domestic affairs are the legitimate concern of all CSCE states, and requests or measures taken to clarify suspect cases can no longer legitimately be rejected by simply referring to the 'non-interference in domestic affairs' clause. This was a clear success for Bonn's policy

Overall, Germany's CSCE policy was marked by a well-defined and comprehensive position regarding assignments, competencies, instruments, and decision-making procedures. It aimed at creating an international institution able to engage in conflict prevention and political crisis management and to foster the process of democratization and the protection of human and minority rights. The CSCE should be an all-European institution capable of making an effective contribution to European security. Germany's institutionalization policy thus rested on an awareness of the policy interdependence in European security affairs that followed the end of the East–West conflict and of the facilitating role of the CSCE in multilateral cooperation on common problems.

This definition of interests and policy preferences produced a policy comprising a great variety of detailed and concrete proposals. Germany claimed the 'copyright' for numerous political initiatives and proposals submitted in negotiations with its partners and allies in the EC/EU and NATO in Brussels or at the CSCE negotiations in Vienna. Most of the time, Bonn's policy was ambitious and robust in comparison with what most of the other participants were ready even to consider, much less adopt, by consensus. German eagerness and determination, however, was not always appreciated by other governments. Bonn's position on the further institutionalization of the CSCE was criticized as 'idealistic', i.e. not in accord with political realities. Despite the immense impact of the German government's institutionalization process, the overall institutional evolution of the CSCE, renamed the Organization for Security and Cooperation in Europe (OSCE) at the Budapest meeting in December 1994, resulted from multilateral negotiations and depended on consensus decisions by all participating states, who numbered thirty-four in 1990 and fifty-five after 1996.

[60] See *FAZ* 5 Oct. 1991: 'Die KSZE durchbricht erstmals das Konsensprinzip'. Concluding Document of the CSCE Meeting on the Human Dimension of the CSCE in Moscow, 3 Oct. 1991.
[61] 'Report on the CSCE Expert Meeting on National Minorities', Geneva, 19 July 1991, in *20 Jahre KSZE 1973–1993* (Bonn: Auswärtiges Amt), 309–17, at 311.
[62] 'Document of the Conference on the Human Dimension of the CSCE in Copenhagen, 29 June 1990', in *Sicherheit und Zusammenarbeit in Europa: Dokumentation zum KSZE-Prozeß 1990/91* (Bonn: Auswärtiges Amt), 35–58.

Bonn's negotiating strategy: no German Sonderweg

How did Germany carry out its ambitious institutionalization policy? Was there a tendency to avoid the traditional practice of holding prior consultations among the Western states in order to agree on a common CSCE policy? What about German tendencies to concentrate on its national interests and to adopt unilateralism as its policy strategy?

Prior consultations with its Western partners clearly remained one of the major features of German policy, and explicitly unilateral actions were rare. But this does not mean that each and every German initiative was coordinated with its EU and NATO partners before being presented in the CSCE-wide negotiations. For example, the various 'models' the German delegation generated and presented in Vienna had been discussed with its Western partners but did not always gain full support or a formal *placet* before they were submitted at CSCE-wide negotiations. On several occasions Germany formed coalitions with the newly democratic states of Central Europe, whose active involvement it viewed as an important contribution to what Bonn saw as the central purpose of the CSCE, the stabilization of Eastern and Central Europe. Such joint actions with these states were the reasons for the impasse on the consensus rule during the Moscow meeting on the human dimension (September 1991), and the attempts to strengthen the competencies of the CPC in autumn 1991 and in spring 1992.[63] In both cases Bonn failed to receive full support from its EC partners for its own proposals and had to compromise. Nevertheless, Germany made clear that it was ready to go beyond the EC position and sympathized with the proposals of the Central and Eastern European states. This strategy of trying to bring in one's own aims and ideas by the back door sometimes irritated its partners. However, because some of the latter occasionally behaved the same way, the German practice could hardly be interpreted as a trend toward a German *Sonderweg* (special path).[64]

Another incentive to avoid unilateral policy was the fact that the CSCE became one of the first four areas for common actions by the EU in the framework of the Common Foreign and Security Policy following the Maastricht Treaty of 1992.[65] The Kinkel-Kooijmans initiative of May 1994 apparently ran counter to this provision, because the foreign ministers publicly presented their proposals for further strengthening the CSCE before a common EU position had been adopted. However, this proposal

---

[63] See Peters (1994: 167–76).   [64] See Heraclides (1993: 86–7).
[65] See Regelsberger (1992).

had undoubtedly been discussed with their partners in advance. This became evident in the 'CSCE-first' idea in the bilateral package proposal, which was worded more cautiously than Kinkel's earlier formulation at the Rome council meeting in December 1993.[66]

Germany's early and emphatic policy in favour of a far-reaching institutional reform of the CSCE, especially the comprehensive July 1990 proposal for a CPC, constrained Bonn's room for political manœuvre. The political suspicion aroused by this proposal and by Genscher's hasty rhetoric about plans to transform the CSCE into an institution overarching the military alliances put Germany very much on the political defensive. This became obvious, for example, when Germany did not nominate a candidate for the post of first CPC director in autumn 1990, when Bonn held back from pushing its strong preference for establishing an 'operational section' at the CPC in autumn 1992, and by its tactical reluctance regarding the plans for creating a 'permanent committee' prior to the Stockholm council meeting in December 1992. This low-profile strategy was adopted in order to avoid burdening its own aims and proposals with the suspicions of its partners about Germany's idealistic CSCE policy, thereby endangering the consensus on these ideas. Even though this strategy meant some restrictions on Germany's political leeway, it was not seriously inconvenient because Germany always lobbied behind the scenes beforehand and was sure most of the time that other governments would officially present its favoured proposals.

3. The CSCE, NATO, and the EC/EU: Complementing or Competitive Frameworks of German Foreign and Security Policy?

How did Germany's policy on institutionalizing the CSCE relate to its policies on NATO and the EC/EU? Was Bonn trying to strengthen the all-European institution at the expense of West European and transatlantic institutions, thereby putting in question the country's traditional Western commitments? Germany's Western partners were for some time, and for a number of reasons, suspicious of Germany's forceful CSCE policy. They were anxious that Germany might be pursuing a CSCE policy running counter to their own political priorities and institutional preferences, which were to maintain NATO and the EC/EU and to keep Germany integrated.

---

[66] Joint German-Dutch agenda for preparing the CSCE summit in Budapest, 20 May 1994, 412–13; *Frankfurter Rundschau* (1 Dec. 1993): 'KSZE will mehr Gewicht'.

The vigorous rhetoric of Chancellor Kohl and Foreign Minister Genscher, as well as the numerous detailed and ambitious proposals in favour of strengthening the CSCE, irritated Germany's Western partners, especially during spring and summer of 1990 and to a lesser extent through the first half of 1991. Was Germany pursuing a hidden agenda, i.e. aiming at unilateral goals under the cover of its institutionalization policy? Did Bonn aim at transforming the CSCE into a full-fledged collective security system? Did Bonn intend to use a strong CSCE as a substitute for the military alliances, at that time the Warsaw Treaty Organization and NATO, or to create a regional United Nations, thus possibly undermining the global organization?

Suspicion was also aroused by the comprehensive CPC proposal that Bonn presented at the Preparatory Committee in Vienna in July 1990. According to the German plan the CPC would be confined to political conflict and crisis management but could address military as well as non-military conflicts. This raised the question of whether the CSCE should in future acquire the military capacities necessary for coping with such assignments. This suspicious interpretation of German intentions was given further plausibility by demands, mainly from Genscher's, for some sort of CSCE security council. Genscher's proposals irritated Germany's Western partners especially because it was not clear whether he was arguing for an independent body entitled to take decisions comparable to the mandate of the UN Security Council, for a council of permanent representatives comparable to the NATO Council, or for an executive body similar to the EC troika. This left abundant room for concern and speculation. Paris and London especially disliked the German proposals because they feared that a CSCE security council with similar competencies to the UN's might call into question their privileged status as members of the UN Security Council. Moreover, his rhetoric about the CSCE as a potential collective security system seemed to challenge the priority of the Western Alliance. Because of the negative reaction to Genscher's statements by Germany's Western partners, the Chancellor ordered the Foreign Minister to avoid ambiguous statements, resulting in a more cautious and pragmatic presentation of Germany's vision of the future of the CSCE in subsequent months.[67]

Doubtless, as this analysis has shown, Germany wanted a strong CSCE. Yet, compared with the institutional quality of the traditional cornerstones of (West) German *Westbindung*, i.e. the European Community and the North Atlantic Treaty Organization, Germany's CSCE policy did not aim at

---

[67] See Teltschik (1991: 183).

an equally strong integration. The institutionalization policy was ambitious compared with those of its Western partners, involving new competencies and even some operational autonomy for the CSCE, but it also displayed a clear preference for intergovernmental structures and international political control of this institution rather than for a supranational organization. With regard to institutional functions and assignments, Bonn aimed at an enhancement of the CSCE that would complement but not compete with those of the EC and NATO. In the German view, the CSCE should take on new assignments in order to safeguard democratization processes and support the social, economic, and political transformation of the Central and East European countries. But the expected contribution of the enhanced CSCE was clearly confined to the realms of conflict prevention and political crisis management, human and minority rights, and peaceful settlement of disputes. Germany did not envision using the CSCE for extensive economic cooperation, for a general political integration, or for operational military security assignments.[68] Overall, the enhancement of the CSCE should not, according to the German proposals, be accomplished at the expense of the traditional institutional cornerstones of German security policy.

Germany's proposals for enhancing the CSCE rested on its view of the institutional form and quality required to address the new all-European security challenges. Bonn wished to render the CSCE useful in acute crisis situations, which meant being able to arrange immediate consultations and make timely decisions. The fact that Genscher usually justified his demand for some sort of 'CSCE security council' by referring to acute crises suggests that Germany's basic aim was indeed to establish a permanently operational CSCE council similar to NATO's but not identical with the UN's. Some East European participants in these discussions believed, nevertheless, that Bonn may have found the UN model attractive, since it would have in a sense raised Germany to the status of an equal power with the permanent members of the UN Security Council, at least on the regional level. The likelihood of such an arrangement was remote, of course, and not only because of the likely objections of Paris and London. Despite its elusive rhetoric, Bonn had never proposed more than a modest CSCE council encompassing representatives from all participating states.

Furthermore, the timing and other circumstances of Genscher's statements shed a different light on Germany's CSCE policy. In the spring of 1990 the partly visionary rhetoric and numerous concrete proposals for

---

[68] See McKenzie (1994: 26–31). Regarding the continuity of German EC/EU policy in view of unification see Gardner Feldman (1994); Bulmer and Paterson (1996).

strengthening the CSCE were no doubt motivated primarily by Bonn's *Deutschlandpolitik*. This policy served to overcome Moscow's opposition to unification and to united Germany's membership in NATO. Moscow had demanded the strengthening of the CSCE as a major precondition for accepting German unification, and Bonn had no reason not to respond to this demand with an aggressive CSCE policy. The CSCE was in any case an important building block for the Germanys in an all-European security structure. German rhetoric about to a collective security system was obviously an instrument of its unification policy and did not signal any loosening of its commitment to the Western Alliance.

Germany's policy envisioned a strengthened CSCE within an all-European security architecture, as Kohl said in his November 1989 plan for German unification and later reiterated regularly. In its concrete proposals, too, Bonn argued repeatedly in favour of cooperation among European security institutions.[69] German CSCE policy was in accord with the common Western aim of establishing a 'network of mutually reinforcing security institutions',[70] in which the CSCE was to play an important but nevertheless a restricted role. The German-American declarations of May and October 1991, which served as reassurance with regard to German intentions and defined the baseline of the common Western position, were an important step towards harmonizing the varying positions of Western governments on the relation among European security institutions. On the one hand, agreement was reached in favour of strengthening the CSCE, entailing concrete next steps but no agreed-on definition of its ultimate role, functions, and structures; on the other hand, the maintenance of NATO and its role as the central Western security institution was reaffirmed so as to allow for no further doubts.[71]

Bonn's commitment to reforming NATO and the EC also helped them survive and adapt to new requirements and reassured the Western partners of Germany's benign intentions. Germany consistently favoured deepening EC integration: e.g. in the German-French initiative of April 1990 to transform the Community into a political union in addition to an economic and

---

[69] See e.g. the proposal on cooperation among institutions submitted by Bulgaria, Germany, Poland, Romania, the CSFR, and Hungary at the CSO meeting in Berlin, 17 June 1991 (Document CSCE/3-CSO.4).

[70] See 'Communiqué of the NATO Council meeting at Copenhagen, 6/7 June 1991', *Bulletin*, 66: 525–9, 'Declaration on Central and Eastern Europe', p. 528, para. 3.

[71] See the joint statement by Hans-Dietrich Genscher and James Baker of 10 May 1991 in Washington, in Auswärtiges Amt, *Mitteilungen für die Presse*, 1104 (11 May 1991); *FAZ* (13 May 1991): 'Baker und Genscher wollen für die NATO eine stärkere politische Rolle'; *Neue Zürcher Zeitung* (16 May 1991): 'NATO und KSZE im europäischen Umbruch'.

currency union. As for NATO, which needed new assignments in order to sustain its legitimacy after the end of the cold war, Bonn and Washington in 1990 took the lead in creating the North Atlantic Cooperation Council, an instrument for political dialogue between NATO countries and the new democracies in Central and Eastern Europe.[72]

Another indicator of the limited role which Bonn ascribed to the CSCE, manifested during the preparations for the Helsinki follow-up meeting in 1992, was Bonn's definition of the relationship of the CSCE to the UN and its plan to make the CSCE an arrangement under chapter 8 of the UN Charter. This meant a clear subordination of the CSCE to the UN. Bonn had no intention of allowing the CSCE to compete with the UN or of questioning the competence of NATO as the chief European military security organization. In Germany's plans, the CSCE would not acquire the authority for *peacemaking* under chapter 8 of the UN Charter but would be restricted to *peacekeeping*. Such peacekeeping operations under the political auspices of the CSCE would be implemented by national militaries and with the support of other institutions, primarily the Western Alliance.

Likewise, Bonn refused to support fully the French plans in late 1991 for a European security pact because they were seen to be directed against the United States and NATO.[73] According to these proposals, put forward at the negotiations in Vienna, the CSCE would become an all-European collective security instrument and be based on a formal treaty according to international law. Bonn rejected similar proposals put forward by Russia, especially during the preparations for the Budapest Review Conference in December 1994, and for the same reasons: NATO's position and the role of the US in European security should not be questioned. In both cases functional and institutional reasons played an additional role. For the Germans, because of the immediate crises in Europe, it was more important to strengthen the operational capacities of the CSCE than to formalize its treaty basis.

4. Conclusion: How Do Institutions Matter?

The CSCE was Germany's prime foreign-policy vehicle for attaining European security through cooperation. In order to facilitate meaningful multilateral cooperation, Bonn sought to render CSCE not just an instrument of

---

[72] See for the significance of the 'German question' during the Maastricht negotiations Janning and Piepenschneider (1993: 43–5); Weidenfeld *et al.* (1991). On the role Germany played with regard to the process of NATO reforms see Karádi (1994: 40–67).   [73] See Peters (1995*b*).

international politics or an arena for cooperation, but a partially independent actor.[74] Security required multilateral cooperation, and in 1989 the CSCE was a promising candidate. However, although highly valued in principle, its institutional features did not match the requirements of the time. Therefore the institution had to be reformed for multilateral action on security risks: the escalation of conflicts arising from societal instability, unsettled minority and human rights issues, and the lack of democratic institutions. Even though Bonn did not intend to transfer sovereign rights to the CSCE, the German government was, to a greater extent than most other governments, ready to subject its own policies to the principles, norms, rules, and decision-making procedures of this institution. But German CSCE policy showed little inclination to loosen its traditional strong institutional ties to the EU and NATO, nor to strengthen the CSCE at the expense of the EC/EU or NATO.

Suspicion and irritation nevertheless occurred; Germany still faces the problem of defining its role and aims in a way compatible with the legitimate interests of other countries. Germany had to conduct a 'balancing policy' of (*a*) taking on new responsibilities while calming anxieties about German great-power aspirations, and (*b*) managing the implicit tension between comprehensive European institutions and its Western institutional commitments. There was in fact no conflict between *Westbindung* and Germany's CSCE policy. Irritation about German strategies and proposals was sometimes a tactic on the part of other governments to limit German influence. Most of the time Germany responded cautiously and was ready to compromise its own priorities while simultaneously trying to keep its aims and proposals on the agenda.

Germany continued its multilateral policy because it believed that European security challenges could not be addressed by any unilateral policy or even by a more powerful united Germany. As the country at the borderline between the wealthy West and the poor East, Germany had an overriding interest in stabilizing the states and societies of Central and Eastern Europe. As such, the CSCE served the purpose of coping fairly with uncertainty.

These challenges require coordinated and cooperative efforts, if indeed they are manageable at all. Bonn's multilateralism can be ascribed to perceived 'problem interdependence' among the European states. The baseline of Germany's national interest was to transform its own preferences into the multilateral interest. Therefore, in Genscher's words, Bonn aimed at engaging the other governments in a dense institutional network based on

---

[74] See Archer (1993: 147–8).

common security interests. The German government tried to convince its neighbours and partners to commit themselves to the same strategy of co-operative security. Bonn's CSCE policy was an attempt to attain a European consensus on:

- how to define the European security agenda based on a common set of principles, norms, and rules;
- how to define the role of the CSCE as a chief instrument for solving collective problems; and
- how to achieve institutional reforms in order to render it a politically effective multilateral instrument.

Germany's proposed strategies for solving collective problems cannot be divorced from its self-interest. Nevertheless, the identification of its national interest with the multilateral interest did not mean unilateral gains. In 1990 Germany sought to use the OSCE as an instrument for harmonizing its goal of unification with other countries' demands for having a say on Germany's future. The other states wanted not to oppose the peaceful unification of Germany but only to keep unified Germany hedged in by institutional frameworks, reassuring them that Germany's institutional embeddedness was accepted by the Germans and that its commitment to multilateralism would continue. Contrary to Germany's tradition of keeping the German question outside the CSCE process, the latter finally indeed served as a substitute for a peace treaty, an *Ersatz-Friedensvertrag*.[75] Germany's goal of gaining European legitimacy for German unification thus accorded with the multilateral interest of all European states.

Multilateralism in general and the CSCE in particular were not mere tactical or instrument features of German policy. After unification Germany sustained its pro-institutional policy, made public statements, and offered concrete proposals at the negotiating table. If the German promotion of the CSCE until 1989/90 had been due only to its dependence during the cold war, the end of bipolarity should have led to a change in Germany's institutional policy. According to neo-realism, systemic changes and the increase in its relative power should have led Germany away from multilateral policies. The continuity in its pro-institutional policy cannot be accounted for by systemic changes.

Overall, Germany's continued strong engagement in the CSCE without compromising the EU and NATO displays the impact of the institution itself on German preferences as well as strategies. Germany's national

---

[75] See Schulz (1989: 78–80).

preferences were to a significant degree defined in terms of gains from multilateral cooperation themselves, not merely gains in unilateral German interests. German national interests were merging with those of its neighbours and partners. The CSCE's role in matching the interdependent security situation and Germany's preference for collective problem-solving meant that CSCE institutionalization was not merely a means, but a German end in itself. The value of the institution for the German government lay in its enabling function for multilateral cooperation: it allowed for a cooperative security strategy which otherwise would not have been possible. Despite the changes in the international environment, the institution indeed kept German preferences and strategies constant. Thus, evidence is provided of the institution's impact on Germany's preferences and—following from this—on its institutional policy strategy.[76] Overall, this investigation of Germany's institutional policy falsifies Krauthammer's, Layne's, and Mearsheimer's predictions that the country would in their terms become a 'great power' de-emphasizing its traditional multilateral foreign policy.

[76] For results of other studies, starting with a similar empirical research question but regarding different policy areas and based on different theory, being compatible with these findings, see Anderson and Goodman (1993); Paterson (1996).

III

Continuity and Change in Security Institutions

8

SPONTANEOUS INSTITUTIONS: PEACEKEEPING AS AN INTERNATIONAL CONVENTION

Christopher Daase

Many institutions in international politics are not deliberately created, but instead evolve spontaneously. From the most basic institution of sovereignty to the subtleties of diplomatic etiquette, international life is governed by rules that no one has designed or negotiated but appear as if they were the product of rational planning or contractual bargaining.

Neo-liberal institutionalists have acknowledged this fact, conceding that international institutions may take the form not only of organizations and regimes but also of conventions, which are 'informal institutions, with implicit rules and understandings, that shape the expectations of actors'.[1] Yet despite this avowal and the pioneering work on conventions conducted in other disciplines,[2] institutionalists in international relations have neglected patterned behaviour[3] and have concentrated on more formal, negotiated institutions, leaving the analysis of conventions largely to constructivists and postmodernists.[4] This self-restriction has deprived institutionalists of the analytical means to explain phenomena that are not easily accounted for by the intentions of their creators or that do not fulfil the usual expectations of efficiency. But the question remains: how and why do

I am indebted to the participants of the CFIA-ATASP workshops, especially to Page Fortna, Gunther Hellmann, Robert Keohane, and Celeste Wallander for helpful criticism. I also thank Lars-Erik Cederman, Susanne Feske, Thomas Gehring, and David Lake for comments and suggestions. The usual caveat applies.

1 Keohane (1989c: 4).

2 See Lewis (1969) on language, Ullmann-Margalit (1978b) on norms, Schotter (1981) on economic activity, Sugden (1986) on property rights and morality.

3 Note, however, the exceptions of Young (1983); Puchala and Hopkins (1983); Kratochwil (1989).

4 See e.g. Wendt (1992) and Ashley (1988) on anarchy, Biersteker and Weber (1996) and Bartelson (1995) on sovereignty, and Der Derian (1987) on diplomacy.

actors in international politics, without either external hegemonic coercion or conscious collective action, develop rules and obey them?

Peacekeeping as a security institution is a case in point. Its evolution has often been described but rarely explained.[5] Nobody founded peacekeeping or explicitly negotiated its rules; yet it is now a convention with distinctive principles, norms, rules, and procedures. During the cold war, these rules were sometimes challenged and not always observed but they proved remarkably stable. Today, however, although highly valued by the international community, peacekeeping appears to be in flux and perhaps in dissolution. The United Nations' increasing willingness to decentralize peacekeeping—to transfer peacekeeping tasks to regional organizations and *ad hoc* coalitions—undermines its institutional homogeneity and legal coherence.

How, then, to explain the appearance, the stability and the change of peacekeeping? Clearly, no agent structured peacekeeping according to a master plan and no group of actors collectively decided on its institutional form. It may, therefore, be more useful to put less analytical stress on instrumental rationality and instead to think of peacekeeping as the spontaneous product of an evolutionary process—that is, to think of peacekeeping as a convention.

In this article, I will explain how conventions regulating political action can evolve without conscious human design, can maintain themselves without the existence of formal enforcement mechanisms, and can change without a plan for further institutional development. I begin by outlining a theory of spontaneous institutions, applying the familiar notion of the invisible hand and linking functional with causal reasoning. Then, I apply this theory to three questions. Why did peacekeeping emerge? Why is it maintained? Why was it transformed? In answering, I look at three periods: the early phase of East–West friction (1947–56), the cold war years (1956–87), and the fading of East–West tensions (1988 to present).

1. Explaining International Conventions: A Theory of Spontaneous Institutions

In focusing on the voluntary self-organization of political life, theorists of international institutions have settled in comfortably with the traditional power-based and rational-choice explanations.[6] In security studies, interest

---

[5] For descriptions of the evolution of peacekeeping see Goulding (1993); Segal (1995); Hill and Malik (1996: 25–58); Durch (1993); United Nations (1996); James (1990).

[6] For an overview, see Kato (1996) and Hasenclever *et al.* (1996).

has thus centred either on organizations like NATO, OSCE, and ASEAN, or on arms control regimes like the NPT, all of which can be explained as either rationally designed solutions to cooperation problems or as institutional manifestations of the power structure.[7]

If, however, institutions 'are persistent and connected sets of rules that prescribe behavioural roles, constrain activity, and shape expectations',[8] then some may be neither the result of intentional action nor the direct effect of structural causes. Institutions like sovereignty, reciprocity, and common law in international politics are neither human artefacts nor natural phenomena but rather what I will call spontaneous institutions.

Conventions as spontaneous institutions

The dichotomy between natural phenomenon and human artefact, although deeply rooted in our modern concept of knowledge,[9] is deceptive. Some things are neither one nor the other, but both. 'The things in this category resemble natural phenomena in that they are unintended and to be explained in terms of efficient causes, and they resemble artificial phenomena in that they are the result of human action, including of course rational human action.'[10] Figure 8.1 attempts to capture this idea.

Conventions obviously belong to the class of spontaneous institutions because they are, in the words of Adam Ferguson, 'the result of human action, but not the execution of any human design'.[11] This makes them resistant to traditional methods of analysis and forces institutionalists to go beyond structural and rational approaches to explain them. For if we

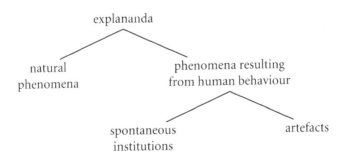

FIGURE 8.1. Modes of Phenomena to be Explained

---

[7] See Walt (1991).   [8] Keohane (1989c: 3).
[9] See Latour (1991); see for the following Keller (1990).
[10] Haakonssen (1981: 24).   [11] Ferguson (1904/1767: 171).

account for conventions in purely structural terms, we adopt a naturalistic world-view in which social effects are the necessary consequences of structural determinants and can be explained by natural laws. One example is Kenneth Waltz's theory that the balance of power would emerge even if no single state aimed to establish it.[12] As he admits, however, this theory is not compulsive and its predictions are indeterminate.[13] Since neo-realists like Waltz conceive of conventions as quasi-natural phenomena, they are led to overstate the causal relation between the structure of the international system and the balance of power, failing to capture the peculiarities of spontaneous institutions.

The same is true of rationalist theories, which explain the existence of institutions by what purposes they serve. 'Rational-choice theory, as applied to social institutions, assumes that institutions can be accounted for by examining the incentives facing the actors who created and maintain them. Institutions exist because they could have reasonably been expected to increase the welfare of their creators.'[14] How can such a theory explain conventions, which are not the result of 'any human design'? Assuming that all institutions are artefacts, rational-choice theories as largely applied in international relations fail to address what is distinctive about spontaneous institutions.

The rejection of structural and rational theories, however, does not mean that causal and functional reasoning have no role to play in explaining international conventions—quite the contrary. As long as no terminology is available to grasp the *tertium quid*—spontaneous institutions—we must resort to a combination of opposites, connecting functional and causal reasoning. Theories that do so are often called 'invisible-hand' theories.

Introducing the invisible hand

The metaphor of the invisible hand stands for the spontaneous development of a social order out of the interaction of individual behaviour. Although antecedents exist,[15] Adam Smith is usually regarded the founder of invisible-hand theory. The *Wealth of Nations* argues that 'every individual . . . intends only his own gain, and he is in this, as in so many other cases, led by an invisible hand to promote an end which was no part of his intention'.[16] This end, of course, is the common welfare.

---

[12] See Waltz (1979: 119).   [13] Ibid. 124.
[14] Keohane (1984: 80).   [15] See Myers (1972).
[16] A. Smith (1976/1776: 456). See also Smith (1969/1759).

It remains controversial whether Smith's idea really constitutes a theory.[17] Carl Menger, for example, voiced doubts, claiming that Smith does not provide an answer to the fundamental question: 'How can it be that institutions which serve the common welfare and are extremely significant for its development come into being without a common will directed toward establishing them?'[18] Friedrich Hayek[19] and Karl Popper[20] subsequently took up the challenge and developed ideas which Robert Nozick, with reference to Smith, termed 'invisible-hand explanations'.[21] Edna Ullmann-Margalit summarizes:

An invisible-hand explanation explains a well-structured social pattern or institution. It typically replaces an easily forthcoming and initially plausible explanation according to which the explanandum phenomenon is the product of intentional design with a rival account according to which it is brought about through a process involving the separate actions of many individuals who are supposed to be minding their own business unaware of and a fortiori not intending to produce the ultimate overall outcome.[22]

Although Smith was not primarily interested in the problem of social self-organization and his concept of the invisible hand did not entail a theory of coordination, his thinking favoured a historic-genetic over a contract-theoretic approach to the development of institutions.[23] This approach consists of three linked propositions:[24] first, that human behaviour often leads to unintended and unforeseen consequences; second, that these unintended consequences sometimes aggregate into an order that appears to be the product of rational planning; and third, that this order is the best participants can hope for. While the first two propositions are unobjectionable, the third is controversial. Spontaneous order may sometimes prove beneficial, but the invisible hand may also produce unwanted effects. And this may happen not only when the invisible hand 'trembles' or 'fails', but also when it works perfectly.[25] Critics of spontaneous-order theory have capitalized on this weakness, attributing it to the alleged functionalism of invisible-hand theories.[26] Explaining the evolution of social institutions by the functional needs of society, they argue, makes suboptimality unexplainable. Indeed Smith and, especially, Hayek may have encouraged this interpretation by stressing the virtuousness of the invisible hand and rejecting any practical interference, out of their deep mistrust of human rationality.

[17] See Rothschild (1994).
[18] Menger (1985/1883: 146).
[19] See Hayek (1967/1973).
[20] See Popper (1965).
[21] Nozick (1974: 18; 1994).
[22] Ullmann-Margalit (1978a: 267).
[23] See Buchanan (1976); Elsner (1989); Coase (1976).
[24] See Vaughn (1989).
[25] See Hahn (1982).
[26] See e.g. J. Knight (1992: 94).

Yet invisible-hand explanations do not necessarily presuppose a naïve functionalism that supplies *ex-post* rationalizations.[27] Rather, they save functional arguments from functionalism by differentiating and integrating reasons and causes within a single analytical framework.

Integrating reasons and causes

Invisible-hand explanations are hybrid, integrating functional and causal reasoning. Disregarding one of the two would deprive the theory of spontaneous institutions of its internal balance and render its explanations susceptible to the naturalistic and functionalist fallacies respectively.

Omitting functional reasoning by ignoring the importance of individual choice and action would prevent the theory from explaining institutional emergence and change. Neo-realists, despite referring to Smith and the invisible-hand motif,[28] are guilty of this fault. Waltz is therefore right to acknowledge that structural theories cannot account for change.[29] But equally distorting is the neglect of causal reasoning by confining oneself to the correlation between problems of collective action and the forms of institutions. This version of invisible-hand theory has aptly been called quasi-functionalist, since it starts reasoning from the effects of an institution rather than from its emergence, and so it fails to expound the causal mechanism by which the institution is brought about.[30]

The interplay of functional and causal mechanisms is constitutive of spontaneous institutions, so in order to explain conventions, they have to be analytically integrated. Figure 8.2 shows three modes of explaining international institutions and indicates how invisible-hand theories combine the other two. To account for the first part of invisible-hand explanations, we look for reasons for actions. Contrary to causal explanations, functional explanations do not include laws or at least have no laws at their centre,[31] even if the premises are restricted to the utility assumptions of rational choice. Game theorists admit that 'the international system, with its established patterns of practice and rules, is significant for defining the individual game model and for deriving conclusions from it'.[32] Acknowledging that 'motivation is more complicated than the simple expected utility

---

[27] See O. E. Williamson (1994: 323). [28] See Waltz (1979: 88–93).

[29] See Waltz (1986: 343). [30] See Heath (1976: 67); Vanberg (1984: 134).

[31] Although we may think of rough laws connecting reasons and actions, these generalizations cannot be sharpened into that 'kind of law on the basis of which accurate predictions can reliably be made': Davidson (1963: 691).

[32] Snidal (1984: 45).

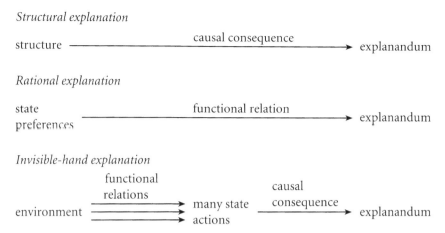

FIGURE 8.2. Three Modes of Explaining Institutions in International Relations

model',[33] the question remains, however, how these patterns and rules are understood and whether it is worth analysing individual motivation beyond self-interest. Philosophically speaking, the question is whether practice and rules embodied as reasons are also causes for action.

To distinguish reasons and causes is to ask for the independent impact of actors' intentions including, but not restricted to, their interests. As Donald Davidson puts it:

When we ask why someone acted as he did, we want to be provided with an interpretation. [. . .] When we learn his reason, we have an interpretation, a new description of what he did which fits it into a familiar picture. This picture certainly includes some of the agent's beliefs and attitudes; perhaps also goals, ends, principles, general character traits, virtues or vices. Beyond this, the re-description of an action afforded by a reason may place the action in a wider social, economic, linguistic, or evaluative context.[34]

But given that reasons explain actions in the rational sense, how can we infer that these reasons also cause the behaviour that constitutes action? There may be many reasons for a single action, only one of them causal; and there may be several reasons for alternative actions, only one of them acted upon. Hence, the connection between reasons and actions cannot be seen as necessary or lawlike. And yet some reasons may indeed cause actions; namely, those that become operative.[35] As Bernard Williams argues, 'if there are reasons for action, it must be that people sometimes act for those reasons,

---

[33] North (1990: 42).   [34] Davidson (1963: 691).   [35] See Mohr (1996: 86–95).

and if they do, their reasons must figure in some correct explanation of their action'.[36]

In order to identify reasons for action, the analyst has to focus on the practical reasoning of actors. In so doing, he or she expands the motivational model beyond narrowly defined self-interest.[37] Once interests, norms, rules, and the like are identified, they become possible reasons for action; once they are operative, they also become causes. For the analysis of institutions, then, it is important to determine why and under what conditions certain reasons become causes on a larger scale.

The second stage of invisible-hand explanations is concerned with the process that aggregates intended actions into unintended results. To know why someone acted as he or she did is to know the intention with which the action was done.[38] But how can we infer from intended actions to unintended consequences? As noted earlier, actions do not follow laws but do have lawlike effects. It is likely that actors doing business try to maximize their profit, but it is not inevitable. There is no law that determines this behaviour. It is equally likely that a state being attacked militarily will defend itself. Yet again, there is no (natural) law that compels a state to do so, and Clausewitz is correct in pointing out that, philosophically speaking, 'war begins only with defense'.[39]

The more often actors act in a specific manner, the more likely it is that they will continue to do so in the future and that others will rely on their doing so. Yet this statement only expresses an empirical observation until one explains how a regularity develops self-enforcement mechanisms, turning a simple behavioural recurrence into an institutional fact. This path, as I will argue in the next section, is better described as the development of a behavioural prototype than as coordination by precedent. The process by which the functional results of intended behaviour aggregate into a structure that is beyond the reach of individual intention (i.e. spontaneous institution) is a causal phenomenon. It can only be explained as a necessary consequence of recurring actions. Even if these causal explanations sometimes seem trivial,[40] they are not only important but are even indispensable for good invisible-hand explanations.

Spontaneous institutions resulting from this process may be difficult to observe but are not therefore insignificant.[41] By setting the framework for choice,[42] spontaneous institutions are the basis for more complex coopera-

---

[36] B. Williams (1981: 102).   [37] See North (1990: 37); Hollis and Smith (1990: 165).
[38] See Davidson (1963: 689).   [39] Clausewitz (1980/1832: 644).
[40] See Keller (1990: 105–21).   [41] See Hasenclever *et al.* (1996: 182).
[42] See North (1990: 36–45).

tion. As Peyton Young comments, 'it would scarcely be an exaggeration to say that almost all economic and social institutions are governed to some extent by conventions'.[43] The procedure I have outlined for analysing conventions reconstructs the path from the reasons of actors on the micro-level to the resulting effects on the macro-level and the latter's feedback to the micro-level. By doing so, invisible-hand explanations represent what Carl Hempel termed 'genetic' explanations, which 'present the phenomenon under study as the final stage of a developmental sequence, and accordingly account for the phenomenon by describing the successive stages of their sequence'.[44] Invisible-hand explanations are, therefore, explanations in the strict sense.

2. The Appearance of Peacekeeping: Explaining Institutional Emergence

To call peacekeeping an international convention is to depart from traditional narratives of its institutional emergence. Most historians of the United Nations date the appearance of peacekeeping to 4 November 1956, when the General Assembly met in an emergency session after the outbreak of the Sinai War and instructed the secretary-general to set up 'an emergency international United Nations Force to secure and supervise' a cease-fire between Egypt and Israel.[45] Three days later the United Nations Emergency Force (UNEF, 1956–67) was created, the first armed force of the United Nations to be interposed between two adversaries. But although UNEF became a model for other UN missions,[46] peacekeeping was not founded or created at this time, if by creation we mean the intended invention of something new. The secretary-general and the member states did not act in a normative vacuum, creating something entirely novel, nor did they intend to form an institution or set a precedent. All they did at the time was cooperate in an urgent matter of international peace and security by extending the established practice of United Nations mediation in order to prevent a Third World conflict from escalating into a superpower confrontation.

Nevertheless, it is not unreasonable to speak of peacekeeping as an institution even in this early stage; an institution, however, that was brought about more by the invisible hand of institutional evolution than deliberately

---

[43] H. P. Young (1996: 105).   [44] Hempel (1965: 447).
[45] Higgins (1969: 231).   [46] See O. R. Young (1967: 135–51).

by the secretary-general or the member states. But this raises a question of definition: what *is* peacekeeping? At what point may we speak of peace-keeping as a convention that has emerged? What are conventions, and how do they differ from simple regularities?

Precedents and prototypes

In his seminal study, David Lewis defined conventions as regularities in behaviour in recurrent situations.[47] In game-theoretic terms, he treats conventions as a function of a specific preference structure among rational actors that maximizes their individual utility. However, as Margaret Gilbert argues, Lewis does not 'make it entirely clear when, precisely, such a regularity is to be taken to exist';[48] that is, when exactly a convention has emerged. Obviously, not every behavioural regularity—eating, sleeping, and sex, for example—is a convention.

At what point does behavioural regularity translate into rule-governed conduct constituting a convention? Lewis addresses this problem by discussing two possible pathways to conventions: agreements and precedents. Conventions arise in coordination games; that is, in non-trivial situations where the predominant interests of actors coincide and at least two proper coordination equilibria exist.[49] The interesting thing about conventions is that they may be tacit: they can exist among actors who have never explicitly agreed to adopt them.

For such conventions to develop, some point of reference is needed indicating the structure of the game and the best way to solve the co-ordination problem. In Thomas Schelling's terms, some prominent or salient event is necessary for the actors to make their choice of strategies.[50] Lewis argues that previous instances of successful cooperation can serve this purpose: 'Coordination by precedent, at its simplest, is this: achievement of coordination by means of shared acquaintance with the achievement of coordination in a single past case exactly like our present coordination problem.'[51]

Lewis does not explain, however, who decides which coordination was successful and thus qualifies as precedent, or why one should expect others to repeat their behaviour in a similar situation. Nor can he prove that a single example of successful coordination will inspire the development of a

---

[47] See Lewis (1969: 36–42).   [48] Gilbert (1989: 326).
[49] For more on coordination games in international relations, see Stein (1983) and Martin (1992*b*).
                                                                 [50] See Schelling (1960: 54–8).
[51] Lewis (1969: 41).

convention. Hence, Gilbert concludes that '*within the framework of game theory*, the assumption that some point is salient gets us nowhere. That is, it does not move the agent's reasoning onto the conclusion: act this way.'[52]

To determine what conventions are and how they differ from behavioural recurrence, it helps to think of them as having evolved rather than having been chosen, however tacitly. Robert Sugden argues that 'a convention can start to evolve as soon as some people believe that other people are following it'.[53] However, this presupposes the idea of a convention before the convention exists (or starts to evolve) and raises the question of where that idea comes from. Sugden appeals to the notion of prominence, thereby reconnecting with choice-theoretic conceptions of focal points and precedents. But if we take his own words seriously—that 'conventions are not chosen; they evolve'[54]—and if we want to escape circular reasoning, then even focal points have to be seen as the 'outcome of an evolutionary process of expectation formation'.[55] For focal points are not necessarily focal by themselves; they *become* focal, just as precedents are not prominent as such, but are made so through common understanding.

In order to account for the emergence of conventions, it makes more sense to focus on the process by which common knowledge about a certain regularity arises (i.e. the evolution of prototypes) rather than on selection strategies of rational actors (i.e. choice among given precedents). Behavioural prototypes evolve when actors repeat one kind of action significantly more often than another, thus setting a self-reinforcing process in motion which makes the *regularity as such* a focal point for further action. It becomes rational to follow a certain rule once more and more actors are doing the same. Such process can be said to be path-dependent in so far as small events and even chance circumstances can produce conduct patterns which, once they prevail, determine the path of further institutional development.[56]

While path-dependent self-reinforcement is a causal phenomenon, the behaviour of actors is not, and the development of conventions remains unpredictable.[57] Their emergence, however, can be traced to the point where behavioural recurrence translates into rule-governed behaviour. The evolution of prototypes explains the process by which reflective knowledge about a certain regularity develops and enters into the practical reasoning of actors, thus constituting an independent reason for action. Accordingly,

[52] Gilbert (1989: 334), emphasis in the original.
[53] Sugden (1989: 93); see also Sugden (1986: 34–54).
[54] Sugden (1989: 93).
[55] H. P. Young (1996: 121).
[56] On path-dependence see Arthur (1994); North (1990).
[57] See H. P. Young (1996: 111).

becoming aware of the virtue of following a rule, rather than discovering the utility of imitating an example, is the inception of a convention.

Rejecting creationism and teleology

The notion of path-dependence implies that history matters. But this does not mean that history alone answers the question of institutional emergence. Thus, in order to explain the appearance of peacekeeping, the analysis of its prehistory has to free itself from prejudgements which could distort the picture.

Static 'working definitions'[58] of peacekeeping are to be avoided, since their ahistoric nature can adulterate the findings. More important than pinpointing terms is tracing their meaning for the actors of the time, thus accounting for their evolution. Existing lists of peacekeeping missions should be used with caution, since differences among them may indicate disagreement over their essentials.[59] This should cast doubts on the stringency of development which the listings imply and which the traditional narrative of peacekeeping assumes. Peacekeeping, this story goes, is the congenial invention of virtuous men in response to East–West frictions that prevented the United Nations from maintaining peace and security through a reinvigorated system of collective security. The actual history is not so simple, however. Peacekeeping was not created but has developed; and it has not developed teleologically but has evolved through trial and error. Two UN missions which are not included in official UN peacekeeping records will point up that indetermination and illustrate the process by which a regularity emerged.

In late 1946, the Greek government, invoking articles 34 and 35 of the UN Charter, asked the Security Council to take measures against communist infiltration across its northern borders. The still feeble, Western-oriented Greek government maintained that Yugoslavia, Albania, and Bulgaria supported fighters waging a guerrilla war against Athens. Within a fortnight the Security Council established a commission consisting of representatives of all its members, which verified the allegations. While debating the commission's report in the Security Council, however, member states sharply disagreed on matters of substance as well as on procedural questions, and when the Soviet Union blocked decisions with its veto the topic was removed from the Security Council's agenda. This enabled the General

---

[58] Durch (1993: 5).
[59] See e.g. the differences in Durch (1993); United Nations (1993); Higgins (1969).

Assembly to act, creating the United Nations Special Committee on the Balkans (UNSCOB, 1947–52) in October 1947 with a mandate to 'observe the compliance by the four Governments concerned with the . . . Committee's recommendations': terminate help to the guerrillas, settle their disputes peacefully, and establish 'normal diplomatic and good neighborly relations'.[60]

UNSCOB consisted of delegates from nine countries, including the Security Council's permanent members. The Soviet Union, Poland, and other communist countries, however, refused to cooperate and called the enabling resolutions illegal, arguing that they were incompatible with the principles of the UN Charter. Nevertheless, the special committee set up military observer groups that scrutinized the region in question and reported its findings directly to the special committee. The committee, in turn, issued its reports not to the Security Council or the secretary-general, as was usually done in later missions, but to the General Assembly. The effectiveness of UNSCOB was severely restricted because Yugoslavia, Albania, and Bulgaria refused to cooperate and denied the United Nations access to their territory. Nevertheless, guerrilla activities finally ceased and the Greek government was consolidated. In 1952 UNSCOB was terminated and became the Balkan subcommittee of the new Peace Observation Commission, created under the Uniting for Peace resolution which was designed to circumvent deadlock in the Security Council.[61]

Although UNSCOB's personnel did not represent the United Nations but their own national governments, UNSCOB was the UN's first attempt to establish a peace mission in the field. Its shortcomings demonstrated 'the importance of obtaining the consent of all local parties before deploying an operation, as well as the necessity for politically impartial conduct once deployed'.[62]

Of similar importance was the United Nations' venture into Indonesia in 1947–51. Violence erupted after the Netherlands accepted Indonesian independence and agreed to the terms of withdrawal in March 1947. The Security Council demanded the termination of hostilities and called upon the career consuls stationed in Batavia to report on the situation.[63] Subsequent resolutions in August 1947 established the Committee of Good Offices (GOC) and attached the UN's first military observers to it. In early 1949, after the situation deteriorated again, the Security Council reaffirmed its call for a political solution and transformed the GOC into the United

---

[60] See Higgins (1969: iv. 18–23).   [61] See Menzel (1971: 38).
[62] Birgisson (1993: 77).   [63] See Higgins (1969: ii. 10).

Nations Commission for Indonesia (UNCI). The military observers appointed to UNCI had to monitor the cease-fire, investigate and report incidents, delineate demilitarized zones, and guard the Dutch nationals who wanted to leave the country. The juridical status of the military observers remained precarious, however, since they continued to serve under national duty even while acting as representatives of the UN Security Council.[64]

The organizational ambiguity of both missions is the reason why UNCI and UNSCOB are not included in official accounts of UN peacekeeping. It is evident, however, that their form and function make them legitimate forerunners of subsequent peacekeeping missions. But they were not without precedent either. The League of Nations had engaged in operations which we would today consider peacekeeping missions. When Poland occupied the Lithuanian capital Vilna in 1920, the League of Nations proposed an international force to replace Polish troops and secure a plebiscite to be carried out under the League's auspices. Poland and Lithuania, however, withdrew their initial consent, and the League discontinued the planning in March 1921.[65] The League's operation in the contested region of Letitia, where Peruvian and Colombian troops were about to fight, went one step further. The League negotiated a settlement, took over the region's governmental control for a year, and finally transferred sovereignty to Colombia in 1934. Whether the military forces attached to the League's transitional commission qualify as truly 'international' in this case is a matter of dispute,[66] since they were exclusively Colombians. The League went even further when, under the provisions of the Versailles Treaty, the Saar Basin was placed under its government in 1920. The mandate included the conduct of a plebiscite that would determine the Saar's future political status. In order to calm tensions and guarantee a free election, the Council of the League created in 1934 not only an international police force but also the first multinational military operation under the auspices of an international organization. This force, consisting of 3,300 soldiers, remained the 'first and last International Force in the service of the League'.[67]

What this historical excursion demonstrates is that the setting up of peace missions after the Second World War by the United Nations did not start from scratch. Rather, there existed an established practice of mediation, interposition, and trusteeship: examples to be followed or avoided. This does not answer the question of why and how peacekeeping appeared, but it allows us confidently to reject creationist and teleological accounts of

[64] For details see A. M. Taylor (1960).   [65] See W. Williams (1971: 39).
[66] See ibid. 42; Bowett (1964: 11); Walters (1952: 592).   [67] Walters (1952: 592).

its institutional emergence. There is no historical evidence, either, that any actor, individual or collective, intentionally created peacekeeping *ex nihilo* or that any identifiable first mission contained a nucleus that gradually unfolded into full-blown peacekeeping.

Following examples and following rules

Clearly we must supplement historical description with genetic explanation in order to understand why the United Nations and its member states decided on one kind of action more often than others and why these decisions accumulated into a convention shaping future decisions. After the Second World War the United Nations tried to draw on the League of Nation's experience in running peace missions. Besides the transition and mediation missions mentioned above, there was also the creation of city regimes in Trieste and Jerusalem on the pattern the League had developed in Danzig. The Versailles Treaty placed the German enclave of Danzig 'under the protection of the League of Nations' and assigned key government functions to the League's Council and a High Commissioner. This made Danzig a 'Free City' and 'the purest example of an "internationalized territory"'.[68] Yet the Nazis undermined the city's status without facing much resistance from the League and eventually annexed Danzig on the first day of the Second World War. After the war Danzig became Polish, but Trieste was made a 'Free Territory', whose 'integrity and independence shall be assured by the Security Council of the United Nations'. As Steven Ratner points out, it was planned that Trieste would follow the example of Danzig 'as an independent state under the guardianship or guarantee of an international organization. Yet Trieste's governor would have greater explicit powers over the internal administration than did the League's High Commissioner for Danzig.'[69] But US–Soviet rivalry prevented the appointment of a governor, and the UN never established any administration. A similar fate met the UN's attempt in 1947 to make Jerusalem 'a *corpus separatum* under a special international regime . . . administered by the United Nations' and distinct from both the proposed Jewish and Arab states in Palestine. As with Trieste, it was planned that a governor would resume extensive governmental functions and that the UN would assure the territorial integrity of Jerusalem and guarantee its special status. But the first Israel–Arab war in 1948 ordained the failure of these plans.

While building on the League's experience in setting up internationalized

[68] Hannum (1990: 378).   [69] Ratner (1995: 98).

territories, the UN had also been prepared to learn the League's lessons by granting the governors greater powers and guaranteeing the security of those entities more boldly. But the examples of Trieste and Jerusalem, along with other unsuccessful attempts to assume civil governance functions in Korea and Namibia, demonstrated that partition rather than international-ization was the order of the day, not only at the centre of the emerging East–West conflict in Europe, but also in its periphery. Common govern-ance was irreconcilable with conflicting claims of being in possession of the one true formula of good governance. This being the case, there was no reason for the UN and its member states to embark again on this futile track, and thus there was no opportunity to develop a causal mechanism that might have made the internationalization of a territory a UN institu-tion or a part of peacekeeping.

Although this path of spontaneous institutionalization was obstructed by negative selection, other paths remained open. When the Security Council established the Truce Commission for Palestine in 1948, it followed the example of UNCI in Indonesia, by calling upon the career consular officers stationed in Jerusalem to report on compliance with the Security Council's strong request for a cease-fire between Jews and Arabs. It further provided the commission and the UN mediator, who was separately appointed by the General Assembly, 'with a sufficient number of military observers'.[70] When an armistice was arranged between Israel and the Arab states in mid-1949, the Security Council terminated the role of the medi-ator, and the truce commission 'became a subsidiary organ of the United Nations with its own well-defined functions'.[71] This strengthened the posi-tion of the secretary-general, who became responsible for the appointment of the staff, issued directives, and received reports from the field. During the course of events, UN activities increased steadily, and without any act of creation[72] the commission became known as the United Nations Truce Supervision Organization (UNTSO), subsequently developing into the organizational centre of other peace missions in the region.

Like UNTSO, the United Nations Military Observer Group in India and Pakistan (UNMOGIP, 1949 to the present) evolved from an earlier fact-finding mission that the Security Council had sent to India and Pakistan in order to 'investigate the facts' and 'exercise mediatory influence' on the disputed territories of Jammu and Kashmir.[73] Although the Soviet Union had insisted on a commission drawn from members of the Security Coun-

---

[70] UN Doc. SC Res. 773, 22 May 1948 and UN Doc. SC Res. 801, 29 May 1948.
[71] Burns (1962: 27).   [72] See Menzel (1971: 50).   [73] UN Doc. SC Res. 650, 10 Jan. 1948.

cil, the United Nations Commission on India and Pakistan (UNCIP) was composed of three members, one selected separately by India and Pakistan, and one agreed on by both. Although UNCIP did not reach a political solution, it facilitated a cease-fire and the drawing of a demarcation line by mid-1949. The Security Council terminated UNCIP and separated political and military tasks by appointing a UN representative to further negotiate a political settlement and creating UNMOGIP to monitor the truce.

Until this point, peace operations of the United Nations had been observer missions and had consisted of unarmed military personnel. When the General Assembly established the first United Nations Emergency Force (UNEF, 1956–67) and agreed to deploy armed units, this was a change. However, the secretary-general insisted, in his second and final report to the Security Council clarifying the parameters of the operation, that it 'would be more than an observer's corps, but in no way a military force temporarily controlling the territory in which it was stationed; nor, moreover, should the Force have military functions exceeding those necessary to secure peaceful conditions'.[74] Certainly, plans had existed to dispatch a UN force 'about the size of a division, with a brigade of tanks, and attached reconnaissance and fighter-aircraft units—the whole organized as an operational force capable of fighting'.[75] None of the permanent members, however, was prepared to take so decisive an action given the explosive situation in other parts of the world (e.g. in Hungary) and the recent experience in Korea, which nobody was eager to repeat. As in the case of the internationalization of territory, the external constraints of the cold war narrowed the range of acceptable solutions, restricting reasons for action and foreclosing causal mechanisms that could have institutionalized robust, enforcement-like measures, as General Burns had proposed.

Yet UNEF proved well-equipped for the functions assigned: (1) to secure and supervise a cease-fire by delineating a buffer zone; (2) to supervise the withdrawal of British, French, and Israeli troops from Egyptian territory; (3) to patrol the border and deter infiltration; and (4) to secure the provisions of the Egypt-Israel Armistice Agreement. In many respects, UNEF thus reflected the existing practice of UN peace missions. The supervision of cease-fires and the creation of buffer zones had been the obligation of UNCI and UNTSO. The monitoring of troop withdrawal was among the functions of UNCI. The patrol of border regions has been for long on the agenda of UNMOGIP and UNTSO and was also part of UNSCOB's mandate. Therefore, when Secretary-General Dag Hammarskjöld defined the

---

74 UN Doc. A/3302, 6 Nov. 1956.   75 Burns (1962: 186).

essential principles of peacekeeping in a report written in the midst of the Suez crisis, he did not invent peacekeeping but summarized an existing practice in order to clarify and operationalize it for a specific purpose, namely to 'define the terms' under which UNEF would operate.

Hammarskjöld conceived of three essential conditions for a peace mission in the Middle East. First, its emplacement and operation had to have the consent of the parties involved and would not entail enforcement action against any party. Second, it would not influence the military or political balance of power among the adversaries. Third, the mission would be temporary.[76] In addition, the secretary-general noted that the General Assembly had asked that the force consist of military units recruited from states other than the five permanent members of the Security Council. What is important about these principles is that Hammarskjöld did not elaborate them by referring to precedents from the recent past. Rather, he drew on an abstract, imaginary body of rules that was distinct from specific cases. In other words, he did not merely codify UNTSO, UNMOGIP, UNCI, etc., but utilized the emergent regularity as a prototype.

It is reasonable, then, to say that peacekeeping as a security institution appeared with UNEF, since it was the first mission that followed rules rather than examples and that appealed to a prototype rather than a precedent. UNEF marks the point where actors realized that this particular form of cooperation embodied the most promising way of dealing with peripheral conflicts under conditions of great-power conflict; it thus marks the emergence of peacekeeping as a convention.

3. The Maintenance of Peacekeeping: Explaining Institutional Stability

Institutions are said to be stable if an equilibrium, once achieved, is maintained by actors complying with the institution's provisions. In the case of peacekeeping, however, it is difficult to see how thirteen missions as diverse as the UN operation in the Congo (ONUC, 1960–4), the mission in the Dominican Republic (DOMREP, 1965–6), and the Second UN Emergency Force in Palestine (UNEF II, 1973–9), for example, could have stabilized a coherent set of rules shaping the expectations of actors during the cold war. And yet peacekeeping was seen during this period as a 'fairly homogeneous

---

[76] UN Doc. A/3302, 2nd and final Report of the secretary-general on the plan for an emergency international UN Force, 6 Nov. 1956.

activity'[77] and consolidated as a convention despite not only the divergence of the missions but also non-compliance with its rules in several cases and even the explicit disagreement of member states over what constitutes peacekeeping proper.

The constancy of its principles, however, is only half of the cold war story of peacekeeping. The other half is the growing unwillingness of the UN member states to implement these principles. From 1974 to the end of the cold war, only one operation, UNIFIL, was set up, though older missions such as UNTSO, UNMOGIP, and UNFICYP remained in place. This withdrawal from peacekeeping weakened the institution, although its institutional form remained intact. The central puzzle of peacekeeping during the cold war period is therefore why it was maintained: why and how did its rules endure when nobody was prepared to follow them?

Conventions and conformity

Institutionalist theory assumes a close relation between the stability of an institution and the conforming behaviour of self-interested actors. As long as an actor cannot do better by pursuing a different strategy, he or she will continue to act in accordance with the institution and will not try to change its rules.[78] The same logic applies to conventions, since the self-enforcing mechanism which sustains the convention's equilibrium is said to depend on each player benefiting by following the convention.[79]

But although the nexus of convention and conformity seems plausible, it does not hold in reality. For conventions, like other institutions, continue to exist even if actors do not conform with their provisions. Steven Krasner may be correct in claiming that 'if there is an international society out there, it has not much more impact on the behavior of states than conventional norms about sex, family, and marriage now have on the behavior of individuals in North America and Europe';[80] but it does not follow that marriage and the family (or, by analogy, international institutions) are non-existent or fading away. Behavioural non-conformity is not directly linked to the existence or the stability of conventions. While one might wonder how long a convention could survive in absence of conformity, 'it appears that a convention can endure without the correlative regularity of behavior'.[81]

To account for this phenomenon, it helps to recall the distinction between conventions and regularities. As elaborated above, conventions

---

77 Goulding (1993: 451). 78 See Axelrod (1984); M. Taylor (1987).
79 See Lewis (1969); Sugden (1986). 80 Krasner (1994: 17).
81 Gilbert (1989: 346).

emerge from regularities, but are not easily reduced to them. Just as a convention is more than the sum of recurrent behaviour, the disappearance of a convention requires more than a reduced regularity. Behaviour that is not in line with a convention's provisions does make the regularity less of a regularity, but does not make the convention less a convention.[82] It only shows that the reason associated with the convention becomes less often operative within the actors' practical reasoning, because, for example, of other reasons overriding it. Only if the reason completely drops out of the deliberative process of rational actors has the convention ceased to exist. But this would be the result of a causal process rather than of a rational decision: the cumulative effect of continued and widespread lack of conformity with a convention's rules.

A given convention, then, may be associated with a strong regularity, meaning that most of the actors conform most of the time with most of the convention's provisions. Other conventions may differ (in one or more respects) in so far as only some of the actors conform some of the time with some of the provisions. In this case, the convention exhibits a rather weak regularity. By differentiating conventions and regularities in this way, it becomes possible to explain why not only repeated implementation but sometimes also violations of conventional rules stabilize a convention, contrary to Lewis's argument that each instance of non-conformity reduces the degree to which a given regularity is a convention. It further helps us understand how the circumvention of a convention leaves its institutional form intact but weakens its authority.

Positive and negative selection

The theory of spontaneous institutions conceptualizes stability as the causal consequence of equable behaviour. It thus avoids the idea of a quasi-natural equilibrium of institutions[83] as well as the assumption that conventions automatically become more stable in the long run.[84] Instead it concentrates on the processes by which certain kinds of action are selected and are either repeated or avoided in similar cases. Positive as well as negative selection can stabilize a convention if conforming behaviour is repeated and thus reinforced and deviating behaviour is avoided and thus barred. Both processes apply to peacekeeping during the early phase of the cold war and contribute to explaining its institutional stability.

Marrack Goulding, former UN Undersecretary-General for Peacekeeping

---

[82] Gilbert (1989: 345).   [83] See e.g. Krasner (1988).   [84] See Kier and Mercer (1996: 93).

Operations, identified five principles of peacekeeping, conceding that 'few of them were formally enacted by the legislative organs of the United Nations. But they came to constitute a corpus of case law or customary practice which was by and large accepted by all concerned.'[85] In one form or another these principles had been part of the UNEF provisions, which are the prototype of peacekeeping as a convention, but only their repetition in subsequent missions—i.e. their reinforcement through positive selection— made them stable rules.

The first principle Goulding notes is that peacekeeping operations are UN operations. The assertion that only organs of the United Nations may establish peacekeeping missions is by no means trivial, given that regional organizations and even *ad hoc* coalitions have assumed that function from time to time. Traditionally, however, peacekeeping missions were regarded as UN activities, carried out under the command and control of the secretary-general, who acted with authority delegated to him by the Security Council.[86] In this respect, the example of Cyprus was pathbreaking, since the mission was established although two alternative ways had been considered to manage the crisis. The United Kingdom, Greece, and Turkey, the guarantor states of the Zurich agreements that had established an independent Republic of Cyprus in 1960, proposed to form an *ad hoc* peacekeeping force under British command in order to separate the warring Greek and Turkish factions and to draw a green line of cease-fire. The agreement was unstable, however, and the British advocated strengthening the force by troops from other NATO countries. Neutral Cyprus, however, rejected the idea of NATO intervention and preferred bringing the issue before the UN.[87] Had the peacekeeping convention not existed, the parties would have made a different decision; yet their implementation of the rule strengthened the regularity underlying it, thus intensifying the rationale for following it the next time.

Goulding's second principle, which has evolved into the central operational rule of peacekeeping, concerns the willingness of parties to cooperate. It holds that before and during the operation the consent of the two sides to the conflict must be assured.[88] This principle is a direct 'lesson'

[85] Goulding (1993: 453). The *exact* number and content of these principles is of course disputed in the literature.

[86] A corresponding complex of rules may be seen in the financing system for peacekeeping missions, since the costs of peacekeeping came to be regarded as 'expenses of the Organization' under Article 17 of the UN Charter.

[87] See Birgisson (1993: 220).

[88] In order to facilitate a legally binding form of consent, the UN has established a model for 'Status of Force Agreements'. See UN Doc. A/45 (594).

from earlier peace missions like UNSCOB and was strictly upheld in the prototypical case of UNEF. When Egypt's President Nasser demanded that the UN withdraw on the eve of the Six Day War in 1967, the secretary-general had little choice but to order UNEF to leave, since Israel was also not prepared to accept the peacekeepers on its territory. The secretary-general has often been criticized for terminating UNEF when war was imminent, and many hold that 'UN credibility was indeed damaged.'[89] Yet one can only speculate about whether the war could have been prevented if the UN forces had not withdrawn, and how peacekeeping would have developed after such a decision. It is a fact, however, that the institutional consequence of the peacekeepers' retreat was a reaffirmation of the principle of consent.

Closely linked to the provision of consent is the third principle: impartial conduct. Impartiality demands that peacekeepers be strictly neutral in fulfilling their mandate and not take sides in the dispute. This is not thought to forbid peacekeepers criticizing or putting pressure on a party that violates agreements; but there is a fine line peacekeepers must observe in order to uphold neutrality. This provision becomes intractable once a peacekeeping force intervenes in an internal conflict, as was evident in the case of the Congo.

The fourth principle applies to national armies as the source for UN personnel. The principle that peacekeepers work under the authority of the United Nations but are to be recruited from the national armies of member states implies the non-existence of a standing UN force for peacekeeping purposes. Furthermore, it guarantees that national governments have the last word on the travel orders of their nationals.[90] A corollary to this principle is that permanent members of the Security Council as well as regional powers having an interest in the conflict are excluded from donating troops for peacekeeping purposes there. This rule started to evolve in 1954 after the Indian Prime Minister succeeded in demanding the withdrawal of the US personnel who had participated in UNMOGIP since 1949. The rule was included in the UNEF provisions and upheld until 1973, when the UN chose a different solution to a similar problem: it allowed the Soviet Union to provide the same number of troops for UNTSO as the United States, which had taken part in the operation since 1948.

The fifth principle concerns the use of force for self-defence only. Although more than 50 per cent of cold war peacekeeping missions consisted of unarmed military observers, this provision became necessary once

---

[89] Ghali (1993: 104).

[90] Within this framework, however, gradations in the transfer of command are possible, which the UN has formalized in standard agreements.

armed units had been deployed. It forecloses by definition enforcement measures that have to be authorized by the Security Council under chapter 7 of the UN Charter. The definition of self-defence is open to dispute, however, and has changed significantly over time.

It is evident, then, that actors repeatedly acting according to the rules of a convention will, intentionally or not, stabilize and strengthen this convention. It is a puzzle, however, why violations sometimes do the same. The United Nations Operation in the Congo (ONUC, 1960–4) clearly stands out among the cold war peacekeeping missions as the largest and bloodiest. Steven Ratner summarizes: 'The UN deployed peacekeepers where the government or secessionists did not want them, rounded up foreign mercenaries, and even closed several airfields and a radio station. With explicit authority from the Council, ONUC defeated the Katangese secession through a series of battles and other armed encounters with the rebels from the summer of 1961 through early 1963.'[91] Yet although ONUC violated nearly all principles of traditional peacekeeping, it did not destabilize or even weaken the convention.

When the Congolese government clarified its initial appeal and called for military assistance against external aggression rather than help in restoring internal order,[92] Secretary-General Hammerskjöld, referring to article 99 and circumventing articles 39, 41, and 42 of the UN Charter, brought the situation to the Security Council's attention and recommended being given the necessary powers to negotiate the terms of military support with the Congolese government. In his request to the Security Council, Hammarskjöld explicitly referred to the principles and rules that had governed UN peacekeeping in Palestine.[93] However, Hammarskjöld did not use UNEF as a precedent legitimizing action, but rather as a prototype demonstrating the practicability of peacekeeping, referring to the 'classic text on UNEF'.[94]

On 14 July 1960, the secretary-general clarified the principles under which ONUC would operate. It would act under the sole authority of the UN but with the consent of the Congolese government; it would not interfere in the internal affairs of the country, for example by joining arms with government forces; it would use force for the purpose of self-defence only. When the Belgian-backed secessionist movement in the south-eastern region of Katanga did not allow UN forces to enter the area to restore government control in August 1960, the mission reached a critical junction.

---

[91] Ratner (1995: 104). [92] See Higgins (1969: iii. 14).
[93] See Menzel (1971: 84). [94] Higgins (1969: iii. 126).

Initially the UN had not considered the consent of the secessionists to be a legal prerequisite for the deployment of peacekeepers; now, however, their lack of cooperation endangered the whole mission. Since the original mandate[95] did not grant permission for the use of force, Hammarskjöld sought additional authority. The Security Council upgraded the mandate several times, finally allowing the secretary-general to 'take vigorous action, including the use of the requisite measure of force, if necessary'.[96] However, the resolution approved of the use of force only to apprehend foreign soldiers and mercenaries, but not to quell the secession, since this could have compromised the United Nations' impartiality.

At the time, ONUC appeared to be a disaster. In retrospect, it was an early mix of peacekeeping and peace enforcement. But although ONUC, as William Durch argues, 'set a potential precedent for coercive UN operations elsewhere',[97] the experience was not repeated. On the contrary, the United Nations did not contemplate the possibility of combat operations for decades and drew the line between peacekeeping and enforcement measures more rigidly than ever. Instead of becoming a precedent, ONUC became an exception. But what is an exception in theoretical terms? It is an action that is *post festum* collectively regarded by actors as violating the principles of an institution and is therefore disapproved. By promising not to repeat the experience, actors try to encapsulate the action in order to minimize its destabilizing effect on the institution as a whole. What is more, it enters into the decision-making process as a 'lesson', thus becoming an independent reason for complying with the convention's terms and, consequently, contributing to the stability of the convention. By becoming an example of how *not* to proceed in peacekeeping operations—that is, by negative selection— ONUC in fact stabilized rather than destabilized peacekeeping as a convention.

Reduced regularity

There is another reason why peacekeeping was maintained during the cold war despite mounting controversy over principles in the wake of the Congo experience. ONUC had stretched the United Nations to the breaking point, politically and financially. The Soviet Union refused to pay its share for the operation, demanding that 'the aggressor nation should pay the cost of liquidating the consequences of its aggression'.[98] Furthermore, Moscow was

---

[95] UN Doc. S/4387, 14 July 1960.
[96] See Higgins (1969: iii. 37–8).   [97] Durch (1993: 8).
[98] UN Doc. SC, Official Report, 18th year, 1038th meeting, 4.

suspicious of the prominent role the secretary-general had assumed and of his proactive approach to the issues. Obviously, the rules established so far for peacekeeping missions offered no guidance for cooperation during turbulent times. Ultimately, however, a compromise was found. The Soviet Union promised vaguely to pay for ONUC and UNEF, while the creation of a 'Special Committee on Peacekeeping Operations' was envisaged which would solve the problems once and for all and place future peacekeeping missions on a sound basis.

The committee, known as the Committee of 33, received a mandate 'to undertake as soon as possible a comprehensive review of the whole operation of peacekeeping operations in all their aspects, including ways of overcoming the present financial difficulties of the organization'.[99] Thus the member states answered the institutional crisis of peacekeeping with a step of forced institutionalization, creating a committee to systematically negotiate the rules for further cooperation. However, the attempt failed. While the Soviet Union and the United States held to their opposing positions on the financing and authority of UN agencies, Canada and the non-aligned members of the committee tried to find common ground. At one point success seemed within reach. By 1969 the committee had developed two models of peacekeeping,[100] and in 1977 it even prepared a Draft Formula for Articles of Agreed Guidelines for United Nations Peacekeeping Operations.[101] The agreement was short-lived, however, and the practice of peacekeeping soon outstripped futile attempts to negotiate its future functions and design its institutional form.

While disagreeing on matters of principle, the member states of the United Nations did cooperate in concrete cases, establishing new peacekeeping missions in West Irian (UNSF, 1962–3), Yemen (UNYOM, 1963–4), and Cyprus (UNFICYP, 1964 to present). By this time, peacekeeping consisted not only of a relatively stable set of principles but also of standardized procedures. The importance of such routine measures can hardly be overemphasized. They were critical in setting up the Second United Nations Emergency Force in Palestine (UNEF II) within two days. When the Israeli forces repelled the Egyptian and Syrian advances in October 1973 and moved deep into Arab territory, the Soviet Union threatened direct military intervention. American troops went on alert. In spite of heated debate in the Security Council, three resolutions were reached, calling for a cease-fire, requesting the secretary-general to dispatch observers to supervise it, and

---

[99] UN Doc. GA Res. 2006 (XIX), 18 Feb. 1965.   [100] UN Doc. A/7742 Appendix.
[101] UN Doc. A/32/394 Annex II, Appendix, 2 Dec. 1977.

establishing a Second United Nations Emergency Force.[102] By drawing the command structure from UNTSO and reinforcing the contingents from UNFICYP, UNEF II was operationally effective within twenty-four hours of the time the decision was made. 'This shows that, though there are no formal agreements or guidelines for peacekeeping operations, institutionalized practice and competent administration are very effective, perhaps more effective than they would be were the Committee of 33 to define the regulations and procedures.'[103]

What the Committee of 33 did, then, was to institutionalize the conflict over principles while allowing cooperation in concrete cases. This cooperation, in turn, stabilized existing principles even though member states, especially the Soviet Union, repeatedly stressed that specific solutions in the field might not set precedents and predetermine results to be negotiated by the committee. In fact, they did just that, not through the visible hand of the committee but through the invisible hand of institutional spontaneity.

Nevertheless, the stability of rules is one thing, the frequency with which they are implemented is another. Actors who sometimes act according to certain rules and sometimes circumvent them may keep the rules stable but reduce the behavioural regularity underlying them. This may weaken a convention even though its rules remain intact. Exactly this happened to peacekeeping, and it is worth noting that this process started with a success.

UNEF II contributed significantly to the growing climate of trust between Egypt and Israel and ultimately led to the peace treaty of March 1979. This success was UNEF's fate. Since the Soviet Union and other Arab countries opposed the accord, the peacekeeping mission could not be renewed in the Security Council and was terminated in 1979. Anticipating events, however, the United States had made preparations for an independent peacekeeping force, the Multinational Force and Observers (MFO), composed largely of US personnel under the authority of a US director general.[104] Its deployment was seen as an exception at the time, yet the same solution was adopted again in 1982, when the United Nations Interim Force in Lebanon (UNIFIL 1978–date) proved unable to evacuate the PLO after Israeli forces had invaded Lebanon and encircled the Palestinians in West Beirut. A non-UN multinational force (MNF), composed of military units from the US, France, and Italy did the job, thus making the earlier MFO a precedent rather than an exception.

---

[102] UN Doc. SC Res. 338, 22 Oct. 1973; UN Doc. SC Res. 339, 23 Oct. 1973; UN Doc. SC. Res. 340, 25 Oct. 1973.

[103] Wiseman (1987: 294).

[104] Ibid. 318.

To the extent that regional organizations (the OAS in the Dominican Republic in 1965, the Commonwealth in Rhodesia/Zimbabwe in 1980, the OAU in Chad in 1980–1 and the Western Sahara in 1981) and *ad hoc* arrangements took on peacekeeping tasks, the UN lost its monopoly in peacekeeping. Indeed, in the period between 1978 and 1988, while three earlier missions (UNTSO, UNMOGIP, UNFICYP), together with two more recent ones (UNDOF, 1974 to present, UNIFIL, 1978 to present), remained in place, no single peacekeeping operation was established under UN auspices. Though the operational principles of peacekeeping remained stable, peacekeeping as a convention was weakened, since its underlying regularity decreased, further reducing incentives to follow its rules. The United Nations had lost the necessary political cohesion to agree on new peacekeeping operations implementing the well-established UN provisions for peace missions around the world. As Henry Wiseman notes: 'The concept of peacekeeping and the Organization itself suffered in consequence.'[105]

This development clearly illustrates that time is not enough to stabilize an institution. Though duration and continuity are important for stability, it is not time itself that 'works on the side of conventions';[106] it is rather the repeated rule-governed and rule-implementing behaviour of actors that reinforces the regularity, which in turn creates incentives to follow the rules, thus strengthening the convention.

4. The Transformation of Peacekeeping: Explaining Institutional Change

Although peacekeeping was not mentioned in the UN Charter, it emerged as a convention and stabilized during the cold war to become one of the central institutions around which member states' expectations on matters of international peace and security converged. With the end of the East–West conflict, the demand for peacekeeping increased significantly, as did the willingness of member states to deploy blue helmets in non-standard situations of civil war and failed states. But instead of strengthening United Nations peacekeeping capabilities—for example, by establishing Rapid Deployment Forces, increasing the secretary-general's room of manoeuvre, or even paying their dues—member states have opted to transfer more and more missions to regional organizations and *ad hoc* coalitions. The

---

[105] Ibid. 289.   [106] Kier and Mercer (1996: 93).

consequence is that peacekeeping as an international security institution is becoming increasingly decentralized and regionalized,[107] thus losing its institutional homogeneity and legal coherence.[108]

While some analysts maintain that this constitutes 'a sea change in the nature and purpose of peacekeeping',[109] others insist that every feature of the 'new peacekeeping' has its forerunner in the history of the United Nations.[110] Both claims have some merit, but neither is easily explained. It is not easy to discover either the causes of change or the reasons for the rediscovery of discarded rules. History alone does not provide the answer why peacekeeping has been transformed. We must resort to theory.

Modes of change

Institutionalist theory maintains that institutions change if they no longer fulfil the needs of their creators. This implies a plan or at least some idea of how existing rules could be altered in order to serve one or another actor's interests more efficiently. But how do *conventions* change, when they have not been created but have evolved? Most theories, and even evolutionary explanations, embrace the idea of adaptive efficiency.[111] Institutions may not be efficient but they are presumed to change for the better since selection works in favour of more efficient alternatives.

However, while it seems plausible that efficient behaviour will have a greater chance of being repeated and reinforced, and inefficient behaviour will induce a search for alternatives or an imitation of more efficient behaviour,[112] this only holds if a shared standard of efficiency exists and if individual efficiency is equivalent to collective efficiency. Where this is not the case, individually efficient behaviour may produce inefficient collective outcomes, and existing institutions could change for the worse.

In order to account for this phenomenon, a theory of institutional change must endogenize efficiency by differentiating individual motives from social effects. Efficiency on the micro-level can thus be separated from efficiency on the macro-level. Such an invisible-hand explanation of institutional change would hold that institutional change is not only the direct result of actors altering existing rules but also the indirect result of their gradual deviance from established practices. Institutional transformation

---

[107] On regionalization of peacekeeping, see Barnett (1995); Rivlin (1992); Smith and Weiss (1997).

[108] On the legal implications, see Higgins (1995: 181).   [109] Ratner (1995: 1).

[110] See Hill and Malik (1996).   [111] See North (1990: 92).

[112] See Elsner (1989: 201).

may, then, be the result of either intended revision or spontaneous change.[113]

Though the notion of spontaneous change is closely connected with informal institutions, both kinds of change, spontaneous and intended, may indeed affect both kinds of institutions, formal and informal. A convention may change without purposive activity by any actor, individual or collective; it may also become subject to revision by actors trying to re-negotiate its rules. Likewise, regimes and organizations may be revised by participants altering their rules, but they may also change spontaneously as actors gradually modify their behaviour.

The theory of spontaneous institutions thus conceptualizes institutional change as the incremental transformation of conventions through continuous marginal adjustments of practice and explains it as the cumulative causal consequence of many separate functional decisions by political actors. At the same time, this theory does not deny other modes of institutional change, and it acknowledges the necessity of combining invisible-hand and intentional-design accounts to understand fully particular cases of institutional change.

The uncertainty zone

Institutions exist in order to reduce uncertainty among interacting agents. They provide guidance for behaviour by specifying the terms of cooperation and shaping actors' expectations. However, institutions never fully exclude uncertainty, for two fundamental reasons: factual indecisiveness and procedural vagueness. Factual indecisiveness means that it is unclear whether a given event is covered by a certain institution. Is, for example, the breakdown of public order in Somalia a case for UN peacekeeping? Because of insufficient information ('What really happened in Somalia?') and conflicting interpretations ('What is public order?'), there is always the possibility of a grey area, in which it is unclear whether a certain institution applies. Yet even when applicability is clear, many institutional rules allow a large discretion in their application. For example, once Somalia is decided to be a case for UN peacekeeping, whose consent is to be obtained? Again, no rule can be sharpened to avoid all vagueness.

Edna Ullmann-Margalit has called these grey areas the 'uncertainty zone' of an institution, since it 'provides no guidance for behavior with regard to cases falling within this zone'.[114] Usually, this zone is kept to a minimum by

---

[113] See Ullmann-Margalit (1990).   [114] Ibid. 578.

providing strict criteria, as in the case of peacekeeping during the cold war. Since peacekeeping was restricted to a narrow range of problems—especially decolonization issues—and operated under the severe restraints of the East–West conflict, the uncertainty zone was limited, allowing only a few cases to call into question peacekeeping practice.

As long as the uncertainty zone of an institution is small—meaning that most events can be clearly decided as cases or non-cases—no pressure to change the institution arises. If the uncertainty zone expands, however—if more and more events arise which are controversial as to whether and how they should be treated—incentives will develop to transform the institution either intentionally (by institutional reform) or spontaneously (by deviating practice).

When the East–West conflict faded, the number of peacekeeping operations expanded dramatically. There were three reasons. First, the Security Council was more capable of agreeing on certain actions in crisis situations. Second, there was widespread optimism that the United Nations could play a much more active role in international security and that peacekeeping could solve a very wide range of urgent problems. Third, there was an increased need for peacekeeping because of the termination of regional conflicts made possible by the end of the cold war and the rise of new conflicts resulting from the breakdown of multi-ethnic communist states like the Soviet Union and Yugoslavia.[115]

These conflicts posed considerable problems for the UN, since most of them fell into a zone of uncertainty, where the applicability of existing institutions was unclear. In this situation peacekeeping was used as a framework, since it provided rules which were firmly established yet flexible enough to be adapted to the new post-cold war environment. By using the convention and gradually departing from its rules, however, peacekeeping was unintentionally transformed in two directions. First, by interfering in the internal matters of sovereign states, peacekeeping expanded its function into the field of trusteeship. Second, by moving towards enforcement, peacekeeping further expanded its task, departing from its former strict rule of non-use of force.

When the United Nations resumed peacekeeping activities in the late 1980s, it was in the least controversial form of traditional peacekeeping: peace observation.[116] The United Nations Good Offices Mission in Afghanistan and Pakistan (UNGOMAP 1988–90), which had to verify the withdrawal of Soviet troops from Afghanistan; the United Nations Iran-

---

[115] See A. Roberts (1994).   [116] See Weiss *et al.* (1994: 63).

Iraq Military Observer Group (UNIIMOG 1988–91), which ensured the maintenance of the cease-fire between Iran and Iraq; the United Nations Angola Verification Mission (UNAVEM I, 1989–91) that facilitated the simultaneous withdrawal of Cuban troops from Angola and South African troops from Namibia, and finally the United Nations Transition Assistance Group (UNTAG, 1989–90) for Namibia, all remained within the limits of traditional peacekeeping and were strictly committed to the peacekeeping principles of consent, impartiality, and the minimal use of force.

UNTAG arguably expanded the functions of peacekeeping in so far as it included electoral matters, human rights, and police and educational functions.[117] In doing so, it set the stage for those peacekeeping missions in connection with the peace process in Central America. The cornerstone of this process was the agreement to cease helping rebel groups or granting them safe havens in one country to carry out guerrilla actions in another. In 1989 the United Nations Observer Group in Central America (UNUCA 1989–92) was set up to supervise this agreement. After the Nicaraguan election, the mandate was expanded to include the demobilization of the Contra rebels. To secure free and fair elections in Nicaragua, another mission, ONUVEN, was created for the first time in UN history to supervise elections within a member state rather than in a non-self-governing territory. Although the secretary-general vindicated this departure from previous practice by emphasizing the international dimension of the election for the Central American peace process, and despite his promise to the General Assembly that ONUVEN would have 'no effect on established practice, nor would a precedent be set for possible further requests', ONUVEN had precisely this effect. As Kier and Mercer note, 'declaring something unique does not make it so'.[118]

With ONUVEN the UN had crossed the line between deploying a peacekeeping mission with an electoral component only in situations with clear interstate dimensions and sending one into an internal conflict. Although it was not the intention of the General Secretary or the member states, this decision changed the rules of peacekeeping. 'By their actions, the member states and Perez de Cuellar signaled their acceptance of the notion of UN missions to oversee elections anywhere.'[119] This was highlighted by the establishment of the United Nations Observer Mission to Verify the Electoral Process in Haiti (ONUVEH, 1990–1), which performed tasks similar to the mission in Nicaragua. In Cambodia as well, elections were the core function of the UN mission, but the United Nations Transitional Authority in

---

[117] Ratner (1995: 123).   [118] Kier and Mercer (1996: 85).   [119] Ratner (1995: 128).

Cambodia (UNTAC, 1992–3) was much more complex, including seven components: human rights, electoral, military, civil administration, police, repatriation, and rehabilitation. From the start, UNTAC assumed administrative authority, exercising key governmental functions and renewing the tradition of trusteeship which the UN had abandoned when peacekeeping was about to emerge.

The second direction in which peacekeeping developed through gradual behavioural adjustments is peace enforcement. It was an often-repeated opinion during the cold war that if the Security Council had been able to agree on more decisive measures, peacekeeping missions would have been much more effective. This time seemed to have come when, on 19 November 1990, the Security Council invoked chapter 7 authorizing member states to use 'all necessary means' to expel Iraq from Kuwait. Though the UN authorized the use of force, it did not direct or control it. Command and control of the Gulf War was in the hands of an *ad hoc* coalition led by the United States. 'The Security Council was essentially a spectator, but U.S. control appeared necessary for reasons of efficiency as well as political support.'[120]

A similar picture emerges from an analysis of peacekeeping missions that included major enforcement actions, especially those in Bosnia and Somalia. On 21 February 1992, the Security Council authorized the deployment of the United Nations Protection Force (UNPROFOR)[121] mandated to create conditions within its area of operation for the safe return of refugees. Worsening conditions, however, led the Security Council to expand UNPROFOR's mandate to 'ensure the delivery of humanitarian assistance'[122] and to formally recognize 'that the situation in Bosnia and Herzegovina constitutes a threat to international peace and security and that the provision of humanitarian assistance in Bosnia and Herzegovina is an important element in the Council's effort to restore international peace and security in the area'.

On 13 August 1992, the Security Council, invoking chapter 7, called upon states 'to take nationally or through regional agencies or arrangements all measures necessary to facilitate in coordination with the United Nations the delivery by relevant United Nations humanitarian organizations and others of humanitarian assistance to Sarajevo and wherever needed in other parts of Bosnia and Herzegovina'.[123] This extremely broad mandate was not meant to apply to UNPROFOR but to independent coalitions of member

---

[120] Weiss *et al.* (1994: 70).   [121] UN Doc. SC Res. 743, 21 Feb. 1992.
[122] UN Doc. SC Res. 761, 29 June 1992.   [123] UN Doc. SC Res. 770, 13 Aug. 1992.

states. Marc Weller holds that the 'aim of this maneuver was quite clearly to transfer enforcement tasks away from the UN Secretariat to organizations which would be less hesitant in using force, if necessary'.[124] However, in order to limit the danger of independent intervention, especially from Islamic countries, this provision was revoked in subsequent resolutions by assigning the task of armed convoy protection to UNPROFOR, thus assuring 'the Security Council's control of the operation'.[125]

In February 1993, the Security Council, specifying UNPROFOR's mandate, cited chapter 7 for the first time.[126] The French Ambassador, who sponsored the resolution after French soldiers had died in hostilities, maintained that this was not meant to transform the operation from peacekeeping to peace enforcement but should rather strengthen the traditional right of self-defence.[127] Chapter 7 was invoked a second time when the Security Council decided to change some parts of UNPROFOR's mandate, especially those concerning the protection of 'safe havens', enabling peace enforcement to take place independent of the parties' consent.[128] In the same resolution, NATO was authorized to use air power in support of UNPROFOR's mandate.

However, in every new resolution on Bosnia extending the right to use force, the Security Council reaffirmed previous resolutions on UNPROFOR. Obviously, the Security Council did not want to alter the mission's character completely by invalidating earlier provisions.[129] Much of UNPROFOR's work, therefore, continued to be based on consent. The effect, however, was that the line between peacekeeping and peace enforcement was blurred, since the reference to chapter 7 permitted UNPROFOR to switch from one to the other.

A similar situation arose when the Security Council established the United Nations Operation in Somalia (UNOSOM I, 1992–3), again referring to chapter 7 and maintaining that the civil war in Somalia posed a threat to international peace and security. Though the belligerents initially agreed to a small force of 500 and some fifty observers, they opposed the 3,000 UN soldiers authorized under Resolution 751.[130] In order to enforce UN resolutions, President Bush moved towards humanitarian intervention

---

124 Weller (1996: 98).
125 Report of the secretary-general, UN Doc. S/24540, 10 Sept. 1992, para. 18.
126 UN Doc. SC Res. 807, 19 Feb. 1993.
127 Remarks of Ambassador Merimée of France, Provisional Verbatim Record of the 3174th Meeting, 19 Feb. 1992, UN Doc. S/PV. 3174, pp. 13–15.
128 UN Doc. SC Res. 836, 4 June 1993.
129 See Tharoor (1995/6: 59).
130 UN Doc. SC Res. 751, 24 Apr. 1992.

by proposing the creation of an Unified Task Force (UNITAF). Once again, a US-led coalition of 28,000 soldiers, authorized by the Security Council,[131] used military force to secure the delivery of humanitarian relief.

After UNITAF ceased operations in May 1993, the second phase of UN peacekeeping in Somalia (UNOSOM II, 1993–5) began. Fifteen hundred US soldiers remained in reserve as a rapid deployment force in boats offshore to be called in by the UN commander in Somalia, who was a NATO general from Turkey. In June 1993 the Security Council adopted a resolution that allowed the arrest and punishment of Somali clan members responsible for killing twenty-five Pakistani peacekeepers.[132] This move of UNOSOM II from peacekeeping to peace enforcement compromised the mission's perceived impartiality and provoked retaliatory attacks on US soldiers, forcing the Council to retreat from its position.[133] In these circumstances the United States, Italy, and Germany announced the withdrawal of their troops once their initial commitment to UNOSOM II expired. Since the secretary-general could not replace these forces, he was forced first to scale back the operation, and finally to terminate it in March 1995.

Both developments—the move toward trusteeship and the move towards enforcement—indicate that the sheer quantity of unconventional cases which the UN faced after the end of the cold war expanded the uncertainty zone of peacekeeping, pushing it toward institutional change. In the course of events, most of the principles of peacekeeping came to be compromised: the principle of non-use of force, the principles of consent and impartiality, and the principle not to deploy troops of the permanent members. The ultimate change, however, which followed from all the preceding ones, was the gradual relinquishment of the United Nation's sole authority over peacekeeping missions.

Regionalizing peacekeeping

By the mid-1990s the extension and perhaps over-extension of peacekeeping became apparent.[134] In March 1995 Secretary-General Boutros Boutros-Ghali declared: 'The number of United Nations operations, the scale of the operations, the money spent on operations cannot keep growing indefinitely. The limits are being reached.'[135] By that time, however, a

---

[131] UN Doc. SC Res. 794, 4 Dec. 1992.		[132] UN Doc. SC Res. 837, 6 June 1993.
[133] UN Doc. SC Res. 885, 16 Nov. 1993.		[134] See Roberts (1994).
[135] Boutros Boutros-Ghali, 'Managing the Peacekeeping Challenge', Speech on 21 Mar. 1995, Yale University, UN Press Release SG/SM/5589.

possible solution had already emerged through the practice of assigning certain functions of peacekeeping to regional organizations or *ad hoc* coalitions. What the secretary-general did was try to channel this drive towards the regionalization of peacekeeping by arranging a dialogue between the UN Secretariat and various regional organizations to discuss their future role in strengthening international peace and security with particular regard to peacemaking, preventive diplomacy, fact-finding, confidence-building, and peacekeeping.[136]

This has led some analysts to argue that regionalization is a deliberate solution, designed to overcome the financial and operational problems of future peacekeeping.[137] However, the regionalization of peacekeeping was only partly intentional. To a larger extent, it was the unintended consequence of the intended behaviour of member states to cooperate more effectively in the new functions of peacekeeping after the cold war.

Wherever the UN resumed quasi-governmental functions, for example in Cambodia, it became a player in the internal power game. Since similar problems occurred in Namibia, Nicaragua, and El Salvador, endangering UNTAG, ONUVEN, and ONUSAL respectively, a pattern seems to be forming. As Ratner argues: 'The intrusive nature of the new peacekeeping prevents the Organization from acting as a neutral player in the sense of having no effect on the ultimate resolution of the dispute.'[138] This, in turn, increases the risk of the United Nations not only being drawn into the internal conflicts of a state but also facing hard choices in cases where consent is fading,[139] thus jeopardizing unanimity among member states. To mitigate this peril was one of the basic reasons why the United Nations teamed up with various regional organizations to carry out difficult peacekeeping missions: e.g. in Cambodia with ASEAN; in the former Yugoslavia with NATO, the EU, and the OSCE; in Haiti, El Salvador, and Nicaragua with the OAS; in Liberia with ECOWAS; in Burundi and Rwanda with the OAU.

An even stronger incentive to make regional organizations or *ad hoc* arrangements a party to UN peacekeeping operations emerged once enforcement measures were envisaged. The UN's experience in Bosnia and Somalia shows that three operational consequences arise once enforcement provisions are included in peacekeeping operations.[140] First, they need more and better equipped troops, sophisticated C^3 facilities, and highly qualified specialists, which makes them more dependent on those countries

---

[136] UN Doc. S/25184, 29 Jan. 1993. UN Doc. S/25996, 15 June 1993
[137] Barnett (1995: 418); see also W. A. Knight (1996).   [138] Ratner (1995: 52).
[139] See Durch (1993: 11).   [140] See Biermann (1995).

that can provide such means. Second, they pose a high risk for UN soldiers, which increases the member states' propensity to interfere in the mission's conduct in order to protect their nationals. Third, because of the high risks involved, member states are reluctant to provide troops for such operations under UN auspices. Hence, the cooperation problems arising from peace enforcement are quite different from the problems that exist under traditional peacekeeping situations and seemed to be better solved within regional organizations and *ad hoc* arrangements than in the traditional framework of the United Nations, with its built-in deficiencies and susceptibility to significant free-riding.[141] The resort to regional organizations and *ad hoc* arrangements for enforcement purposes can therefore be explained by the desire of member states to cooperate efficiently by minimizing the risks arising from the functional extension of peacekeeping.

5. Conclusion

The emergence, stability, and transformation of peacekeeping as a convention is very well explained as an unintended effect. Critics may object that this finding is not very surprising, accustomed as they are to astonishing insights on the effects of the 'invisible hand' in Bernard Mandeville's *Fable of the Bees*[142] or in Smith's more scholarly *The Wealth of Nations*.[143] The core idea is that evil may breed good, that bad actions may produce beneficial outcomes. Some analysts, therefore, see the explanatory power of invisible-hand theories as in part a function of their surprise effect. The more the results are unexpected, given certain premises, they argue, the more astonishing and 'telling' an invisible-hand explanation is.[144] This, however, is a purely aesthetic argument; the real value of invisible-hand explanations lies not in surprise, but in the methodological insight that, in order to explain many institutions, the motives of individual behaviour have to be distinguished from their social effects.

As developed in the previous sections, this approach to institutional analysis does not hinge on unrealistically strong assumptions about rationality and common knowledge. At the same time, it does not dispense with rationality altogether. By combining reasons and causes in a single analytical framework, the theory of spontaneous institutions promises a comprehensive yet elegant and parsimonious explanation of conventions.

---

[141] See Barnett (1995: 427).
[143] See A. Smith (1976/1776).

[142] See Mandeville (1924/1732).
[144] See Ullmann-Margalit (1978a: 267).

9

US NON-PROLIFERATION CAMPAIGNS AND THEIR IMPACT ON INSTITUTIONAL CHANGE

Henning Riecke

1. Introduction

Nuclear non-proliferation has been one of principal objectives of United States foreign and security policy. Both the build-up of non-proliferation institutions and unilateral or collective efforts against potential nuclear proliferators and their programmes have been crucial elements of American strategy. The non-proliferation regime would not be what it is today without these American efforts. However, the effects of US campaigns against alleged defectors are not always positive. This needs to be explained.

Unilateral American non-proliferation campaigns in the 1990s were directed at signatories of the Nuclear Non-Proliferation Treaty (NPT) suspected of conducting nuclear weapons programmes, like North Korea and Iran, or at former Soviet republics that held nuclear weapons on their territory while their membership in the non-proliferation regime was uncertain. The US sought to stabilize the non-proliferation regime and to maintain the reliability of cooperative behaviour. However, Washington faced a problem: its unilateral strategies disregarded regime rules and thus risked undermining the regime's effectiveness.

This chapter deals with the puzzling fact that the United States sometimes violated the rules of the non-proliferation regime in order to increase its effectiveness. Under what conditions does unilateral action enhance the

I would like to thank all participants in the Joint Conferences for their helpful criticism of earlier versions of this paper: in particular, Robert O. Keohane and Celeste Wallander for detailed comments, and Jeff Legro, Gunther Hellmann, and David A. Lake for remarks made as discussants at the Center for International Affairs, Harvard University, and at the ISA Annual Meeting in Toronto, 1997.

effectiveness of the regime? Which rules must be observed if the regime is not to be jeopardized? What, in general, is the impact of unilateralism on the regime?

The puzzle is deepened by the fact that it is the US which sometimes proceeds unilaterally, outside institutional processes. As the most influential actor within the regime, the US could use this advantage to stabilize its rules. Hegemonic stability theory ascribes an important role to powerful actors, or 'hegemons', in upholding cooperation.[1] Even in institutional theory, where the existence of a hegemon is neither sufficient nor necessary to explain the rise and stability of institutions,[2] support by powerful states is still important for the stability of the regime.[3]

The main argument of this chapter is that unilateralism or small-group action can have a positive effect on a regime provided its principled rules are not transgressed and the preferences of other relevant actors are not violated. Unilateral action that violates the procedural rules of a regime may strengthen the effectiveness of the regime, but only when compatible with the regime's fundamental principles and norms. The effectiveness of the non-proliferation regime depends largely on the degree of compliance by the US with these principled rules, since the United States is still the most effective stabilizer of the non-proliferation regime.

The conditions under which unilateral stabilization efforts are successful is an understudied issue. The present volume sets out to pay attention to reciprocal interactions between institutions and national policy and the impact of such national policy on the institutions themselves.[4] Accordingly, this chapter looks at the effects of unilateral state activities on the viability of institutions and the norms and principles they enshrine. The term 'unilateralism' will refer to policies that are conducted outside agreed-upon institutional procedures.

To examine how US policies impinge on the effectiveness of the non-

---

[1] On hegemonic stability see Kindleberger (1974); Gilpin (1975); Krasner (1976). For criticism, see Keohane (1980); Snidal (1985); Haggard and Simmons (1987: 500–4).

[2] See Keohane (1984: ch. 3). In this article this school of thought is named 'institutional', though other branches of institutionalism exist. Institutionalism has also been called 'contractualism', see Keohane (1995: 36); Hasenclever *et al.* (1996: 184). In institutionalist theory, the term 'institution' subsumes conventions, regimes, and organizations. In this paper, the term 'institution' is used accordingly with reference to sets of rules governing behaviour in general, whereas 'regime' refers to the subgroup of agreed upon institutions incorporating principled and procedural rules, one of which is the non-proliferation regime. See Keohane (1989*c*: 4).

[3] See Keohane (1989*c*: 6).

[4] Introduction, pp. 12–13.

proliferation regime, the puzzles sketched out above need first to be elaborated theoretically. Patterns of unilateral political action and their institutional impact are analysed in the following section. Next, the efforts of the United States to persuade Ukraine to sign the NPT as a non-nuclear-weapon state will be examined, along with the US–North Korean negotiations to terminate the crisis around that country's nuclear programme, and Washington's isolation campaign toward Iran. Though not entirely comparable, these cases show certain parallels which do allow them to be used as case studies.[5] Finally, the impact of the United States' unilateral policy actions on the regime's effectiveness will be discussed and compared with other effects of these crises.

2. Powerful States' Unilateralism and Institutional Change

Institutionalist change under the institutionalist paradigm

The institutionalist argument focuses on the institution's functions in facilitating cooperation. Institutions are 'persistent and connected sets of rules (formal and informal) that prescribe behavioral roles, constrain activity, and shape expectations'.[6] Institutions do this through the principled and procedural rules they incorporate. These rules help states trust in another's cooperative behaviour but do not guarantee cooperation, since national preferences may sometimes induce states to disregard these rules. Institutions increase the costs of defection that otherwise may seem rational in pursuit of short-term gains. To encourage adherence, institutions provide credible information on the implementation of agreements by the regime's participants, thus raising the costs of secret defection. In addition, institutions may threaten sanctions for defection.

The non-proliferation regime comprises several subregimes and agencies that are designed to implement the provisions of the NPT. The treaty codifies a trade-off between nuclear weapon states (NWS) and those without these capabilities, in which the latter renounce a nuclear option and the former promise not to assist in the development of nuclear weapons. The

---

[5] The case constituted by India's and Pakistan's nuclear testing in May 1998 is not included in this article because India and Pakistan are not members of the non-proliferation regime, so it is harder to invoke its rules against them.

[6] Keohane (1989*c*: 3).

NWS commit themselves to embark on a path of disarmament. The non-nuclear weapons states (NNWS) are granted international assistance for the peaceful use of nuclear energy and are obliged to accept safeguards administered by the International Atomic Energy Agency (IAEA). Other elements of the non-proliferation regime are export-control regimes implemented by the Nuclear Suppliers Group, a system of negative and positive security guarantees given by the NWS, and several nuclear-weapons-free zones. The central authority for enforcing the NPT provisions is the UN Security Council. As these institutions are closely linked to each other, the non-proliferation regime should be treated as a single institution with a few principled and many procedural rules.

The distinction between principled and procedural rules is important. Principled rules, or norms, provide a frame of reference that shapes the expectations of the participants about others' behaviour. They express a collective understanding of the function of cooperation within the non-proliferation regime as well as shared beliefs about appropriate behaviour. Procedural rules are the means agreed upon to achieve this purpose and to secure the cooperative behaviour of all participants.

The principled rules, codified by the NPT, are the focal point for expectations about the participant's behaviour. They include a renunciation of the nuclear option by the NNWS, the freedom to use civil nuclear energy as long as this use is safeguarded by the IAEA, and a commitment on behalf of all participants to help prevent the spread of nuclear weapons. In order to enable states to take the risk of renouncing the nuclear option while the possibility still exists that other participants might not cooperate, sophisticated procedural rules concerning all aspects of the regime have been established. When designed appropriately, procedural rules reflect the principled rules. They include monitoring and sanctioning mechanisms as well as decision-making procedures in case of defection. In the non-proliferation regime, the IAEA's procedural rules combine verification with mechanisms for involving the international community in deciding about sanctions in cases of detected defection. Regular review conferences provide for the adaptation of the regime itself.[7]

Principled rules play a more important role in solving collective action problems. The prescription of behaviour and the stability of expectations rest on these rules. The procedural rules assure their implementation. Information, even if it is comprehensive and intrusively collected, is worthless if a clear framework of assessment is lacking. Sanctions must be fairly and

---

[7] See Müller (1989).

consistently applied in light of established principles. The quality of the principled rules is thus decisive for the functioning of the non-proliferation regime.

In this article, institutional change is identified not as a change in the purpose of the non-proliferation regime but as a change in its norms and procedures.[8] Variations in the commonality and specificity of principled and procedural rules will be assessed according to whether they strengthen or undermine the institution's effectiveness. From the institutionalist perspective, the demand for effective institutions should lead to the adaptation of existing ones when the latter become ineffective. The question is when unilateral activities lead to increased effectiveness.

Unilateral policies

In this article, the term 'unilateralism' or 'unilateral policy' refers to actions conducted outside agreed-upon multilateral procedures. The contrast is with action conducted entirely within institutional principles and procedures. Therefore, 'unilateral' actions need not be those of only one state: several states may act unilaterally in a given instance, together or separately. One actor starts a campaign outside established institutional procedures and perhaps rallies other relevant players to share costs and responsibilities. This kind of unilateralism refrains from consultation within the regular institutional decision-making bodies and defies their rules, either principled or procedural, for achieving a negotiated solution.[9]

Institutional shortcomings can motivate powerful states to act outside institutional procedures. A state with a sophisticated intelligence capability may be able to gather information more easily than an international agency. Sanctions on a rogue state are usually designed very cautiously in order not to impinge too much on national sovereignty, so they are not always very effective. A powerful participant may be able to replace frail sanctions with robust inducement or coercion. Consultation and conflict-management mechanisms work slowly and on a low administrative level. A powerful actor can open up new channels of communication among a small number of relevant states or initiate high-level talks to speed up decision-making.

Under conditions of asymmetrical power, rules can be instruments of both regulation and domination. Powerful states can use these rules to exert their dominance in institutional cooperation or, more subtly, through

---

[8] See Ch. 1 above.
[9] For a definition of unilateralism, see also Czempiel *et al.* (1994: 1).

agenda-setting. Since these rules are the standards of behaviour, they are also an important instrument of leadership. But a powerful state cannot neglect the path of cooperative behaviour set by institutional constraints once these rules have reached a certain degree of commonality. Rule conformity will then be regarded by others as criterion of the regime's legitimacy and will be a precondition of its international acceptance.

Unilateral action may be aimed at enforcing institutional decisions, reversing defections, or pursuing national interests. The main subject of this article is unilateralism aimed at enforcing the non-proliferation regime. Under these circumstances, the powerful actor has an interest both in upholding the institution and in bearing the costs of stabilizing its norms.[10] Three kinds of unilateralism for the sake of the institution are conceivable.

First, a powerful actor may find unilateral or small-group action appropriate when a state participating in the regime has to be persuaded to return to a norm-oriented policy. Multilateral institutional procedures are often slow. Decision-making bodies can be paralysed by competing national preferences which impede effective sanctions against the defector. Unilateral policies will also be more probable when the institution does not encompass instruments for effective sanctioning. The powerful state can deal directly with a defecting state or try to isolate it internationally. It can threaten coercion or promise compensation, and can link the state's behaviour to punishment or reward in other areas. However, in pursuing such a strategy, a powerful state will need both some institutional backing to increase the legitimacy of its actions and some collaboration with other relevant actors to share costs and responsibilities. It will seek support in the form of a resolution or mandate from an authorizing institution such as the UN Security Council, which in turn will limit its room for unilateral manoeuvring. Unilateral action of this type may also be aimed at getting a state to join an institution.

The distinction between crisis and routine is relevant here. A crisis is characterized by threat, surprise, and temporal urgency.[11] An institutional crisis occurs when the stability of an institution is threatened, for instance by a member state's sudden defection. For more long-term changes, routine conditions lead to institutional adaptation governed by procedural rules (such as regular review conferences); states should be able to deal with non-crisis challenges by following agreed procedures. The time factor is the most important distinguishing feature between the two. Unilateral policies, cir-

---

[10] On the stabilizing function of a single actor in institutions, see Gehring (1995: 211–15).

[11] For a concept of 'crisis' that embraces these three features, see Hermann (1969: 414). For a discussion of the concept of crisis decision-making, see Bühl (1988: 26–34).

cumventing institutions that might react too slowly, may therefore be rational in a crisis situation.

A second possible rationale for unilateralism is that the institution's procedures may not provide the means to reliably verify participants' compliance with the rules. A powerful state may be able to perform this task more effectively with national means, supplementing the institution's information collection and distribution capacities. This implies some inequality, however, since the other participants cannot verify the powerful state's own compliance. This imbalance may threaten the principle of sovereign equality and bring criticism not only from defectors but also from members cherishing equal status.

A third norm-enforcing strategy justifies a deliberate breach of the rules with the argument that it causes less damage than obeying the rules would have, and may even stimulate their reformulation.[12] A relevant actor could also behave far 'above' a norm by setting an example of self-restriction, accepting short-term costs, or trying to persuade or force other participants to adopt the new, more stringent policy. These strategies fail, however, if the other participants decline to renegotiate the norm. In this case, the damage to institutional cooperation will be severe.

Unilateral policies as a causal factor in institutional change

Unilateral strategies can terminate a crisis or remedy institutional flaws. But, the impact of unilateral stabilization on institutional dynamics is more complex. On the one hand, in addition to solving a crisis threatening the foundations of the regime, agreements reached outside its institutional framework may also serve as a catalyst for the development of new and more appropriate principled rules; or they may make stricter principled rules more feasible politically. Unilateralism can thus have an innovative effect on the regime. On the other hand, unilateralism can devalue an institution by circumventing its agreed procedures. When a powerful state's actions conflict with the institution's functions, negative effects are to be expected.

If a powerful state acts on its own, it may violate principled rules that oblige participants to place their activities under multilateral verification or that entitle only multilateral bodies to impose sanctions. This could deal a severe blow to members' confidence in the reliability of the regime. It may

---

[12] See Martin (1992*b*: 776–7); also Gehring (1995: 214). For an introduction into the concept of 'justified disobedience' in international trade, see Hudec (1990).

also generate competition between institutional and unilateral strategies, reducing the value of the regime to other member states, who might prefer relying on powerful states to investing in the institution.

Unilateral policies also contradict the notion of sovereign equality on which cooperation in the non-proliferation regime is based. In any unilateral or small-group activity, narrow perceptions and preferences will influence policies and outcomes. If this bias is very visible (for example, when more pressure or sanctions are applied to some states than others), it will undermine acceptance of principled rules and reduce the value of the institution. The institution will lose its legitimacy and its rules their binding force. American support of Israel—a NWS outside the non-proliferation regime—creates the impression that the principle of non-proliferation is important in some cases but not in others. The negative impacts of unilateral action can, however, be mitigated. The positive effects of unilateral action basically rest on the fact that the powerful state assumes the political and material costs for increasing the institution's effectiveness, assuring norm-oriented behaviour on the part of all participants and thus strengthening the regime's norms.

The foregoing discussion is summarized in the following hypothesis. Unilateral action by a powerful state or group of states increases the functional effectiveness of an institution if, both in the way the crisis is managed and in its outcome, (i) the principled rules are not violated, and (ii) other relevant actors' preferences are not disregarded.

3. US Campaigns Against Alleged Defectors

In the 1990s, the nuclear non-proliferation regime is facing a number of severe challenges. Not all of them were caused by the end of the cold war. After the demise of the Soviet Union, the United States is the only remaining major power with the ability to assure the functioning and further development of the existing institutions dealing with nuclear non-proliferation.[13] Though a nuclear attack on US territory is not very likely, the United States wants to prevent the spread of nuclear and other weapons of mass destruction (WMD), especially in regions of conflict where American troops abroad and those of their allies could be threatened or American reputation in the region could be seriously impaired. In particular, US ability to use

---

[13] For a comprehensive assessment of the changing nature of the issue of nuclear non-proliferation, see Bailey (1993); Fischer (1992); Krause (1998); Müller (1997).

conventional weapons in military operations in unstable regions or against pariah states would be severely circumscribed if an opponent was thought to be equipped with WMD.[14] Thus, the non-proliferation regime is of the highest importance for the last remaining superpower.

While the non-proliferation regime is today nearly universally supported, a few states do wish to acquire nuclear and other WMD. On the one hand, nuclear proliferation is more difficult to prevent than forty years ago. Advances in nuclear technology and ease in global distribution have enabled a growing number of threshold states to develop the technology necessary for a military nuclear programme and to sell this technology on the international market. A related threat is the smuggling of nuclear materials and know-how from the former Soviet Union. On the other hand, the development of nuclear capabilities is much more expensive and difficult to conceal now than in the past because of the verification provisions. In an ongoing process of adaptation, certain limits on the regime's effectiveness have been identified and continually improved. Nuclear proliferation will not happen as frequently today as it did in the 1960s, but in order to prevent it, the existing non-proliferation regime has to be prepared, its constraints directed against those who wish to acquire nuclear capabilities and against those who can supply the necessary technology.

1991 was a year of change for two reasons. First, the Gulf War disclosed that Iraq, an NPT signatory, had conducted a nuclear weapons programme, shielded from the regular IAEA safeguards. This revelation corroborated earlier suspicions. The international community was put on notice to rethink the efficiency of the non-proliferation regime's rules. Second, the break-up of the Soviet Union generated fears that its nuclear weapons and its vast stockpiles of fissile material might not be secure in the future. Potential nuclear proliferants could acquire technology and material much faster by purchasing them from the newly independent republics of the Community of Independent States (CIS) than through indigenous development.

Iraq also showed the limits of even American intelligence capabilities, which had delivered enough information to raise suspicions about a military application of nuclear technology but had not detected the actual scale of the programme. Only after the UN Security Council's special commission UNSCOM had inspected Iraq's nuclear facilities did it become clear that Iraq had done research in all technologies concerning uranium enrichment

---

[14] This motive also works the other way round and increases the incentives of pariah states to acquire or develop weapons of mass destruction. See Council on Foreign Relations (1995: 4–5).

and had pursued a comprehensive nuclear weapons programme, the advanced state of which surprised the international community.[15] The North Korean crisis and the alleged nuclear aspirations of Iran demonstrate that an NPT signatory under IAEA safeguards could develop nuclear weapons in a parallel programme and that other proliferants might follow a similar path, taking advantage of the fairly weak verification procedures to hide their military ambitions.

The issue of denuclearization in the former Soviet republics forced the US government to expend considerable money and energy to help safeguard the nuclear complex in the CIS.[16] At the meeting of the UN Security Council on 31 January 1992, the United States initiated a regulation in which it was stated that 'the proliferation of all kinds of weapons of mass destruction constitutes a threat to international peace and security'. This resolution contains the key words from the UN Charter that can trigger chapter 7 measures and is designed for future UN Security Council activities targeting the proliferation of WMD.[17] Several US initiatives were directed at establishing tighter export controls, thereby instrumentalizing foreign trade for non-proliferation purposes.[18] In the summer of 1992, President Bush started a so-called Non-Proliferation Initiative aimed at streamlining inter-administrative coordination within the US government.[19]

For the Clinton administration, non-proliferation became a top foreign-policy priority. The President outlined the goals and principles of his government's non-proliferation policy in a speech before the UN General Assembly on 27 September 1993. He expressed strong support for the non-proliferation regime, the IAEA safeguard system, and an indefinite extension of the NPT. Furthermore, he proposed to begin negotiations for a global ban on the production of fissile material for military purposes. In his speech, Clinton sketched out parts of the Presidential Decision Directive

---

[15] Iraq is said to have conducted a 'crash program' to construct a nuclear explosive device as late as Apr. 1991, when operation Desert Storm had already started. See US Department of Defense (1996: 18–20). On the UN special commission UNSCOM, carrying out the destruction of Iraq's capabilities concerning weapons of mass destruction, see Butler and Frick (1994) and Tucker (1996).

[16] Since 1992, the Pentagon annually appropriates $400 million for disarmament assistance on the territory of its former adversary. See Allison *et al.* (1993); Falkenrath (1994); US Congress (1994); US Department of Defense (1995).

[17] See extracts from the resolution S/PV.3046 in *UN PPNN Newsbrief*, 17 (Spring 1992): 15.

[18] For US export control policies designed to prevent nuclear non-proliferation, see Long (1994).

[19] The Central Intelligence Agency established a Non-Proliferation Center to enhance American intelligence capabilities for detecting nuclear proliferation. See Dembinski (1994*a*: 325).

No. 13, which he signed the same day and which sets out guidelines for the non-proliferation policy of his administration.[20] Also in the autumn of 1993, Secretary of Defense Les Aspin presented the Pentagon's Defense Counterproliferation Initiative (DCP) to his NATO colleagues.[21] This was designed to prevent proliferation with a combination of political and military means if it cannot be prevented by export controls and safeguards alone, and to decrease the vulnerability of US armed forces to an attack with WMD. Though this strategy's emphasis on military means drew some criticism from the allies, its principles also had a bearing on NATO's non-proliferation policy.[22]

Today Washington conducts a dual-track non-proliferation strategy. US diplomats work simultaneously on the adaptation of the regime's different components to changing international conditions and on crisis-management procedures to persuade potential defectors to adhere to their commitments. In cases when rogue states were to be pushed towards norm-oriented behaviour, the United States was particularly involved—not only as a stabilizer of the regime, but also as an important actor in the regional conflict.

The case of Ukraine

A challenge for the non-proliferation regime, only foreseeable shortly beforehand, occurred after the collapse of the Soviet Union at the end of 1991. Soviet strategic nuclear weapons were deployed in Russia, Belarus, Kazakhstan, and Ukraine. Apart from the sudden emergence of new NWS entangled in potential conflicts with Russia, a number of risks resulted from this situation. In all four republics, custody of the nuclear weapons was insecure, and nuclear scientists as well as military personnel were insufficiently paid. So illicit export of nuclear technology from the CIS states and a migration of nuclear experts to potential nuclear-weapons states threatened the balance of the non-proliferation regime, along with the risk

---

[20] 'Clinton Warns of Perils Ahead Despite Cold War's End', speech by US President Bill Clinton at the United Nations, 9 Sept. 1993, US Policy Information and Texts No. 99: 3–7. Wolfsthal (1993: 22). For a critique, see Arms Control Association (1993).

[21] See Rühle (1994) and 'USA bekämpfen Verbreitung von Massenvernichtungswaffen. Ausführungen von Verteidigungsminister Aspin' Amerika dienst 50.

[22] See 'Declaration of the Heads of State and Government' participating in the meeting of the North Atlantic Council held at NATO Headquarters, Brussels, on 10–11 Jan. 1994. *NATO Review*, 42/1: 30–3 (32). Two NATO working groups were established to examine the political and military means to react to the threat of nuclear proliferation. See also Joseph (1996); Carter and Omand (1994); Riecke (1997: 211–18).

of nuclear accidents and unauthorized or accidental launch of delivery vehicles.[23]

Only Russia was regarded as the legal successor state to the USSR and as a NPT signatory. The nuclear status of the other three states was not clear at the time of their secession. The issue was tricky not only because of their unclear NPT membership but also because the ratification process of the Strategic Arms Reduction Treaty I (START I), which the United States and the USSR had signed in 1991, was still on hold. Both had agreed to reduce the number of their strategic nuclear delivery systems to 1,600, carrying no more than 6,000 warheads. Moscow and Washington thus faced the task of convincing the three states to cooperate concerning adherence to the NPT as NNWS, to transfer their strategic weapons to Russia for dismantling, and to maintain agreed verification and monitoring procedures. The idea was to win their lasting support for the principled rules of nuclear renunciation. Russia and the USA used the START treaty as a vehicle to accomplish the complete denuclearization of the non-Russian republics, though Ukraine, especially, was for a long time reluctant to conform.[24]

In the Ukrainian Declaration on State Sovereignty of 16 July 1990, it was stated that Ukraine would not accept, produce, or build nuclear weapons. The parliament declared in October 1991 that Ukraine would sign the NPT as a NNWS. But the founding documents of the CIS, in which the status of the strategic nuclear forces was to be clarified, produced a confusing situation.[25] Although these documents created a supranational CIS authority to control nuclear weapons, they also contained language by which Ukraine agreed to obligations only a NWS could undertake. They therefore did not settle the status of the nuclear weapons on Ukrainian soil.

The United States was quick to negotiate an additional agreement with

---

[23] See Campbell *et al.* (1991); Falkenrath (1994: 23–35); US Congress (1994: 13–33).

[24] At the time of the dissolution of the USSR, 218 delivery vehicles equipped with 1,734 warheads were deployed in Ukraine. These were 130 missiles of the SS-19 type, 46 SS-24s, and 42 bombers. The Soviet tactical weapons that Ukraine held were transferred to Russia by May 1992. See *The Arms Control Association Fact Sheet* (Nov. 1994), based on testimony by Assistant Secretary of Defense Ashton B. Carter before the Senate Foreign Relations Committee on 4 Oct. 1994. The transfer of tactical weapons began before the disruption of the USSR. Ukraine tried to delay this process in Mar. 1992 but met firm opposition from Western leaders. See Falkenrath (1994: 3).

[25] The 'Agreement on the Creation of the CIS', signed 8 Dec. 1991 by the presidents of the four republics, stated that the former Soviet nuclear weapons would serve the collective security of all CIS countries. The 'Agreement on Joint Measures in Relation to Nuclear Weapons', signed 21 Dec. 1991, by the same states, contained 'no first use' pledges and language, conforming to Art. 1 NPT; and the 'Agreement Between Member States of the CIS on Strategic Forces', signed in Minsk on 30 Dec. 1991, had a time frame regarding the transfer of nuclear weapons to Russian territory. Kiev agreed to transfer these systems by 1994. See US Congress (1994: 77–8); Zaborsky (1994: 3–5); Falkenrath (1994: 5).

the four former Soviet republics. The Lisbon Protocol, signed 23 May 1992, resolved that the four states were successor states of the USSR regarding the START agreement and were bound by the treaty's constraints and verification procedures. Furthermore, it was emphasized that the three non-Russian states should adhere to the NPT in the 'shortest possible time'.[26] The ambiguity of this protocol, making the former Soviet republics equal partners in START I while at the same time obliging them to become NNWS, was the result of a compromise between the concern not to legitimize their possession of nuclear weapons and the need to acknowledge their demand for independence and equal sovereign rights with Russia. President Kravchuk confirmed in a subsequent letter Ukraine's obligation to become a NNWS and to fulfil START and the Lisbon Protocol. He claimed, however, that it had the right to exercise 'control over the non-use of nuclear weapons deployed on its territory'.[27] Kravchuk assumed ownership of nuclear weapon components and delivery systems and wanted to reserve a veto power for Ukraine.

Kravchuk's commitment to renounce a military nuclear option was subsequently the object of heated criticism on the domestic stage. Some policymakers had reconsidered their earlier support for the non-proliferation regime. Strong pro-nuclear sentiments, not only among conservative politicians in the Rada, were expressed in several hearings and decisions of the parliament, in one of which (on military doctrine) Ukrainian ownership of the nuclear weapons on its territory was reasserted.[28] The nuclear weapons were perceived as a useful asset, with a possible military value in a conflict with Russia, whose future political course was unpredictable. They also had a potential to promote Ukraine's standing in the international community or to serve as a bargaining chip for soliciting military and economic assistance.[29] Furthermore, Kiev realized that the fissile material within the warheads was a valuable commercial good.[30]

On 13 November 1993, the Rada finally ratified START I and the Lisbon Protocol, but added thirteen reservations. It delayed the NPT's accession until the START agreement was implemented and stated that only a portion

---

[26] See 'Protocol to the Treaty Between the USA and the USSR on the Reduction and Limitation of Strategic Offensive Arms', Lisbon, 23 May 1992. *Arms Control Today*, 22/5: 34–5.

[27] Ibid. 35.

[28] See Zaborsky (1994: 14); Falkenrath (1994: 6).

[29] For the debate on the nuclear weapons option, see Blank (1994: 10–17).

[30] In Feb. 1993, the US signed a treaty with Russia to buy, over the next two decades, 500 tons of blended-down, highly enriched uranium (HEU) for about $12 billion. This deal could have caused the Rada to claim 'ownership' of former Soviet nuclear weapons. See Falkenrath (1994: 41–3).

of the nuclear weapons on Ukrainian soil would be subject to elimination, implying that Ukraine had only to dismantle the share of the nuclear weapons it actually owned, as the Soviet Union had agreed to do concerning the strategic weapons in START I.[31] Furthermore, the implementation of the dismantling was made contingent on three conditions.[32]

First, the Rada demanded that the renunciation of nuclear weapons be preceded by security guarantees. The weak positive security guarantees the nuclear powers had given to all NNWS were not regarded as sufficient. Kiev preferred a legally binding document. Second, Ukraine asked for financial aid to ease the burden of the disarmament measures. Ukraine wanted to persuade the US to increase the amount of money from the Nunn-Lugar assistance programme already earmarked for helping it with the costs of disarmament. While the United States estimated these costs at $175 million annually, the Ukrainian authorities thought they were much higher, in the range of $2 to $2.8 billion.[33] Third, Ukraine should receive fair compensation for the valuable fissile material and technical components it was to deliver. In the Massandra Agreement of September 1993, Moscow had already agreed to convert the HEU from the Ukrainian warheads into reactor-grade uranium and return it to Ukraine after the latter had put its nuclear facilities under IAEA safeguards. Kiev's demands also included amends for the tactical nuclear weapons removed to Russia in May 1992. As Ukraine was dissatisfied with the solutions reached, the two following months were filled with tense negotiations between Ukraine, Russia, and the US.

In a Trilateral Agreement, signed in January 1994, Russia and the United States agreed both to remove Kiev's strategic incentives for keeping the nuclear weapons and to compensate it for the material losses resulting from the transfer.[34] Ukraine committed itself to eliminating all nuclear warheads on its territory in the seven-year period provided by START, 200 of which had to be transferred to Russia within ten months. Russia was made responsible for the compensation of nuclear warheads HEU in the form of 100 tons of nuclear fuel rods in the same period, thus giving up the linkage with the IAEA safeguards Moscow had made in the Massandra Agreement. To ease this, the US agreed to pay $60 million for the nuclear fuel delivered by Russia under the terms of the HEU deal.[35] In a secret bilateral agreement

[31] Falkenrath (1994: 11).
[32] See Zaborsky (1994: 27).
[33] Ibid. 24.
[34] Trilateral Statement by the Presidents of the United States, Russia and Ukraine, 14 Jan. 1994, in *Arms Control Today*, 24/1: 21.
[35] See Zaborsky (1994: 27).

between Russia and Ukraine, the latter is thought to have promised the dismantling of all warheads in a three-year period. As compensation for the tactical nuclear weapons already removed, Moscow wrote off a share of Kiev's debt for oil and natural gas that it had delivered in recent years.[36]

The presidents of Russia and the US reaffirmed their commitments, made in the context of the CSCE, concerning Ukraine's sovereignty and independence as well as the inviolability of its existing borders. They further stated that they would refrain from economic pressure and reiterated their promise not to use nuclear weapons against Ukraine and to assist it if it were attacked or threatened with nuclear weapons. Washington, finally, provided $175 million in disarmament assistance and promised to increase these funds later. During the visit of President Kravchuk to Washington in March 1994, President Clinton announced that the United States would double its denuclearization assistance.

On 3 February 1994, the Rada approved the ratification of START I and the Lisbon Protocol but delayed the NPT accession until November of the same year (and, with this, the entry-into-force of START). In September, Ukraine signed the safeguards agreement with the IAEA. With regard to security guarantees, Ukraine has not gained as much as it did from the Trilateral Agreement. More rewarding were the economic benefits, though even these were not a triumph for Ukraine. Since the country is highly dependent on Russian energy and Western economic aid and good trade relations,[37] any delay in the elimination of nuclear weapons would have resulted in high economic costs, while Ukrainian nuclear capabilities would probably have not been of much use. What Kiev won was fair compensation for the material value it handed over to Russia and some international consideration of its security concerns.

In its first non-proliferation campaign after the end of the cold war, Washington acted without invoking institutional procedures simply because there were none. Since the former Soviet republics had not been signatories to the NPT, no sanctions by the UN Security Council were available. Washington did the job with the smallest possible number of partners. It rallied the support it needed—of the EU, which delayed economic assistance, and of Great Britain, which joined in giving the security guarantees that Kiev demanded. Washington assumed the largest share of the costs. Without adhering to institutional procedures, its campaign was facilitated by the fact that it was conducted by all sides in the spirit of

---

[36] Falkenrath (1994: 11).
[37] The EU delayed its assistance programme until Ukraine has signed the NPT.

and with reference to the principled rules of the non-proliferation regime. This heightened the pressure on Ukraine (which, at the moment of its foundation, had expressed its support of the NPT) and made it easier for the US to win the assistance of other relevant actors.

The North Korean Crisis

The crisis over the alleged nuclear weapons programme of the Democratic Peoples Republic of North Korea (DPRK) demonstrated the weaknesses of the institutions concerned even as it provided an opportunity for unilateral or small-group action to manage the conflict. In the late 1970s, the DPRK had rapidly increased the scope of its nuclear programme, which was originally based on technological cooperation agreements with the Soviet Union and China dating from the 1950s and was later continued autonomously. One expert cites Russian intelligence information that one motive for these efforts was to develop a military nuclear programme.[38] Pyongyang signed the NPT in 1985, after Moscow made it a precondition for the further supply of nuclear-power plants.

The obligatory nuclear safeguards agreement with the IAEA was then delayed until early 1992. The agreement was preceded by an intense campaign by the United States, the Republic of (South) Korea (ROK), and Japan, in which Washington reaffirmed its strong ties with Seoul but also extended a couple of incentives to North Korea, including the withdrawal of US tactical nuclear weapons from the South and the cancellation of US-ROK manœuvres (which had been under discussion in Washington for quite a while). Direct talks between the US and North Korea were initiated, and Japan delayed its diplomatic recognition of the DPRK until the nuclear issue was resolved.[39] The fact that Washington and its partners brought Pyongyang to accept the obligatory IAEA inspections did not defuse all suspicions against the country. It was still possible that the North was secretly conducting a nuclear-weapons programme even while trying to gain international recognition. Only inspections could yield the necessary information about the full scope of the country's nuclear activities.

The crisis climaxed after IAEA routine inspections began in May 1992. That autumn, the agency detected a discrepancy in the North's nuclear

---

[38] Among other factors, the programme was motivated by South Korean conventional superiority, its military nuclear ambitions, and the US nuclear umbrella extended over the South as well as the annual US–South Korean 'Team Spirit' manœuvres. Furthermore, the DPRK lost the Soviet Union as military ally in 1990. See Mazar (1995: 18–19); Mansourov (1995: 26, 55–6).

[39] See Mazar (1995: 55–77).

inventory. The amount of plutonium North Korean engineers extracted from a so-called radiochemical laboratory at the Yongbyon facility was probably larger than Pyongyang had reported. In February 1993, Hans Blix, the agency's general director, demanded special inspections[40] beyond the routine safeguards at two additional sites the North Koreans had declared to be military warehouses, and not part of their nuclear facilities. These buildings were thought to be possible storage sites for irradiated nuclear waste. The suspicion that the radionuclear laboratory might be a reprocessing plant and that two undeclared sites existed were provided by US intelligence. Its observation of the Yongbyon facilities over a long period via satellite is an example of a powerful state supplementing the functions of an institution with its own information capabilities.[41] North Korea objected to the special inspections, in breach of the non-proliferation regime's procedural rules.

As the conflict escalated, the instruments available to the IAEA and the UN Security Council were tested and failed to solve the problem. The agency cannot punish a defecting member state effectively itself; it can only withhold its technical assistance. According to the IAEA statute, having received notice of non-compliance, the director general has to inform the IAEA Board of Governors as well as the UN General Assembly and the UN Security Council, the latter being the 'organ bearing main responsibility for the maintenance of international peace and security'.[42] The IAEA Board and the Security Council demanded in February and March 1993 that Pyongyang provide access to the two waste sites for the agency's inspectors. On 12 March 1993, the DPRK announced its withdrawal from the NPT after a notification period of ninety days.[43] This step accentuated the crisis and increased pressure for a timely solution. The Board of Governors stated on 1 April that North Korea no longer abided by the Safeguards Agreement and that the IAEA could not guarantee that no fissile material was being extracted clandestinely.[44] On 11 May the UN Security Council repeated its demand for inspections and asked the DPRK to reconsider its NPT

---

[40] The IAEA's authority to conduct special inspections in case the routinely collected information was insufficient to fulfil its verification tasks is based on arts. 73 and 77 of the model safeguard agreement between the IAEA and the NPT member states, see 'The Structure and Content of Agreements between the Agency and States Required in Connection with the NPT' (INFCIRC 153); Howlett and Simpson (1995: E15–E26, at E22–E23).

[41] See Dembinski (1994*b*); Berry (1995: 6); Mazarr (1995: 94–9).

[42] Statute of the International Atomic Energy Agency, Art. III.B.4 and XII.C. Howlett and Simpson (1995: D1–D9 (D1, D6)).

[43] See Berry (1995: 8 ff.).

[44] See Dembinski (1994*b*: 27).

withdrawal. The resolution was adopted 13 votes to 0, China and Pakistan abstaining. The resolution did not threaten sanctions.[45] In late May the US and North Korea agreed to hold negotiations on the issue.[46]

The US tried to induce the DPRK to return to the regime, admit IAEA inspections, and resume the dialogue between the two Koreas. Washington wanted to reinstal the principled rule that nuclear technology may only be used by a NPT participant under IAEA safeguards. In a statement following the negotiations in June, both countries agreed to a set of broader principles and North Korea suspended its NPT withdrawal. After the talks in July, a possible solution—replacement of the graphite-moderated reactors at Yongbyon with less proliferation-prone light water reactors (LWR)—was developed. North Korea agreed to resume consultations with South Korea and the IAEA. Nevertheless, the US still insisted that the IAEA inspect the two sites in question. On the occasion of a visit to South Korea in July, President Clinton stated that the North's defection was unacceptable and indicated that any development and use of nuclear weapons would be punished militarily.[47]

The impasse between the DPRK and the IAEA continued. The haggling about inspections went on. They were first allowed on a limited scale by Pyongyang, then impeded and linked to success in the ongoing talks with the United States. Their progress was accompanied by increasingly 'all-or-nothing' demands by the IAEA for wider access to the DPRK's nuclear facilities, affirming North Korea's principled obligation to accept safeguards for its nuclear energy programme.

In autumn 1993, however, Washington departed from its position that the safeguards agreement had to be fulfilled in order to verify Pyongyang's past behaviour. To avoid the dilemma—that a fruitless insistence on revealing the amount of plutonium possibly removed in the past from its reactors might cause North Korea to refuse any verification of its future nuclear activities—Washington assumed a more pragmatic position and conceded in late December that the North would allow routine inspections but that the special inspection of the two facilities in question should wait until progress in the US–DPRK high-level talks had been achieved. The exact schedule of the inspections was to be agreed between the North and the

---

[45] UN Security Council Resolution 825 (1993) of 11 May 1993, in *Vereinte Nationen*, 41: 217–18.

[46] The negotiations were held in New York on 2–11 June and in Geneva on 14–19 July 1993. They were conducted by Kang Sok Chu, First Deputy Minister of Foreign Affairs and Robert Gallucci, Assistant Secretary of State for Politico-Military Affairs. See Berry (1995: 11).

[47] See Berry (1995: 11–15).

IAEA. In return the US would suspend the 1994 'Team Spirit' manœuvre. Pyongyang's withdrawal from the NPT was not reversed.[48]

The agency was clearly not satisfied with this agreement and insisted on a larger scope of inspections. In February 1994, however, the IAEA relented and agreed to the package negotiated between the USA and North Korea.[49] The Board of Governors again transferred the issue to the Security Council, which agreed to a watered-down statement by the Council's President, demanding that Pyongyang fulfil its safeguard obligations. Chinese reservations prevented the adoption of a Council resolution.[50]

A new urgency arose when in May 1994 the DPRK shut down its small 5 MW reactor in Yongbyon and began to remove 8,000 fuel rods. This would eliminate the IAEA's ability to verify that no plutonium was extracted during an earlier shutdown in 1989. The principled rule on safeguards would be jeopardized. The US subsequently threatened to submit a resolution to the UN Security Council asking for economic sanctions (passage of which was not too probable because of Chinese objections). After further criticism from the IAEA Board, North Korea announced its withdrawal from the agency as well. During this stalemate, former US President Jimmy Carter, with the approval of President Clinton, visited North Korea to find a way out of the crisis. Carter extracted a commitment from the North Korean president, Kim Il Sung, to hold a summit meeting with his Southern counterpart, to resume talks with the US, and to freeze his country's nuclear programme during the talks. Carter is said to have coerced Washington to drop its insistence on inspections about past production.[51]

Thereafter, the US and the DPRK negotiated in Pyongyang and Berlin a Framework Agreement, signed in October 1994. It stipulated that the DPRK's graphite-moderated reactors be replaced with two LWRs, a deal worth approximately $4 billion. Washington had finally dropped its demand that Pyongyang allow inspections before the bilateral negotiations could begin. The reactor replacement was to take place in three phases within a ten-year schedule. In the first phase, North Korea had to suspend its nuclear programme while the US and its partners constructed the first LWR. In the second phase, to begin in five years, IAEA inspectors would be allowed to inspect the waste sites, to which the North had heretofore prohibited access. The DPRK would then remove the 8,000 fuel rods from the cooling ponds where they were stored and were being monitored. In this phase, the first LWR would start to produce electricity and the construction

---

48 See Mazarr (1995: 144).   49 Sigal (1998: 90–122).
50 See Berry (1995: 123–4).   51 See Mazarr (1995: 157–63); Sigal (1998: 129–68).

of the second LWR would begin. In the third phase, when the second LWR went on-line, the graphite-moderated reactors would be dismantled. Other commitments in the agreement were that the USA would compensate the DPRK for lost energy in the form of heavy oil supplies and would recognize North Korea diplomatically.[52] The costs of the agreement were borne by the US, South Korea, and Japan, who formed a special organization to carry out the reactor deal, the Korean Peninsula Energy Development Organization (KEDO).[53] The European Union decided in 1996 to participate as an equal partner in this agreement with an annual contribution of ECU 15 million.[54] Furthermore, the USA gave North Korea negative security assurances, i.e. a commitment not to threaten it with nuclear weapons or to use them against the North. The US and the DPRK pledged to normalize their relations and stated that the dialogue between the two Koreas that had ceased during the crisis was resumed.

In reaching the Framework Agreement, the US acted on the basis of the principled non-proliferation rules, with one exception: the principled rule on safeguards was applied rather loosely and outside the relevant procedural rules. The US–North Korean agreement generated both relief and criticism. Some experts contended that the inspection rights of the IAEA were weakened. While monitoring the reactor exchange, the agency was not allowed for another five years to inspect the radioactive waste extracted from the so-called radionuclear laboratory, which would have given a hint of how many extractions had been made and how much plutonium had been separated. Until the reactors were replaced, i.e. for a five-year period, the regulatory IAEA safeguards were suspended and substituted by the agency's monitoring of the reactor exchange deal.[55] This change of rules had not been decided by the IAEA's Board of Governors, but had been imposed by an agreement among a few member states.

Suspicions against Iran

A case of less successful diplomacy was the US campaign to isolate Iran and to prevent Russia from supplying nuclear technology to that country.

[52] See *PPNN Newsbrief*, 28 (4th quarter 1994): 1–4, 27–8.

[53] See 'U.S., North Korea Resolve Dispute Over Supplier of Nuclear Reactors', *Arms Control Today* (July/Aug. 1995), 23.

[54] Interview with an official from the European Commission, Brussels, 17 Feb. 1997. See also *PPNN Newsbrief*, 37 (1st quarter 1997): 8, naming an amount of $19 million.

[55] For a critical assessment of the Framework Agreement, see Bailey (1995: 141–3); Oh and Grubel (1995: 105–11). A more positive view is taken by the Council on Foreign Relations and Seoul Forum for International Affairs (1995: 8–13).

Washington suspected that Iran was developing WMD and delivery systems. Beginning in the early 1980s, the US undertook various diplomatic efforts to prevent foreign assistance for Iran's nuclear energy programme, which Washington suspected had a hidden military purpose.

Iran has been since 1970 a signatory of the NPT and in 1974 signed a safeguard agreement with the IAEA. Its multidimensional civilian nuclear programme is still in its early stages.[56] Iran possesses a few small research reactors and has two power plants under construction, which were supplied originally by a German contractor, Siemens KWU. Construction was halted after the Islamic revolution in 1979, and parts of the sites were destroyed in the war with Iraq. By autumn 1991, after Germany had redefined its export principles and in accordance with American requests, Siemens KWU decided not to complete the project.[57] Teheran then tried to complete the construction and further develop its nuclear programme without German assistance. American diplomatic efforts aimed mainly at impeding any nuclear trade with Iran. A country should not acquire sensitive technologies under safeguards and later use them for clandestine military purposes, a proliferation path that seemed possible in Iran.

Iran entertained an ambiguous attitude towards the military nuclear option. Teheran persistently states that it has no intention of acquiring nuclear weapons and pursues a policy of transparency concerning its nuclear programme. At the end of 1991, the president of Iran's Atomic Energy Organization invited a team of four staff members of the IAEA, headed by the deputy director general, to inspect the Iranian nuclear programme. The team visited several facilities and was granted access to all the sites it had selected. In a press statement it stated that 'the activities reviewed by the team at the above-mentioned facilities and sites were found to be consistent with the peaceful application of nuclear energy'.[58] But at the February 1992 meeting of the agency's Board of Governors, the US rebuffed the report of the IAEA Secretariat on this visit as 'naïve'.[59] Iran, to counteract the growing reluctance of the West to trade with Iran, has persistently stated that it will accept any kind of international supervision of its nuclear imports and is willing to have IAEA inspectors permanently stationed in Iran at that country's expense.[60]

Iran's intentions, however, are ambiguous. In contradiction of its non-proliferation commitments, President Rafsandjani advocated an Iranian nuclear bomb in 1988. In 1991, Iran's Vice President, Ayatollah Mohajerani,

---

[56] See Cohen (1995).
[58] See *PPNN Newsbrief*, 17 (Spring 1992): 12–13.
[60] See *PPNN Newsbrief*, 22 (2nd quarter 1993): 7.

[57] See Koch and Wolf (1997: 127).
[59] See Preisinger (1993: 15).

stated that if Israel possessed nuclear weapons, the Muslim states should have them, too.[61] In early 1993, several Western and even Russian intelligence sources were cited in the German press reporting that for a decade Iran has pursued the development of nuclear weapons and has experimented with enrichment and reprocessing technologies, which are prerequisites for a military nuclear programme.[62] Iranian acquisition of nuclear warheads from Kazakhstan or Tadjikistan was reported, though no proof was found.[63] In early 1992, the US extended its embargo against Iraq to Iran and passed the Iran-Iraq Arms Non-Proliferation Act, in which all countries are requested not to transfer any nuclear goods or technology to the two countries.[64] Secretary of State Warren Christopher charged in May 1995 that since the mid-1980s, 'Iran has had an organized structure dedicated to acquiring and developing nuclear weapons.'[65]

US diplomacy, however, could not stop Russian-Iranian nuclear co-operation, which resulted in an agreement worth $1 billion in early 1995. Russia agreed to complete the construction of one of the unfinished light water reactors at Bushehr and to supply other facilities, including another 1,000 MW LWR, two 440 ME units, and a gas centrifuge. This enrichment equipment would enable Iran to produce weapons-grade, highly enriched uranium (HEU). In spring 1995, US officials pressed Russia to stop this deal. It did not, however, have much leverage against a great power's craving for foreign currency. Any form of blackmailing—for example, cutting off assistance, such as the annual $400 million denuclearization aid or the $375 million economic aid promised for 1995—would have hurt American interests as well.[66] Warren Christopher and his Russian counterpart, Andrei Kozyrev, established a Joint Working Group to discuss proliferation risks. Through this institution the US hoped to convince Russia of the dangerous implications of its deal with Iran.[67] In April, US Secretary of Defense William J. Perry presented American intelligence information in Moscow, which backed the US accusations. Russian intelligence reports had at this time dropped their earlier assessment that Iran was a potential proliferant. The US administration used both 'blackmailing' and 'back-scratching'

[61] See Cohen (1995: 15); *PPNN Newsbrief*, 16 (Winter 1991/2): 10.

[62] See *PPNN Newsbrief*, 21 (1st quarter 1993): 14.

[63] Ibid.; Dembinski (1994a: 335).

[64] See *PPNN Newsbrief*, 21 (1st quarter 1993): 3.

[65] Office of the Spokesman, Press Briefing by Secretary of State Warren Christopher on the President's Executive Order on Iran, US Department of State, 1 May 1995, quoted in Albright (1995: 49).

[66] See 'Christopher Says Russia May Pay High Price for Chechen War', *New York Times* (*NYT*) (23 Mar. 1995).

[67] See 'U.S.–Russian Intersection: The Romance is Gone', *NYT* (27 Mar. 1995).

linkages to convince Russia about the seriousness of the Iranian threat. It offered to cooperate with Moscow on reactor construction and waste management to the tune of $100 million and to compensate the losses incurred by the Russian Atomic Energy Ministry by cancelling the Iranian deal. Also, possible Russian participation in KEDO, the organization dealing with the North Korean reactor replacement, was hinted at.[68] A few days later, Washington threatened not to renew the existing nuclear cooperation agreement and to withhold new joint projects.[69] The result was only a partial success. At a US–Russian summit in Moscow on 10 May, the Russian government finally announced that it would not supply the gas centrifuge but would continue with the rest of the deal. The Russians argued that the reactors were of the same type as those to be constructed in North Korea, in effect accusing Washington of hypocrisy.[70]

China also provides reactor technology to Iran. According to a ten-year-old cooperation agreement, it supplies Iran with a small research reactor and equipment for experiments with electromagnetic uranium enrichment technology. Another agreement between Beijing and Teheran to supply two 330 MW pressurized water reactors dates from the summer of 1992, but China probably needs Western technology to complete this deal. In April 1995, at the beginning of the NPT Review and Extension Conference, Secretary of State Christopher tried without success to persuade the Chinese Foreign Minister Qian Qichen that China should stop the project.[71] The Chinese-Iranian deal seems to have collapsed in the summer of 1995 because of differences over the conditions of the trade, the site of the construction, and Iran's liability.[72]

Again, the IAEA—at least according to the American perception—could not sufficiently fulfill its functions of information-gathering and verification, so Washington relied on its own sources and acted unilaterally. American apprehensions about Iran are based on intelligence material concerning Iran's procurement patterns that are not available to the IAEA. Washington's accusations, however, were not supported by the findings of IAEA inspections. Because of this missing legitimization, the US had difficulty convincing other countries to withhold nuclear technology and expertise from Iran. Germany, France, and others experienced severe

[68] See 'U.S. gives Russia Secret Data on Iran to Fight Atom Deal', *NYT* (3 Apr. 1995).

[69] See 'U.S. Warns Russia Again on Iran Deal', *NYT* (9 Apr. 1995).

[70] Albright (1995: 49). Preceding the summit, Western and Israeli sources charged that Iran was in reach of nuclear weapons, claims that were not backed by the IAEA findings. See *PPNN Newsbrief*, 29 (1st quarter 1995): 8–7; 30 (2nd quarter 1995): 14–16.

[71] See *PPNN Newsbrief*, 19 (Autumn 1992): 4; 23 (3rd quarter 1993): 9; Cohen (1995).

[72] See *PPNN Newsbrief*, 32 (4th quarter 1995): 7.

pressure to withdraw from the construction of power reactors in Bushehr, but Russia and China took over the task. Their deals are none the less in compliance with the rules of the NPT.

The US campaign has devalued the IAEA procedures designed to uncover illicit nuclear activities. It violated the principled rule that nuclear trade should not be hindered as long as the recipient state cannot be proven to have pursued military applications of nuclear technology. Washington chose not only to put this rule aside unilaterally, it also tried to impose its behaviour on others. The 1996 Congressional decisions on sanctions against companies trading with Cuba, Iran, and Libya, which contain a strong extraterritorial element, alienated partners and allies and led to an open confrontation with the US.[73] These US laws could not prevent a $2 billion investment in Iran by the French company Total and the Russian Gazprom.[74] It is thus not surprising that a new approach seems to be gaining support in Washington. While Iran's conventional and naval build-ups receive increasing attention, security experts in the US capital, including former National Security Advisors Brzezinski and Scowcroft, suggest a more moderate strategy of economic incentives toward Iran as well as acceptance of the deal with Russia.[75] In June 1998 Washington dropped its tough position towards Iran and showed a willingness for constructive dialogue over several issues.[76]

4. Conclusions

The three cases discussed have illustrated the importance of unilateral or small-group activities for institutional stability and change. Moreover, there was a certain inevitability about the US engagement. In all cases, the US was an important actor without which a political solution was inconceivable. Furthermore, the US was the most prominent supporter of the non-proliferation regime since the 1960s, a depository state of the NPT, and a supplier of intelligence information to the IAEA. The impact of the US campaigns can be summarized as follows.

American policy in the CIS had an outright positive effect on the regime

---

[73] See Stern (1997).

[74] See Fitchett (1997).

[75] See Brzezinski *et al.* (1997) and *PPNN Newsbrief*, 38 (4th quarter 1997): 16.

[76] See 'USA wollen Beziehungen zu Iran normalisieren', *Tagesspiegel* (19 June 1998); 'Iranischer Hardliner deutet Dialog mit den USA an', *Tagesspiegel* (27 June 1998).

as a whole. After some suspicions about Kiev's ability and willingness to assure the ratification and implementation of the trilateral agreement, Ukraine fulfilled its commitments. It and the other CIS republics acceded to the NPT as non-nuclear weapon states, thus increasing the commonality of principles of the treaty and strengthening its universality. The proliferation calculus of neighbouring states was not altered by new nuclear 'haves' in an unstable region. The principled rules about nuclear non-proliferation— though in reality a violation of the non-proliferation rules by Ukraine was not possible—did indeed constrain this country even before it signed the NPT. Its refusal to adhere would have exposed it to strong international pressure and isolation. The procedural rules were strictly enforced and their commonality enlarged. That their application was made possible in the Ukraine has removed a possible threat to the nuclear bargain. The effectiveness of the non-proliferation regime was increased: The nuclear trade-off is still intact and the IAEA has the ability to verify the nuclear activities of the new members.

With the DPRK Framework Agreement among a few member states of the non-proliferation regime, its procedural rules were violated. The safeguard system is obligatory for all NPT signatories. The principled rules did, however, provide a basis for US activities that were conducted in the spirit of the NPT commitments. With regard to the procedural rules, however, Washington walked a tightrope, since the acceptance of international inspections is an integral part of the NPT trade-off. The North Korean deal made it impossible for the IAEA to fulfil its verification mission in a dangerous case. If Pyongyang really has separated plutonium and hidden it with the intention of building a nuclear explosive device, the agency will not be able to detect the amount of weapons-grade fissile material diverted until the next century. The costly Framework Agreement, however, was probably more beneficial than damaging for the regime. Though the alleged defector was rewarded with technological assistance, a breach of the principled rules of nuclear renunciation was avoided. This would have increased the incentives of some of its neighbours to rethink their position concerning nuclear weapons. The US chose to break the procedural rules on safeguards, and to put in question the principled rule about allowing civilian use of nuclear energy only under safeguards, rather than leave North Korea entirely unconstrained.

The impact of the campaign on the regime's effectiveness is as yet ambiguous: though the commonality of the principled rule not to acquire nuclear weapons has been kept from weakening, the IAEA's effectiveness has suffered in two ways. First, the past conduct of the DPRK cannot be monitored, so the possibility of weapons-grade fissile material hidden in Pyongyang's closet is still there. For a couple of years, the IAEA has no way to alleviate these suspicions. The US campaign did not complement the institution's functions but undermined them. Second, by illustrating the IAEA's weaknesses, the North Korean policy has shown that even NPT signatories can acquire nuclear weapons as long as they are independent of foreign assistance and skilfully hide their activities even from satellite surveillance. The same holds true for Iran, if that country has actually pursued a nuclear weapons programme and if its defection is detected too late. Altogether, however, the effect of the North Korean solution on proliferation incentives has been positive.

US policy concerning Iran can be perceived as in violation of both the principled and procedural rules. As long as Teheran sticks to its commitments, there is no multilaterally accepted basis for Washington's unilateral action. The United States broke the principled rule that civilian use of nuclear energy is permitted and should be furthered as long as safeguards are in place. In suspending this rule, its authority has been weakened. This is no judgement about the validity of US suspicions, which are based on national intelligence information. Through the coercive character of the US campaign, not only the alleged defector but also any company doing business with it has been hurt. This raises doubts about the benefits of US efforts to stabilize the non-proliferation regime. Its effectiveness was decreased; the campaign showed that Washington still tries to make use of international institutions for its own purposes. This bias can have a sobering effect on those looking for cooperative ways to solve problems. The fact that Washington denies Teheran the same light water reactor technology it has provided to Pyongyang clearly fosters this ambivalence. US challenges to the investigative abilities of the IAEA have put the effectiveness of the agency in doubt. Had Washington discarded its normative framework less bluntly and responded to the perceived flaws of the institution with a more diplomatic approach, this damage could have been avoided.

The overall effects of US non-proliferation campaigns thus can be summarized in three sets of causalities. First, US campaigns decreased the incentives for proliferation. By removing suspect states from the list of possible nuclear 'haves' they have prevented changes in other threshold countries' calculus concerning the bomb.

Second, American efforts against proliferants have increased the demand for specific institutional operations. In particular, the commonality of the principled rule not to acquire nuclear weapons has been strengthened. The US campaigns have called attention to the fact that nuclear proliferation, rare as it may be, is a serious international risk, not only for the states of the region in which the proliferator is situated but for all members of the international community. The situation in North Korea has shown that military options for coping with proliferants are not very viable. Although a powerful state can cover the costs of bilateral crisis management, the instruments best suited to handle this risk are the IAEA's verification procedures, restrictive export controls, and effective action by the UN Security Council. The success of the US initiative to direct the attention of the Security Council towards the non-proliferation issue resulted in increased demand for multilateral institutional means to avoid reliance on US policies and priorities. Washington's campaign against Iran, which has thrown a shadow on US leadership in the non-proliferation regime, could have a contrary although minor effect.

Third, concerning procedural rules, positive and negative effects have been visible. The sophistication of Iraq's hidden nuclear weapons programme showed that Washington could not rely exclusively on its own sources. The Korean case emphasized the safeguards' shortcomings. Special inspections could not be enforced against the DPRK's will by either the IAEA or US pressure but gained new importance in the ongoing IAEA reform process. The '93+2' programme, which will both streamline the agency's procedures and equip it with new instruments, states that comprehensive surveillance procedures on a member state's nuclear programme are its prime objective, since past inspections of the possible diversion of fissile material from the nuclear fuel cycle only had a limited range. The programme entails a right of the agency to conduct more intrusive inspections on short notice and to use more sophisticated technologies of environmental monitoring.[77] US intelligence information has shown that the IAEA's abilities were too restricted to provide credible verification. Its functions can hardly be replaced by national efforts if a deterioration of the IAEA's effectiveness is to be avoided. The reform programme undertakes to handle the risk of unauthorized diversion through a greater degree of specificity in the procedural rules. But there are limits to institutional adaptation.

Another issue in this programme is giving the IAEA a capacity to use intelligence information provided by member states. The IAEA has established a small office in the UN General Secretariat to evaluate information received from the US and other countries. This body, however, has no strong

---

[77] For the IAEA Board of Governors' '93+2', see Diamond (1997). For the IAEA's enhanced capabilities of evaluating information on nuclear programmes, see Fischer (1996: 71); Killinger (1995); US Congress (1995).

position within the agency and is 'hidden' in the budget. The use of third-party information has been criticized by some developing countries, since it opens up the possibility that some developed countries, especially the US, may make use of the agency for national purposes.[78] On balance, however, an impartial assessment of these intelligence data by the IAEA and the dispersion of these findings to other member states would enhance the agency's effectiveness in fulfilling its informational function.

It could be an indication of a strong demand for a neutral and unrestrained IAEA that one of the documents from the 1995 NPT Review Conference clearly stated that the agency 'is the competent authority responsible for verifying and ensuring . . . compliance with its safeguards agreements. . . . Nothing should be done to undermine the agency in this regard.'[79] The US crisis management in North Korea has set new standards for specificity. There is, however, still a concern about use of the agency for national purposes. US intelligence information might not in any case be welcome.

The stabilizing role of the US and its partners has been an integral part of the non-proliferation regime. The success of stabilization policies and the positive impact they have on the non-proliferation regime are, however, constrained by cooperation problems which this regime has been established to solve.

[78] See Dembinski (1994a: 16). For the concept of third-party intelligence evaluated by the agency, see Fainberg (1993).

[79] 'Principles and Objectives for Nuclear Non-Proliferation and Disarmament', para. 9, NPT/CONF/L5, New York, 9 May 1995.

10

THE MYTH OF THE ASEAN WAY? EXPLAINING THE EVOLUTION OF THE ASEAN REGIONAL FORUM

Alastair Iain Johnston

1. Introduction

At first glance, one wonders why the ASEAN Regional Forum even exists at all. The ARF, set up in 1993 and the only multilateral security institution in the Asia-Pacific region at present, is so underinstitutionalized the members don't even call themselves members. The correct term is 'participants'. 'Membership' sounds too permanent. The ARF's first meeting lasted three hours. It now meets once a year for about a day. There is no secretariat. It doesn't call the groups that do intersessional work 'working groups'. This, too, sounds too permanent. Rather they are called 'intersessional support groups' (ISG) and 'intersessional meetings' (ISM). This is because 'meetings' do not sound very institutionalized.

Why would such an amorphous institution be set up in the first place? For one thing, among the now twenty-one states in the ARF there are vast differentials in material power, and their security interests are varied and often conflictual. There is not much agreement on what the principal regional security problems are, though many argue that East Asia is in one of its most peaceful periods in many decades. For another, many ARF participants are in the midst of rapid economic development. They are collectively reaping the benefits of individual trade and investment

Many thanks to the following people for their comments and criticisms of this paper: Celeste Wallander, Helga Haftendorn, Robert Keohane, Tom Christensen, Peter Katzenstein, Michael Griesdorf, Lisa Martin, Paul Evans, Yuen Foong Khong, and participants in the 'Security Institutions' workshops. I have not followed all of the suggestions, but they have all made me think harder about the subject. I am also very grateful to the Olin Institute of Strategic Studies and the United States Institute for Peace for funding some of this research.

liberalization policies. They are caught, in what Drysdale and Garnaut call an economic 'prisoner's delight':[1] states in the region are individually pursuing economic liberalization strategies with little coordination while apparently unconcerned about defection by others. Given the diversity of security interests in the region, the relatively low level of imminent interstate violence (especially in Southeast Asia), and the rapid economic growth in the region, it is hard to see why there would be any demand for the ARF, even as underinstitutionalized as it is.

The ARF is a security institution worth studying, however. Krasner bifurcates institutionalist theory into two camps: those who focus on how institutions constrain agent choice, given a constant set of preferences—an economistic or contractualist camp; and those who focus on how institutional features and agent interests are mutually constitutive, both evolving in directions that were not entirely anticipated at the start—a sociological camp.[2] The boundaries within and between these approaches are not always entirely clear, but as a general rule the former is the predominant strain. The institutional evolution of the ARF so far raises some interesting questions for contractual institutionalist theory. The literature tends not to focus so much on how institutions change preferences, or it takes a traditionally liberal stance by looking at how interaction changes domestic balances of power among actors whose preferences are given. This has led to a rather limited notion of the effects of institutions on actors. It essentially downplays the possibility of socialization, since actor preferences are given prior to social interaction in an institution and do not change as a result of *social* processes generated by this interaction.[3] From this perspective an institution simply places exogenous constraints on actors in the form of monitoring, rewarding, or sanctioning procedures. Usually, these are material not

---

[1] Drysdale and Garnaut (1993: 187).

[2] Krasner (1983*b*: 361–3).

[3] See the Introduction by the editors, which clarifies the language of 'interests' and 'preferences' as used in this volume. In their view, strategies can be changed through involvement institutions. For changing 'interests' or 'preferences', it is not clear what the causal mechanism would be, and whether the process would be endogenous to the institution itself or a function of shifting domestic coalitions. They may look first to a change in distribution of power among political élites/decision-makers—élite replacement—due to some effect of an institution (e.g information about policy failure, or the distribution of institutions benefits). Other scholars with choice-constraints predilections argue that it is wiser to assume fixed interests for methodological reasons: holding preferences constant makes it easier to differentiate between the effects of institutions on strategies and on preferences; in addition it is methodologically tricky to 'observe' preferences and changes in them because one can never tell whether the action observed reflects true preferences or are themselves a product of strategic interaction. See Frieden (1997). These are helpful caveats, but they do end up diverting scholars away from looking hard for changes in preferences through social interaction.

social constraints.[4] Yet it is precisely in institutions that conditions for the socialization of actors ought to be ripe. For example, social interaction is intensive and relatively structured. Moreover, institutions generally have some identifiable, corporate normative trait, goal, or identity. There are often opportunities, certainly many attempts, to use technical, issue-specific, or highly authoritative and legitimate information to convince, persuade, and otherwise change the normative and causal beliefs of actors in the institution. Behaviour is carefully scrutinized by others. And other actors frequently try to use these institutions to change the preferences of others. Often the interaction inside institutions is in small groups, generating a range of interpersonal pressures to conform.

Contractual institutionalist theory, then, tends not to ask how actors are socialized by institutions. That is, institutions are rarely treated as *social* environments where group interaction creates social pressures, incentives, and environments conducive to persuasion and/or pro-social conformity. This is, however, a central focus of social constructivist inquiry.[5] The ARF story suggests that by starting instead with the assumption that actor interests may be changed by social interaction inside institutions, one opens the door to understanding how institutions themselves change. Moreover, one is forced to reconsider the definition of 'optimal' institutional design favoured by standard institutionalist theory—namely, that institutional form is due to the solution of a given security problem. Instead, an optimal institution becomes one that is most likely to change actor interests in ways that maximize the likelihood that it will voluntarily accept maximally constraining commitments. Put differently, extremely underinstitutionalized arrangements may in some cases be effective in constraining highly opportunistic behaviour. If this is the case, then in policy terms one may not need to build especially intrusive monitoring and sanctioning institutions to elicit cooperation from potential defectors.

My argument is as follows. The ARF was set up in the first place because,

---

[4] Contractual institutionalism, in principle, does not rule out the possibility that sanctions could be social ones, presumably where actors are 'shunned', 'criticized', 'labelled', etc. Some institutionalists argue that a concern for a cooperative reputation is a non-material interest as well. But practically speaking, mainstream institutionalist research has mostly focused on material constraints, and institutional theory has not gone very far in theorizing about why social sanctions would work in the absence of material ones. Moreover, changed behaviour through social incentives is not the same thing as changed behaviour through re-evaluation of desires, wants, and preferences due to persuasion. The latter is not really explored much theoretically by constractual institutionalism. Finally, at the bottom of arguments about reputation-as-incentive is the assumption that reputations are instruments for gain in other (largely material) exchanges, not ends desirable in and of themselves.

[5] Sterling-Folker (1997); Finnemore (1996); Wendt (1994, 1997); Ruggie (1993).

given the multiplicity of state interests in the region, there was sufficient uncertainty about the regional security environment to create a demand for some mechanism to increase predictability. There was also enough interest in preserving economic prosperity in the region such that purely realpolitik mechanisms for reducing uncertainty—arming and allying—were ruled out as too costly. The low level of institutionalization in the ARF at first was also a result of the lack of consensus about which security problem required what solution. States did not know if they were in an *n*-person prisoners' dilemma, an assurance game, a coercive suasion game, or some issue-specific combination. But even a weak institution, supporting sustained interaction among senior officials, could provide information to clarify and change estimations about intentions. The key target here was China. For most states in the region China is the source of greatest uncertainty.[6] The marginal benefits of new information about China are quite high for weak states around its periphery. The institution therefore had to ensure China's participation. China has been historically suspicious of multilateral institutions that might constrain its ability to maximize relative power and autonomy. Therefore, the institution had to be non-threatening, thus weakly institutionalized. Even though a range of institutional variants were proposed and were acceptable, in principle, to many states, ASEAN leadership of the ARF became the logical institutional form because the 'ASEAN Way's' stress on consensus decision-making and weak institutionalization ensured the ARF would be minimally threatening to China. When China's preferences were figured in, no other configuration of leadership or institutionalization was acceptable to all states.

The subsequent evolution of the ARF is a story about path-dependence and mutual constitution. The nature of the ARF itself created conditions for movement towards greater institutionalization and a more intrusive security agenda.[7] When eighteen Asian-Pacific countries under ASEAN auspices agreed in 1993 to set up the ARF there was no agreed-upon organizational plan or agenda. By 1997, the ARF had in place a series of intersessional governmental working groups examining everything from templates for defence white papers, to military observers at military exercises, to the South China Sea, to nuclear weapons free zones, to peacekeeping standby arrangements. There is now a complex division of labour between track I (official) and track II (non-governmental) processes that allow controversial issues to be examined in a less controversial way.

---

[6] G. Smith (1996: 38).

[7] 'Intrusive' refers to issues that impinge on concrete material power capabilities, their configuration, distribution, and use.

Most interestingly, these features of the ARF today were, or would have been, considered too institutionalized, too formalized, too intrusive when the ARF was first set up. But the ARF's institutional design, such as it was, has changed, in an albeit small way, beliefs in China among key actors about interests *vis-à-vis* regional security institutions and issues. It has influenced these beliefs through the ARF's dialogue process by socializing those in charge of ARF policy in China. This has allowed incremental institutionalization over time in ways that were probably not possible, nor predicted, initially. The ASEAN Way has also created opportunities for the agenda to be captured by actors with preferences for greater multilateral institutionalization. There is, then, a feedback or mutually constitutive relationship between the initial ARF structure, change in China's overall comfort level with this structure, and institutional change in the ARF.

This article begins with a brief account of the origins of the ARF. It then moves to a discussion of why an ARF constrained by the 'ASEAN Way' became a point of agreement in 1993. I look next at the institutional and agenda features of the ARF and then suggest how these created conditions for a shift towards greater institutionalization. I then briefly address alternative arguments, and offer some comments on the implications for institutional theory.

2. A Brief History of the ARF

There had been serious proposals for a post-cold war regional multilateral security institution of some kind floating around the Asia-Pacific for a few years prior to the formation of the ARF.[8] In 1990 the Canadian government set up the North Pacific Cooperative Security Dialogue, gathering together scholars and officials in their personal capacities from nine countries in the north Pacific. But there was little chance of the initiative being institutionalized at the official level, given the adamant opposition of the Bush administration to multilateral security institutions in the region.

Then in 1991, Japan's then Foreign Minister Taro Nakayama proposed an official regional security dialogue to be held under the auspices of the annual ASEAN post-ministerial conference (PMC). The ASEAN PMC traditionally brought together ASEAN with its seven dialogue partners (Canada, US, Australia, New Zealand, Japan, South Korea, and the EU) and five consultative partners (Russia, China, Vietnam, Laos, New Guinea) to discuss

---

[8] The following draws largely from Leifer (1996); G. Smith (1996); Acharya (1996).

non-security issues in the region. Nakayama proposed putting security issues on the agenda. This was rejected at the time by ASEAN, which itself had traditionally kept controversial security issues off its intra-ASEAN agenda. However, the ASEAN ISIS (a grouping of ASEAN foreign policy think-tanks with close government ties) essentially appropriated Nakayama's proposal and put together a paper suggesting an expanded ASEAN-led regional security dialogue. The paper was circulated at an ASEAN summit meeting in January 1992, where the heads of government agreed to begin a foreign-minister-level ASEAN security dialogue, held eventually in May 1993. At the May meeting, Singapore, evidently with the quiet urging from the Australians and Americans, recommended expanding the intra-ASEAN security dialogue to the PMC structure. So at the July 1993 ASEAN PMC, foreign ministers of the eighteen states agreed to set up a separate meeting, to be held in July 1994, specifically for discussing security issues and to be called the ARF.[9] At the time, however, there was no clear sense of the design or agenda for the institution.[10]

It is worth noting ASEAN calculations because the relatively sudden turn around in ASEAN views on the desirability of a multilateral security institution has a bearing on the form and agenda of the ARF. Essentially, geopolitical changes in the early 1990s focused ASEAN attention on the high level of uncertainty in its security environment and on the absence of any mechanisms for reducing this unpredictability and for handling regional disputes.[11]

First, was the growth in Chinese power. ASEAN options were limited: it did not have the aggregate military capabilities to balance against China. Confrontational policies would also reduce investment and trade opportunities with the PRC. It made more sense, then, to use China's interest in economic development and cooperation to constrain its behaviour. This could be done through institutional engagement. The arguments made in ASEAN for engagement ran the gamut of propositions that institutional theory has about what institutions can do: acquire more information about Chinese intentions; link China's security interests to economic interaction with ASEAN making it more costly to 'defect' against ASEAN interests in security affairs; and change Chinese definitions of their own interests. These arguments took on more urgency with the collapse of the Soviet Union in

---

[9] With Burma and Vietnam's entry into ASEAN and the acceptance of India as a dialogue partner in 1996, there are currently 21 participants.

[10] *Far Eastern Economic Review* (5 Aug. 1993): 11.

[11] See the ASEAN ISIS Memorandum 'Enhancing ASEAN Security Cooperation' (5 June 1993), p. 2.

1991; it raised the possibility that regional conflicts, suppressed to some extent by the cold war, might surface with a vengence.

Finally, shortly after the Soviet collapse, the US withdrew its forces from the Philippines. There was a more or less common view in ASEAN that the US had to maintain its forward military presence in East Asia to constrain both China and Japan. But there was less agreement on what form this US presence should take. Thailand was less keen on US prepositioning of military supply ships in the Gulf of Thailand for instance, but Singapore, Indonesia, and Malaysia all supported some kinds of basing rights for the US navy. ASEAN generally agreed that regional security dialogues had to keep the US interested in staying in the region. The ASEAN calculus was helped by the Clinton administration's endorsement of multilateral security as a key component of US strategy in the region.

These geopolitical developments led to a relatively high level of dissensus in the region about what precisely the primary security problems were. To be sure there was overall agreement that the South China Sea was a potential flashpoint. A sample of 358 country-specific statements on security issues in East Asia, based on a survey of news reports about the ARF from *The Straits Times* (Singapore), *Far Eastern Economic Review* (Hong Kong) and *Nexis-Lexis* from 1993 to 1996, indicates the largest portion of all the references to security problems in the region in 1993 ($n = 73$) was to the South China Sea issue (23.3 per cent). After that the next most frequently identified security problems were the proliferation of weapons of mass destruction (15.1 per cent), then Korea (12.3 per cent) and China (12.3 per cent).[12]

But this ranking is unstable across time. The Kendall's W (coefficient of congruence across k-samples of ranked observations) for the most frequently mentioned issues in 1993–6 (Burma, Cambodia, China, Korea, South China Sea, weapons of mass destruction) indicates there was little consistency in the ranking of these issues across time (Kendall's W = .52, p = .063). As Figure 10.1 indicates, in 1993–4 there is a fairly consistent frequency distribution in the ranking of different security issues. If there had been a convergence of views over time about the salience of particular issues one would expect a peaking of one or two critical issues across states over time. While the South China Sea emerges even more clearly as the predominant issue in 1995, this is due mainly to the temporary salience of the Mischief

---

12 Each separate report was coded for statements relating to regional security problems. These were then disaggregated into statements identified with particular states. There were 358 coded statements about individual security issues. Many thanks to Anna Angelova, Matt Stephenson, and Theresa McNiel for compiling and coding the reports.

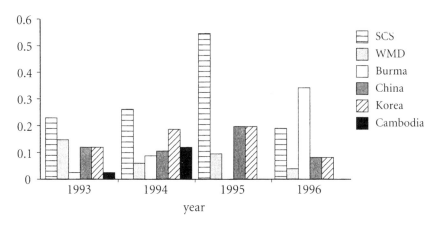

FIGURE 10.1. Relative Frequencies of Security Issues

Reef incident. By 1996, the question of Burma had captured the attention of states due to the increased repression there. The only thing states agreed upon was that there was no consensus on how to resolve these conflicts.[13] Cambodia, for instance, was essentially a coordination game. The South China Sea issue, however, is a question of sovereignty and territory, essentially zero-sum, and perceived that way by key players. Thus strategic uncertainty convinced ASEAN to take the initiative in setting up a regional institution. But because this institution would involve a wide range of states with disparate interests, because Chinese participation was essential, and because a critical goal was to figure out what indeed the nature of the security game in East Asia was, it made sense to make participation relatively costless.

The decision to support a weakly institutionalized forum was not an ahistorical response to perceptions of the uncertainty of the security environment, however. There were alternative models 'out there'—ranging from a wholesale reproduction of CSCE processes, to the Australian and the Canadian proposals for a less institutionalized but comprehensive Conference on Security Cooperation in Asia (CSCA), to virtually invisible structures such as the ARF. The preferences of ASEAN states, however, was influenced by their own habits of dialoguing. ASEAN itself even after almost three decades was loosely structured with a small secretariat: decisions were reached by consensus, and controversial issues were shelved in the interests of community-building. Thus in the absence of a consensus about the

---

[13] Author's interviews with Canadian and Singaporean embassy officials in Beijing in Apr. 1996 confirmed the lack of consensus about the degree of conflict of interests in the region.

security problems in the region, in order to ensure the legitimacy of its leadership role in any regional security institution, and in order to ensure maximum sustainability of such an institution, the 'ASEAN Way' became the organizing principle behind the ARF. Fortunately this choice was an optimal one: though probably unintended by ASEAN at the time, the initial parameters have allowed for the ARF's further institutional development.

3. The 'ASEAN Way' as a Point of Agreement

The ARF and the ASEAN Way became a point of agreement for states because of uncertainty about the nature of the security game. Abstractly put, most states wanted information primarily about Chinese intentions that could clarify appropriate collective or individual responses. But they also wanted a mechanism for possibly changing Chinese interests. As the ASEAN Secretary-General Ajit Singh noted shortly after the decision to set the ARF was made, 'The whole thing [ARF] is premised on the fact that we want to have a more stable and predictable order in South East Asia.' Singapore's Lee Kuan-yew noted, 'If you have a China out to make mischief, that increases the costs. Why not hoist this fellow on board.'[14] One senior Singaporean official acknowledged that China probably wished to establish a regional hegemony, but held out the hope that this hegemony could be pushed and pulled towards a more 'benign', American-style hegemony.[15] The ARF therefore had to be designed to make China's participation less costly for it than remaining outside the institution.

ASEAN was well aware of China's wariness of multilateral institutions.[16] Beijing had in the past clearly expressed a preference for dealing with ASEAN states bilaterally over disputes in the South China Sea. Chinese commentary on proposals in the early 1990s for regional security dialogues routinely indicated that multilateral bargaining situations were disadvantageous for China. Thus the promise that the ARF would be extremely loosely organized, would operate by consensus determined by ASEAN

---

[14] Cited in Antolik (1994: 118).

[15] I do not want to leave the impression that everyone in ASEAN intended to try to alter Chinese interests. Some were more sceptical about this possibility than others. Even these people, however, do not necessarily have an interest in openly defining the security problem as a suasion game. The concern is that by focusing on a China threat ARF will lose its focal point status and ASEAN will lose its leadership status in regional security affairs.

[16] The following two paragraphs draw from G. Smith (1996: 30); Leifer (1996: 26–7), and the author's interviews with a former US government figure involved in Asia policy, Beijing, June 1996, and with Canadian and Singaporean embassy officials, Beijing, June 1996.

chairs, and that the agenda would not involve formal commitments to security cooperation, ensured that from China's perspective participation was low cost. This promise was all the more credible when it was clear that states who did not share the enthusiasm for the ASEAN Way were none the less willing to live with it. To be sure, other states typically less patient with the ASEAN Way, particularly the US, Canada, Australia, and South Korea, expressed some concern that this kind of ARF would be so underinstitutionalized as to be ineffective, and therefore politically hard to support domestically. But they were all willing to accept the pace of institutionalization established by the accommodation of China. Indeed, they saw this as price for the existence of the institution in the first place.[17] The fact that Western states had a quiet desire to push the ARF in the direction of a CSCE-style institution underscored that the ASEAN Way was a compromise for them.

In sum, China's preferences became the basis of a point of agreement. While an ASEAN-style institution was not the best outcome for activist states such as Canada and Australia, it was better than none at all. A CSCE-type institution was not the best in ASEAN's view, but it was likely preferable to none at all. Thus, arguably, either of these types of institutions was preferred by all non-China actors to the absence of an institution that might both reduce uncertainty and change Chinese calculations.[18] For the PRC, however, initially no institution was better than any kind of forum, but an ASEAN-style institution was preferred to a CSCE one. It would ensure that the US could not dominate a regional security institution. Participation would also help demonstrate China's status quo intentions, thus reinforcing its carefully orchestrated post-June 1989 diplomatic breakout strategy. China outside of the ARF, or China responsible for the ARF being stillborn, would be costly to China's image as a peaceful regional power. There was, initially, no particular internalized commitment in China to multilateralism *per se* as a legitimate or efficient form of cooperation.

---

[17] As one Canadian diplomat noted, the ASEAN Way is a catchphrase for a pace that the PRC is comfortable with. The promise of a slow pace in the ARF is the only reason China came to the table. Author's interview with Canadian embassy officials, Beijing, Apr. 1996.

[18] Had ASEAN and the activists states agreed to the ASEAN Way because of some characteristic 'prominence and conspicuousness' other than China's preferences, one could argue the initial ARF would have constituted a focal point rather than a point of agreement. On the these features of a focal point, see Schelling (1960: 54, 57) and Morrow (1994: 96). This underscores, however, the conceptual problems in distinguishing between the two types of agreements: another actor's strong preference can itself be a 'prominent and conspicuous' coordination point for actors who are relatively indifferent between two outcomes as long as there is prior agreement that the strong-preference actor should be part of a group, community, or contract.

Once the initial structure and agenda of the ARF became a point of agreement, how did this shift over time? That is, how did the initial structure of the ARF encourage a particular pattern of social interaction that allowed institutional change? Concretely, how did the ARF change China's 'comfort level'? Here the story shifts to the initial institutional features of the ARF.

4. The 'Structure' of the ARF

Norms of national independence

The ARF explicitly endorses sovereignty-centric norms designed to preserve the independence and autonomy of participant states. This was an extension of intra-ASEAN norms. Since a number of ASEAN states were creations of colonialism—multi-ethnic spaces where national identity construction was the primary task of political élites—they have been acutely sensitive to external challenges to domestic political order and legitimacy. Thus their rules of interstate interaction have stressed non-interference in internal affairs, respect for sovereignty and independence, and the shelving of controversial issues. ASEAN leaders have been determined to preserve fragile, post-colonial domestic status quos and thus have no incentive to raise volatile bilateral issues that might set off domestic crises. Norms of national sovereignty and non-interference in internal affairs, therefore, make sense for ASEAN leaders.

These norms were embodied in ASEAN's 1976 Treaty of Amity and Cooperation (TAC),[19] and the First ARF in 1994 agreed to endorse the principles of the TAC as a code of conduct for relations among ARF states.[20] These principles were subsequently embodied in a paper by ASEAN ISIS submitted for approval at the Third ARF in 1996.[21] The most prominent of these principles were sovereignty, equality, independence, respect for territorial integrity and unity, non-interference in internal affairs, the right to chose one's social system, etc. These were norms that the Chinese regime, faced in particular with perceived American threats to unity (support for Taiwan) and domestic political order (human rights), wholly endorsed.[22]

Consensus

ARF decisions are determined by consensus, not unanimity. This is an

---

[19] Leifer (1996: 12–15).   [20] ARF (1995a: 4).   [21] ASEAN (1996).
[22] For a typical defence of more absolutist notions of sovereignty see Li (1992).

extension of intra-ASEAN decision-making norms. For ASEAN the rule stemmed from the fear of leaving any member state dissatisfied enough that it might accentuate interstate conflicts. Consensual decision-making is a logical mechanism for reassuring member states that the institution will not threaten sovereignty or national unity. The rule was expressly written into the Chair's statement summarizing the consensus at the Second ARF meeting in Brunei in 1995: 'Decisions of the ARF shall be made through consensus after careful and extensive consultations among all participants.'[23] The statement, in turn, reflected the ARF Concept Paper, a blueprint for the ARF's institutional and agenda evolution. The Concept Paper, while compiled by the Brunei foreign minister, in fact balanced Chinese concerns about faster institutionalization with US, Australian, and Canadian preferences for a more formal and intrusive organization and agenda.[24] But on procedural matters the paper reflected ASEAN (and Chinese) preferences: 'The rules of procedure of ARF papers shall be based on prevailing ASEAN norms and practices: Decisions should be made by consensus after careful and extensive consultations. No voting will take place.'[25]

At first glance, consensus decision-making would appear to be a suboptimal decision-making rule for a diverse group of actors. While it is more efficient than a unanimity rule, there is always the risk that individual actors can acquire informal veto power if whoever is in charge of determining when a consensus exists is committed to near-unanimity, is weak, or is beholden to particular actors. Studies of consensus decision-making among political parties in Swiss canton governments suggest, however, that consensus rules are likely to reduce intergroup conflicts in systems with 'strong subcultural segmentation' (e.g. diverse subgroups as in the ARF).[26] Even in PD-like or suasion-like games, consensus processes—despite feeble monitoring, adjudication, and enforcement mechanisms—can provide some of the mechanisms that institutional theory argues are functionally appropriate.[27] The expansion of discussion and research functions in consensus-seeking institutions can variously: create new expert constituencies with new, shared, understandings of the nature of the security problem; create issue linkages; reveal 'true' intentions; and provide forums for persuasion that lead to changes in preferences. These in turn can lead to redefinitions of the game being played.

Consensus is also a robust decision rule. As Steiner's study of Swiss federalism suggests, once decision-makers operate by consensus they are

[23] ARF (1995*a*).   [24] ARF (1995*b*).   [25] Ibid. 6.
[26] Steiner (1974).   [27] Martin (1993); Wallander (1999).

likely to stick with it.[28] If they interact enough personally they may develop a degree of intragroup solidarity that would be threatened by wins and losses associated with majoritarian voting. Alternatively, a consensus decision reduces the risk of ending up on the losing side. Losing internationally can have domestic political costs. It could be harder to maintain a domestic consensus for an international institution if one appears to lose badly from time to time.

Consensus decision-making requires that the chair be highly legitimate, since it must decide when a consensus has been reached. The decision has to be respected even by those who are not entirely happy with the outcome.[29] In this respect since ASEAN's leading role is considered legitimate, and acceptable to all sides, decisions to declare consensus are generally authoritative. This means, of course, that some chairs may have the authority to declare premature consensuses, or they may be open to pressure from more activist states to push the envelope on institutional structure and agenda.

The ARF's consensus decision rule was an attractive feature for China. While the PRC could not veto the chair's declaration of consensus, the norm at least required extensive consultation before any decisions. Consensus also ensured that China would not be on the losing side in any majoritarian voting system. This was probably important for those in the Ministry of Foreign Affairs handling ARF diplomacy. It would have been much harder to sell the benefits of the ARF in the policy process in Beijing if China's leaders had evidence that China was losing in recorded voting procedures.

Thin institutionalization

ARF participants have agreed to keep the institution barely institutionalized for the time being. As the ARF II Chair's statement noted: 'In the initial phase of the ARF, no institutionalization is expected. Nor should a Secretariat be established in the near future.'[30] Logistical work for the annual meeting is the responsibility of the foreign ministry bureaucracy of the ASEAN state that is chairing that particular year's ARF meeting. This informality is not entirely out of deference to China. In the absence of an ARF secretariat, it would make sense for the ASEAN secretariat to handle some of the preparations for security dialogues. There are apparently intra-ASEAN rivalries that prevent the secretarial work being handled by the

---

[28] Steiner (1974: 269–71).   [29] Jenks (1965: 55–63).   [30] ARF (1995*b*: 6).

ASEAN secretariat, however. ASEAN ministries of defence, for example, may be reluctant to transfer responsibilities for security dialogues to the ASEAN secretariat.

ARF members agreed at their first meeting in 1994 that ASEAN 'undertakes the obligation to be the primary driving force'. This was repeated in the Chair's statement from the Second and Third ARF meetings as well.[31] The ARF also officially promises, in essence, to evolve at the speed most suitable for the most reluctant player. As the Chair's statement in 1994 declared: 'The ARF process shall move at a pace comfortable to all participants.'[32] Together, ASEAN's leading role coupled with the 'comfortable pace' norms do two things. They reassure China mainly that there will be no immediate institutionalization that might reduce its autonomy, and they ensure ASEAN leadership—the two elements that made the ARF focal point attractive to the widest range of states.

But there is another less obvious consequence of ASEAN leadership that is reassuring to China. The fact that the ARF is the *ASEAN* Regional Forum means that its agenda is limited geographically primarily to Southeast Asian issues. It is not ASEAN's mandate to deal directly with volatile Northeast Asia issues like Korea or Taiwan or territorial disputes between China and Japan. The ARF's agenda was thus initially constrained by the geographical limits of its mandate, limits set by ASEAN leadership. But this only accentuated the ARF's acceptability to Beijing.

The relationship between Track I and Track II [33]

Right from the start, the ARF had a close relationship with Track II security dialogues. For one thing, proposals for an ARF-like institution came largely from the Track II community in ASEAN, Canada, and Australia. For another, many of the officials involved in Track I activities are unofficially involved in Track II as observers or in their 'personal' capacities. This is evident from the membership lists of the various national committees in the Council of Security Cooperation in the Asia-Pacific (CSCAP), the premier security Track II organization in Asia-Pacific.[34] Thus, ideas de-

---

[31] ARF (1995*a*: 2; 1996*a*: 2).

[32] ARF (1995*a*: 2).

[33] Track II refers to non-official dialogue processes and institutions—i.e. dialogues that include a substantial number of government officials acting in a non-official or observer capacity, but recognized by governments as serving the purposes of Track I (formal governmental) processes. This distinguishes Track II from unofficial or purely non-governmental activities.

[34] For example, 50% of the board of directors of the US national committee of CSCAP have

veloped at the Track II level can move quickly to Track I. This means that states with particularly active or authoritative Track II communities (e.g. Canada, Australia), regardless of the relative power of the state, can help define the Track I agenda.

The ARF has officially sanctioned these linkages. At the 1995 meeting, the ARF agreed that its activities should move along both tracks. To ensure that Track II activities do not get too far ahead (with the implied threat that these might then push the envelope in Track I), the ARF Chair is to ensure that ARF-related Track II activities 'result from full consultations with all ARF participants'.[35] The Chair will also be the 'main link' between the two tracks.

The ARF is increasingly reliant on Track II activities to generate ideas about its structure and agenda. ARF Track II activities come in three forms. The first are ARF-sponsored Track II meetings: those in 1996 in Paris and Moscow were on preventive diplomacy and confidence-building measures (CBMs) respectively. At the Paris meeting in November, for instance, the Chair's statement recommended that the ARF consider taking a proactive role in preventive diplomacy through the provision of ARF Chair's 'good offices'. The proposal was influenced by a paper from a Singaporean academic with support from Australian, Canadian, Philippines, US, and Singaporean participants. China, along with India, Vietnam, Malaysia, and Indonesia, was less enthusiastic, but none the less accepted the consensus decision. The paper had originally been written for the CSCAP CSBM meeting just prior to the Paris working group.[36]

The second form are activities undertaken parallel to, or in support of, the ARF without the ARF's prior formal endorsement. For example, after the First ARF in 1994, Australia, Canada, and South Korea had pressed the ARF to set up intersessional meetings officially so as to sustain the momentum coming out of the annual ARF meetings. The idea was rejected at that time (though accepted in 1995). Consequently, the three states ran informal intersessionals on their own initiative: Australia convened a workshop on CBMs in November 1994; Canada and Malaysia co-hosted a workshop on PKO activities in March 1995; and South Korea hosted a workshop on preventive diplomacy in May 1995.[37] The results of the workshops

worked in government. The US CSCAP also has a category called observers who are current government officials (US CSCAP, 1997). The Chinese CSCAP national committee includes an Assistant Foreign Minister, the senior specialist on American, European, and arms control affairs in the PLA General Staff Department, as well as the Foreign Ministry's senior functional level officer handling ARF affairs (PRC CSCAP [1997]).

[35] ARF (1995*a*: 3).   [36] *PacNet* (1996).   [37] G. Smith (1996: 30–1).

were acknowledged and commended in the Chair's statement at the 1995 ARF.[38]

The third form is CSCAP. CSCAP was created in 1993 as an umbrella organization for thirteen national CSCAP committees. While it is not the only Track II process around, it is the largest and most organized, with national CSCAP committees collaborating in working groups on topics such as CSBMs. The relationship between CSCAP and the ARF has been rather ambiguous. Neither the 1995 nor 1996 ARF Chair's statement specifically names CSCAP as the primary forum for ARF Track II activities, although the 1995 Concept Paper does identify it and ASEAN ISIS as two potential brainstrusts for the ARF. Its absence from the Chair's statements reflected, most likely, Chinese objections at that time to handing Track II responsibilities to an organization in which China was not a member.[39]

None the less, CSCAP appears to be emerging as a potential ideas factory for the ARF, somewhat analogous to the non-governmental Pacific Economic Cooperation Council's relationship to APEC. It is clear that many of the agenda items on the ARF have appeared first or are most fully developed in CSCAP working groups and memoranda. Indeed, CSCAP papers are regularly circulated to ARF participants.

Whether by design or not, the evolving relationship to Track II contributes to the ARF's stability as a focal point for states in the region. First it reassures states that the 'ASEAN Way' will remain the predominant organizing ideology of the ARF. Second, it allows for the evolution in institutional structure and agenda in ways that keep more activist states comfortable with the pace as well. Because the ARF Chair is the primary link between Track II and Track I, the Chair can decide just how far to push controversial Track II ideas onto Track I. This means ideas that might not get on the Track I agenda may well do so, depending on the Chair's activism. It also means, however, that some states are less worried that activists in Track II will hijack the Track I agenda.

In addition, issues that are too controversial for Track I can be moved into Track II rather than being discarded entirely. This sustains the momentum behind issues that the ARF might otherwise be compelled to abandon at the

---

[38] ARF (1995*a*: 5).

[39] China's membership had been held up as the rest of CSCAP debated how to handle Taiwan's application for membership. The PRC refused to set up a national committee until it was satisfied Taiwan could not participate formally. This decision was made in late 1996; the PRC subsequently put together its national committee and formally applied to join CSCAP. Author's interview with Canadian academic involved in Track II activities, Jan. 1997, and email correspondence with an Australian government official involved in ARF policy-making, Feb. 1997.

Track I level.[40] Given the myth of the official-unofficial identities of Track I and II activities, an issue is never really not within Track I's sphere of attention. This means that states are more likely to get used to an issue being part of their interaction than if it were initially considered illegitimate.

Track II can also 'filter' or sanitize proposals that would otherwise be deemed more controversial by dint of who made them.[41] *Who* makes a proposal can sometimes be more controversial than the *content* of the proposal itself.[42] But if proposals are 'depersonalized' through the Track II consensus process and then again through the ARF Chair's personal endorsement, and then again through the Chair's determination of consensus in the Track I level, much of the controversiality can be filtered out. Thus Track II can help define a Track I agenda that might not have otherwise appeared.

The Track I/II relationship in the ARF, therefore, is an example of how minor institutional innovations can have major intersubjective effects. Simply calling an issue a Track II one, to be handled unofficially or informally by many of the same people who represent their states officially in Track I, can create a focus on a particular issue. Some countries quite explicitly recognize that this official/unofficial Track I/II division is a fiction. Yet as long as this myth of difference is not explicitly challenged, and is reproduced through the descriptive language used and through the superordinate-subordinate relationship between ARF and Track II activities, then the destabilizing effect of controversial issues is reduced. Chinese officials have stated openly that CSCAP's unofficial nature was a fiction because of the presence of so-many government officials in their 'personal capacities'. None the less the Chinese government has played along. In a statement of support for links to Track II, it noted, 'Issues not discussed or needing further discussions because of disagreement' can be put into Track II forums.[43] The net result of this deliberate coordination behind the myth is to reinforce the robustness of the ARF and its 'way', reducing fears of defection from the institution even as the institution changes.

This brings us finally to a core issue: how have these institutional characteristics of the ARF promoted evolution and innovation in structure and agenda? The story here shifts to China's changing comfort level in the ARF.

---

[40] This leeway given to Track II activities is symbolized by the fact that the ARF cannot call Track I working groups 'working groups', but it uses this term for ARF-sponsored Track II working groups.

[41] 'Filter' is Paul Evan's term. I am indebted to him for his insights into Track II.

[42] Desjardin (1996).

[43] China (1996: 2).

4. China's Changing Comfort Level[44]

As I indicated above, from the start ARF participants have been keenly sensitive to how to keep the ARF attractive to Beijing. Thus there were explicit references to establishing 'comfortable pace' norms in the annual Chair's statements and in the Concept Paper. But what does 'comfort level' mean, and how might it change?

Comfort level simply refers to a utility distribution that is dependent on levels of institutionalization. That is, an actor has a particular distribution of utility associated with particular levels of institutionalization.[45] Different states may have different distributions of utility. Figure 10.2 would represent a state that is sceptical of the value of high levels of institutionalization. Figure 10.3 might reflect the interests of a committed multilateral activist.

Greater willingness to accept institutionalization would be indicated by a change in Actor 1's distribution curve whereby it comes to believe that the absence of an institution is less valued than before and the presence of one

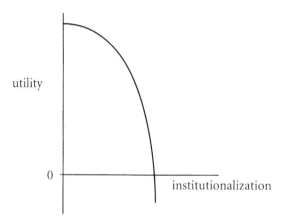

Figure 10.2. Actor 1: The Sceptic

[44] Important note: from here on in, when I refer below to 'China' or 'Chinese' 'changing comfort levels' in an aggregate sense I am referring mainly to those in the ARF decision-making processes unless otherwise indicated. That is, I do not claim that all constituencies or decision-makers in China have been socialized to accept multilateralism as a legitimate feature of regional security structures. However, those in the political leadership who believe China's participation is good for diffuse reputational and image reasons have also exhibited an 'increased comfort level'.

[45] I am subsuming, for the moment, the intrusiveness of the agenda within the level of institutionalization.

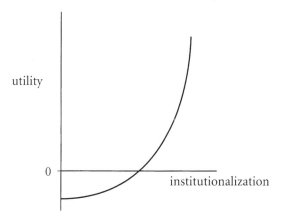

FIGURE 10.3. Actor 2: The Activist

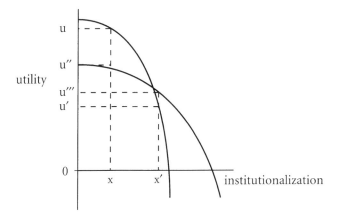

FIGURE 10.4. Changing Comfort Levels

becomes more valued than before, moving towards a shape more consistent with the Activist's curve. In Figure 10.4, for example a comfort level at time t would provide utility u for level of institutionalization x, and u′ for level x′. An increased comfort level at time t+1 would provide a lower level of utility u″ for level x, and a higher level of utility u‴ for utility x′.[46]

---

[46] I have not modelled here the factors that might encourage the sceptic to enter an institution in the first place nor the factors that might then get it to accept some institutionalization given the shape of the curve in Fig. 10.4 (since, in this case, the actor is indifferent between no and low institutionalization). If the sceptic were to 'move first' of course, there would be no institution. But I assume here for illustrative purposes (and indeed empirical accuracy) that the activists move first, implicitly or explicitly establishing linkages with other 'goods' valued by the sceptic.

A shift in the comfort level could result from a range of factors: convincing information that fears of even small amounts of institutionalization are exaggerated; increasing image costs from backing out and sabotaging the institution as it becomes more legitimate to a wide range of other players; changing levels of identification with other potential institutional partners (and hence a desire to emulate activists); persuasive information that more institutionalization is a 'good' in and of itself, etc. All of these factors are functions of time and social interaction within the institution.

In China's case, its interest in low levels of institutionalization has been changing, made possible by an initially positive comfort level with the institutional features of 'ASEAN Way'. The utility of no institutionalization is dropping, while the utility of some institutionalization is increasing. When proposals for a regional security institution were floated in the early 1990s, China's utility distribution was essentially one where no institutionalization was better than even a little bit. Thus there was no point of agreement with activists or other states—the range of institutionalization the PRC was willing to accept never overlapped the range of institutionalization desired by multilateralist activists states, like Canada and Australia, at a level of utility that all were willing to accept.

Since it was in the activists' interests to try to encourage China's acceptance of institutionalization, however, the 'activists' basically had to accept *temporarily* a lower level of institutionalization (an ARF defined by the 'ASEAN Way') even if the utility was perceived to be low. This was acceptable only because it was seen as part of an extended strategy of trying to change China's interests.[47] The goal was to provide China with some gains to help increase its comfort levels. The point of agreement was relatively stable because if one moved towards greater institutionalization, one would not get Chinese cooperation, and if one moved towards less institutionalization, one would get efforts by 'activists' to push for more institutionalization in the face of Chinese opposition. This would create image problems for China, which might spill over into other issue areas (e.g. it would confirm 'the China threat'; it might contribute to the aggregation

---

[47] This is a critical point. Neither the establishment of the ARF as a point of agreement with China, nor movement of this point towards higher levels of institutionalization by increasing China's comfort level, would have made sense if at least some states did not believe that institutions can change interests. States do intend, and try, to change other's intentions. That is what much of diplomacy is about. Expending so much energy trying to do so would not make sense without some belief in some probability of success. Thus, states often see social interaction as a tool of persuasion and transformation, a feature of institutions that choice-constraints institutional theory neglects.

of countervailing power against China, among other negatives). A temporary 'shift' in the activists' curve meant, basically, there was a higher level of utility for a lower level institutionalization. This would characterize, for instance, the US and Canadian and Australian recognition that perhaps to go slow was healthier for the ARF at that moment.

Note then what is changing through ARF interaction. The changing level of Chinese comfort entails, essentially, a redefinition of the game being played, a change in China's ranking of outcomes from a clear preference for no institutionalization to a preference for a moderate level of institutionalization.[48] This new preference is a function of what Cohen and Axelrod call 'positively surprising' consequences: when the ability of actors to project out the consequences of their behaviour is limited (by limited information or limited information processing capabilities), action can lead to unanticipated positive consequences where the expected utility of the act is less than the actual utility. An actor will come to desire or prefer this surprising outcome. This is not simply an instance where new information clarifies the game being played. Rather it leads to a realization that the new outcome is not, in fact, undesirable.[49]

The 1996 ARF Chair's statement hinted that the institutional evolution of the ARF was in fact due to this process of changing Chinese comfort levels through interaction: 'It is therefore worth noting that increasing comfort levels among participants at the Third ARF demonstrates that the ARF is progressing at a good pace. Future meetings should try to build upon this demonstrated base of friendly and frank discussions among the participants and this will in turn pave the way for agreements on substantive issues in the coming years.'[50] It seems China agreed with this assessment. In a statement prior to the Third ARF in 1996, the Chinese government expressed support for the pace of the ARF's development: the present 'operational mode and organizational form are working well'.[51]

---

[48] I realize that for many game theorists what I call a 'preference' here is considered a 'strategy'. In fact, as the editors note in the Introduction, the difference between the two concepts is artificial and depends on the level of ends and means one is examining. For game theorists, the outcome of strategic interaction between two players is the product of a particular strategy pair. States are said to have preferences over outcomes. Yet if a multilateral institution is itself a product of a particular strategy pair, then it seems to me multilateralism can be a preference. Of course, multilateralism can also be a strategy at a higher level of interaction where the 'goal' is some more abstract good, such as security. But since security is a grand preference of most states, to limit preferences to things as abstract as security, welfare, peace, etc., means that no outcome below this level can be called a preference. Everything becomes strategy. I think this reduces the utility of the term preference, and ignores the fact that actors can come to internalize multilateralism, unilateralism, and bilateralism as legitimate, taken-for-granted ends in themselves.

[49] Cohen and Axelrod (1984: 31).   [50] ARF (1996a: 9).   [51] China (1996: 1).

How, then, did the ARF process change Chinese assessments of the utility of the ARF? The answer to this is veiled by the mysteries of the Chinese policy process, but it appears to have been a function of two separate variables. The first has been the emergence of a small group of policy-makers who have developed a somewhat more deeply normative commitment to multilateralism because it is 'good' for Chinese and regional security. The evidence is only indirect.[52] ARF policy in China was put in the hands of the Comprehensive Division of the Asia Department of the Foreign Ministry. The Division had only about eight to ten (overworked) officers. A couple of these officers did the preparatory work for ARF meetings and Track II activities. Initially, in ARF activities the Chinese representatives were unaccustomed to the give and take of corridor debate and negotiation. They also came to the discussions with a watchful eye for developments that might impinge on sensitive security or domestic political issues. Over time, however, with experience in informal discussion, familiarity with the ARF norms of interaction, these officers have become much more engaged, relaxed, and flexible.

Most interesting has been their apparent endorsement, within limits, of multilateralism as being compatible with Chinese security interests. One foreign diplomat in Beijing, who has interacted with these MFA officers extensively, even suggested that their agenda is to tie China gradually and innocuously into regional security institutions so that some day China's leaders will be bound by the institutions. They see ARF involvement as an process of educating their own government. According to another close observer of Chinese multilateralism, these individuals are groping intellectually towards variations of common or cooperative security. The main conduit for the infusion of these sorts of ideas, into this group at least, has tended to be experience in Track I and II, and not so much the absorption of academic literature on multilateralism. The Canadian government has decided to invest in this community of proto-multilateralists: in January 1997 it ran a two-week seminar programme on the theory and practice of regional multilateralism for some of these individuals and for others from Chinese intelligence and the military. It seems this group's influence over Chinese ARF policy may be helped by further institutional change in China.

---

[52] The following comes from the author's interviews with Canadian and Singaporean embassy officials, Beijing, Apr. 1996; with a Chinese intelligence analyst involved in ARF policy process, Beijing, July 1996; and with a prominent Canadian academic involved in Track II activities, Jan. 1997; with a Japanese Foreign Ministry official involved ARF policy, Oct. 1998; with a Canadian embassy official, Beijing, Nov. 1998; and with Chinese academics involved in research on multilateralism for the Foreign Ministry, Nov. 1998. See also G. Smith (1996).

In January 1998, the Asia Department set up a separate division just to handle ARF and Track II diplomacy.

There is some intriguing concrete evidence of the commitment these individuals have in protecting the policy from domestic political critics—hence an indication of their growing normative stake in the ARF. A senior Canadian official involved in ARF diplomacy has reported that the Chinese delegates to ARF discussions apparently do not report back to Beijing any reference by other delegations to the CSCE as a possible model for the ARF. The CSCE is not just a symbol of a more intrusive, constraining regime, it is also a regime that deals with human rights.[53] Downplaying this information, then, was important to preserve support or acquiescence for further institutionalization of the ARF. Other Canadian diplomats have reported that sometimes the multilateralists in the MFA will help other states frame proposals for ARF-related activities in ways that will make these more acceptable in Beijing. While only anecdotal, this evidence suggests that over time the character of Chinese obstruction or resistance in its ARF diplomacy 'on the ground' has shifted from protecting given Chinese 'interests' to protecting Chinese multilateral diplomacy from potential domestic opposition. Tentatively speaking, one could plausibly see this as diplomacy more empathetic with the institution and less empathetic with other PRC constituencies that may have different views of the value of multilateralism. In other words it may reflect an emergent solidarity with the institution and its participants.

The second variable is image. None of these concrete manifestations of Chinese comfort levels would last if the political leadership were not at least willing to acquiesce to creeping multilateralism in day-to-day policy. While the proto-multilateralists in the ARF policy process appear to have supported China's continuing involvement for normative reasons, for the *political leadership* in Beijing this acquiesence is encouraged by a concern about China's international image. As China becomes more committed to institutional and agenda change in the ARF, the ARF becomes a more credible and legitimate regional institution. This means the costs of backing out of or sabotaging the institution increase. Low-key, iterated, consensus-based interactions can create a social environment in which defection carries heavier opprobrium costs. China has come under pressure to produce Defence White Papers and to accept potentially more intrusive CBMs. The costs of refusing are very diffuse, but real none the less. The ARF has no sanctioning or side payment capacity. No other state has threatened

---

[53] G. Smith (1996: 22).

sanctions or offered side payments to keep China involved in the ARF. Yet, time and again in interviews with people involved in the interagency policy process on arms control and regional security in 1996, sometimes explicitly sometimes implicitly, the informants would reveal how sensitive the top leadership was to the appearance of obfuscation and isolation in high-profile international institutions. The coercive nature of the ARF as an institution is thus more a function of what Young calls a diffuse sense of 'social disgrace' than of a concrete material cost-benefit calculus.[54]

Thus socialization in the norms of multilateralism through the ARF and related processes may help explain the increasing comfort level of the PRC 'on the ground' and among the functional specialists in the policy process. This increasing comfort level has allowed the ARF structure and agenda to develop in ways that would have been unacceptable at the start in 1993. This has contributed to the ARF's legitimacy (a wide range of states are clamouring to get in as participants). This legitimacy, in turn, has increased both the normative costs and the diffuse reputational costs to China's image from backing out, obstructing, or sabotaging the institution. Concretely, China's changing comfort level has allowed the following changes in the ARF institution and agenda.

Institutional structure

The major innovation occured at the Second ARF in 1995. The ARF agreed to set up two kinds of working groups to undertake intersessional discussions that could not be handled in the annual day-long foreign ministers' meeting. Canada and Australia had floated proposals at the First ARF in 1994 for Track I intersessional work, but these had been rejected at the time, primarily because of Chinese objections.[55] In 1995 the proposal was put on the ARF agenda again.[56] Much of the initiative to keep the issue on the

---

[54] Young (1992); Susskind (1994); Cialdini (1984). That is, this concern about image is not simply an interest in short-term deception (e.g. designed to cover up short-run defection strategies). Nor does it appear to be diffusely deceptive (e.g. to build image capital to cover up defection in the long run). Rather it appears that many believe China's identity as a legitimate world power rests to an increasing degree on whether it behaves the way other major powers behave, namely as a player in all the major institutions governing global order. This argument is consistent with Chayes and Chayes contention (1996: 27) that sovereign identities are increasingly tied to a state's status in the complex of international regimes that regulate interstate relations. It is clear that diffuse reputation or image concerns have been a concrete constraint on preventing outright defection from the ARF and other multilateral institutions.

[55] Leifer (1996: 32).

[56] This time both ASEAN and Australia claimed to have raised the issue. Author's interview with Singaporean embassy official, Beijing, Apr. 1996; email correspondence with Austrialian government official involved in ARF policy, Jan. 1997.

agenda was taken by the Chair, the Brunei foreign minister. The ARF agreed to set up a Track I intersessional process, but compromised over the label and the mandate. China objected to the term 'working groups' and to an indefinite timeframe because both smacked of thicker institutionalization, and it wanted only to set up two intersessional groups. This led to the creation of three groups categorized under two types—two intersessional meetings (ISM), one on peacekeeping operations (PKO), the other on search and rescue (SAR); and one intersessional support group (ISG) on CBMs. It was understood that the ISMs were to be the more impermanent of the two types. Their mandate was only to meet once in 1996, and the Third ARF would then decide whether or not to extend their lives. The ISG was viewed as a potentially more extended process, since it was taking up the complex and sensitive issue of CBMs. Each group would be co-chaired by an ASEAN state and one other initiating state. The PRC accepted, though apparently was not overly enthusiastic.[57]

The ISG and ISMs finally provided the ARF with a process for much more detailed investigation of solutions to security problems in the region. This allowed states with particular expertise and or interest to influence intersessional work. Thus Canada co-chaired the PKO ISM, Japan co-chaired the CBM ISG, while the United States co-chaired the SAR ISM. In each case, the agenda was negotiated well in advance, as requested by China.[58] For example, when Canada established the agenda for the ISM on PKO it had to compromise with China on the wording of at least one agenda item, PKO Standby Arrangements (the preposturing of a division level force ready for PKO operations). The Chinese side asked that 'standby arrangements' be dropped, because the military did not want even the hint that it might have to tie itself to PKO operations in the region. Canada renamed the item 'PKO arrangements' and left the content pretty much alone.[59] Interestingly enough, later in the Third ARF Chair's statement the document asked participants to consider involvement in PKO 'standby arrangements'.[60] Evidently China was eventually willing to put aside its opposition to the term for the sake of consensus.

[57] Much of the above paragraph came from author's interviews with Canadian embassy officials, Beijing, Apr. 1996; G. Smith (1996: 32–3); and email with Australian government official involved in ARF policy, Jan. 1997.

[58] The time was needed in part because the Comprehensive Division in the MFA Asia Department did not have the expertise or personnel to thoroughly assess the pros and cons of proposals quickly. In addition, the Chinese response had to be coordinated across units, in particular with the PLA. This was a delicate task, since the MFA officers believed the PLA was a potential spoiler of greater Chinese involvement. Thus great care had to be taken to ensure the PLA was on board.

[59] Author's interview with Canadian embassy officials, Beijing, Apr. 1996.

[60] ARF (1996a).

Despite the tentativeness with which the ARF set up the ISMs and ISG in 1995, the ARF in 1996 extended the mandates and timeframe for all three, and endorsed the groups' concrete recommendations. Most surprising to ARF participants, but consistent with the argument about China's increasing comfort levels, China offered at the 1996 ARF to co-chair a ISG on CBMs with the Philippines in March 1997. China is now part of the inter-sessional process in a way no one imagined possible in 1993.

Agenda

Here there have been a number of innovations that were either rejected in 1993 and 1994, or were viewed as too controversial. All of these reflect some give by the Chinese.

(1) Nuclear testing: Despite its sensitivity to criticism on this score, the Chinese did not disrupt consensus when the 1995 and 1996 Chair's statements indirectly criticized both China (and France) for their nuclear-testing programmes.[61]

(2) Preventive diplomacy: In the ARF context, 'preventive diplomacy' generally refers to using the Chair's good offices to investigate or mediate disputes, sending ARF special representatives on fact-finding missions, moral suasion, and third-party mediation. The PRC has traditionally been uneasy with a more active ARF role in preventive diplomacy because of the potential for 'internationalization' of core security issues.[62] None the less, the ARF formally took up the issue at its Track II working group on preventive diplomacy in November 1996 in Paris. The idea had already been raised in the ARF Concept Paper in 1995, but it was confined to the Annex B list of CBMs, a list of more intrusive and controversial CBMs relegated to the indefinite future. Interestingly, the explicit mandate of the Paris working group was to propose a list of relevant preventive diplomacy CBMs for the agenda of the ISG in March 1997: recall the Chinese had already offered to act as a co-chair for this ISG. The fact that the ARF took up these issues in 1997 suggests, again, a changing degree of Chinese comfort with the evolving agenda.

(3) The South China Sea: China's long-time preference has been to resolve

---

[61] ARF (1995*a*: 7; 1996*a*: 3).

[62] China is not alone. South Korea apparently is leary of giving the ARF a preventive diplomacy role if this means ASEAN might try to involve itself in Northeast Asian issues. Author's interview with prominent Canadian academic involved in Track II activities, Jan. 1997.

this issue in bilateral discussions with other claimants, where its bargaining leverage is greatest. It has tried assiduously in the past to prevent what it calls the multilateralization of the issue. It was considered a major conceptual breakthrough, then, when the SCS was put on the Second ARF agenda in 1995 (apparently with considerable American effort). The Chinese did not use this as a reason for objecting to the Chair's declaration of consensus. Nor was China willing (or able) to prevent the statement from pointedly encouraging all claimants to reaffirm their commitment to ASEAN's 1992 Declaration on the South China Sea, this after China's unilateral grab of the Mischief Reef in February 1995. The Declaration called on all states to respect the non-use of force and to refrain from unilateral actions. The Third ARF Chair's statement again touched on the SCS issue—this time welcoming China for its commitment in 1995 to resolve SCS disputes according to international law, but also pointedly commending the Indonesian workshop on the South China Sea for its work on conflict-management issues.[63] The workshop was set up in 1992 and is funded by Canada. The Chinese had been unhappy with this and had tried to pressure the Canadians to stop funding. By the Third ARF, apparently, China did not believe it was necessary to oppose consensus on this issue.

(4) Confidence-building measures: China has traditionally been sceptical about the value of CBMs, to the extent these are deemed asymmetrically intrusive. Concerning military transparency, for instance, the predominant argument has been that as a weak power *vis-à-vis* other major powers, China should be less transparent in the hope that strong states overestimate their capabilities. In addition, China has criticized the notion that one can transplant CSCE-type CBMs to the Asia-Pacific. Multilateralists like the Canadians and the Australians, on the other hand, had a repertoire of concrete CBM proposals, based in part on CSCE models. And they were ready to raise these on every possible Track I and II occasion.

The First ARF was relatively silent on CBMs. However, by the Second ARF, under Brunei's leadership, the ARF had endorsed the ARF Concept Paper that laid out a timetable for implementing a wide variety of CBMs. These, all voluntary, would be taken from the Annex A list and included: statements on security perceptions and defence policies; enhanced military-to-military exchanges; observers at military exercises; promotion of the principles of the ASEAN TAC and the ASEAN Declaration on the South China Sea; exchanges of information on PKO activities. At the ISG on CBMs in January 1996, states presented Defence White Papers and statements about

---

[63] ARF (1996*a*: 4).

security perceptions. But no comments on or criticisms of the content were permitted. There were complaints outside the ARF that the Chinese presentation—a White Paper on Arms Control—was not especially detailed or credible.

By the Third ARF, with the results in from the ISG on CBMs, the list of CBMs recommended in the Chair's statement lengthened and deepened. While Defence White Papers and statements on security policies were still voluntary there were hints of an emerging template.[64] 'Such papers could also cover defense contacts and exchange programmes undertaken by participants.'[65] The statement also hinted that, unlike in the ISG, the content of these papers would also no longer be off-limits to discussion. 'Exchanges of views on the information provided in such statements and papers should be encouraged in future ARF dialogues.'[66] On military observers at exercises and prior notification of military exercises, the statement noted that states were encouraged to exchange information about their ongoing observer and prior notification activities 'with a view to discussing the possibilities of such measures in selected exercises'.[67] The March 1997 ISG on CBMs co-chaired by China and the Philippines pushed this further. The agenda for the meeting called for reaching consensus on the invitation of observers to joint military exercises and the prior notification of joint military exercises.[68] Interestingly, while ASEAN and China tend to decry the validity of a CSCE template for the Asia-Pacific, the CBMs that are now either on the table in the ARF ISG or endorsed in the ARF Concept Paper Annex B, are not much different in kind from the first generation of CBMs under the CSCE.[69] Indeed, perhaps in an indication of its rising comfort level on the CBM issues, in a statement on the Third ARF agenda in April 1996 China drew attention to its just-completed multilateral CBM treaty with Russia, Kazakhstan, Kyrgyzstan, and Tajikistan. This treaty is, essentially, a CSCE-type agreement with specific rules on prior notification of military exercises of particular sizes, invitations to military observers, limits on the size of military exercises within a certain distance of the border, etc. While the Chinese statement does not say the treaty is fully applicable to the Asia-

---

[64] For which activists were pushing hard. See for instance CSCAP Memorandum No. 2, 'Asia-Pacific Confidence and Security Building Measures' (1995), p. 4.

[65] ARF (1996*a*: 4).   [66] Ibid. 5.   [67] Ibid. 6.

[68] The agenda focus on 'joint' exercises had been set by China, and it ran into opposition from the US and its allies, as they are the ones who run 'joint exercises'. China does not. The ISG failed to reach consensus on the issue. While this was a setback for the CBM process, a range of alternative proposals was floated for implementing other versions of this kind of CBM. The Chinese ran into heavy criticism for this proposal, and it is likely that it in subsequent meetings it will have to accept modifications that are not so obviously self-serving.

[69] See Desjardin (1996: 7).

Pacific, it does note that it will have a positive impact in the region.[70] One of the dividing lines between multilateralists and sceptics in the ARF policy process in Beijing is over the applicability of the treaty to the region. In essence this reflects a debate on the applicability of the CSCE model. That some involved in ARF policy-making apparently now support some version of this model suggests there is some ideational basis for China's increasing comfort levels in the ARF.

None of this means that China does not ever get its way. Clearly, despite the changes, the institutionalization and agenda of the ARF are not moving as fast as some countries would like. But often the limits to Chinese comfort levels tend to show up in the language adopted, rather than in the concrete content of discussions. While preventive diplomacy is on the agenda, the Chinese have been reluctant to support conflict-resolution roles for the ARF. The 1995 ARF Concept Paper had divided the timeline for ARF development into three phases: CBM phase, development of preventive diplomacy phase, and a phase for the development of conflict-resolution mechanisms. When the Second ARF Chair's statement endorsed the Concept Paper, however, 'conflict resolution' was changed to 'the elaboration of approaches to conflict'. The Chinese had objected to 'conflict resolution mechanisms' because the term implied giving the ARF a mandate to intervene in conflicts that the Chinese might want to keep bilateral.[71]

5. Objections to the Argument

Overall, the evidence suggests that China's increasing comfort level with the ARF has allowed the ARF to evolve towards somewhat higher levels of institutionalization and somewhat more intrusive agenda issues. My argument has rested on claims about the particular characteristics of China's socialization in the ARF that makes participation at once more reassuring and withdrawal or obstruction more costly. Neither effect is attributable to specific gains in relative military power, nor to side payments or threats of sanctions put in place by the institution or any of its participants.

Indeed, variants of neo-realist material power and interest arguments have very little to say about changing Chinese 'comfort levels' and the evolution of the ARF. The ARF is not being manipulated by the most powerful players in the Asia-Pacific subsystem. Much of the agenda and institutional

---

[70] China (1996: 3).
[71] Author's interview with Singaporean embassy official, Beijing, Apr. 1996; China (1996: 3).

structure is pushed by multilateral activitists such as Canada and Australia. Regionally powerful states like China clearly have not got their way on all issues or even on the most sensitive ones. Indeed, precisely because of the form of the ARF, the agenda can be captured by actors regardless of their material 'power' capabilities. The ARF and the ASEAN Way opened the door to multilateral activists—actors with special authoritative knowledge that makes it both probable and legitimate for them to influence the agenda (e.g. Canada and PKO). There are also no changes in material power distributions in the time period that can explain demonstrable changes in Chinese comfort levels.

Nor is China's changing comfort level merely a deceptive strategy by a realpolitik actor for increasing relative power without provoking resource-draining counterbalancing reactions from other states. If this were all only deception, we would expect that as the ARF handles increasingly intrusive and sensitive issues that may impinge on core interests or relative power issues the PRC should balk at further change in the institution and agenda. In other words, the comfort level and the level of institutionalization/ agenda should be negatively related. Yet, change in the ARF and change in China's comfort levels are, to this point, positively related. That the ARF is already discussing the South China Sea in multilateral terms, intrusive CBMs, and preventive diplomacy mechanisms is evidence of this.

Nor is the ARF designed to balance against a Chinese threat, nor is it being used by China to balance against a US threat.[72] To be sure, some in ASEAN and in the US see the ARF as a tool for tying China into institutions that can then create costs for the reckless use of Chinese power in the future. But the use by realpolitik actors of a still relatively unrestrictive multilateral institution with no strict blueprint for future development to balance against a threat is something Walt would certainly not expect. Realpolitik actors should have no faith in such an institution in the first place.

For most states, there is no clear consensus on what the threat is—China? a security dilemma? the interactive effects of unfettered major power interests? The ARF is a tool for acquiring some of the information necessary for making this judgement and, for some states, for actively changing the

---

[72] Chinese security policy is not one of balancing in the Waltzian sense. The elements of balancing behaviour (e.g. increases in military expenditures, military contingency planning) that might be consistent with Waltz all began prior to the change in the global distribution of power with the collapse of the USSR. Other balancing elements are missing. China is not trying to reduce security externalities produced by trade relations with the US. Nor is China trying very hard to undermine US alliance structures in East Asia or build its own. If, over all, China's security policy is not consistent with Waltzian balancing arguments, there is no reason to believe its ARF policy is. See Johnston (1998).

environment. Thus it cannot be a mere instrument of threat balancing. Interestingly, even after the Mischief Reef in February 1995 (where the Philippines discovered a small Chinese naval post in disputed reefs near the Philippines) and the Chinese missile exercises directed at Taiwan after Lee Denghui's visit to Cornell University in the summer of 1995, there was no discernible shift in the motivation of most ARF members. If smaller states in the region were balancing against threat, one would have expected to see either the abandonment of the ARF as a credible tool to deal with Chinese power, or a more concerted effort to use the ARF to constrain Chinese power. Yet there were was no obvious burst of proposals to turn the ARF into a monitoring and sanctioning institution directed at China. Singaporean Prime Minister Goh Chok Tong summarized the predominant reaction: 'It is important to bring into the open this underlying sense of discomfort—and even insecurity—about the political and military ambitious of China.' However, he went on, 'It is not preordained that Chinese military power will turn into a threat.'[73] There is still a sense among many players that the ARF can create a Chinese stake in institutionalized dialogue. This is not the reaction one would expect from Waltzian or Waltian realpoliticians. This is not to say that the nature of the security game is settled, and states are generally reassured about China. But neither have most states concluded the game is a coercive suasion game or an n-person prisoners' dilemma; there are enough signals coming from China through its behaviour in the ARF to suggest dialoguing, persuasion, and appeals to image have not been ineffective.

A materialist choice-constraints, contractual institutional explanation does not capture the dynamics of the story either. This approach assumes states have some sort of agreement about the nature of the game being played. It then assumes that rational actors should *try* to put a functionally efficient institution in place. It then assumes that the rules of the institution constrain states in such a way that defection becomes too costly and cooperation become relatively more attractive. The exogenous (dis)incentives could be material or reputational. These assumptions may help explain why an institution makes sense in the first place, but they do not clarify all the plausible paths in its evolution. For contractual institutionalism a positive change in institutions comes through a process of adjusting from a suboptimal to a more efficient structure.[74] But the process is often attributed to

[73] *FEER* (3 Aug. 1995).

[74] The language of functional optimality and efficiency is especially apparent in Martin's discussion of the hypothesized 'fit' between different types of security problems and different types of institutional solutions. See Martin (1993: 107–8).

exogenous variables such as domestic political change, higher levels of interdependence, or the unintended effects of autonomous changes in technology. Institutional change as a result of socialization is ruled out by fixed or exogenously given interests.

Alternatively, for contractual institutionalism behavioural change can come about through new information provided by the institution about the intentions and strategies of other players. Thus materialist institutionalist arguments about China's 'comfort level' would focus on the provision of reassuring information by the ARF about (*a*) the non-threatening nature of the ARF agenda and institution, and (*b*) the intentions of most other states in the institution. Once this information was communicated through China's initial involvement in the ARF, Chinese decision-makers realized that the institution would not threaten fundamental interests. Initial suspicions were thus put aside.

China's changing comfort in the ARF level, however, is neither a function of institutional constraints on choice nor the provision of new information. The ARF has very few hard institutional constraints; there are no threats of sanctions or promises of material side payments in place in the ARF. As for reputational constraints, clearly a portion of the Chinese decision-making élite (though not the ARF functional specialists in the Ministry of Foreign Affairs) did feel constrained by the impact on China's image as a responsible major power if China were to back out of an increasingly legitimate institution. But it is important to distinguish conceptually (despite the difficulties of doing so empirically) between a concern for reputation and one for image: the former refers to an externally directed desire to develop the perception among observers of an interest in cooperation, but perception for the purposes of benefiting from an imminent, discrete, and obvious exchange. The latter refers to an internally directed desire to meet the more diffuse social-status expectations to accrue more generalized social back-patting benefits. Without this distinction reputational concerns as constraints on defection become unfalsifiable because one could always argue that in the back of the minds of decision-makers is a desire to use a cooperative reputation instrumentally in some exchange somewhere at some time.

The question, of course, is: if the extant constraints that do exist were lifted would China revert to prior behaviour? Suppose at the ISG on CBMs in Beijing in March 1997, the consensus had been that the ARF should no longer ask for voluntary defence or security white papers. A choice-constraints model would suggest we should not expect to see a Chinese white paper of any kind in the future. A more nuanced argument about the

institutional construction of interests would predict the continued production of white papers not just because these ensure that others provide
reassuring information as well, but also because white papers are appropriate behaviours for members of the institution. Obviously we cannot run
this test, except in a counterfactual way, but it is a scientifically valid
question in principle. We could ask whether this norm of transparency is
manifesting itself in other environments that are even less constraining
than the ARF, even in a limited way. There is evidence to suggest it is: the
Chinese nuclear-weapons programme, for instance, for the first time allowed Western government and non-governmental arms control experts to
tour its R&D city in October 1996 as a special event at the tail end of the
Pugwash-connected ISODARCO Arms Control Seminar.

As for reputational constraints, it is unlikely that a short-term concern
for reputational benefits applicable to other specific opportunities for
exchange was the driving force behind China's *continued* (as opposed to
initial) participation in the ARF. No other states, particularly those who
could provide the most concrete costs or benefits to China—the US and
Japan, for example—were linking ARF participation to other areas of cooperation such as trade. Indeed, the US government and congress have been
somewhat ambivalent about the value of the ARF. Rather diffuse image and
status factors—related to the evolving legitimacy of the ARF—were present
after China began participating in the ARF.

The 'new information' explanation is problematic because it under-
estimates the uncertain status of 'new information'. From the constructivist
perspective, information is interpreted and the same information can be
interpreted differently in the context of similar institutional rules and structures. Empirically we know that the same information will be interpreted
differently depending on whether it comes from 'people like us' (the information is more authoritative and persuasive) or comes from a devalued
'other'.[75] Economic transactions, for instance bargaining over price where
people exchange information relating to their preferences and their 'bottom
line', vary dramatically depending on whether or not the parties are
friends—friends offer higher payments and lower prices than strangers.[76]
That is, social context is an important variable in how well information
reduces uncertainty in a transaction, and in which direction this uncertainty is reduced (e.g. clarifying the other as a friend or adversary).

Thus, if China's ARF decision-makers were realpolitik opportunists (that
is, if they believed they were playing a prisoners' dilemma game in some

[75] Kuklinski and Hurley (1996: 127).   [76] Halpern (1997: 835–68).

form in East Asia), new information would be interpreted through these lenses. As I noted earlier, there is solid evidence from China's pronouncements and the interpretations of these by other states in the region that China initially looked upon multilateral institutions with a great deal of scepticism, and that its basic preferences were prisoners' dilemma ones. Now, it is probably true that the initial signals provided by a underinstitutionalized and non-intrusive ARF in 1994 would have been interpreted as non-threatening by realpoliticians. But as the ARF agenda and institution evolved, the signals should have been interpreted with increasing alarm by realpoliticians, since the trend lines were towards issues and procedures that could place some limits on relative military power. Yet, for a small group of China's ARF policy-makers these signals were reinterpreted in less, not more, threatening ways. The fact that this group of policy-makers eventually believed this information *was* reassuring while still expressing concern that others in the policy process, with more realpolitik views of multilateralism, might see this information as less reassuring, suggests that information provided by institutions is often not self-evident. Yet the proto-multilateralists did not enter the ARF with this more sanguine interpretation of this 'new information'. Rather, the interpretation came from socialization inside the ARF.

6. Conclusion: Constructed Institutionalism?

There are a number of implications for institutional theory that arise from the ARF story. First, the mutually causal relationship between institutional design, actor comfort levels, and institutional change in the ARF suggests that institutional theory might usefully accommodate insights from social constructivism. The ARF story illustrates how institutions become more valued over time because they provide information about identities. This information permits a re-evaluation of one's own definition of interests. This is how I take Keohane's comment that institutions develop in a cooperative manner because they allow actors to '*know* their partners, not merely *know* about them'[77]—a statement with which constructivists would have no problem. The ARF case suggests that to figure out how actors come to 'know' each other and change their own beliefs about their interests, even in a limited way, institutional theory needs to focus carefully on the empirics of social interaction: conferencing, dialoguing, and consulting. How

---

[77] Keohane (1995: 163).

do these activities affect actor definitions of the game and where their interests lie?[78]

The ARF case does not undermine liberal arguments that domestic political variables help explain changing state interests inside institutions. But it does suggest that there is a logical symbiotic relationship between change in policy process and change in definitions of interest. Any shifts in the definitions of interests by the small group of Chinese multilateralists in the ARF policy process would not have mattered if they had been shut out of this process or if the military's voice had become the predominant one. Again, however, there is a degree of path-dependence here that complicates the causal process in the creation of the ARF, the emergence of these multilateralists, the effects on Chinese comfort levels, and institutional change in the ARF. Policy was initially in the hands of proto-multilateralists in the Asia Department of the Ministry of Foreign Affairs, because the ARF in 1993 was considered an 'Asian' diplomatic issue but did not fit neatly into the country desk structure of the Department. So it was allocated to the catch-all Comprehensive Division. The rising importance of the ARF, and China's increasing level of activism, provided incentives for the emergent multilateralists to ensure that detailed policy stayed in their hands. The decision in January 1997 to set up a special division devoted entirely to regional security dialogues (thus giving ARF policy a higher formal status than it had in the Comprehensive Division) was probably pushed by the MFA to ensure that it continued to be the predominant voice even as the ARF increasingly touches on the military's concerns. But the ARF specialists' incentive to institutionalize their role in policy further would probably have been lower had these individuals not developed a concept of Chinese interests that focused on the ARF's benefits to Chinese security.

Second, the ARF story suggests that under conditions of uncertainty about the game being played, weakly institutionalized structures with no particular functional, problem-solving solution-seeking mission can none the less be optimal institutions for clarifying the environment. States under conditions of uncertainty do not automatically reach for neo-realist tools.[79]

---

[78] There is, in fact, a vast literature in social psychology on the processes of political and normative persuasion through small-group interaction, and through the manipulation of both material and social rewards and punishments. Contractual institutionalists and social constructivists have, for the most part, ignored this literature—the former perhaps because of the difficulties of dialogue across the rational choice-psychology divide; the latter perhaps because of suspicions about the hardcore positivism of much of experimental social psychology. For examples of this literature see Sears and Funk (1991); Schwarz *et al.* (1991); Cialdini (1984); Gerard and Orive (1987); Barnum (1997); Shelly and Webster (1997).

[79] See also Wallander (1999) for empirical verification of this.

Uncertainty does not dictate unilateral self-help strategies. Status quo states will often want to clarify their environment first through the creation of institutions. This suggests why the international system is plagued by fewer security dilemmas than neo-realists expect.[80] Actors who are unclear about the game being played can, by virtue of the nature of the institution, be socialized into believing the game is the one assumed by the institution. Even if the game is, say, a PD-type environment, the application of an institution appropriate for that game—highly developed and unbiased mechanisms for monitoring and sanctioning—might not be appropriate *if* actors also assume that interests can change. If prisoners' dilemma preferences can be changed, then the optimal institution may be one where participation to the potentially most non-cooperative state is attractive (thus there must be weak or low monitoring and sanctioning mechanisms), but is also iterated, intense, public, and full of statements about appropriate social norms. Since many states do start from the assumption that interests can be changed this would suggest that weak institutions are always a good place to start when players are uncertain about the nature of the game *and* when they suspect the game may be a conflictual one.

Put another way, institutions designed to acquire information about the game being played, although appropriate for an assurance environment (like the ARF), may be able to deal with emergent collaboration problems as well, under specific conditions. If the legitimacy of the institution in the eyes of potential defectors is high, then to challenge the institution itself will carry a high cost. In the ARF case, for instance, the legitimacy of an ASEAN-led ARF is relatively high in the eyes of potential defectors like China and the US. For both this is better than an ARF led by the other, and is better than no ARF at all. Defecting carries a large cost: it signals a normative rejection of multilateralism in Asia-Pacific, which itself is a signal that the state is a potential threat (the game would be clarified as a coercive suasion game). It carries the risk that ASEAN leadership will fail, opening the door to efforts by the other to dominate the remnant institution. These costs ensure that the ASEAN Way remains the ideology of institutional development, even if not the content, and thus ensures the longevity of the institution.

So the ARF as an institution is increasingly legitimate. States are increasingly focusing their multilateral security resources and efforts on the ARF. But their consensus behind the ARF legitimacy has come prior to consensus on many of the details of its functional features and the efficacy

---

[80] Self-described realists are coming to this conclusion as well. See Glaser (1994/5) and Schweller and Priess (1997).

of its actions. This is not what a choice-constraint institutionalist should expect. The legitimacy of the institution should follow from not precede consensus about its efficacy in solving the 'security problem'. This suggests that waiting to determine whether an institution 'works' before according it legitimacy and resources, as US diplomacy is often wont to do, can be mistaken. An institution can not work unless it is highly legitimate. It is hard to imagine that China could have ever offered to co-host an ISG-like forum on CBMs prior to its experience in the ARF.

In a sense, constructivist-oriented institutionalists who believe institutions and interests are mutually constitutive can, by dint of their theory, be more patient about institutional design than the choice-constraint theorists. The latter have to determine what game is being played before they can determine an optimal design. This can be a frustrating task in the policy world, especially once one leaves the comfort of two-player game metaphors and enters a world of twenty-one players with vast discrepancies in histories, interests, material power capabilities, and issue-specific authority. All of this suggests that the static definition of 'functional efficiency' used by many institutionalists (e.g. that there is one institutional arrangement that is conducive to one pareto-optimal equilibrium) needs rethinking in more dynamic ways. Perhaps functional efficiency should be reconceived as the institutional *design* and *process* that is most likely to alter actor interests in ways that produce a 'game' that maximizes utility among all possible (or likely) games. Put another way, an efficient institution is one that is most likely to alter interests in ways that produce the most cooperative environment for the actors concerned (whether a collective security environment, or an intra-alliance environment).

Third, even weakly institutionalized structures can create conditions for dialogue, persuasion, and socialization that lead to higher levels of institutionalization. Institutionalist theory needs to develop a fuller understanding of socialization whereby preferences are altered, not just strategies closed off, if only because actors often explicitly try to use institutions to change others' preferences.[81] This socialization process is critical for understanding how focal points and points of agreement are created and change. If actors form institutions because they do not know what the game is, then the process of developing common knowledge about the game is in fact a socialization process.[82] Common knowledge (a game-theoretic term for social or cultural knowledge) is what creates focal points and points of agreement. Interaction can create crisper expectations about who others are

---

[81] Krasner (1983*b*); Caporaso (1993).   [82] Berger and Luckman (1966); Alker (1996).

and what they want. But this is not just a process of bringing static identities into clearer focus. Rather it is a process of changing these identities as well (or at least, of trying to change them). Put another way, the process of clarifying the game is sometimes a process of changing it.

What about the question in the title? Myths are stories whose elements of truth are exaggerated to bind people to a common, simple, easily reproduced group identity. This identity allows the group to cohere and evolve. The ASEAN Way is mythic in the sense that its elements allowed states to converge on an agreement that established an extremely low level of institutionalization with a very non-instrusive agenda. These institutional features, in turn, created a process of social interaction that appears to have allowed further institutional movement. What makes the ASEAN Way mythic is that the movement it has generated, if present trends continue, promises to negate it, as the ARF converges, tentatively, with European-like models.

Perhaps even this is too bold a statement. This article draws on only three years of data points. Information about the intentions of states provided through interaction in the ARF may be sending signals that states are in fact in an emergent assurance game. But this is only one source of information. Information coming from outside the ARF—from potentially volatile bilateral relations such as the US–China or China–Japan relationships—is less consistent with this message. What could unravel the evolution of the ARF, this delicate process of clarifying the environment as an assurance game, is extra-ARF conflict, for instance another round of Chinese missiles at Taiwan or a clash of Sino-Vietnamese naval forces in the South China Sea. Then 'informational clarification' could convince states that the game is a conflictual one, or a game requiring coercive collective responses. If this were to occur, the ARF would not survive along its present trajectory. In this sense, the ARF is not shielded from realpolitik clashes of power and interest. But it is fair to say that the the existence of the institution itself has made this kind of behaviour less legitimate.

CONCLUSIONS

Robert O. Keohane, Helga Haftendorn,
and Celeste A. Wallander

International security institutions are 'imperfect unions'. They often do not have highly elaborate and systematic organizational features, they nearly always evolve and change in ways unanticipated by the states that create and support them, and they do not always elicit perfect compliance from self-interested states. Sometimes states ignore the norms and procedures embodied in these institutions, sometimes states' interests diverge too much to permit agreement on how these institutions might be used to cope with security problems, and sometimes institutional forms themselves hinder effective cooperation. Without a doubt, power and selfish national interests remain important in security relations.

Nevertheless, this volume shows that security issues in the modern world are highly institutionalized. As both the most highly institutionalized and most successful multilateral alliance in history, NATO holds a prominent place in the history of the cold war. It is now being transformed, as Celeste Wallander and Robert Keohane argue, into a security management institution designed to cope with risk rather than threat. Christopher Daase shows that United Nations peacekeeping emerged during the cold war as a set of conventions—a 'prototype'—for coping with peripheral conflicts. It has been extended to internal conflicts, not entirely successfully, since 1989. As Louise Richardson demonstrates, in the years after 1815 the Concert of Europe carried out similar functions to those performed by contemporary international organizations, providing access to decision-making by states not directly involved in a conflict, offering assurance to members about each others' intentions, and requiring conformity to institutional norms as a condition for acceptance as a member in good standing. As the larger number of security institutions—including OSCE and ARF as well as NATO and the UN—suggests, it would be wrong to believe that security is a non-institutionalized domain of anarchy, contrasting with political economy.

On the contrary, contemporary security politics cannot be coherently de-scribed without taking into account international security institutions.

What does it mean to think about security in institutional terms? This book has argued that institutional theory can illuminate security issues. The first contribution of institutional theory is to help explain the character-istics of institutions and how they change over time. Institutions can be negotiated at an international conference, pursuing purposes that are explicitly sought by representatives of governments, non-governmental organizations, and other actors. Such institutions, which include the United Nations and NATO, can be viewed as *designed*. Other institutions, however, emerge in response to unanticipated situations: as Daase argues with re-spect to UN peacekeeping, these institutions may evolve spontaneously as conventions. A key point, however, is that whether institutions are created by negotiation or emerge incrementally from practice, they typically change over time in ways that were originally unanticipated. New situations arise that demand action, and participants perceive existing institutions as adaptable to deal with these contingencies. Institutions evolve in a path-dependent way, in the sense that previous contingencies create (or fail to create) institutional capabilities that alter the incentives facing key actors, including states, international bureaucracies, and non-governmental or-ganizations. The ongoing transformation of NATO from alliance to security management institution provides a case in point.[1]

Institutional change takes place in part as a result of such changing in-centives. The core of institutional theory specifies how institutional charac-teristics affect strategies of states, and therefore outcomes. The key insight of institutional theory is that the rules and practices of institutions can affect the choices faced by states and their incentives to select one alternative or another. Institutions set agendas and define who has access to forums for decision-making. Their rules may provide focal points for coordination when many solutions are possible in principle but cooperation requires that states agree on which one to use. Institutions may reduce uncertainty about other members' present behaviour and likely future actions, and they may

---

[1] We do not know of any situations in which a security management institution evolved into an alliance, becoming exclusive and threat-oriented after having been inclusive and risk-oriented. Such a change could presumably only occur when the threatening state left the organization, or was expelled. One could imagine the League of Nations having become an alliance of Britain, France, and Russia against Germany in the late 1930s, had Britain and France not followed a policy of appeasement. The United Nations seemed in 1950 to be becoming an alliance against the Sino-Soviet bloc, with its refusal to seat representatives of the People's Republic and UN-sponsored intervention in Korea to stop the North Korean invasion (assisted by the Soviet Union). But neither the League nor the UN became an alliance in the end.

also reduce the costs of negotiating and enforcing agreements. Occasionally, international institutions exert power over states—as the United Nations did with respect to Iraq in the wake of the Gulf War—but more often they enable states better to achieve their own objectives through co-operation.[2]

Understanding how international institutions affect state behaviour requires clarity about the relationship between ends and means for states. Concepts such as 'interest' are inherently ambiguous.[3] In our Introduction we used the metaphor of a long 'ends-means chain' linking the most fundamental goals of states with a series of means, which themselves become goals at the next level. We used this metaphor to distinguish between 'preferences'—fundamental 'tastes' associated with a particular society and form of government that persist over time—and 'strategies' to realize those preferences. The United States could be said to have a preference for peaceful relations with other democracies based on the principles of no changes in the territorial status quo and freedom of movement world-wide for civilians pursuing peaceful commercial or personal objectives. As a fundamental means to achieving such an end, the United States may seek to remain the world's only superpower. At a more specific level, United States strategies to achieve its fundamental objectives may include such diverse activities as promoting general adherence to neo-liberal principles of economic exchange, organizing UN action against Iraq's 1990 invasion of Kuwait, enacting unilateral economic sanctions, or even engaging in unilateral military intervention.

Institutionalist theory based on broad assumptions of rational behaviour argues that institutions can affect state *strategies*. It takes fundamental preferences as given. The logic is to ascertain whether, given unchanging preferences, institutional change affects the incentives that states have to behave in specific ways. No attention is paid in this formulation to changes in preferences. Indeed, both institutionalist theory and the economic theory to which it is deeply indebted, are reluctant to explain behavioural change on the basis of changes in preferences, since it seems all too easy after the fact to ascribe behavioural change to some *unobserved* changes in tastes.

However, it would be hard to deny that the preferences of states can change, sometimes dramatically. For instance, changing social attitudes in Britain and France after the Second World War altered these countries'

---

[2] For a recent review, see Lake (1996).

[3] In *After Hegemony*, Robert Keohane referred to institutions changing state interests, an argument that has been often misinterpreted. In the terms used in this volume, his argument was that institutions could change state strategies, not that they altered state preferences.

preferences about colonialism; and the end of legal discrimination on the basis of race in the United States, during the 1950s and 1960s, shifted United States preferences about international human rights conventions. German preferences about territorial acquisitions and the use of force changed dramatically after the defeat of Nazism, and the most fundamental objective of the government in Moscow—that the Soviet Union be preserved —disappeared almost overnight in 1991. These changes are not accounted for by institutional theory, although whether they are explained better by changes in domestic politics or by theories emphasizing the social construction of norms remains contested.[4]

This conclusion is organized around three themes. We first consider how our studies of security institutions inform the understanding of institutional characteristics and change. Second, we focus on the findings on the effects of institutions on security strategies. Finally, we return in more depth to the issue of changes in preferences, briefly introduced above. Rationalist and constructivist perspectives offer different insights on these problems— insights that are in some ways conflicting, but which may be able to be fruitfully combined.

1. Institutional Characteristics and Change

In thinking about the characteristics of institutions, it is important at the outset to differentiate their central, defining norms and principles from their secondary norms. As John Ruggie pointed out some time ago, such an analysis enables the observer to distinguish changes within a regime from change of regimes.[5] In his chapter Henning Riecke uses a similar distinction, between principled and procedural rules, to analyse United States actions with respect to the Non-Proliferation (NPT) regime. In the case of North Korea, he argues, the United States broke procedural rules but upheld principled ones by entering into a Framework Agreement with the People's Republic. In his analysis of UN peacekeeping, Daase argues that the fundamental principles of peacekeeping changed in the 1990s, including those of non-use of force and of consent and impartiality. The result was a transformation of peacekeeping towards an essentially different set of practices, involving peace enforcement by regional groups not under the sole authority of the United Nations.

---

[4] Katzenstein (1996); Moravcsik (1997).   [5] Ruggie (1983).

Understanding the characteristics of international institutions, and how they change, requires an examination of the relationship between the function to be served by the institution (from the standpoint of powerful states) and its form; and how external forces and processes internal to the institution interact over time.

Characteristics: form follows function

A 'first cut' at understanding institutional characteristics is that form will follow function. Some institutions will be designed to serve particular purposes sought by powerful states, given the nature of their environment; others will evolve in ways that are shaped by such purposes. The papers in Part I emphasize this relationship. Wallander and Keohane develop a functional framework that links features of the environment, such as problem durability and issue density, to the institutionalization of security coalitions. Richardson demonstrates that the form taken by the Concert of Europe—for example, the Congress system—reflected agreement (or disagreement) on the functions to be performed by the institution. Carsten Tams argues that conflicting state policies with respect to a European Security and Defense Identity (ESDI) reflect differences of view about the function that ESDI should perform.

Other papers in the volume also echo this theme. For instance, Helga Haftendorn shows how the changing institutional repertoire of the 'Quad' reflected the changing functions that it performed for its members: Germany, the United States, Britain, and France. Iain Johnston discusses how the low degree of institutionalization of the ASEAN Regional Forum (ARF) reflected its major function of bringing China into regional discussions; since China was extremely wary of formal institutions, this function determined the form that the ARF would take.

Identifying the functions to be performed by a security institution and then interpreting its form as a response is reasonable enough, but does not by itself provide a basis for generalization and systematic comparison. Each function, and each form, may appear unique; and it is hardly surprising that they are connected. Furthermore, the argument in a given case can easily be circular, if the observer simply infers function from form. In that case, there would be no way to disconfirm the proposition that function follows form. Generalization and systematic comparison require categories that can used for a variety of cases.

A step towards generalization and theoretical analysis can be taken by recognizing that security issues are inherently characterized by uncertainty.

Uncertainty is not always the key obstacle to cooperation, but it is always present. Hence, information is of critical importance to the actors in security politics; and in so far as international institutions can either provide information about others' behaviour, or increase one's own credibility, they can be valuable. Institutions—whether dealing with security or not—are created largely to enable states and other actors to reduce or at least to cope more effectively with uncertainty.[6] Information need be neither symmetrical nor provided solely by institutions, as Riecke shows in the case of the US influence on nuclear non-proliferation. But symmetrical and institutional sources of information are more likely to be seen as credible and unbiased (all things being equal), and therefore to be effective.

Uncertainty takes different forms in different situations. In the Introduction we discussed four different types of situation, each with a different type of uncertainty. Collaboration games such as Prisoners' Dilemma are characterized by uncertainty about whether players will keep their commitments. In coordination problems, however, the uncertainty is about whether any agreement can be negotiated; once it has been reached, compliance with commitments is fairly well assured. In suasion problems, the uncertainty concerns whether the state with a dominant strategy to cooperate can prevent others from free-riding through linkage. Finally, for players that view a situation as one of assurance, the only uncertainty is whether other players both share this assessment and are confident that their own partners will cooperate.

The Concert of Europe could be seen as a response to a collaboration game among the major powers: each could have a preference for remaining part of the Concert (others would cooperate by regarding one as a great power entitled to special privileges), while pursuing its own unilateral policies. The Concert when it operated well—as in the separation of Belgium from the Netherlands in 1831—provided incentives for members to moderate their policies in return for maintaining their status in the 'club'. As described by Haftendorn, the Quad began as an informal response to coordination problems, but became more institutionalized as the allies faced a collaboration problem in the late 1950s: risks existed that members would defect from agreed-upon policies.[7]

UN peacekeeping also combined elements of collaboration with coordination games: members sought to coordinate either on joint action in peripheral trouble spots or on no action at all. Sometimes there may have been an incentive to defect—to let others take the burdens while reaping

---

[6] Keohane (1984: chs. 4–6).   [7] Haftendorn, in Ch. 7, pp. 168–171.

benefits themselves—but the more crucial negotiations were often about whether to intervene collectively at all.

NATO's practices with respect to Germany's increased power during the years of the cold war, in contrast, could be seen as responses to an assurance situation: Germany wanted to cooperate with its allies but needed to assure them of its benign intentions. Likewise, the Conference on Security and Co-operation in Europe (CSCE) sought to reassure states in Central and Eastern Europe that they would face a benign security environment; and ARF sought to assure Asian states about each other's intentions and capabilities. Finally, United States demands for 'burden-sharing' from its NATO allies reflected a worry that it was engaged in a suasion game where its preference for defending Europe could be used by European allies as an excuse for 'free-riding'.

As Lisa Martin has emphasized, the institutional requirements for cooperative action differ depending on the kind of game that is involved.[8] Where there are incentives for defection, as in collaboration and suasion games, institutional arrangements may have to be quite strong, so that defection is deterred, or at least detected and punished. But where the goal is coordination or assurance, a lower degree of institutionalization may suffice. This perspective helps us to understand why NATO was much more highly institutionalized than the CSCE/OSCE or the ARF.

Change: limits and openings

In shaping institutional change, external and internal factors interact. Institutional change is limited by external constraints. For instance, as Riecke shows, the Non-Proliferation Treaty (NPT) regime is strongly affected by the actions of the United States, whether within the regime framework or outside of it. Britain's special relationship with the United States, and its distinctive history, affect its willingness to participate in ESDI, and therefore the shape that ESDI takes. The cold war disabled much UN peacekeeping as a result of superpower rivalry. All international institutions are limited by the preferences, strategies, and power of states.

External limiting factors not only imply that institutionalization will sometimes be modest, but that from the standpoint of regime effectiveness, high institutionalization is not necessarily optimal. There were too many fundamental normative disagreements between Great Britain and the eastern monarchies in the Concert of Europe for the Congress system to

---

[8] Martin (1992*b*).

work well, as Richardson shows. Any highly institutionalized system for congresses that could authorize joint intervention to suppress liberal movements would have been opposed by Great Britain. The Quad, as described by Haftendorn, thrived as a very quiet institution, whose growth was constrained by its members' focus on consultation with respect to Berlin and Germany, and their desire not to infringe on NATO. The ASEAN Regional Forum has only been able to exist and have some impact at a very low level of institutionalization, in view of China's resistance to a clear institutional structure or a high profile for this organization.

More interesting than the fact that international institutions are limited by the power, preferences, and strategies of states, are the *openings* that sometimes appear for institutional innovation. The most dramatic instance of such innovation is how UN peacekeeping evolved, under pressure especially of Israeli-Arab crises, to a well-understood convention, albeit one that was not foreseen in the United Nations Charter. The outbreak of a serious war that both the United States and the Soviet Union wished to stop, provided an opportunity for Lester Pearson and Dag Hammersjköld to enhance UN peacekeeping capabilities. Another example is provided by NATO, which continues its transformation: from a pure alliance in its earliest years, to a hybrid alliance/security management institution after Germany's incorporation, towards a post-cold war security management institution after 1990, as Wallander and Keohane argue. Finally, Haftendorn clearly shows that the Quad had both an engagement and a confidence-building effect that increased its value to its members, and thus their reliance on it.

Institutions can also facilitate structural changes. Christian Tuschhoff argues that NATO institutions made it easier for Germany's partners to accept the increases in its power that occurred as it regained economic strength and political self-confidence after its defeat in the Second World War. Non-institutional factors contributed to German power, but institutions helped make that new situation a stable equilibrium rather than a source of instability. Similarly, in the years after 1815, the Concert of Europe helped France regain its status as a great power, without alarming its former enemies.

2. The Impact of Institutions on Strategies

In so far as students of international security issues have focused on institutions at all, they have emphasized the role of alliances. Alliances have multiple functions, as Paul Schroeder has shown,[9] but they are in large part designed to affect the strategies of non-members: to deter them from attacking members of the alliance, to intimidate them into making concessions, or to prevent them from using threats of force for political gain. The chapters in this volume do not have much to add to the literature on how alliances affect the strategies of non-members. Instead, the focus here is on how security institutions—alliances or not—affect relationships among their own members.

Christopher Gelpi provides systematic and dramatic evidence about the impact of alliances on mediation of international disputes. He finds that the interaction between a mediator's alliance ties and its military capacity strongly affects the success of mediation attempts: the most successful mediators in international crises are great powers allied to one of the disputants. Furthermore, the evidence indicates that this success results principally from these mediators putting pressure on *their own allies* in the course of the dispute, rather than from the mediator siding effectively with its ally against the other state. Alliances seem to enhance the effectiveness of mediation strategies, when pursued through pressure on states' own partners.

More consistent with the intentions of institution-builders are the assurance functions of security institutions. Security management institutions, as defined by Wallander and Keohane, are inclusive, designed to deal with risk among members. In substantial measure, they constitute responses to games of assurance. The Concert of Europe performed assurance functions, as argued by Richardson. Tuschhoff and Haftendorn discuss how NATO and the Quad, respectively, performed assurance functions with respect to the rise of German power after 1955. The CSCE was designed to assure governments and peoples in Central and Eastern Europe about the stability of their region. And the principal task of the ARF seems to be the attempt to assure Asian countries about each other's intentions, with special reference to China.

Institutions, of course, do not always have the effects on strategies for which their proponents hope. UN peacekeeping has not led to systematic, predictable UN-run intervention in internal conflicts; indeed, the United Nations has often avoided involvement in situations, especially in Africa, that were quite as horrible in human terms as those cases where peacekeeping forces were employed. The European Security and Defence Identity has been more a ghostly shadow than a robust child, as a result of differences

---

[9] Schroeder (1994a).

in preferences and strategies among major European states. And the non-proliferation regime, while holding together, has done so only in conjunction with unilateral actions—sometimes supportive, sometimes destructive—by the United States.

3. Rationalism, Constructivism, and the Impact of Institutions on Preferences

Realism and neo-realism have made enduring contributions to the study of international relations. Realism's emphasis on 'anarchy' (the absence of common governance) and on the power and preferences of states remains valid at the end of the twentieth century. Concerns about physical security against attack and the threat of attack have not vanished from history after the cold war, although they have taken new forms. World order, new or old, remains elusive. As a series of cautionary tales, the lore of realism needs to remain part of our consciousness.

Yet realism does not constitute a satisfactory theory of world politics. The problem is not so much that realism failed to predict the end of the cold war: neither did any other theory, and in any case, the collapse of the Soviet Union was a classic conjunctural event, resulting from the coming together of separate developments.[10] A more serious theoretical failing of realism is that it is underspecified, failing to make clear and falsifiable predictions. But that deficiency is also shared by its competitors. Rationalist theory, drawing on game theory, shows that multiple equilibria are typical of interesting situations in world politics. Constructivists approaches have eschewed prediction for *post hoc* interpretation.

The more serious inadequacy of realism as compared with rationalism and constructivism is its inattention to issues of information and institutions. Realism argues that state behaviour is fundamentally determined by the interaction between interests and power capabilities. For realism, material interests reflect preferences for survival and sometimes for more power for its own sake, along with power-aggregating strategies to attain these preferences. But power is an ambiguous term, as generations of political scientists have discovered. The ability of A to influence B does not bear a direct relationship to the resources that A can bring to bear on the issue, but also depends on the opportunity costs facing both parties, the common knowledge they have about the situation, including each other's

---

[10] See Hirschman (1970), on conjunctural events and their unpredictability.

preferences, and other aspects of the context.[11] Game theory has shown how crucial information is to any strategic interaction: unless information conditions are specified, it is impossible to make valid predictions about behaviour.[12] Knowing preferences and power resources is difficult enough; but even if we knew them for a given situation, we would not be able to anticipate what would happen.

Rationalist theory has therefore moved beyond the confines of realism. It focuses not only on the structure of power in 'anarchy' but on strategic interaction, given different power, preferences, and information conditions. One result of this emphasis on information is to focus on institutions, since institutions provide information of various kinds to actors. In this sense, institutional theory incorporates much of realism but supersedes it by offering a richer specification of the institutional and informational environments within which strategic interaction takes place.[13]

Yet rationalist theory has the key limitation that it does not seek to explain preferences, or (as we have defined them) fundamental tastes. They are a starting-point for analysis, taken as given exogenously. Assuming fixed preferences is a sort of self-denying ordinance for rationalist theory: it forces the analyst to look for variations in the environment, associated with variations in costs and benefits, as explanations for variations in strategies. This precept has been productive. Since untestable claims that 'preferences must have changed' are unacceptable, analysts have been compelled to look elsewhere—in institutional arrangements and information conditions, for example—for explanations of changes in strategies. When analysts argue that fundamental preferences change—as Peters does with respect to German policy and CSCE and Johnston does about the ASEAN Regional Forum—the rationalist alternative constitutes an obvious counterhypothesis: that only strategies are changing, in response to shifts in the environment that change the patterns of costs and benefits. For the story of 'changing preferences' to be convincing, it has to be shown that the more modest 'changing strategies' account fails to explain the behaviour under scrutiny.

However, state preferences may fundamentally change over time, as we assumed at the outset of this chapter. Political science needs a better way to understand how fundamental preferences change. A plausible place to begin such an exploration is to acknowledge that human beings construct social reality: that some features of reality depend on the relationship between the feature itself and human perception of it. In the United States,

---

11 March (1966); Baldwin (1979).   12 Morrow (1994: esp. ch. 8).
13 Keohane (1989c).

green pieces of paper engraved with the heads of famous Americans count as money. It is an *institutional fact*, therefore, that these pieces of paper can be exchanged for valuable goods and services. Institutional facts are reflections of 'a collectively recognized status to which a function is attached'— as in the example that a dollar counts as a means to buy the daily *New York Times* in Boston. And which objects perform the functions in question is a matter of convention.[14]

Institutional facts can change not because any material condition shifts, but because beliefs change. Institutional facts that have been dramatically altered in the past include chattel slavery, colonialism, and (in many societies) the legal subordination of women. The Soviet Union was an institutional fact in the 1980s, but collapsed almost overnight when state leaders were no longer willing to use terror to keep it in place, and people, hating the system and recognizing this new reality, acted to bring it down.[15] Nazi Germany was an institutional fact, which had immense consequences for the peoples of Europe; the Federal Republic is a very different kind of institutional fact, with very different principles, functions, and status hierarchies—and very different implications for its neighbours.

In the terms we have used above, political systems viewed as institutional facts define preferences. Societies with different functions, practices, and status hierarchies develop different preferences about their relationships with their neighbours. We know, for instance, that democracies behave very differently from non-democracies in international relations, quite in contradiction to the precepts of realism.

What is less clear is how to account for these variations in the preferences of states. One account simply extends rationalistic and institutional theory to the domestic level: to understand state preferences, in this view, one has to understand domestic politics.[16] This way of viewing the problem assumes that *individual* preferences do not change (consistent with rationalistic theory) but observes that 'state preferences' are only aggregates of those of individuals. Hence 'state preferences' really represent the results of strategies pursued by individuals, typically through groups and organizations, at the domestic level. The rationalistic research programme should, in this view, jettison the unsustainable assumption that states have preferences or act rationally, but transfer the basic principles of rationalistic analysis to the individual level, focusing particularly on domestic politics.

---

[14] Searle (1995: esp. 37–51).
[15] On the Soviet Union as an institutional fact, see Searle (1995: 92); on cascade effects as a result of changes in willingness to use force, see Kuran (1995).
[16] Milner (1997); Moravcsik (1997).

In contrast, constructivist theory seeks to show that cognitive or subjective factors are ultimately responsible for variation in behaviour. As John Ruggie says, 'At bottom, constructivism concerns the issue of human consciousness, the role it plays in international relations, and the implications for the logic and methods of social inquiry of taking it seriously.'[17] People are seen as following not merely a 'logic of consequences' but a 'logic of appropriateness'. They construct their own realities from a mixture of observation and normative preferences; they hold principled beliefs, which affect their behaviour; they follow precedents and rules-of-thumb; and they seek to construct institutions that will facilitate implementation of actions reflecting those beliefs.[18]

The differences between rationalism and constructivism are not as stark as they are sometimes portrayed. Both approaches are incomplete, as the study of conventions (exemplified in Daase's essay on UN peacekeeping) indicates. Conventions evolve as a result of incremental processes that combine elements of calculation with shared beliefs, analogies, and expectations based in part on moral conceptions.[19] Even if participants in these processes behave rationally, knowing that they are rational will not enable us to explain their behaviour, unless we know a lot more about the context within which they operate. Game theory recognizes the existence of multiple equilibria (in the folk theorem) and the importance of the assumption of common knowledge; the opening for constructivists comes not by denying that people often behave rationally, but by trying to understand how people's beliefs enable them to concert their expectations and reach solutions to problems where no game-theoretic equilibria exist. Institutionalism and constructivism also are linked in the importance they attribute to how states value institutions, especially for their role in making states' behaviour accountable to one another. As Haftendorn and Johnston demonstrate, patterns of mutual understanding and respect evolve over time—as states are socialized within an institution—and influence future behaviour. States chose to cooperate even in cases when a short-term rational cost-benefit analysis (as the US might have made after the end of the cold war, withdrawing from the entanglements of NATO) would have advised them to prefer unilateral to multilateral actions. Rationalism and constructivism begin with divergent premisses, but they are complementary.

We will not even begin to resolve the issues between rationalism and

[17] Ruggie (1998: 35).
[18] Katzenstein (1996); March and Olsen (1998); Finnemore (1996).
[19] Sugden (1989).

constructivism here, much less to construct a synthesis. Most of this book is thoroughly rationalist, seeking to show that institutional theory is essential to understand contemporary security issues, yet in some chapters a constructivist approach is used to generate additional insights. In this final discussion we seek to emphasize our view that in the future the most interesting conversations will not be between realism and rationalist institutionalism, but between a broader rationalist-institutionalist research programme, extending downward to domestic politics and laterally to transnational and transgovernmental relations, and the emerging constructivist approach. Crucial to this debate will be the question of how essential it is for understanding variation and change in world politics to understand variations in human consciousness, given a set of material conditions. We hope that in the decades to come, this debate will enrich our understanding of institutional facts and norms, just as the realist-institutionalist debate has illuminated the impact of information and institutions on world politics.

REFERENCES

Acharya, Amitav (1996). 'The New Frontier of Multilateralism: Canada and the ASEAN Regional Forum' (paper prepared for the Canadian International Development Agency, Nov.).

Akten (1994). *Akten zur Auswärtigen Politik der Bundesrepublik Deutschland*, i. *1. Januar bis 31. Mai 1963*, ed. im Auftrag des Auswärtigen Amts vom Institut für Zeitgeschichte (Munich: Oldenbourg).

Akten (1995). *Akten zur Auswärtigen Politik der Bundesrepublik Deutschland, 1964*, ii. *1. Juli bis 31. Dezember*, ed. im Auftrag des Auswärtigen Amts vom Institut für Zeitgeschichte (Munich: Oldenbourg).

Albrecht, Ulrich (1992). *Die Abwicklung der DDR: Die '2+4' Verhandlungen. Ein Insiderbericht* (Opladen: Westdeutscher Verlag).

Albright, David (1995). 'The Russian Iranian Reactor Deal', *Nonproliferation Review*, 2/3: 49–51.

Alker, Hayward (1996). 'Beneath Tit for Tat', in Hayward Alker, *Rediscoveries and Reformulations: Humanistic Methodologies for International Studies* (Cambridge University Press), 303–31.

Allison, Graham T., Ashton B. Carter, Steven E. Miller, and Philip Zelikow (1993). *Cooperative Threat Reduction: From Pledges to Deeds* (CSIA Studies in International Security, 2; Cambridge, Mass.: Center for Science and International Affairs).

Anderson, Jeffrey J., and John B. Goodman (1993). 'Mars or Minerva? A United Germany in a Post-Cold War Europe', in Robert O. Keohane, Joseph S. Nye, and Stanley Hoffmann (eds.), *After the Cold War: International Institutions and State Strategies in Europe, 1989–1991* (Cambridge, Mass., and London: Harvard University Press), 23–62.

Anderson, Matthew (1979). 'Russia and the Eastern Question 1821–1841', in Alan Sked (ed.), *Europe's Balance of Power, 1815–1845* (London: Macmillan), 79–97.

Antolik, Michael (1994). 'The ASEAN Regional Forum: The Spirit of Constructive Engagement', *Contemporary Southeast Asia*, 16/2 (Sept.): 117–36.

Archer, Clive (1993). *International Organizations* (London and New York: Routledge).

ARF (1995*a*). 'Chairman's Statement of the Second ASEAN Regional Forum' (Brunei, 1 Aug.).

ARF (1995*b*). 'The ASEAN Regional Forum: A Concept Paper' (mimeographed statement).

ARF (1996*a*). 'Chairman's Statement of the Third ASEAN Regional Forum' (Jakarta, 23 July).

ARF (1996*b*). 'Concept Paper of Co-Chairs: ARF Intersessional Support Group on Confidence Building Measures' (Jakarta, 22 July).

Arms Control Association (1993). 'The Administration's Non-Proliferation and Export Control Policy', *Arms Control Today*, 23/9: 9–13.

Art, Robert J. (1994). 'A Defensible Defense: America's Grand Strategy after the Cold War', *International Security*, 15: 5–53.

Arthur, W. Brian (1994). *Increasing Returns and Path Dependence in the Economy* (Ann Arbor: The University of Michigan Press).

Ashley, Richard K. (1988). Untying the Sovereign State: A Double Reading of the Anarchy Problematique', *Millennium*, 17: 227–62.

Asmus, Ronald D., Richard L. Kugler, and F. Stephen Larrabee (1993). 'Building a New NATO', *Foreign Affairs*, 72: 28–40.

Assembly of Western European Union (1995). *New Trends in North American Countries' Foreign Policy and their Implications for Transatlantic Co-operation in Security and Defense Matters, with Particular Reference to the United States*, Report submitted on behalf of the Political Committee by Lord Finsberg, Rapporteur, Document 1457 (15 May 1995).

Auswärtiges Amt (1991) (ed.). *Deutsche Außenpolitik 1990/91. Auf dem Weg zu einer Europäischen Friedensordnung: Ein Dokumentation* (Bonn: Auswärtiges Amt).

——(1995). *Außenpolitik der Bundesrepublik Deutschland: Dokumente von 1949–1994.* (Cologne: Verlag Wissenschaft und Politik).

Axelrod, Robert (1984). *The Evolution of Cooperation* (New York: Basic Books).

——and Robert O. Keohane (1985). 'Achieving Cooperation under Anarchy: Strategies and Institutions', *World Politics*, 38: 226–54.

Bailes, Alyson J. K. (1995). 'Sécurité européenne: Le Point de vue britannique', *Politique étrangère*, 60: 453–71.

Bailey, Kathleen C. (1993). *Strengthening Nuclear Non-Proliferation* (Boulder, Colo.: Westview).

——(1995). 'The Nuclear Deal with North Korea: Is the Glass Half Empty or Half Full?', *Comparative Strategy*, 14: 137–48.

Baldauf, Jörg F. (1984). 'Implementing Flexible Response: The US, Germany, and NATO's Conventional Forces', Ph.D. thesis. Massachusetts Institute of Technology, Cambridge, Mass.

Baldwin, David A. (1979). 'Power Analysis and World Politics: New Trends vs. Old Tendencies', *World Politics*, 31: 161–94.

Barnett, Michael (1995). 'Partners in Peace? The UN, Regional Organizations, and Peace-Keeping', *Review of International Studies*, 21: 411–33.

Barnum, Christopher (1997). 'A Reformulated Social Identity Theory', in *Advances in Group Processes*, xiv (New York: JAI Press Inc.), 29–57.

Bartelson, Jens (1995). *A Genealogy of Sovereignty* (Cambridge: Cambridge University Press).

Bartsch, Sebastian, and Axel Sauder (1994). 'Die rechtlichen Grundlagen der ausländischen Truppenstationierung in Deutschland im Wandel der politischen

Rahmenbedingungen', in Gunther Hellmann (ed.), *Alliierte Präsenz und deutsche Einheit: Die politischen Folgen militärischer Macht* (Baden-Baden: Nomos), 127–54.

Bennett, D. Scott, and Allan Stam (1996). 'How Long has this been Going on: The Duration of Interstate Wars, 1816–1985', *American Political Science Review*, 90 (June): 239–57.

Berger, Peter, and Thomas Luckman (1966). *The Social Construction of Reality* (New York: Anchor Books).

Bercovitch, Jacob, Ted Anagnoson, and Donnette Wille (1991). 'Conceptual Issues and Empirical Trends in the Study of Successful Mediation', *Journal of Peace Research*, 28(1):

Berkovitch, Peter, and Allison Houston (1996). 'The Study of Mediation: Theoretical Issues and Empirical Evidence', in J. Bercovitch (ed.), *Resolving International Conflicts* (Boulder, Colo.: Lynne Rienner), 7–18.

Berry, William E., Jr. (1995). *North Korea's Nuclear Program: The Clinton Administration's Response*. Institute for International Security Studies, US Air Force Academy, Colorado (INSS Occasional Paper, 3, Proliferation Series).

Betts, Richard K. (1992). 'Systems for Peace or Causes of War? Collective Security, Arms Control, and the New Europe', *International Security*, 17: 5–44.

Biermann, Wolfgang (1995). 'Old UN Peacekeeping Principles and New Conflicts: Some Ideas to Reduce the Troubles of Post-Cold War Peace Missions', *European Security*, 4: 55–70.

Biersteker, Thomas J., and Cynthia Weber (1996) (eds.). *State Sovereignty as Social Construction* (Cambridge: Cambridge University Press).

Birgisson, Karl T. (1993). 'United Nations Special Committee on the Balkans', in William J. Durch (ed.), *The Evolution of UN Peacekeeping: Case Studies and Comparative Analysis* (New York: St Martin's Press), 77–83.

Blake, Robert (1967). *Disraeli* (New York: St Martin's Press).

Blank, Stephen J. (1994). *Proliferation and Nonproliferation in the Ukraine: Implications for European and U.S. Security* (Carlisle Barracks, Pa.: Security Strategic Studies Institute, US Army War College).

Bowett, Derek W. (1964). *United Nations Forces: A Legal Study* (New York: Praeger).

Bozo, Frederic (1992). 'French Security Policy and the New European Order', in Colin McInnes (ed.), *Security and Strategy in the New Europe* (London and New York: Routledge), 197–216.

Brand, Christoph-M. (1993). *Souveränität für Deutschland: Grundlagen, Entstehungsgeschichte und Bedeutung des Zwei-plus-Vier-Vertrages vom 12. September 1990* (Cologne: Wissenschaft und Politik).

Brecher, Michael, and Jonathan Wilkenfeld (1996). *International Crisis Behavior Project* (Ann Arbor: Inter-University Consortium for Political and Social Research).

Bridge, F. R., and Roger Bullen (1980). *The Great Powers and the European States System 1815–1914* (London: Longman).

Brouillet, Alain (1988). 'Mediation as a Technique of Dispute Settlement: Appraisal and Prospects', in Ramesh Thakur (ed.), *International Conflict Resolution* (Boulder, Colo.: Westview).

Brown, Michael E. (1995). 'The Flawed Logic of NATO Expansion', *Survival*, 37: 34–52.

Brzezinski, Zbigniew (1995). 'A Plan for Europe', *Foreign Affairs*, 74: 26–42.

—— Brent Scowcroft, and Richard Murphy (1997). 'Differentiating Containment', *Foreign Affairs*, 76/3: 20–30.

Buchanan, James M. (1976). 'Public Goods and Natural Liberty', in T. Wilson and A. S. Skinner (eds.), *The Market and the State: Essays in Honour of Adam Smith* (Oxford: Clarendon Press).

Bueno de Mesquita, Bruce (1981). *The War Trap* (New Haven: Yale University Press).

Bühl, Walter L. (1988). *Krisentheorien: Politik, Wirtschaft und Gesellschaft im Übergang* (Darmstadt: Wissenschaftliche Buchgesellschaft).

Bull, Hedley (1977). *The Anarchical Society: A Study of Order in World Politics* (New York: Columbia University Press).

Bulmer, Simon, and William E. Paterson (1996). 'Germany in the European Union: Gentle Giant or Emerging Leader?', *International Affairs* (Cambridge), 72: 9–32.

Bundesministerium der Verteidigung (1994). *Weißbuch zur Sicherheit der Bundesrepublik Deutschland und zur Lage der Bundeswehr* (Bonn: Presse- und Informationsamt der Bundesregierung).

Burns, E. L. M. (1962). *Between Arab and Israeli* (London: George G. Harrap).

Butler, Peter von, and Helmut Frick (1994). 'Langzeitverifikation im Irak: Entstehung und Entwicklung des Konzepts, Instrumente und Probleme der Implementation', in Hans Blix *et al.* (eds.), *Probleme der nuklearen Nichtverbreitungspolitik. Beiträge zur internationalen Diskussion* (Forschungsinstitut der Deutschen Gesellschaft für Auswärtige Politik e.V. and Kernforschungszentrum Jülich GmbH, Arbeitspapiere zur Internationalen Politik, 83; Bonn: Europa-Union), 72–100.

Butterworth, Robert, and Margaret Scranton (1976). *Managing Inter-State Conflict, 1945–1974* (Pittsburgh, Pa.: University Center for International Studies).

Campbell, Kurt M., Ashton B. Carter, Steven E. Miller, and Charles A. Zraket (1991). *Soviet Nuclear Fission: Control of the Nuclear Arsenal in a Disintegrating Soviet Union* (Center for Science and International Affairs Studies in International Security, 1, Nov.; Cambridge: CSIA).

Caporaso, James A. (1993). 'International Relations Theory and Multilateralism: The Search for Foundations', in John Gerard Ruggie (ed.), *Multilateralism Matters: The Theory and Praxis of an Institutional Form* (New York: Columbia University Press), 51–90.

Carnevale, Peter, and Sharon Arad (1996). 'Bias and Impartiality in Mediation', in J. Bercovitch (ed.), *Resolving International Conflicts* (Boulder, Colo.: Lynne Rienner).

——and D. G. Pruitt (1992). 'Negotiation and Mediation', *Annual Review of Psychology*, 43: 531–82.

Carnovale, Marco (1993). *The Control of NATO Nuclear Forces in Europe* (Boulder, Colo.: Westview Press).

Carstens, Karl (1993). *Erinnerungen und Erfahrungen*, ed. K. von Jena and R. Schmoeckel (Boppard am Rhein: Harald Boldt).

Carter, Ashton B., and David B. Omand (1994). 'Countering the Proliferation Risks: Adapting the Alliance to the New Security Environment', *NATO Review*, 42/5: 10–15.

CDU-Bundesgeschäftsstelle (1992a). *Sicherheitsvorsorge für eine neue Zeit: Beschluß des Bundesfachausschusses Sicherheitspolitik der CDU vom 4. Juni 1992* (Bonn: CDU).

——(1992b). *Gemeinsam Verantwortung in Europa und in der Welt wahrnehmen* (Bonn: CDU).

Chayes, Abram, and Antonia Handler Chayes (1996). *The New Sovereignty: Compliance with International Regulatory Agreements* (Cambridge, Mass.: Harvard University Press).

China (1996). 'Chinese Position on Issues Relating to the Third ARF Meeting' (Beijing, Apr.).

Chirac, Jacques, and Helmut Kohl (1996). 'Gemeinsame Botschaft von Bundeskanzler Dr. Helmut Kohl und dem Präsidenten der Französischen Republik, Jacques Chirac, an den amtierenden Vorsitzenden des Europäischen Rates und Ministerpräsidenten von Irland, John Bruton, 9. Dezember 1996', *Bulletin*, 102 (11 Dec.): 1105–8.

Choi, Ajin (1997). 'Democracy, Alliances, and War Performance in International Conflicts, 1816–1992', paper presented at the Annual Meeting of the American Political Science Association 28–31 Aug., Washington, DC.

Cialdini, Robert B. (1984). *Influence: The New Psychology of Modern Persuasion* (New York, Quill).

Clark, John (1989). *British Diplomacy and Foreign Policy 1782–1865* (London: Unwin Hyman).

Clarke, Michael (1995). 'British Policy Options', in Christoph Bluth, Emil Kirchner, and James Sperling (eds.), *The Future of European Security* (Aldershot: Dartmouth), 47–63.

Claude, Inis L. (1962). *Power and International Relations* (New York: Random House).

Clausewitz, Carl von (1980) [1832]. *Vom Kriege*, ed. Werner Hahlweg (Bonn: Dümmler).

Coase, Ronald H. (1976). 'Adam Smith's View of Man', *Journal of Law and Economics*, 19: 529–46.

Cohen, Avner (1995). 'The Nuclear Equation in a New Middle East', *Nonproliferation Review*, 2/2: 2–30.

Cohen, Michael D., and Robert Axelrod (1984). 'Coping with Complexity: The

Adaptive Value of Changing Utility', *The American Economic Review*, 74/1: 30–42.

Coolidge, Archibald Cary (1919). *Claimants to Constantinople* (Cambridge, Mass.: Harvard University Press).

Coriat, Benjamin (1997). 'Globalization, Variety, and Mass Production: The Metamorphosis of Mass Production in the New Competitive Age', in J. Rogers Hollingsworth and Robert Boyer (eds.), *Contemporary Capitalism: The Embeddedness of Institutions* (Cambridge and New York: Cambridge University Press), 240–64.

Cornish, Paul (1996). 'European Security: The End of Architecture and the New NATO', *International Affairs*, 72: 751–69.

Council on Foreign Relations (1995). *Nuclear Proliferation: Confronting the New Challenges*, Report of an Independent Task Force on Nuclear Proliferation (New York: CFR).

——and Seoul Forum for International Affairs (1995). *Success or Sellout? The U.S.–North Korean Nuclear Accord: Report of an Independent Task Force* (New York: CFR).

Craig, Gordon A. (1960). 'The System of Alliances and the Balance of Power', in J. P. T. Bury (ed.), *The New Cambridge Modern History*, x (Cambridge: Cambridge University Press), 246–73.

——(1972). *Europe 1814–1914*, 2nd edn. (Hinsdale, Ill.: Dryden).

Cruttwell, Charles Robert Mowbray Fraser (1936). *The Role of British Strategy in the Great War* (London: The University Press).

Czempiel, Ernst-Otto, Kerstin Dahmer, Mattias Dembinski, and Kinka Gerke (1994). *Die Weltpolitik der USA unter Clinton. Eine Bilanz des ersten Jahres* (PRIF-Report, 1/2; Frankfurt am Main: Peace Research Institute Frankfurt).

Daalder, Ivo H. (1991). *The Nature and Practice of Flexible Response: NATO Strategy and Theater Nuclear Forces since 1967* (New York: Columbia University Press).

Daase, Christopher (1992). 'Bedrohung, Verwundbarkeit und Risiko in der "Neuen Weltordnung": Zum Paradigmenwechsel in der Sicherheitspolitik', in Bernhard Moltmann (ed.), *Sicherheitspolitik in den 90er Jahren: Politische und ethische Positionsbestimmungen für die Bundeswehr* (Frankfurt am Main: Haagen und Herchen), 68–83.

Daugherty, William H. (1993). 'System Management and the Endurance of the Concert of Europe', in Jack Snyder and Robert Jervis (eds.), *Coping with Complexity in the International System* (Boulder, Colo.: Westview), 71–106.

Davidson, Donald (1963). 'Actions, Reasons, and Causes', *The Journal of Philosophy*, 60: 685–700.

Dembinski, Matthias (1994a). 'Weltordnung und Sicherheit: Amerikanische Nonproliferationspolitik nach dem Ende des Ost-West-Konfliktes', in M. Dembinski, Peter Rudolf, and Jürgen Wilzewski (eds.), *Amerikanische Weltpolitik nach dem Ost-West-Konflikt* (Baden-Baden: Nomos), 307–47.

——(1994*b*). *Testfall Nordkorea: Die Wirksamkeit des verbesserten IAEO-Safeguardsystems* (Ebenhausen: Stiftung Wissenschaft und Politik, Forschungsinstitut für Internationale Politik und Sicherheit, SWP-IP 2849).

——(1996). *Nukleare Abrüstung und Nichtverbreitung: Positionen der Regierung Clinton* (Ebenhausen: Stiftung Wissenschaft und Politik, Forschungsinstitut für Internationale Sicherheit, S409).

Der Derian, James (1987). *On Diplomacy: A Genealogy of Western Enstrangement* (Oxford: Basil Blackwell).

Desjardin, Marie-France (1996). 'Rethinking Confidence Building Measures: Obstacles to Agreement and the Risk of Overselling the Process', *Adelphi Paper*, 307.

Diamond, Howard (1997). 'IAEA Approves "93+2" Protocol: Awaits Adoption by Member States', *Arms Control Today*, 27/4: 27, 30.

Dixon, William J. (1996). 'Third-Party Techniques for Preventing Conflict Escalation and Promoting Peaceful Settlement', *International Organization*, 50: 653–82.

Dockrill, Michael L., and J. Douglas Goold (1981). *Peace without Promise: Britain and the Peace Conferences, 1919–23* (Hamden, Conn.: Archon Books).

Dockrill, Saki (1991). *Britain's Policy for West German Rearmament 1950–1955* (Cambridge: Cambridge University Press).

Drysdale, Peter, and Ross Garnaut (1993). 'The Pacific: An Application of a General Theory of Economic Integration', in C. Fred Bergsten and Marcus Noland (eds.), *Pacific Dynamism and the International Economic System* (Washington, DC: Institute for International Economics), 183–224.

Duffield, John S. (1995). *Power Rules: The Evolution of NATO's Conventional Force Posture* (Stanford, Calif.: Stanford University Press).

Durch, William J. (1993). 'Introduction', in William J. Durch (ed.), *The Evolution of UN Peacekeeping: Case Studies and Comparative Analysis* (New York: St Martin's Press), 1–15.

Edmonds, Robin (1991). *The Big Three: Churchill, Roosevelt, and Stalin in Peace and War* (New York: W. W. Norton).

Edwards, Geoffrey (1997). 'The Potential and Limits of the CFSP: The Yugoslav Example', in Elfriede Regelsberger, Philippe de Schoutheete de Tervarent, and Wolfgang Wessels (eds.), *Foreign Policy of the European Union. From the EPC to CFSP and Beyond* (Boulder, Colo., and London: Lynne Rienner), 173–95.

Edwards, Geoffrey, and David Sanders (1994). 'Consensus and Diversity in Elite Opinion: The Views of the British Foreign Policy Elite in the Early 1990s', *Political Studies*, 41: 413–40.

Efinger, Manfred, Volker Rittberger, Klaus Dieter Wolf, and Michael Zürn (1990). 'Internationale Regime und Internationale Politik', in Volker Rittberger (ed.), *Theorien der Internationalen Beziehungen: Bestandsaufnahme und Forschungsperspektiven* (Politische Vierteljahresschrift, 21/1990; Opladen: Westdeutscher), 263–85.

Elman, Colin, and Miriam Fendius Elman (1997). 'Diplomatic History and International Relations Theory: Respecting Difference and Crossing Boundaries', *International Security*, 22/1 (Summer): 5–21.

Elrod, Richard B. (1976). 'The Concert of Europe: A Fresh Look at an International System', *World Politics*, 28 (Jan.): 159–74.

Elsner, Wolfram (1989). 'Adam Smith's Model of the Origins and Emergence of Institutions: The Modern Findings of the Classical Approach', *Journal of Economic Issues*, 23: 189–213.

European Yearbook (1992, 1994). (Dordrecht, Boston, and London: Martinus Nijhoff).

Fainberg, Anthony (1993). *Strengthening IAEA Safeguards: Lessons from Iraq* (Stanford, Calif.: Center for International Security and Arms Control, Stanford University).

Falkenrath, Richard A. (1994). *The United States, the Former Soviet Republics and Nuclear Weapons: Problems and Policies of Denuclearization* (CSIA discussion paper; Cambridge, Mass.: Center for Science and International Affairs, Harvard University).

Fearon, James D. (1994*a*). 'Domestic Political Audiences and the Escalation of International Disputes', *American Political Science Review*, 88: 577–92.

——(1994*b*). 'Signaling Versus the Balance of Power and Interests: An Empirical Test of a Crisis Bargaining Model', *The Journal of Conflict Resolution*, 38 (June): 236–70.

——(1995). 'Rationalist Explanations for War', *International Organization*, 49(3): 379–414.

——(1998). 'Bargaining, Enforcement and International Organization', *International Organization*.

Feis, Herbert (1967). *Churchill, Roosevelt, Stalin: The War they Waged and the Peace they Sought* (Princeton: Princeton University Press).

Ferguson, Adam (1904) [1767]. *An Essay on the History of Civil Society* (Edinburgh: University Press).

Finnemore, Martha (1996). *National Interests in International Society* (Ithaca, NY: Cornell University Press).

Fischer, David A. V. (1992). *Stopping the Spread of Nuclear Weapons: The Past and the Prospects* (London: Routledge).

——(1996). 'New Directions and Tools for Strenghtening the IAEA Safeguards', *Nonproliferation Review*, 3/2: 69–76.

Fisher, Roger, and Loraleigh Keashley (1991). 'Potential Complementarity of Mediation and Consultation Within a Contingency Model of Third Party Consultation', *Journal of Peace Research*, 28: 29–42.

——Andrea Schneider, Elizabeth Borgwardt, and Brian Ganson (1997). *Coping with International Conflict* (Upper Saddle River, NJ: Prentice-Hall).

Fitchett, Joseph (1997). 'France Hopes to Isolate U.S. on Iran Deal', *International Herald Tribune* (1 Oct.).

Foreign and Commonwealth Office (1996). *A Partnership of Nations: The British Approach to the European Union Intergovernmental Conference 1996* (London: FCO).

Foreign Broadcast Information Service (1993–6): *China; Asia-Pacific* (Washington, DC: Government Printing Office).

Foreign Relations of the United States (FRUS) (1993). *1958–1960*, xiii. *West Europe and Canada* (Washington, DC: Government Printing Office).

——(1994). *1961–1963*, xiii. *West Europe and Canada* (Washington, DC: Government Printing Office).

Freedman, Lawrence (1989). *The Evolution of Nuclear Strategy*, 2nd edn. (Houndsmill and London: Macmillan).

French, David (1995). *The Strategy of the Lloyd George Coalition, 1916–1918* (Oxford: Clarendon Press).

Frieden, Jeffry A. (1999). 'Actors, Preferences and International Relations', in David A. Lake and Robert Powell (eds.), *Strategic Choice and International Relations* (Princeton: Princeton University Press).

Gaddis, John Lewis (1997). 'History, Theory and Common Ground', *International Security*, 22/1 (Summer): 75–85.

Gardner Feldman, Lily (1994). 'Germany and the EC: Realism and Responsibility', *Annals*, 531: 25–37.

Garnham, David (1994). 'Ending Europe's Security Dependence', *Strategic Studies*, 17: 125–42.

Garrett, Geoffrey, and Barry Weingast (1993). 'Ideas, Interests and Institutions: Constructing the European Community's Internal Market', in Judith Goldstein and Robert O. Keohane (eds.), *Ideas and Foreign Policy: Beliefs, Institutions and Political Change* (Ithaca, NY: Cornell University Press), 173–206.

Gärtner, Heinz (1996). 'Case-by-Case Action and Case-by-Case Neutrality: European Security Models and Options for the New "Neutral" EU Members—the Austrian Example', in *Visions of European Security—Focal Point Sweden and Northern Europe* (Stockholm: Olof Palme International Center).

Gartner, Scott Sigmund, and Randolph M. Siverson (1996). 'War Expansion and War Outcomes', *Journal of Conflict Resolution*, 40 (Mar.): 4–15.

Gehring, Thomas (1995). 'Regieren im internationalen System: Verhandlungen, Normen und Internationale Regime', *Politische Vierteljahresschrift*, 36: 197–219.

Gelpi, Christopher (1997). 'Crime and Punishment: The Role of Norms in Crisis Bargaining', *American Political Science Review*, 91 (June): 339–60.

Genscher, Hans-Dietrich (19 Oct. 1989). 'Sicherheit für die 90er Jahre: Mut zur gemeinsamen Zukunftsverantwortung. Statement at a conference of the Institute for East-West-Security-Studies (New York) in Frankfurt am Main', in *Umbruch in Europa. Die Ereignisse im 2. Halbjahr 1989* (Bonn: Auswärtiges Amt), 45–56.

——(1. Jan. 1990). 'Statement in Potsdam', in Walther Stützle (ed.), *Abschied von der alten Ordnung: Europas neue Sicherheit?* (Gütersloh: Bertelsmann), 20–9.

Genscher, Hans-Dietrich (13 Feb. 1990). 'Statement at the "Open-skies" Conference in Ottawa', *Bulletin*, 25 (15 Feb. 1990), 195–8.

—— (23 Mar. 1990). 'Die deutsche Vereinigung als Beitrag zur europäischen Stabilität. Statement to the WEU Assembly in Luxemburg', *Bulletin*, 40 (27 Mar.): 309–13.

——(6 Apr. 1990). 'Die Zukunft eines europäischen Deutschland. Speech given at association of American newspaper chief editors in Washington, DC. In (parts) *Deutsche Außenpolitik 1990/91: Auf dem Weg zu einer Europäischen Friedensordnung: Eine Dokumentation* (Bonn: Auswärtiges Amt), 103–5.

——(11 Apr. 1990), 'Statement to the CSCE Conference on Economic Cooperation in Bonn', *Bulletin*, 46 (19 Apr. 1990): 364–8.

——(5 June 1990). 'Statement at the Second Conference on the Human Dimension of the CSCE in Copenhagen', in *Deutsche Außenpolitik 1990/91: Auf dem Weg zu einer Europäischen Friedensordnung: Eine Dokumentation* (Bonn: Auswärtiges Amt), 117–19.

——(28 June 1990). 'Statement to the Deutschen Gesellschaft für Auswärtige Politik in Bonn', *Mitteilung für die Presse* (Bonn: Auswärtiges Amt, 1136/90).

——(1 Aug. 1990). 'Statement on the Occasion of the 15. Anniversary of the Signing of the Helsinki Final Act', *Bulletin*, 98 (14 Aug.): 834–5.

——(20 Sept. 1990). 'Erklärung der Bundesregierung zum Vertrag über die abschließenden Regelungen in bezug auf Deutschland. Statement to the German Bundestag', *Bulletin*, 113 (21 Sept.): 1185–8.

——(10 Sept. 1991). 'Statement at the CSCE meeting on the Human Dimension in Moscow', *Bulletin*, 100 (18 Sept. 1991): 797–9.

George, Alexander L. (1997). 'Knowledge for Statecraft: The Challenge for Political Science and History', *International Security*, 22/1 (Summer).

Gerard, Harold B., and Ruben Orive (1987). 'The Dynamics of Opinion Formation', *Advances in Experimental Social Psychology*, 20 (New York: Academic Press), 171–202.

Gerhold, Dankward (1992). 'Armaments Control of Germany: Protocol II of the Modified Brussels Treaty', in Fred Tanner (ed.), *From Versailles to Baghdad: Post War Armament Control of Defeated States* (Geneva: United Nations), 71–99.

Ghali, Mona (1993). 'United Nations Emergency Force I: 1956–1967', in William J. Durch (ed.), *The Evolution of UN Peacekeeping: Case Studies and Comparative Analysis* (New York: St Martin's Press), 104–30.

Gilbert, Margaret (1989). *On Social Facts* (London and New York: Routledge).

Gilpin, Robert (1975). *U.S. Power and the Multinational Corporation* (New York: Basic Books).

——(1981). *War and Change in World Politics* (Cambridge: Cambridge University Press).

Glaser, Charles L. (1993). 'Why NATO is Still Best: Future Security Arrangements for Europe', *International Security*, 18: 5–50.

——(1994/5). 'Realists as Optimists: Cooperation as Self-Help', *International Security*, 19/3 (Winter): 50–90.

Goldstein, Judith, and Robert O. Keohane (1993) (eds.). *Ideas and Foreign Policy: Beliefs, Institutions, and Political Change* (Ithaca, NY: Cornell University Press),

Gordon, Philip H. (1995). *France, Germany and the Western Alliance* (Boulder, Colo.: Westview).

Gormly, James L. (1990). *From Potsdam to the Cold War: Big Three Diplomacy, 1945–47* (Wilmington: Scholarly Resources).

Goulden, John (1996). 'The WEU's Role in the New Strategic Environment', *NATO Review*, 44: 21–4.

Goulding, Marrack. (1993). 'The Evolution of United Nations Peacekeeping', *International Affairs*, 69: 451–64.

Grabbe, Hans-J. (1983). *Unionsparteien, Sozialdemokratie und Vereinigte Staaten von Amerika, 1945–1966* (Düsseldorf: Droste).

Grant, Robert P. (1996). 'France's New Relationship with NATO', *Survival*, 38: 58–80.

Greco, Ettore (1995/6). 'Nature and Classification of New Security Challenges in Europe', in Gianni Bonvicini (ed.), *A Renewed Partnership for Europe. Tackling European Security Challenges by EU-NATO Interaction* (Baden-Baden: Nomos), 15–38.

Greiner, Christian (1993). 'Die militärische Eingliederung der Bundesrepublik Deutschland in die WEU und die NATO 1954 bis 1957', in Hans Ehlert, Christian Greiner, Georg Meyer, and Bruno Thoß, *Die NATO Option: Anfänge westdeutscher Sicherheitspolitik 1945–1956*, iii, ed. vom Militärgeschichtlichen Forschungsamt (Munich: Oldenbourg), 561–850.

Grieco, Joseph M. (1988). 'Anarchy and the Limits of Cooperation: A Realist Critique of the Newest Liberal Institutionalism', *International Organization*, 42: 485–508.

——(1996). 'State Interests and Institutional Rule Trajectories: A Neorealist Interpretation of the Maastricht Treaty and European Economic and Monetary Union', *Security Studies*, 5: 261–306.

Gulick, Edward Vose (1965). 'The Final Coalition and the Congress of Vienna, 1813–1815', in C. W. Crawley (ed.), *The New Cambridge Modern History*, ix (Cambridge: Cambridge University Press), 639–67.

——(1967). *Europe's Classical Balance of Power* (New York: Norton).

Haakonssen, Knud (1981). *The Science of a Legislator: The Natural Jurisprudence of David Hume and Adam Smith* (Cambridge: Cambridge University Press).

Haber, Stephen H., David M. Kennedy, and Stephen D. Krasner (1997). 'Brothers under the Skin: Diplomatic History and International Relations', *International Security*, 22/1 (Summer): 34–43.

Hafner, D. L. (1980). 'Castlereagh, the Balance of Power and Non-Intervention', *Australian Journal of Politics and History*, 26: 71–84.

Haftendorn, Helga (1989). 'Außenpolitische Prioritäten und Handlungsspielraum: Ein Paradigma zur Analyse der Außenpolitik der Bundesrepublik Deutschland', *Politische Vierteljahresschrift*, 30: 1, 32–49.

——(1991). 'The Security Puzzle: Theory-Building and Discipline-Building in International Security', *International Studies Quarterly*, 35: 3–17.

——(1996*a*). 'Das institutionelle Instrumentarium der Alliierten Vorbehaltsrechte: Politikkoordinierung zwischen den Drei Mächten und der Bundesrepublik Deutschland', in H. Haftendorn and H. Riecke (eds.), '. . . *Die volle Macht eines souveränen Staates . . .': Die Alliierten Vorbehaltsrechte als Rahmenbedingung westdeutscher Außenpolitik* (Baden-Baden: Nomos), 37–80.

——(1996*b*). *NATO and the Nuclear Revolution: A Crisis of Credibility, 1966–1967* (Oxford: Clarendon Press).

——(1997). 'The Post-Cold War Atlantic Alliance', *The Madeline Feher European Scholar Lecture* (Ramat Gan: The Begin-Sadat Center for Strategic Studies).

——and Otto Keck (1997) (eds.). *Kooperation jenseits von Hegemonie und Bedrohung: Sicherheitsinstitutionen in den internationalen Beziehungen* (Baden-Baden: Nomos).

——and Henning Riecke (1996) (eds.). '. . . *Die volle Macht eines souveränen Staates . . .': Die Alliierten Vorbehaltsrechte als Rahmenbedingung westdeutscher Außenpolitik 1949–1990* (Baden-Baden: Nomos).

Haggard, Stephen, and Beth A. Simmons (1987). 'Theories of International Regimes', *International Organization*, 41: 491–517.

Hahn, Frank (1982). 'Reflections on the Invisible Hand', *Lloyds Bank Review*, 144: 1–21.

Hall, Peter A., and Rosemary C. R. Taylor (1996). 'Political Science and the Three New Institutionalisms', *Political Studies*, 44: 936–57.

Halpern, Jennifer J. (1997). 'Elements of a Script for Friendship in Transaction', *Journal of Conflict Resolution*, 41/6 (Dec.): 835–68.

Hannum, Hurst (1990). *Autonomy, Sovereignty, and Self-Determination: The Accommodation of Conflicting Rights* (Philadelphia: University of Pennsylvania Press).

Hanrieder, Wolfram (1989). *Germany, America, Europe: Forty Years of German Foreign Policy* (New Haven: Yale University Press).

Hart, H. L. A. (1961). *The Concept of Law* (Oxford: Clarendon Press).

Hart, Jeffrey (1976). 'Three Approaches to the Measurement of Power in International Relations', *International Organization*, 30/2 (Spring): 289–305.

Hasenclever, Andreas, Peter Mayer, and Volker Rittberger (1996). 'Interests, Power, Knowledge: The Study of International Regimes', *Mershon International Studies Review*, 40: 177–228.

Hayek, Friedrich August von (1967). 'The Results of Human Action But Not of Human Design', in *Studies in Philosophy, Politics and Economics* (London: Routledge and Kegan Paul).

——(1973). *Law, Legislation and Liberty*, i (Chicago: University of Chicago Press).

Hayes-Renshaw, Fiona, and Helen Wallace (1997). *The Council of Ministers* (New York: St Martin's Press).

Heath, A. (1976). *Rational Choice and Social Exchange: A Critique of Exchange Theory* (Cambridge: Cambridge University Press).

Hellmann, Gunther (1996). 'The Making of a European Foreign and Defence Identity: Neo-realist and Constructivist Perspectives', in Snezana Trifunovska (ed.), *The Transatlantic Alliance on the Eve of the New Millennium* (The Hague: Kluwer Law International), 167–80.

——and Reinhard Wolf (1993). 'Neorealism, Neoliberal Institutionalism, and the Future of NATO', *Security Studies*, 3/1 (Autumn): 3–43.

Hempel, Carl G. (1965). *Aspects of Scientific Explanation* (New York: The Free Press).

Heraclides, Alexis (1993). *Helsinki-II and its Aftermath: The Making of the CSCE into an International Organization* (London and New York: Pinter).

Hermann, Charles F. (1969). 'International Crisis as a Situational Variable', in James N. Rosenau (ed.), *International Politics and Foreign Policy* (New York and London: Free Press and Collier-Macmillan), 409–21.

Hertslet, Edward (1875). *The Map of Europe by Treaty*, i (London: Butterworths).

Herz, John H. (1951). *Political Realism and Political Idealism* (Chicago: University of Chicago Press).

Higgins, Rosalyn (1969). *United Nations Peacekeeping 1946–1967: Documents and Commentary*, i (London: Oxford University Press).

——(1995). *Problems and Process: International Law and How we Use it* (Oxford: Clarendon Press).

Hill, Christopher (1996). 'Sharpening Contradictions', in Christopher Hill (ed.), *The Actors in Europe's Foreign Policy* (London: Routledge), 68–89.

Hill, Stephen M., and Shahin P. Malik (1996). *Peacekeeping and the United Nations* (Aldershot: Dartmouth).

Hinsley, F. H. (1963). *Power and the Pursuit of Peace* (Cambridge: Cambridge University Press).

Hirschman, Albert O. (1970). 'The Search for Paradigms as a Hindrance to Understanding', *World Politics*, 22: 329–43.

Hoffmann, Stanley (1993). 'French Dilemmas and Strategies in the New Europe', in Robert O. Keohane, Joseph S. Nye, and Stanley Hoffmann (eds.), *After the Cold War: International Institutions and State Strategies in Europe, 1989–1991* (Cambridge, Mass., and London: Harvard University Press), 127–47.

Holbraad, Carsten (1970). *The Concert of Europe* (London: Longman).

Holbrooke, Richard (1995). 'America: A European Power', *Foreign Affairs*, 74: 38–52.

Hollis, Marting, and Steve Smith (1990). *Explaining and Understanding International Relations* (Oxford: Oxford University Press).

Holsti, Kalevi J. (1984). 'Who got What and How: The CSCE Negotiations in Retrospect', in Robert Spencer (ed.), *Canada and the Conference on Security and*

Co-operation in Europe (Toronto: Toronto University, Center for International Studies), 134–66.

Holsti, Kalevi J. (1991). *Peace and War: Armed Conflicts and International Order 1648–1989* (Cambridge: Cambridge University Press).

Horsley, William (1992). 'United Germany's Seven Cardinal Sins: A Critique of German Foreign Policy', *Millennium*, 21: 225–42.

Howlett, Darryl A., and John Simpson (1995) (eds.). *Briefing Book, ii. Treaties, Agreements and Other Relevant Documents. Programme for Promoting Nuclear Non-Proliferation*, 3rd edn. (Southampton: Mountbatten Center for International Studies: an updated version of the documentary part of Howlett and Simpson (eds.), *The Nuclear Non-Proliferation: A Reference Handbook*, London: Longman, 1992).

Hudec, Robert E. (1990). 'Thinking about New Section 301: Beyond Good and Evil', in Jagdish Bhagwati and Hugh T. Patrick (eds.), *Aggressive Unilateralism: America's 301 Trade Policy and the World Trade System* (Ann Arbor: University of Michigan Press), 113–59.

Huth, Paul K., Christopher Gelpi, and D. Scott Bennett (1993). 'The Escalation of Great Power Militarized Disputes: Testing Rational Deterrence Theory and Structural Realism', *American Political Science Review*, 87 (Sept.): 609–23.

'In Frieden leben' (1991). 'Entschließung des Bremer Parteitages der SPD vom 31. Mai 1991' (1991), *Blätter für deutsche und internationale Politik*, 36: 894–6.

Ingram, Edward (1997). 'The Wonderland of the Political Scientist', *International Security*, 22/1 (Summer): 53–63.

International Institute of Strategic Studies (IISS) (1993). *The Military Balance 1993–1994* (London: Brassey's).

James, Alan (1990). *Peacekeeping in International Politics* (London: Macmillan).

Janning, Josef, and Melanie Piepenschneider (1993). *Deutschland in Europa: Eine Bilanz europäischer Einigungspolitik* (KAS, Deutschlandreport, 19; Melle: Verlag Ernst Knoth).

Jenks, C. Wilfred (1965). 'Unanimity, the Veto, Weighted Voting, Special and Simple Majorities and Consensus as Modes of Decision in International Organizations', in *Cambridge Essays in International Law: Essays in Honour of Lord McNast* (London: Steven's and Sons).

Jervis, Robert (1976). *Perception and Misperception in International Politics* (Princeton: Princeton University Press).

——(1978). 'Cooperation under the Security Dilemma', *World Politics*, 30: 167–214.

——(1983). 'Security Regimes', in Stephen D. Krasner (ed.), *International Regimes* (Ithaca, NY, and London: Cornell University Press), 173–94.

——(1986). 'From Balance to Concert: A Study of International Security Cooperation', in Kenneth Oye (ed.), *Cooperation Under Anarchy* (Princeton: Princeton University Press), 58–79.

Johnston, Alastair Iain (1998). 'International Structures and Chinese Foreign

Policy', in Samuel S. Kim (ed.), *China and the World*, 4th edn. (Boulder, Colo.: Westview Press).

Joseph, Robert (1996). 'Proliferation, Counter-Proliferation and NATO', *Survival*, 38: 111–30.

Karádi, Matthias Z. (1994). *Die Reform der Atlantischen Allianz. Bündnispolitik als Beitrag zur kooperativen Sicherheit in Europa?* (Münster: Lit).

Kato, Junko (1996). 'Institutions and Rationality in Politics: Three Varieties of Neo-institutionalists', *British Journal of Political Science*, 26: 553–82.

Katzenstein, Peter J. (1996) (ed.). *The Culture of National Security: Norms and Identity in World Politics* (New York: Columbia University Press).

Kaufmann, William W. (1964). *The McNamara Strategy* (New York: Harper & Row).

Keashley, Loraleigh, and Roger Fisher (1996). 'A Contingency Perspective on Conflict Interventions: Theoretical and Practical Considerations', in J. Bercovitch (ed.), *Resolving International Conflicts* (Boulder, Colo.: Lynne Rienner).

Kelleher, Catherine M. (1975). *Germany and the Politics of Nuclear Weapons* (New York: Columbia University Press).

——(1987). 'NATO Nuclear Operations', in Ashton B. Carter, John D. Steinbrunner, and Charles A. Zraket (eds.), *Managing Nuclear Operations* (Washington, DC: Brookings Institutions), 445–69.

Keller, Rudi (1990). *Sprachwandel: Von der unsichtbaren Hand in der Sprache* (Tübingen: Francke).

Keohane, Robert O. (1980). 'Theory of Hegemonic Stability and Changes in International Economic Regimes, 1967–1977', in Ole Holsti (ed.), *Change in the International System* (Boulder, Colo.: Westview), 131–62.

——(1982). 'The Demand for International Regimes', *International Organization*, 36: 325–55.

——(1984). *After Hegemony: Cooperation and Discord in the World Political Economy* (Princeton: Princeton University Press).

——(1989a). 'International Institutions: Two Approaches', in Keohane, *International Institutions and State Power* (Boulder, Colo.: Westview), 158–82.

——(1989b). *International Institutions and State Power: Essays in International Relations Theory* (Boulder, Colo.: Westview).

——(1989c). 'Neoliberal Institutionalism: A Perspective on World Politics', in Robert O. Keohane, *International Institutions and State Power: Essays in International Relations Theory* (Boulder, Colo.: Westview), 1–20.

——(1995). 'The Analysis of International Regimes: Towards a European-American Research Programme', in Volker Rittberger (ed.), *Regime Theory and International Relations* (Oxford: Clarendon Press), 23–45.

——and Joseph S. Nye (1977). *Power and Interdependence* (Boston: Little, Brown).

——and Nye (1993). 'Introduction: The End of the Cold War in Europe', in Keohane, Nye, and Hoffmann (eds.), *After the Cold War* (Cambridge, Mass.: Harvard University Press).

Keohane, Robert O., and Elinor Ostrom (1995) (eds.). *Local Commons and Global Interdependence: Heterogeneity and Cooperation in Two Domains* (London: Sage).

——Joseph S. Nye, and Stanley Hoffmann (1993) (eds.). *After the Cold War: International Institutions and State Strategies in Europe, 1989–1991* (Cambridge, Mass.: Harvard University Press).

Kier, Elisabeth, and Jonathan Mercer (1996). 'Setting Precedents in Anarchy', *International Security*, 20: 77–106.

Killinger, Mark H. (1995). 'Improving IAEA Safeguards through Enhanced Information Analysis', *Nonproliferation Review*, 3/1: 43–8.

Kindleberger, Charles P. (1974). *The World in Depression, 1929–1939* (Berkeley, Calif.: University of California Press).

King, Gary, Robert O. Keohane, and Sidney Verba (1994). *Designing Social Inquiry: Scientific Inference in Qualitative Research* (Princeton: Princeton University Press).

Kinkel, Klaus (1990). 'Die deutsche Vereinigung als Beitrag zur europäischen Stabilität, Rede des Bundesministers des Auswärtigen vor der WEU-Versammlung in Luxemburg', *Bulletin*, 40 (27 Mar.): 309–13.

——(1992). 'Statement to the 47. General Assembly of the United Nations, New York, 23 Sept.', *Bulletin*, 102 (25 Sept.): 949–51.

——(1994*a*). 'Deutschland in Europa: Zu den Zielen der deutschen Präsidentschaft der Europäischen Union', *Europa-Archiv*, 49: 335–42.

——(1994*b*). 'Rede von Bundesminister zur deutschen Außenpolitik in einer neuen Weltlage vor der Deutschen Gesellschaft für Auswärtige Politik am 24. August 1994 in Bonn', *Europa-Archiv*, 18: D540–4.

——(1994*c*). 'Stärkung der KSZE als gesamteuropäische Sicherheitsinstitution', Statement to the Permanent Committee of the CSCE in Vienna, 17 May, *Bulletin*, 46 (20 May): 411–12.

——(1994). 'Rede von Bundesminister Klaus Kinkel zur deutschen Außenpolitik in einer neuen Weltlage, gehalten vor der Deutschen Gesellschaft für Auswärtige Politik e.V. (DGAP) am 24. August 1994 in Bonn (excerpts)', *Europa-Archiv*, 18: D540–4.

——and Hervé de Charette (1996). 'Leitlinien zur Gemeinsamen Außen- und Sicherheitspolitik, verabschiedet anläßlich des Seminars der Außenminister Deutschlands und Frankreichs, Klaus Kinkel und Hervé de Charette, am 27. Februar 1996 in Freiburg', *Internationale Politik*, 51/8: 84–6.

Kissinger, Henry (1957). *A World Restored* (Boston: Houghton Mifflin).

——(1982). *Years of Upheaval* (Boston: Little, Brown, and Co.).

——(1994). *Diplomacy* (New York: Simon & Schuster).

Klauer, Vera (1997). 'Bedingungen institutioneller Leistungsfähigkeit am Beispiel des Konfliktes im ehemaligen Jugoslawien', in H. Haftendorn and O. Keck (eds.), *Kooperation jenseits von Hegemonie und Bedrohung* (Baden-Baden: Nomos), 233–54.

Knight, Jack (1992). *Institutions and Social Conflict* (Cambridge: Cambridge University Press).

Knight, W. Andy (1996). 'Towards a Subsidiarity Model for Peacemaking and Preventive Diplomacy: Making Chapter VIII of the UN Charter Operational', *Third World Quarterly*, 17: 31–52.

Knorr, Klaus (1976) (ed.). *Historical Dimensions of National Security Problems* (Lawrence, Kan.: University of Kansas Press).

Koch, Andrew, and Jeannette Wolf (1997). 'Iran's Procurement Program: How Close to the Bomb?', *Nonproliferation Review*, 5/1: 123–35.

Kohl, Helmut (28 Nov. 1989). 'Zehn-Punkte-Programm zur Überwindung der Teilung Deutschlands und Europas. Statement to the Deutschen Bundestag', in *Umbruch in Europa: Die Ereignisse im 2. Halbjahr 1989: Eine Dokumentation* (Bonn: Auswärtiges Amt), 111–21.

——(3 Feb. 1990). 'Statement to the World Economic Forum in Davos', *Bulletin*, 21 (6 Feb.): 165–9.

——(19 Mar. 1990). 'Statement to the CSCE Economic Forum in Bonn', *Bulletin*, 37 (20 Mar.): 285–8.

——(3 Apr. 1990). 'Der Standort eines geeinten Deutschland in einem künftigen Europa, Rede des Bundeskanzlers in Cambridge', *Bulletin*, 43: 333–6.

——(21 May 1990). 'Statement at the Conclusion of the Disarmament Conference of the Interparliamentary Union in Bonn', in *Deutsche Außenpolitik 1990/91: Auf dem Weg zu einer Europäischen Friedensordnung: Eine Dokumentation* (Bonn: Auswärtiges Amt), 114–16.

——(17 July 1990). 'Bilanz und Perspektiven der Politik der Bundesregierung. Statement to the Bundespressekonferenz in Bonn', *Bulletin*, 93 (18 July): 801–4.

——(22 Nov. 1990). 'Statement at the Deutscher Bundestag on the Paris CSCE summit', *Bulletin*, 136 (23 Nov.): 1405–8.

——and Jacques Chirac (1995). 'Schreiben des deutschen Bundeskanzlers und des französischen Staatspräsidenten, Helmut Kohl und Jacques Chirac, an den amtierenden Vorsitzenden des Europäischen Rates, den spanischen Minister-präsidenten Felipe Gonzáles, veröffentlicht am 6. Dezember 1995 in Bonn und Paris (excerpts)', *Internationale Politik*, 51/8: 80–1.

Krasner, Stephen D. (1976). 'State Power and the Structure of International Trade', *World Politics*, 28: 317–47.

——(1982). 'Structural Causes and Regime Consequences: Regimes as Intervening Variables', *International Organization*, 36: 185–205.

——(1983*a*) (ed.). *International Regimes*. (Ithaca, NY: Cornell University Press).

——(1983*b*). 'Regimes and the Limits of Realism: Regimes as Autonomous Variables', in Krasner (ed.), *International Regimes* (Ithaca, NY: Cornell University Press).

——(1988). 'Sovereignty: An Institutional Perspective', *Comparative Political Studies*, 21: 66–94.

Krasner, Stephen D. (1991). 'National Power and Global Communications', *World Politics*, 43: 336–66.

——(1994). 'International Political Economy: Abiding Discord', *Review of International Political Economy*, 1: 13–20.

Kratochwil, Friedrich V. (1989). *Rules, Norms, and Decisions: On the Conditions of Practical and Legal Reasoning in International Relations and Domestic Affairs* (Cambridge: Cambridge University Press).

——(1993). 'Contract and Regimes', in Volker Rittberger (ed.), *Regime Theory and International Relations* (Oxford: Oxford University Press).

Krauthammer, Charles (1989). 'Return of the German Question', *Time Magazine* (25 Sept.): 33.

Krause, Joachim (1998). *Strukturwandel der Nichtverbreitungspolitik: Verbreitung von Massenvernichtungswaffen und die weltpoltische Transformation* (Schriften des Forschungsinstitutes der Deutschen Gesellschaft für Auswärtige Politik e.V.; Munich: R. Oldenbourg).

Kugler, Richard L. (1993). *Commitment to Purpose: How Alliance Partnership Won the Cold War* (Santa Monica, Calif.: Rand).

Kuklinski, James H., and Norman L. Hurley (1996). 'Its a Matter of Interpretation', in Diana C. Mutz, Paul M. Sniderman, and Richard Brody (eds.), *Political Persuasion and Attitude Change* (Ann Arbor: University of Michigan Press), 125–44.

Kupchan, Charles A., and Clifford A. Kupchan (1991). 'Concerts, Collective Security, and the Future of Europe', *International Security*, 16/1 (Summer): 114–61.

——and——(1995). 'The Promise of Collective Security', *International Security*, 20/1 (Summer): 52–62.

Kuran, Timur (1995). *Public Truths, Private Lies: The Social Consequences of Preference Falsification* (Cambridge, Mass.: Harvard University Press).

Lake, David A. (1996). 'Anarchy, Hierarchy and the Variety of International Relations', *International Organization*, 50: 1–34.

Langer, William (1931). *European Alliances and Allignments* (New York: Knopf).

Langghut, Gerd (1991). 'Deutschland, die EG und die Architektur Europas', *Außenpolitik*, 42: 136–45.

Langhorne, Richard (1981/2). 'The Development of International Conferences 1648–1830', *Studies in History and Politics*, 2/2: 61–91.

——(1986). 'Reflections on the Significance of the Congress of Vienna', *Review of International Studies*, 12: 313–24.

Latour, Bruno (1991). *Nous n'avons jamais été modernes: Essai d'anthropologie symétrique* (Paris: Éditions La Découverte).

Lauren, Paul Gordon (1983). 'Crisis Prevention in Nineteenth-Century Diplomacy', in Alexander George (ed.), *Managing U.S.–Soviet Rivalry: Problems of Crisis Prevention* (Boulder, Colo.: Westview), 31–64.

Layne, Christopher (1993). 'The Unipolar Illusion: Why New Great Powers Will Rise', *International Security*, 17: 5–51.

Leifer, Michael (1996). 'The ASEAN Regional Forum: Extending ASEAN's Model of Regional Security', *Adelphi Paper*, 302.

Leimbacher, Urs (1995). 'Die deutsch-französische Zusammenarbeit in der Gemeinsamen Außen- und Sicherheitspolitik der Europäischen Union', in *Handeln für Europa: Deutsch-französische Zusammenarbeit in einer veränderten Welt* (Opladen: Centre d'Information et de Recherche sur l'Allemagne Contemporaine), 28–51.

Lellouche, Pierre (1996). *Légitime défense: Vers une Europe en sécurité au XXIème siècle* (Paris: Patrick Banon).

Levy, Jack S. (1997). 'Too Important to Leave to the Other: History and Political Science in the Study of International Relations', *International Security*, 22/1 (Summer): 22–33.

Lewis, David (1969). *Convention: A Philosophical Study* (Cambridge, Mass.: Harvard University Press).

Lewis, Jeffrey (1998). *The Institutional Problem-Solving Capacities of the Council: The Committee of Permanent Representatives and the Methods of Community* (Discussion Paper 98; Cologne: Max-Planck-Institut für Gesellschaftsforschung).

Li Shisheng (1992). 'Guanyu guoji xin zhixu ji ge wenti de tan tao', [Discussion of several questions relating to the new international order], *Shijie jingji yu zhengzhi* [World Economics and Politics],10.

Livre blanc sur la défense (1994). (Paris: Union Générale d'Éditions).

Lockhart, J. G. (1934). *The Peacemakers, 1814–1815* (New York: Putnam).

Long, William J. (1994). 'Global Security, Democratization, and Economic Development after the Cold War: New Goals for U.S. Export Control Policies', in Gary K. Bertsch, Richard T. Cupitt, and Steven Elliott Gover (eds.), *Cooperation in International Export Controls: Prospects for the 1990s and Beyond* (Ann Arbor: University of Michigan Press), 59–85.

Lynn-Jones, Sean M., and Joseph S. Nye (1988). 'International Security Studies: A Report of a Conference on the State of the Field', *International Security*, 12: 5–27.

McCalla, Robert B. (1996). 'NATO's Persistence after the Cold War', *International Organization*, 50: 445–75.

McGowan, Patrick, and Robert M. Rood (1975). 'Alliance Behavior in Balance of Power Systems: Applying a Poisson Model to Nineteenth Century Europe', *American Political Science Review*, 69/3: 859–70.

McKenzie, Mary M. (1994). *Germany and the Institutions of Collective Security in Europe* (Report 36; Frankfurt am Main: Hessische Stiftung Friedens- und Konfliktforschung).

Mager, Olaf (1990). *Die Stationierung der britischen Rheinarmee: Großbritanniens EVG-Alternative* (Baden-Baden: Nomos).

Mahncke, Dieter (1972). *Nukleare Mitwirkung: Die Bundesrepublik Deutschland in der atlantischen Allianz, 1954–1970* (Berlin and New York: Walter deGruyter).

Mandeville, Bernard de (1924) [1732]. *The Fable of the Bees: Or, Private Vices, Public Benefits*, ed. F. B. Kaye (Oxford: Oxford University Press).

Mansourov, Alexandre Y. (1995). 'The Origins, Evolution and Current Politics of the North Korean Nuclear Program', *Nonproliferation Review*, 2/3: 25–38.

March, James (1966). 'The Power of Power', in David Easton (ed.), *Varieties of Political Theory* (Englewood Cliffs, NJ: Prentice-Hall).

——and Johan Olsen (1998). 'The Institutional Dynamics of International Political Orders', *International Organization*, 52: 4.

Martin, Lisa L. (1992*a*). *Coercive Cooperation: Explaining Multilateral Economic Sanctions* (Princeton: Princeton University Press).

——(1992*b*). 'Interests, Power, and Multilateralism', *International Organization*, 46: 765–92.

——(1993). 'The Rational State Choice of Multilateralism', in John Gerard Ruggie (ed.), *Multilateralism Matters: The Theory and Praxis of an Institutional Form* (New York: Columbia University Press), 91–121.

——(1995). 'Heterogeneity, Linkage and Commons Problems', in R. O. Keohane and E. Ostrom (eds.), *Local Commons and Global Interdependence* (London: Sage), 71–91.

Mazarr, Michael J. (1995). *North Korea and the Bomb: A Case Study in Nonproliferation: New Nonproliferation* (New York: St Martin's Press).

Mearsheimer, John J. (1990). 'Back to the Future, Instability in Europe after the Cold War', *International Security*, 15/1 (Summer): 5–56.

——(1994/5). 'The False Promise of International Institutions', *International Security*, 19 (Winter): 5–49.

Medlicott, W. N. (1963). *The Congress of Berlin and After*, 2nd edn. (Hamden, Conn.: Archon Books).

Megens, Ine [1994]. *American Aid to NATO Allies in the 1950s: The Dutch Case*, Ph.D. thesis (Groningen: Thesis Publishers).

Meier-Dörnberg, Wilhelm (1983). 'Politische und militärische Faktoren bei der Planung des deutschen Verteidigungsbeitrages im Rahmen der EVG', in *Entmilitarisierung und Aufrüstung: Vorträge zur Militärgeschichte*, iv (Bonn and Herford: Verlag E. S. Mittler & Sohn), 184–208.

——(1990). 'Die Planung des Verteidigungsbeitrages der Bundesrepublik Deutschland im Rahmen der EVG', in Köllner, Klaus A. Lutz-Meier, Wilhelm Meier-Dörnberg, and Hans-E. Volkmann, *Die EVG-Phase: Anfänge westdeutscher Sicherheitspolitik 1945–1956*, ii (Munich: Oldenbourg), 605–756.

Mellisen, Jan (1993). *The Struggle for Nuclear Partnership: Britain, the United States and the Making of an Ambiguous Alliance 1952–1959* (Groningen: Styx).

Menger, Carl (1985) [1883]. *Investigations into the Method of the Social Sciences with Special Reference to Economics* (New York: New York University Press).

Menon, Anand (1995). 'From Independence to Cooperation: France, NATO and European Security', *International Affairs*, 71: 19–34.

Menzel, Eberhard (1971). 'Die militärischen Einsätze der Vereinten Nationen zur Sicherung des Friedens', *Jahrbuch für internationales Recht*, 15: 11–137.

Milgrom, Paul R., Douglass C. North, and Barry R. Weingast (1990). 'The Role of

Institutions in the Revival of Trade: The Law Merchant, Private Judges, and the Champagne Fairs', *Economics and Politics*, 2: 1–23.

Milner, Helen V. (1997). *Interests, Institutions and Information: Domestic Politics and International Relations* (Princeton: Princeton University Press).

Mohr, Lawrence B. (1996). *The Causes of Human Behavior: Implications for Theory and Method in the Social Sciences* (Ann Arbor: University of Michigan Press).

Moravcsik, Andrew (1997). 'Taking Preferences Seriously: A Liberal Theory of International Politics', *International Organization*, 51: 513–54.

Morrow, James (1991). 'Alliances and Asymmetry: An Alternative to the Capability Aggregation Model', *American Journal of Political Science*, 35 (Nov.): 904–34.

——(1994). *Game Theory for Political Scientists* (Princeton: Princeton University Press).

Müller, Harald (1989). 'Regimeanalyse und Sicherheitspolitik: Das Beispiel Nonproliferation', in Beate Kohler-Koch (ed.), *Regime in den internationalen Beziehungen* (Baden-Baden: Nomos), 277–313.

——(1997). 'Neither Hype nor Complacency: WMD Proliferation after the Cold War', *Nonproliferation Review*, 4/2: 62–71.

——and Mitchell Reiss (1995). 'Counterproliferation: Putting New Wine in Old Bottles', *Washington Quarterly*, 18: 143–54.

Myers, M. L. (1972). 'Philosophical Anticipations of Laissez-Faire', *History of Political Economy*, 4: 163–75.

Nadeau, Remi (1990). *Stalin, Churchill, and Roosevelt Divide Europe* (New York: Praeger).

NATO Information Service (1989). *The North Atlantic Treaty Organization: Facts and Figures*, 11th edn. (Brussels: NATO Information Service).

Nicolson, Harold (1946). *The Congress of Vienna* (New York: Harcourt Brace).

North, Douglass C. (1990). *Institutions, Institutional Change and Economic Performance* (Cambridge: Cambridge University Press).

Northedge, Fred, and Michael Donelan (1971). *International Disputes: The Political Aspects* (London: Europa Press).

Nötzold, Jürgen (1993). 'Europas Zukunft: Nationalstaatliches Handeln, übernationale Integration und die Interessen Deutschlands', in Albrecht Zunker (ed.), *Weltordnung oder Chaos?* (Baden-Baden: Nomos), 37–53.

Nozick, Robert (1974). *Anarchy, State, and Utopia* (Oxford: Basil Blackwell).

——(1994). 'Invisible-Hand Explanations', *American Economic Review*, 84: 314–18.

Nuclear History Program (n.d.). *Deutsche Dokumente aus dem Bundesverteidigungsministerium, 1956–1967*, declassified by Reiner Pommerin, ed. Gabriele Brenke (Bonn: Nuclear History Program).

——(1989/90a). *Die Nuklearpolitik der Bundesrepublik Deutschland* [Oral history, testimony by General ret. Graf Jojann A. von Kielmannsegg; Dr Ulrich Sahm; General ret. Johannes Steinhoff; General ret. Heinz Trettner; Ambassador ret. Dr Hans-Georg Wieck; General ret. Harald Wust on July 13, 1987] (Bonn: Nuclear History Program).

Nuclear History Program (1989/90*b*). *Zeitzeugenbefragung der 'Flugzeugführer'* [Oral history on 29 May 1989] (Bonn: Nuclear History Program).

Nuti, Leopoldo (1989). ' "Me Too Please": Italy and the Politics of Nuclear Weapons, 1945–1975', *Diplomacy and Statecraft*, 4/1 (Mar.): 144–8.

——(1994). 'A Risky Shortcut to Prestige: Italy and the US MRBMs SM 78 Jupiter', paper presented at the final review meeting in the NHP's MRBM (Jupiter) Project, Ebenhausen, 7–9 July.

Nye, Joseph S. (1990). *Bound to Lead* (New York: Basic Books).

——(1995). 'East Asian Security: The Case for Deep Engagement', *Foreign Affairs*, 74 (July–Aug.): 90–102.

Oh, John C. H., and Ruth M. Grubel (1995). 'The North Korean Nuclear Weapons Crisis: The United States and its Policy Options', *Korea Observer*, 26/1: 97–116.

Osgood, Robert E. (1962). *NATO: The Entangling Alliance* (Chicago: University of Chicago Press).

Osiander, Andreas (1994). *The States System of Europe 1640–1990* (Oxford: Oxford University Press).

Osterheld, Horst (1992). *Außenpolitik unter Bundeskanzler Ludwig Erhard 1963–1966* (Düsseldorf: Droste).

Ott, Marvin (1972). 'Mediation as a Method of Conflict Resolution', *International Organization*, 26/4: 595–618.

PacNet (1996). 'Chairman's Statement' and 'Commentary', 47 (22 Nov.).

Papayouanou, Paul A. (1995). 'The Process of Alliance Formation: A Signaling Game Approach', unpublished MS.

Paterson, William E. (1996). 'Beyond Semi-Sovereignty: The New Germany in the New Europe', *German Politics*, 5: 167–84.

Pedlow, Gregory W. [1997] (ed.). *NATO Strategy Documents 1949–1969* (Brussels: NATO Information Service).

Peters, Ingo (1993*a*). 'Sicherheit in Europa nach dem Ost-West-Konflikt: Der KSZE-Prozeß als regionale Sicherheitsinstitution', in Christopher Daase *et al.* (eds.), *Regionalisierung der Sicherheitspolitik* (Baden-Baden: Nomos), 89–108.

——(1993*b*). 'Sicherheitspolitische Vertrauensbildung im neuen Europa: Herausforderungen und Entwicklungen in der VSBM-Politik', in Erhard Forndran and Hartmut Pohlman (eds.), *Europäische Sicherheit nach dem Ende des Warschauer Paktes* (Baden-Baden: Nomos), 363–89.

——(1994). 'Normen- und Institutionenbildung der KSZE im Widerstreit politischer Interessen', in Bernard von Plate (eds.), *Europa auf dem Wege zur kollektiven Sicherheit? Konzeptionelle und organisatorische Entwicklungen der sicherheitspolitischen Institutionen Europas* (Baden-Baden: Nomos), 155–86.

——(1995*a*). 'CSCE', in Emil Kirchner, Christopher Bluth, and James Sperling (eds.), *Britain and Germany in the New Europe* (Aldershot: Dartmouth), 67–84.

——(1995*b*). 'CSCE and Peacekeeping: An Institution and its Instrument as

"Victims" of Conflicting State Interests', in David Haglund and Hans-Georg Ehrhart (eds.), *The 'New Peacekeeping' and European Security: German and Canadian Interests and Issues* (Baden-Baden: Nomos), 107–26.

Philippi, Nina (1997). 'Frankreichs Rolle im ruandischen Bürgerkrieg: Eine Wende in der französischen Afrika-Politik?' in Hans W. Maull, Michael Meimeth, and Christoph Neßhöver (eds.), *Die verhinderte Großmacht: Frankreichs Sicherheitspolitik nach dem Ende des Ost-West-Konflikts* (Opladen: Leske und Budrich), 223–42.

Phillips, W. A. (1914). *The Confederation of Europe* (London: Longmans).

Philpott, William James (1996). *Anglo-French Relations and Strategy on the Western Front, 1914–18* (London: Macmillan).

Plantin, Marie-Claude (1993). 'Une ambition française: La Promotion de l'UEO comme bras armé d'une identité européenne de sécurité et de défense', *Arès*, 14: 85–103.

Pond, Elizabeth (1993). *Beyond the Wall: Germany's Road to Unification* (Washington, DC: The Brookings Institution).

Popper, Karl R. (1965). *Conjectures and Refutations* (New York: Harper).

Powell, Robert (1990). *Nuclear Deterrence Theory: The Search for Credibility* (Cambridge: Cambridge University Press).

——(1996). 'Uncertainty, Shifting Power and Appeasement', *American Political Science Review*, 90/4 (Dec.): 749–64.

PRC CSCAP [1997]. 'Preliminary List of Members of CSCAP China Committee'.

Preisinger, Johannes (1993). *Deutschland und die nukleare Nichtverbreitung: Zwischenbilanz und Ausblick* (Forschungsinstitut der Deutschen Gesellschaft für Auswärtige Politik e.V., Arbeitspapiere Internationale Politik, 76; Bonn: Europa-Union Verlag).

Princen, Thomas (1991). 'Camp David: Problem Solving or Power Politics as Usual?', *Journal of Peace Research*, 28: 57–69.

Puchala, Donald J., and Raymond F. Hopkins (1983). 'International Regimes: Lessons from Inductive Analysis', in Stephen D. Krasner (ed.), *International Regimes* (Ithaca, NY: Cornell University Press).

Rademacher, Fritz, and Heinrich Rentmeister (1990), *Rüstungskontrollverifikation durch die Westeuropäische Union (WEU)* (Ebenhausen: SWP-S 359; Stiftung Wissenschaft und Politik).

Raiffa, Howard H. (1982). *The Art and Science of Negotiation* (Cambridge: Harvard University Press).

Randzio-Plath, Christa (1992). 'Deutschland und Frankreich zwischen Maastricht und dem Binnenmarkt', *Aus Politik und Zeitgeschichte*, 42: 28–35.

Rasmussen, Eric (1989). *Games and Information* (Cambridge: Cambridge University Press).

Ratner, Steven R. (1995). *The New UN Peacekeeping: Building Peace in Lands of Conflict after the Cold War* (New York: St Martin's Press).

Regelsberger, Elfriede (1992). 'Die Gemeinsame Außen- und Sicherheitspolitik nach Maastricht: Minimalreform in neuer Entwicklungsperspektive', *Integration*, 15: 83–93.

Richardson, Louise (1993). 'British State Strategies after the Cold War', in Robert O. Keohane, Joseph S. Nye, and Stanley Hoffmann (eds.), *After the Cold War. International Institutions and State Strategies in Europe, 1989-1991* (Cambridge: Harvard University Press), 148–69.

——(1996). *When Allies Differ: Anglo-American Relations during the Suez and Falklands Crises* (New York: St Martin's Press).

Riecke, Henning (1997). 'Nukleare Nichtverbreitung als Aktionsfeld von NATO und GASP', in H. Haftendorn and O. Keck (eds.), *Kooperation jenseits von Hegemonie und Bedrohung* (Baden-Baden: Nomos), 91–232.

Rifkind, Malcolm (1993). 'A Decade of Change in European Security', in *Brassey's Defence Yearbook 1993*, ed. The Centre for Defence Studies, King's College London (London and New York: Brassey's), 19–29.

Risse-Kappen, Thomas (1988). *The Zero Option: INF, West Germany, and Arms Control* (Boulder, Colo.: Westview).

Rivlin, Benjamin (1992). 'Regional Arrangements and the UN System for Collective Security and Conflict Resolution: A New Road Ahead?', *International Relations*, 11: 95–110.

Roberts, Adam (1994). 'The Crisis in UN Peacekeeping', *Survival*, 36: 93–120.

Roberts, Brad (1995). 'Revised Task Force Report No. 2: The Asia-Pacific and the Global Treaty Regime: The Agenda After NPT Expansion' (US CSCAP, 23 Apr.).

Ropers, Norbert, and Peter Schlotter (1992). *Die KSZE: Multilaterales Konfliktmanagement im weltpolitischen Umbruch* (Report 11/12; Frankfurt am Main: HSFK).

Rosecrance, Richard (1992). 'A New Concert of Powers', *Foreign Affairs*, 71/2 (Spring): 64–82.

Rosenberg, David A. (1986). 'Reality and Responsibility: Power and Process in Making of United States Nuclear Strategy', *The Journal of Strategic Studies*, 9/1 (Mar.): 35–52.

Rotfeld, Adam Daniel (1991). 'New Security Structures in Europe: Concepts, Proposals and Decisions', in Stockholm International Peace Research Institute (ed.), *World Armaments and Disarmaments* (Oxford: Oxford University Press), 585–600.

Rothschild, Emma (1994). 'Adam Smith and the Invisible Hand', *American Economic Review*, 84: 319–22.

Ruggie, John Gerard (1983). 'International Regimes, Transactions and Change: Embedded Liberalism in the Postwar Economic Order', in Stephen D. Krasner (ed.), *International Regimes* (Ithaca, NY: Cornell University Press), 195–232.

——(1993). 'Multilateralism: The Anatomy of an Institution', in Ruggie (ed.), *Multilateralism Matters: The Theory and Praxis of an Institutional Form* (New York: Columbia University Press), 3–47.

——(1998). 'What Makes the World Hang Together? Neo-utilitarianism and the Social Constructivist Challenge', *International Organization*, 52/4 (Fall).

Rühle, Michael (1994). 'View from NATO: NATO and the Coming Proliferation Threat', *Comparative Strategy*, 13: 313–20.

Salter, J. A. (1921). *Allied Shipping Control: An Experiment in International Administration* (Oxford: Clarendon Press).

Sauder, Axel (1995). *Souveränitat und Integration: Französische und deutsche Konzeptionen europäischer Sicherheit nach dem Ende des Kalten Krieges (1990–1993)* (Baden-Baden: Nomos).

Scharpf, Fritz W. (1994). 'Die Politikverflechtungsfalle: Europaische Integration und deutscher Föderalismus im Vergleich', in Scharpf, *Optionen des Föderalismus in Deutschland und Europa* (Frankfurt and New York: Campus), 11–44.

Schelling, Thomas C. (1960). *The Strategy of Conflict* (Cambridge, Mass.: Harvard University Press).

Schmidt, Peter (1995). *European Security and Defense Identity (ESDI): A Brief Analysis from a German Point of View* (Ebenhausen: Stiftung Wissenschaft und Politik).

Schotter, Andrew (1981). *The Economic Theory of Social Institutions* (Cambridge: Cambridge University Press).

Schrader, Lutz (1993). 'Mitterrands Europapolitik oder der lange Abschied vom Gaullismus', *Aus Politik und Zeitgeschichte*, 32: 213–25.

Schroeder, Paul W. (1976). 'Alliances, 1815–1945: Weapons of Power and Tools of Management', in Klaus Knorr (ed.), *Historical Dimensions of National Security Problems* (Lawrence, Kan.: University of Kansas Press), 227–62.

——(1977). 'Alliances as Tools of Management', in Klaus Knorr (ed.), *Economic Issues and National Security* (Lawrence, Kan.: Regent's Press of Kansas).

——(1986). 'The Nineteenth Century International System: Changes in the Structure', *World Politics*, 39: 1–26.

——(1987). 'The Collapse of the Second Coalition', *Journal of Modern History*, 59 (June): 244–90.

——(1988). 'An Unnatural "Natural Alliance": Castlereagh, Metternich and Aberdeen in 1813', *International History Review*, 10/4 (Nov.): 522–40.

——(1992). 'Did the Vienna Settlement Rest on a Balance of Power?' *American Historical Review* (June): 683–706.

——(1993). 'The Transformation of Political Thinking 1787–1848', in Jack Snyder and Robert Jervis (eds.), *Coping with Complexity n the International System* (Boulder, Colo.: Westview), 47–70.

——(1994*a*). 'Historical Reality vs Neo-realist Theory', *International Security*, 19/1 (Summer): 108–48.

——(1994*b*). *The Transformation of European Politics 1763–1848* (Oxford: Clarendon Press).

——(1997). 'History and International Relations Theory: Not Use or Abuse, but Fit or Misfit', *International Security*, 22/1 (Summer): 64–74.

Schulz, Eberhard (1989). 'Die deutsche Frage im KSZE-Prozeß', in Eberhard Schulz (ed.), *Die deutsche Frage und die Nachbarn im Osten* (Munich: Oldenbourg), 65–80.

Schwartz, David N. (1983). *NATO's Nuclear Dilemmas* (Washington, DC: Brookings Institution).

Schwartz, Thomas Alan (1991). *America's Germany: John J. McCloy and the Federal Republic of Germany* (Cambridge: Harvard University Press).

Schwarz, Norbert, Herbert Bless, and Gerd Bohner (1991). *Advances in Experimental Social Psychology*, xxiv (New York: Academic Press), 161–201.

Schweller, Randall L., and David Priess (1997). 'A Tale of Two Realisms: Expanding the Institutions Debate', *Mershon International Studies Review*, 41 (May): 1–32.

Seaman, L. C. B. (1955). *From Vienna to Versailles* (New York: Harper and Row).

Searle, John R. (1995). *The Construction of Social Reality* (New York).

Sears, David O., and Carolyn Funk (1991). 'The Role of Self-Interest in Social and Political Attitudes', *Advances in Experimental Social Psychology*, xxiv (New York: Academic Press), 2–92.

Segal, David R. (1995). 'Five Phases of United Nations Peacekeeping: An Evolutionary Typology', *Journal of Political and Military Sociology*, 23: 65–79.

Seton-Watson, R. W. (1972). *Disraeli, Gladstone and the Eastern Question* (New York: Norton).

Shanks, Cheryl, Harold K. Jacobson, and Jeffrey H. Kaplan (1995). 'Inertia and Change in the Constellation of International Governmental Organizations, 1981–1992', *International Organization*, 50/4: 593–628.

Shelly, Robert K., and Murry Webster, Jr. (1997). 'How Formal Status, Liking, and Ability Status Structure Interaction', *Sociological Perspectives*, 40/1: 81–107.

Shepsle, Kenneth A. (1986). 'Institutional Equilibrium and Equilibrium Institutions', in Herbert Weisberg (ed.), *Political Science: The Science of Politics* (New York: Agathon).

Shevardnadze, Eduard (1989). 'Sieben Punkte zur Deutschlandpolitik. Statement to the Political Committee of the European Parliament in Brussels, 19 Dec.', in *Umbruch in Europa: Die Ereignisse im 2. Halbjahr 1989: Eine Dokumentation* (Bonn: Auswärtiges Amt), 146–53.

Sigal, Leon V. (1998). *Disarming Strangers: Nuclear Diplomacy with North Korea* (Princeton: Princeton University Press).

Sked, Alan (1979) (ed.). *Europe Balance of Power 1815–1848* (London: Macmillan).

Slim, Randa (1992). 'Small State Mediation in International Relations', in J. Bercovitch and J. Rubin (eds.), *Mediation in International Relations* (New York: St. Martin's Press).

Smith, Adam (1969) [1759]. *The Theory of Moral Sentiments* (New York: Liberty Classics).

——(1976) [1776]. *An Inquiry into the Nature and Causes of the Wealth of Nations*, ed. R. H. Campbell, A. S. Skinner, and W. B. Todd (Oxford: Clarendon Press).

Smith, Alastair (1996*a*). 'Alliance Formation and War', *International Studies Quarterly*, 39 (Dec.): 405–26.

——(1996*b*). 'To Intervene or Not to Intervene: A Biased Decision', *Journal of Conflict Resolution*, 40 (Mar.): 16–40.

Smith, Bradley F. (1996). *How the Allies Traded Intelligence, 1941–1945* (Lawrence, Kan.: University of Kansas Press).

Smith, Edwin M., and Thomas G. Weiss (1997). 'UN Task-Sharing: Towards or Away from Global Governance?', *Third World Quarterly*, 18: 595–619.

Smith, Gary (1996). 'Multilateralism and Regional Security in Asia: The ASEAN Regional Forum and APEC's Geopolitical Value', draft paper (CFIA, Harvard University, June).

Snidal, Duncan (1984). 'The "Game Theory" of International Politics', in Kenneth A. Oye (ed.), *Cooperation under Anarchy* (Princeton: Princeton University Press).

——(1985). 'Limits of Hegemonic Stability Theory', *International Organization*, 39: 579–614.

Snyder, Glenn H. (1984). 'The Security Dilemma in Alliance Politics', *World Politics*, 36: 461–95.

——(1990). 'Alliance Theory: A Neorealist First Cut', *Journal of International Affairs*, 44: 103–23.

Stark, Hans (1992). 'Dissonances franco-allemandes sur fond de guerre serbo-croate', *Politique étrangère*, 57: 339–47.

Stein, Arthur A. (1982). 'Coordination and Collaboration: Regimes in an Anarchic World', *International Organization*, 36: 115–40.

——(1983). 'Coordination and Collaboration: Regimes in an Anarchic World', in Stephen Krasner (ed.), *International Regimes* (Ithaca, NY: Cornell University Press), 115–40.

——(1990). 'Why Nations Cooperate: Circumstance and Choice', in *International Relations* (Ithaca, NY, and London: Cornell University Press).

Steiner, Jurg (1974). *Amicable Agreement versus Majority Rule: Conflict Resolution in Switzerland* (Durham, NC: University of North Carolina Press).

Sterling-Folker, Jennifer (1997). 'Realist Environment, Liberal Process, and Domestic-Level Variables', *International Studies Quarterly*, 41/1 (Mar.): 1–26.

Stern, Brigitte (1997). 'Einseitige Wirtschaftssanktionen: Helms-Burton, D'Amato und die Europäer', *Internationale Politik*, 52/4: 7–12.

Stinchcombe, Arthur (1968). *Constructing Social Theories* (New York: Harcourt, Brace and World).

Strauß, Franz-Josef (1989). *Die Erinnerungen* (Berlin: Siedler).

Stromseth, Jane E. (1988). *The Origins of Flexible Response: NATO's Debate over Strategy in the 1960s* (London: Macmillan Press).

Stulberg, Joseph B. (1987). *Taking Charge/Managing Conflict* (Lexington, Mass.: Lexington Books).

Sugden, Robert (1986). *The Economics of Rights, Cooperation and Welfare* (London: Basil Blackwell).

Sugden, Robert (1989). 'Spontaneous Order', *Journal of Economic Perspectives*, 3: 85–97.

Susskind, Lawrence (1994). *Environmental Diplomacy: Negotiating More Effective Global Agreements* (London: Oxford University Press).

Taylor, A. J. P. (1971). *The Struggle for Mastery of Europe 1848–1918* (Oxford: Oxford University Press).

Taylor, Alastair M. (1960). *Indonesian Independence and the United Nations* (London: Steven & Sons).

Taylor, Michael (1987). *The Possibility of Cooperation* (Cambridge: Cambridge University Press).

Taylor, Paul (1990). 'A Conceptual Typology of International Organization', in A. J. R. Groom and Paul Taylor (eds.), *Frameworks for International Co-operation* (New York: St Martin's Press), 12–26.

Teltschik, Horst (1991). *329 Tage: Innenansichten der deutschen Einigung* (Berlin: Siedler).

Temperley, Harold (1925). *The Foreign Policy of Canning, 1822–1827* (London: Bell).

——and Lillian M. Penson (1966) (eds.). *Foundations of British Foreign Policy, from Pitt (1792) to Salisbury (1902): Old and New Documents Selected and Edited* (New York: Barnes and Noble).

Tharoor, Shashi (1995/6). 'Should UN Peacekeeping go "Back to Basics"?', *Survival*, 37: 52–64.

Thelen, Kathleen, Sven Steinmo, and Frank Longstreth (1992). *Structuring Politics: Historical Institutionalism in Comparative Analysis* (Cambridge: Cambridge University Press).

Touval, Saadia (1975). 'Biased Intermediaries: Theoretical and Historical Considerations', *Jerusalem Journal of International Relations*, 1 (Fall): 51–69.

——(1982). *Peace Brokers: Mediators in the Arab-Israeli Conflict, 1948–1979* (Princeton: Princeton University Press).

Touval, Saadia, and I. William Zartman (1985). *International Mediation in Theory and Practice* (Boulder, Colo.: Westview).

Trebesch, Herbert (1988). *Informationsunterlagen zur Nuklearpolitik der Bundesrepublik Deutschland* (Bonn: Nuclear History Program).

Tucker, Johnathan B. (1996). 'Monitoring and Verifcation in a Noncooperative Environment: Lessons from the U.N. Experience in Iraq', *Nonproliferation Review*, 3/3: 1–14.

Tuschhoff, Christian (1990). *Die MC 70 und die Einführung nuklearer Trägersysteme in die Bundeswehr* (Ebenhausen: Stiftung Wissenschaft und Politik).

——(1993a). 'Die politischen Folgen der Streitkräfte-Reform der NATO', *Aus Politik und Zeitgeschichte*, B 15-16/93 (9 Apr.): 28–39.

——(1993b). 'Machtverschiebungen und zukünftige Bruchstellen im Bündnis: Die politischen Folgen der Truppenpräsenz nach den NATO-Reformen', in Gunther Hellmann (ed.), *Alliierte Präsenz und deutsche Einheit: Die politischen Folgen militärischer Macht* (Baden-Baden: Nomos), 365–401.

——(1993*c*). 'Multilaterale Verteidigungskooperation in der NATO und amerikanisch-deutscher Machttransfer', in Gustav Schmidt (ed.), *Ost-West-Beziehungen: Konfrontation und Détente 1945–1989*, ii (Bochum: Universitäts-verlag Dr. N. Brockmeyer), 253–71.

——(1994). *Causes and Consequences of Germany's Deployment of Nuclear Capable Delivery Systems, 1957–1963* (Maryland, Md.: Nuclear History Program).

US Congress (1994). *Proliferation and the Former Soviet Union* (Office of Techno logy Assessment; Washington, DC: GPO).

——(1995). *Nuclear Safeguards and the International Atomic Energy Agency. Summary* (Office of Technology Assessment; Washington, DC: GPO).

US Department of Defense (1995). *Cooperative Threat Reduction* (Washington, DC: GPO).

——(1996). *Proliferation: Threat and Response* (Office of the Secretary of Defense; Washington, DC: GPO).

US Department of State (1985). *Documents on Germany 1944–1985* (Department of State Publication No. 9446; Washington, DC: GPO).

——(1993). *Foreign Relations of the United States (FRUS), 1958-1960* (Washington, DC: GPO).

Ulam, Adam B. (1974). *Expansion and Coexistence: Soviet Foreign Policy 1917–73*, 2nd edn. (Fort Worth, Tex.: Holt, Rinehart, and Winston).

Ullmann-Margalit, Edna (1978*a*). 'Invisible-Hand Explanations', *Synthese*, 39: 263–91.

——(1978*b*). *The Emergence of Norms* (Oxford: Oxford University Press).

——(1990). 'Revision of Norms', *Ethics*, 100: 756–67.

United Nations (1996). *The Blue Helmets: A Review of UN Peacekeeping*, 3rd edn. (New York: UNO).

US CSCAP [Council on Security Cooperation in the Asia-Pacific] (1997). 'USCSCAP Board of Directors'.

Vanberg, Viktor (1984). 'Unsichtbare-Hand Erklärung und soziale Normen', in Gesellschaft für Wirtschafts- und Sozialwissenschaften (ed.), *Normengeleitetes Verhalten in den Sozialwissenschaften: Schriften des Vereins für Sozialpolitik* (Berlin: Duncker und Humblodt), 115–46.

Vaughn, Karen I. (1989). 'Invisible Hand', in *The New Palgrave: The Invisible Hand*, ed. John Eatwell, Murray Milgate, and Peter Newman (New York: Norton), 168–72.

Vetschera, Heinz (1994). 'Die Rolle der KSZE als Einrichtung kooperativer Sicherheit im Rahmen des "Interlocking Institutions"-Konzept', in Bernard von Plate (ed.), *Europa auf dem Wege zur kollektiven Sicherheit? Konzeptionelle und organisatorische Entwicklungen der sicherheitspolitischen Institutionen Europas* (Baden-Baden: Nomos), 95–154.

Voss, T. (1982). 'Rational Actors and Social Institutions: The Case of the Organic Emergence of Norms', in W. Raub (ed.), *Theoretical Models and Empirical Analyses* (Utrecht), 76–100.

Wallace, William (1992). 'British Foreign Policy after the Cold War', *International Affairs*, 68: 423–42.

Wallander, Celeste A. (1999). *Mortal Friends, Best Enemies: German-Russian Cooperation after the Cold War* (Ithaca, NY: Cornell University Press).

——and Robert Keohane (1995). 'An Institutional Approach to Alliance Theory', *Center for International Affairs, Working Paper Series, Harvard University*, 95(2).

Waller, Bruce (1974). *Bismarck at the Crossroads* (London: Athlone Press).

Walt, Stephen M. (1987). *The Origins of Alliances* (Ithaca, NY, and London: Cornell University Press).

——(1991). 'The Renaissance of Security Studies', *International Studies Quarterly*, 35: 211–39.

——(1997). 'Why Alliances Endure or Collapse', *Survival*, 39: 156–79.

Walters, F. P. (1952). *A History of the League of Nations*, 2 vols. (London: Oxford University Press).

Waltz, Kenneth N. (1979). *Theory of International Politics* (Reading, Mass.: Addison-Wesley).

——(1986). 'Reflections on Theory of International Politics: A Response to my Critics', in Robert O. Keohane (ed.), *Neorealism and its Critics* (New York: Columbia University Press), 322–45.

——(1993). 'The Emerging Structure of International Politics', *International Security*, 18/2 (Fall): 44–79.

Ward, A. W., and Gooch, G. P. (1922) (eds.). *The Cambridge History of British Foreign Policy*, i. *1783–1815* (New York: Macmillan).

——and——(1923) (eds.). *The Cambridge History of British Foreign Policy*, ii. *1815–1866* (New York: Macmillan).

Webster, C. K. (1921) (ed.). *British Diplomacy 1813–1815: Select Documents Dealing with the Reconstruction of Europe* (London: Bell).

——(1931). *The Foreign Policy of Castlereagh 1812–1815* (London: Bell).

——(1934). *The Congress of Vienna 1814–1815* (London: Bell).

Weidenfeld, Werner (1994) (ed.). *Maastricht in der Analyse: Strategien und Optionen für Europa* (Gütersloh: Bertelsmann).

Weidenfeld, Werner, *et al.* (1991). *Die doppelte Integration: Europa und das größere Deutschland* (Gütersloh: Verlag Bertelsmann).

Weilemann, Peter R. (1990). 'Der deutsche Beitrag zur Überwindung der europäischen Teilung: Die zehn Punkte von Bundeskanzler Helmut Kohl', *Außenpolitik*, 41: 15–30.

Weiss, Thomas G., David P. Forsythe, and Robert A. Coate (1994). *The United Nations and Changing World Politics* (Boulder, Colo.: Westview).

Weller, Marc (1996). 'Peace-Keeping and Peace-Enforcement in the Republic of Bosnia and Herzegovina', *Zeitschrift für ausländisches öffentliches Recht und Völkerrecht*, 56: 70–177.

Wendt, Alexander (1992). 'Anarchy is What States Make of it', *International Organization*, 46: 391–425.

—— (1994). 'Collective Identity Formation and the International State', *American Political Science Review*, 88 (June): 384–96.

Williams, Bernard (1981). 'Internal and External Reasons', in *Moral Luck: Philosophical Papers 1973–1980* (Cambridge: Cambridge University Press).

Williams, Michael C. (1997). 'The Organizations of Security: Elements of a Theory of Security Organizations', *Cooperation and Conflict*, 32: 287–307.

Williams, Phil (1985). *The Senate and U.S. Troops in Europe* (New York: St Martin's Press).

Williams, Walter (1971). *Intergovernmental Military Forces and World Public Order* (Leiden).

Williamson, Oliver E. (1985). *The Economic Institutions of Capitalism* (New York: Free Press).

—— (1994). 'Visible and Invisible Governance', *The American Economic Review*, 84: 323–6.

Winrow, Gareth (1994). 'NATO and Out-of-Area: A Post-Cold War Challenge', *European Security*, 3: 617–38.

Wiseman, Henry (1987). 'The United Nations and International Peacekeeping: A Comparative Analysis', in I. J. Rikhye and K. Skjelsbaek (eds.), *The United Nations and the Maintenance of International Peace and Security* (Dordrecht: Martinus Nijhoff), 263–333.

Wolfers, Arnold (1962). *Discord and Collaboration: Essays on International Politics* (Baltimore and London: Johns Hopkins Press).

Wolffsohn, Michael (1992). 'Der außenpolitische Weg zur Deutschen Einheit: Das Ausland und die vollendeten Tatsachen', in Eckhard Jesse and Armin Mitter (eds.), *Die Gestaltung der deutschen Einheit: Geschichte—Politik—Gesellschaft* (Bonn: Bundeszentrale für politische Bildung), 142–62.

Wolfsthal, John B. (1993). 'President Clinton Unveils New Non-Proliferation, Export Policies', *Arms Control Today*, 23/9: 22.

Yost, David S. (1991). 'France and West European Defence Identity', *Survival*, 33: 327–51.

Young, H. Peyton (1996). 'The Economics of Convention', *Journal of Economic Perspectives*, 10: 105–22.

Young, Oran R. (1967). *The Intermediaries: Third Parties in International Crises* (Princeton: Princeton University Press).

—— (1992). 'The Effectiveness of International Institutions: Hard Cases and Critical Variables', in James N. Rosenau and Ernst-Otto Czempiel (eds.), *Governance without Government: Order and Change in World Politics* (Cambridge: Cambridge University Press), 160–94.

—— (1983). 'Regime Dynamics: The Rise and Fall of International Regimes', in Stephen D. Krasner (ed.), *International Regimes* (Ithaca, NY: Cornell University Press).

Young, Thomas-D. (1996). 'German National Command Structures after Unification: A New General Staff?', *Armed Forces and Society*, 22/3 (Spring): 379–417.

Zaborsky, Victor (1994). *Nuclear Disarmament and Nonproliferation: The Evolution of the Ukrainian Case*, discussion paper (Cambridge, Mass.: Center for Science and International Affairs, Harvard University).

Zelikow, Philip, and Condoleezza Rice (1995). *Germany Unified and Europe Transformed: A Study in Statecraft* (Cambridge, Mass., and London: Harvard University Press).

INDEX

Printed in the USA/Agawam, MA
January 22, 2013

572142.021